Paris Inside Out

The Insider's Handbook to Life in Paris

SIXTH EDITION

David Applefield

The Globe Pequot Press

GUILFORD, CONNECTICUT

For Julia, Alexandre, Anna, and Ernesto

The author wishes to thank Shari Leslie Segall, Lucas Klein, Dale Gershwin, Lisa Nesselson, Sandra Kwock Silve, Lori Thicke, Marie Doezema, Julia Price, and the U.S. Office of American Services for their invaluable editorial input.

All interior photos © Dorothea Resch
Text design by Sandra Burr

ISSN 1541-079X
ISBN 0-7627-1232-5

Manufactured in the United States of America
Sixth Edition/First Printing

Contents

The prices and rates listed in this guidebook were confirmed at press time. We recommend, however, that you call establishments before traveling to obtain current information.

Welcome to
Paris Inside Out

I have been living in Paris for just about twenty years and have watched a lot of people come and go. I also enjoy all sorts of relationships and friendships with people who have come and stayed. Paris, I like to say, is a city you have a lifelong relationship with. When Bogart said, "we'll always have Paris," he spoke from authority. The question, though, is not the love affair you may or may not have with this city; it's the everyday. It's not the joy or the design, the art, or the beauty; it's figuring out how to participate in the workplace, in your neighborhood, at a party, in a public place. Do I know how to be in my local Monoprix supermarket?

Guidebooks have a life of their own, as do cities and the authors that live in them. In the last edition of this guide I stated that I have "witnessed dramatic growth and change both within myself and within this great city." Change since 2000 now seems even more striking. The geopolitics of the world have shifted, and living overseas comes with a new tone of caution. We have a new currency in France and the European Union, the euro. France has survived another presidential election. The Internet has penetrated deeper into French life. The relationship between the European Union and North America has matured and yet the cultural gaps have even widened.

Changes in *Paris Inside Out* must be reported, too. First, I have incorporated highly detailed photographs to render the observations I make with words even more graphic and visual. I'm pleased to introduce you to the photographic work of my collaborator Dorothea Resch, whose task it was to capture the small but vital parts of Parisian life in images that speak French.

Second, because of the rapidity of change in information, I have shortened or eliminated long lists of numbers and moved them to a database on www.paris-anglo.com, where they will be updated regularly. Additionally, I have included new articles on the subject of translation, on bicycling in Paris, on bringing your pet to France, on discovering Asian Paris, and more. Lastly, I've added a detailed index useful for navigating through the book.

As the adventure of living in an overseas, adopted culture away from the comfort and predictability of home deepens, so does your understanding of the experience. Living in a foreign country is tantamount to starting life again as an adolescent. The world is fresh again with adventure and confusion, and wisdom is acquired only through the gradual shedding of innocence. Not everyone is ready and prepared for a second adolescence, and admittedly the process comes with its bumps and knocks. But on the whole the chance to take on a new existence in Paris is a gift that should be seen as fortuitous.

When I arrived for the first time in 1978 with a one-way ticket, four battered duffel bags, and a typewriter, I had no idea either how long I'd stay or how I'd support myself. Equipped only with the address of a friend of a friend scribbled on a piece of paper, a few hundred dollars in traveler's checks, and about three sentences of French, including *"J'aime ta jupe"* (I like your skirt), which wasn't all that helpful, I landed at the Gare du Nord in the somber grayness of a typical Parisian October. I'm still here.

The process of writing about the experience of living in, studying in, and working in Paris has been inspired directly from the trials of figuring it out myself. It became evident that there was a great divide between the mass of information available on the subject and an insider's manual on what to really expect and how to use that information. It is from this need that this guide is motivated. Information changes and grows, but what must remain constant (if you hope to be happy and successful in your new life) is your openness to the crude fact that things work differently here, and that information is always culturally relative. Whenever possible, I try to fill the gaps between facts and data with the cultural underpinnings that make life in a foreign city both so trying and so fascinating. Often you won't feel like being a social anthropologist when you just want your electricity turned on or a green salad served without the dressing, or your driver's license renewed without an argument. Admittedly, daily life in Paris, especially in the beginning, requires a serious dose of philosophy and humor. The act of writing about living here has helped me realize how absurd life can be everywhere. Ultimately living in Paris will oblige you to contemplate your native culture and to examine yourself and the assumptions you came with. No wonder Paris has been the cradle of existential thinking.

What you may not see now but will understand quickly after being in Paris awhile is that the logic and practicality of moving abroad clashes with the reality of doing it. The foreign city you visit and the one you live in are two different beasts. You'll soon come to see that the idea of living somewhere as glorious as Paris and actually living there are at odds. How are you going to tell all those jealous friends and professional acquaintances back home who oohed and aahed with envy at your move that it's actually pretty hard adjusting to daily life in the French capital? Don't spoil the myth. "So how's life in Paree?" *"Magnifique,"* will be your reply as you purse your lips.

It's true that the city's reputation is larger than life, and the myths that drive that reputation are cloaked in glamour and fantasy. Your job is to sort out the fiction from the reality without spoiling the true beauty and style that Parisian life encompasses. The key to this is careful preparation based on good information and a lot of personal courage. Living away from your first home, culture, country, language, things, and currency, and away from the support of family and friends and familiar gestures and dumb TV shows, demands a strong will and an inner sense of security and balance.

Paris is a city you return to over the course of your life, a place in which you take stock of your unfulfilled ambitions, a place you chain to your memory, where bittersweet sentimentality runs freely and the pleasure of melancholia returns each time, a city you take a loved one to for a meal, the place you discover your own lips and the sound of your voice, a town to spend your honeymoon in, a memory you name a child after. Paris for the world is a proper noun meaning beauty, art, romance, elegance, design, class, style, literature, history, bohemian self-discovery, love. I heard myself actually say to the creative director of Hallmark cards at a book fair recently: "Paris is not a city, it's a feeling." I try to make that the motto for living here, and I venture to guess that if you think of your new home in those terms, the psychic scrapes and bruises of figuring out this place will remain *pas grave.*

As a transplanted Parisian, I have tried to put myself directly in your shoes. You want your questions answered. And you want full information, not half information. If you need a special permit to work in France, as important as knowing the hard data is knowing that the lines will be long and that if you don't reach the front before 4:00 P.M. you have to start all over the next day. Or that the snicker of the clerk processing your *dossier* (the French love this word; it means file in administrationese) is not because you did something wrong, but simply an indication of the impersonal treatment that the public is regularly treated to in France. You need to know that a beer consumed at the zinc bar in a café is half the price of the same beer served at a sidewalk table in the same café. You might want to ask for your *baguette coupée en deux* next time, or know how to deal with the concierge in the building you're staying in. It is in this spirit that commentary has been directed. If at times the tone sounds harsh and the criticism barbed, it's not because of cynicism; it's proof of Parisian blood. Parisians love to complain *(se plaindre),* and after a certain number of months in Paris, you'll gain the privilege too.

Parisians also love to seduce *(séduire)* and to please *(plaire).* In fact, the key to successfully living, studying, working, and playing in Paris is learning the art of both. In French, to seduce and to please does not mean to trick, nor does it imply hypocrisy. It is more the result of successful charm. It is learning how to stay at all costs on the good side of the "other." Once the atmosphere for charm has been broken, you can be certain that the experience will be negative. This holds true from buying a cake to getting a job.

Everything in this book you eventually would have learned anyway. But *Paris Inside Out* should save you many hours and lots of euros. It will facilitate your integration into French life and hopefully reduce the frustration of finding yourself alone, dependent, tongue-tied, and handicapped by a totally new setting that you'll at first think of as "foreign." But remember, everything around you is native; it's you that's foreign—whether you come from New York City, London, Toronto, Dubai, Bombay, Sydney, or Stockholm. Paris is capable of confusing and exhilarating you.

A word on tone. Although the guide tries not to be overly American in its orientation and cultural and linguistic references, it was unavoidable that the book lean a bit that way. You are what you are. While aspiring to address all new residents, the guide had to be created with its largest readership in mind.

With that said, let me conclude with this: In a world of rapid change and shifting geopolitical policies and attitudes, living outside of one's culture has never been more challenging. It takes patience and wisdom to figure out. Living in another country is a process of losing your innocence all over again. This exciting path, with its share of awkward moments, should create a profusion of pleasurable and thought-provoking experiences.

I'm open to helping you as Paris becomes yours. To those who've written over the past months and years, I thank you.

David Applefield
david@paris-anglo.com
Globe Pequot Press

The Author's Credo for Survival in Paris

+ Start with an apology or ask permission.
+ Respect the authority and wait to be acknowledged.
+ Hold to form. Charm your way.
+ Never raise your voice.
+ Never ask for a person's name.
+ Never ask for a supervisor.
+ Never curse in English.
+ Never disagree. Always agree, but repeat what you want.
+ Never moralize.
+ Never intimate that things are better at home.
+ Say you are sorry when you're really not.
+ Order another *express* (coffee).

Introduction

Getting oriented as quickly as possible is key to feeling comfortable and moving from the status of short-term visitor to long-term resident. Most of the cultural, geographic, and social references in the media and in daily life will seem foreign to you at first, but you'll quickly start understanding who is who and what is what. Don't fret—this process takes time. A basic knowledge of a few key facts can be a helpful start. Here are some statistics and bits of background info that will help you situate yourself in France:

Capital: Paris
Form of Government: Republic
Official Currency: the euro
Official Language: French
Regional Languages: Basque, Breton, Catalan, Corsican, Provençal, Alsatian
Surface Area: 551,965 sq km
Gross National Product: $8,850 US per inhabitant
Population: 58,609,285 (July 1997 est.)

	City	Metropolitan
Paris	2,188,918	9,960,000
Marseilles	800,550	1,087,276
Strasbourg	252,338	388,483
Lyon	415,487	1,214,869
Toulouse	358,688	608,427
Nice	342,391	474,459
Bordeaux	210,336	685,456
Lille	363,653	950,265

Nantes	244,952	492,212
Grenoble	150,758	400,141
Toulon	167,550	437,493

Paris Statistics

+ Paris is one of the most densely populated cities in Europe with more than 50,000 inhabitants per square mile.
+ The average family size in France is 1.8 children.
+ The average age of the population is thirty-seven.
+ The average life expectancy in France is eighty-one for women and seventy-three for men.

Religions

+ Catholic: 50 million (90%); 1 out of 5 French claims to be "practicing."
+ Muslim: 1.7 million
+ Protestant: 1 million
+ Jewish: 700,000

Ethnic Mix

(Source: *Ministère de l'Intérieur et de l'aménagement du territoire*)
(Official estimation of population legally residing in France as of 31 December 1992)

Portuguese 700,729
Algerian 585,846
Moroccan 441,000
Italian 268,047
Spanish 246,342
Tunisian 178,217
Turkish 147,558
British 59,790
Yugoslav 58,742
Belgian 57,574

German 57,670
Polish 46,193
Cambodian 40,738
Vietnamese 39,059
Senegalese 39,319
Malian 31,886
American (USA) 27,053
Cameroonian 15,672
Irish 4,778

Most Common French Names

Of the 250,000 family names in France, the most common are:

Martin
Bernard
Moreau
Durand
Petit

Dubois
Michel
Marie
Thomas
Richard

In French your name *(nom)* refers to your surname; your first, or given, name is your *prénom.* When writing their name on a form, French students often follow the administrative formality of last name first, e.g. Dupont, Jean. Last names and city names are almost always written in capital letters *(majuscule).* Many people in France have *noms composés,* compound, hyphenated first names, such as Jean-Marie, Marie-Thérèse, or Jean-Claude. As a result of marriage and mixed cultural backgrounds, numerous people have compound last names as well.

Common References to France and Its Institutions in the Press

Le Quai d'Orsay	Ministry of Foreign Affairs
l'Hexagone	France
l'Elysée	the president's official residence
Matignon	the Premier Ministre's residence
le Quai des Orfèvres	police headquarters
Place Vendôme	Ministry of Justice
La dame de fer	Eiffel Tower

Common Symbols of the French Republic

+ Flag: blue, white, and red as three vertical stripes, created by Lafayette in 1789.
+ RF: these letters stand for République Française.
+ Liberté, Egalité, Fraternité: the philosophic slogan of the country.
+ La Marseillaise: the national anthem.
+ Marianne: the muse of the country, whose portrait and bust is found in every city hall in France and on many French stamps.
+ Le Coq: the cock, symbol of the French people, from the Latin gallus and signifying the Gauls, the ancestors of modern France.
+ The Ship: a symbol for the city of Paris.

French Elections /Terms in Office

In France you have to be eighteen years old and a French citizen to vote. Women voted for the first time in France in 1945.

Presidential elections	7 years (Constitutionally becoming 5 years after 2002)
National elections (*députés*)	5 years
Senate elections ($^1/_3$ every 9 years)	9 years
Regional elections	6 years
Cantonale (county) elections	6 years
Municipal elections	6 years
European elections	5 years

Converting Measurements and Sizes

Metric System: Conversions

1 mile = 1.6 kilometers
1 kilometer (1000 meters) = $^5/_8$ mile (0.62 mile)
(to calculate miles multiply kilometers by 0.6)
1 yard = 0.914 meters
1 meter = 39.37 inches, or 3.28 feet
1 inch = 2.54 centimeters
1 centimeter (100 millimeters) = 0.394 inches
1 acre = 0.405 hectares
1 hectare = 2.47 acres

Weights

1 kilogram (kg) = 2.2 pounds
1 livre (demi-kilo) = 1.1 pounds
1 ounce = 28.35 grams

1 pound = 453.59 grams
1 pint = 0.473 liters
1 gram = 0.035 ounce
1 liter = 33.185 ounces

Measurements

1 liter = 0.265 U.S. gallon

1 gram = .033 ounce

Conversions for Cooking

1 ounce = 30 grammes (g.)
3.5 oz. = 100 grammes
1 pound = 454 grammes
1 tbsp = 15 grammes

1 cup = nearly 1/4 litre (l.)
$4^1/_3$ cups = 1 litre
$^1/_3$ cup minus 1 tbsp = 100 grammes
1 pint = 0.473 liter
1 quart = 0.946 liter
1 gallon = 3.785 liters

Clothing Sizes

Women

France	36	38	40	42	44	46	48
US	6	8	10	12	14	16	18
UK	8	10	12	14	16	18	20

Men's suits

France	48	50/52	54	56	58/60		
US	38	40		42	44	46	
UK	38	40		42	44	46	

Women's Shoes

France	36	37	38	39	40	41	42
US	5	6	7	8	9	10	11
UK	3	4	5	6	7	8	9

Men's Shoes

France	42	43	44	45	46	48	50
US	9	10	11	12	13	14	16
UK	8	9	10	11	12	13	14

Men's shirts

France	36/37	38	39/40	41	42/43	44		
US	14.5		15	15.5		16	16.5	17
UK	14.5		15	15.5		16	16.5	17

Commas vs. Decimal Points

In writing numbers and prices, the French use commas where you use decimal points—$100.00 is written $100,00. Twenty-five euros and fifty cents is written as 25,50 euros. A thousand euros and fifty cents is written 1.000,50 euros. And the French use periods where you use commas. $1.200.000,00 is the French version of 1,200,000.00. So be careful with numbers, especially when it's time to pay.

Survival Tips

Dates: In France, the date 1/3/03 does not mean January 3, 2003, but March 1, 2003.

Time of Day: Generally expressed by the 24-hour clock. Thus, 8:00 A.M. = 8h, or 8h00, and 8:00 P.M. = 20h or 20h00.

Midnight = 24h, 24h00, or minuit; noon =12h, 12h00, or midi.

12:30 A.M. = 0h30; 5:00 P.M. = 17h or 17h00.

Currency: As of January 4, 1999, the euro became the official currency in twelve European countries, France included. Until January 1, 2002, the French franc remained in circulation with all cash transactions continuing to be conducted in this currency. After February 17, 2002, the French franc was no longer accepted by merchants. All goods and services are now priced and marked in euros and references to the franc are quickly dwindling. The euro, pegged at the fixed rate of 6.55957 FF and rounded out to the third decimal, initially worth about 10 percent less than the U.S. dollar, reached par in mid-2002. Attention: The rate fluctuates.

The euro is divided into one hundred cents, or centimes. Coins consist of one, two, five, ten, twenty, and fifty centimes, and one and two euro pieces. The cents, or centimes, are distinquished from the euro coins by size, ridges, and tint. The front of the euro coins are identical in all of the European Union euro zone; however, the backs have been slightly localized for each country. Euro coins and notes are freely interchangeable in all euro zone countries: Belgium, Luxembourg, Holland, Greece, Austria, Germany, Finland, Spain, France, Portugal, Ireland, and Italy. Euro banknotes come in five, ten, twenty, fifty, one hundred, two hundred, and five hundred euro denominations.

Districts: The twenty districts that make up Paris are called *arrondissements* and are indicated in postal addresses as the last digits of a postal code. The first two digits are the *département* code, which in the case of Paris also corresponds to the city. Paris always begins with 75. For example, 75005 = Paris's fifth district; 75020 = Paris's twentieth district. See map for a breakdown of Paris by *arrondissement*.

Electric Current: France's system is 220 volt, 50 cycles. To use standard American 110 volt, 60 cycle, British 250 volt, 60 cycle, or other appliances, you will need a plug adapter and a transformer that is appropriate for the wattage of the appliance. The plug adapter alone is not sufficient and its use will result in grilled appliances. Some 220-volt appliances have a combination 50/60 cycle motor that allows them to operate in France without any problems. Many new computers have built-in current transformers, but many still do not, so beware. Take no chances. Lamps from the United States will work without a transformer with 220-volt bulbs. Clock radios work but the clock part is not always reliable due to the variations in wattage. Plug adapters and transformers, once found nearly exclusively in the basement of the BHV *(Bazar de l'Hôtel de Ville)* on the rue de Rivoli, may now be found in most department stores and electronics shops, although the BHV does have a special section for adapting foreign telephones, answering machines, fax/computer equipment, and other appliances. Note that in France there are two types of light bulbs and corresponding sockets, vis and ballonnet; the first screws in and the second hooks into the socket.

Floor Numbers: The floor in which you enter a building is not the first floor, but the *rez-de-chausée* (RC). In France the street level is not officially an *étage* (floor). Thus the *premier étage* (first floor) is actually the second level of the building, one floor up from the *rez-de-chaussée*. Most prewar Paris apartment buildings have six floors of apartments, plus a seventh floor of *chambres de bonnes* (maids' rooms), which now are rented as small studios for lower rents.

Paper Size/Format: In France standard paper size for typing and photocopying is called A4 or 21 x 29.7 cms. This is slightly longer than the American standard size of 8$^1/_2$ x 11 inches. Half of A4 is called A5 and twice the size of A4 is B3.

Holidays

Holidays in France bring out two typically French traits: the respect for ceremony and ritual, and the joy of not having to work. The French custom of taking a long weekend *(faire le pont,* or "making a bridge from the holiday to the weekend")— actually an extended weekend created when a holiday falls on a Thursday or Tuesday—is an occasion for most Parisians to exit to the countryside. The month of May is particularly affected because of high frequency of holidays. Beware of heavy traffic on the *autoroutes,* the *Périphérique,* and at the main *portes* (gateways to the city). This is good news for those who stay in the city, because the pace of Paris slows down remarkably, leaving the tourists and others to enjoy the reduced traffic and noise. Being aware of holidays helps you stay in touch with the rhythms of French life (see Annual Events). Plan your activities around these dates since many shops, restaurants, and museums close on public holidays.

The French are rather conscious of the Christian calendar, with each day assigned to a different saint. Best known is *la Sainte Catherine* on November 25, the day that all twenty-five-year-old, single women are presented with funny hats and have dances held in their honor. New Year's Eve is called *la Saint-Sylvestre.* The French are also conscious of the Moslem calendar in some areas.

The French also celebrate April Fool's Day *(le premier avril)* with jokes and pranks, namely hanging paper fish *(poisson d'avril)* on the backs of friends and strangers.

Workweek

From 1982 to 1999 the official French workweek was thirty-nine hours. After a long and heated public debate as to the wisdom and economic repercussions of the move, the workweek was reduced to thirty-five hours as a means of creating new jobs. Industry and companies have gradually phased in the new thirty-five-hour week without reducing salaries.

Vacation Time

French law guarantees everyone who works five weeks of paid vacation. *Les vacances (congés payés)*, a cherished institution among the French, is a right, not a privilege. People in France live for *les vacances;* the entire year of work is often organized around the sacred period of nonwork. *Les vacances* are not a negotiable benefit. If you are legally employed in France, you are entitled to your paid vacation, and if you are employing people in France, you are legally obliged to allow for these weeks of paid leave. In general the French are willing to trade higher wages for security and benefits, which they see as a higher priority in assuring quality of life. What one plans to do on one's vacation, or what one has just finished doing, is usually the subject of casual conversation for at least four months of the year. In fact vacation plans are often made as early as February for the August break and spoken about for months following the vacation.

Paris traditionally empties out in August, with July being the second heaviest vacation month, although in recent years, especially among people who are in business, there has been a trend away from the long August break. In any case, avoid traveling on July 1, July 30, August 1, and August 30. Or else be prepared to leave in the predawn hours. The fifteenth of each summer month is a difficult traveling day as well. School vacations *(vacances scolaires)* are nationally coordinated with all schools within each of three zones of France sharing the same dates. Similarly, train and domestic flight schedules are divided into blue, red, and white days on the calendar, with blue days being the cheapest for travel. Check these with a travel agent. The airports, especially Orly, can be an absolute mob scene due to the great French tradition of everyone leaving town at the same time. Vacations of up to four consecutive weeks are becoming somewhat less frequent although still the norm for many. Although Anglo-Saxons, especially Americans, admire this "luxury," those who are self-employed or have started businesses in France are often frustrated by the difficulty of getting anything done during the holiday period. Eventually you'll learn that it's better to follow the crowd than fight it. Don't try to pull off overly ambitious projects in the month of August. There's no shame or violation of the work ethic to shut down your business, abandon the mail, and forget the phone messages for a month. *Au contraire,* the French believe that a holiday must be long enough to break the stressful patterns of work.

Aside from the five-week vacation, which most people divide between summer and winter (three to four weeks in summer, one to two in winter), here is a list of holidays and their respective customs.

Public Holidays

January 1: *Jour de l'an* (New Year's Day)*
This day is generally devoted to visiting parents and older relatives and exchanging gifts. *Concièrges* expect to be tipped at this time. Postal workers, firefighters, street cleaners, etc., solicit their New Year's gifts as early as November, offering dingy and tacky calendars with sappy pictures of flowers and cats in exchange for year-end tokens of appreciation (*étrennes*/cash).

Late March/April: *Pâques* (Easter)
First Sunday following the full moon of the spring equinox.

Monday after Easter: *Lundi de Pâques* (Easter Monday)* (*Note:* Good Friday is not a national holiday.)

May 1: *Fête du Travail* (Labor Day)*
May 1 was designated an International Labor Day in 1888 and is observed in France as a legal holiday (celebrated everywhere in the world except the United States). Labor groups generally parade in different sections of Paris. A custom in France on this day is to present *muguets* (lilies of the valley), for good luck *(porte bonheur)* and happiness, to friends and loved ones. Everyone is entitled to pick wild *muguets,* found in the forests surrounding Paris. May 1 is the only day of the year that anyone can sell *muguets* or other flowers without a license. Small bunches of the dainty white flowers cost from 2 euros up. The streets are littered with rustic stands, folding tables, crates, etc. as people peddle their *muguets.*

May 8: *Victoire 1945* (V-E Day)*
Défilés (parades) take place throughout the city, the largest and most impressive on the Champs-Elysées.

Sixth Thursday after Easter: *Ascension* (Ascension Day)*

Last Sunday in May: *Fête des Mères* (Mother's Day)

Second Monday after Ascension: *Pentecôte* (Pentecost)*

Two or three weeks after Mother's Day: *Fête des Pères* (Father's Day)

July 14: *Fête nationale/14 juillet* (Bastille Day)*
Celebrations begin on the thirteenth and include fireworks and street dances. Lively parties take place at most firehouses. Admission is free to performances in all national theaters July 14. Fireworks fly high over Trocadéro and other key locations after dark.

August 15: *Fête de l'Assomption* (Feast of the Assumption)*
Christian holiday commemorating the assumption of the Virgin Mary. Celebrations such as harvest festivals and the blessing of the sea happen on this day.

November 1: *Toussaint* (All Saints' Day)*
Halloween, the North American celebration related to this Christian holiday, is not officially acknowledged in France, although in the last few years, it has caught on as a huge unofficial holiday. Numerous restaurants and shops display pumpkins. Even the local supermarkets have capitalized on the orange and witchy

aesthetics of the occasion. But Parisians have not yet caught on to the "trick or treat" part of the tradition. A word on buying pumpkins: In Paris, pumpkins are often darker in color, flatter, and deeply ridged, making the carving of jack-o'-lanterns more difficult. They cost about 1,50 euros a kilo, a hefty and culturally alienating sum if you're used to having a fat one around for Halloween.

November 2: *Jour des Morts* (All Souls Day)*

It is the custom in France to visit the graves of relatives on the day before the *Jour des Morts* or on the day itself to place flowers on the graves. Chrysanthemums, the seasonal flowers before greenhouses existed, are the traditional flowers used on this day. Don't even consider offering chrysanthemums when invited to people's homes for dinner, etc.

November 11: *Fête de l'Armistice* (Veterans Day)*

December 24 and 25: *Noël* (Christmas)*

It is the time to eat the holiday foods at the traditional Christmas dinner (*le réveillon*): *boudin blanc* (white sausage), *foie gras*, pheasants, *saumon fumé* (smoked salmon), *huîtres* (oysters), and *bûches de Noël* (yule log–shaped cake).

December 31: *Saint-Sylvestre* (New Year's Eve)

Like everywhere, Parisians eat and drink heartily to bring in the New Year. Massive midnight traffic jams at Corcorde, Odéon, Etoile, and the Bastille are to be expected. The Champs-Elysées is closed to motorized traffic. Kissing a stranger at midnight is more or less tolerated.

National public holiday (most schools and businesses are closed).

Annual Events

The *Office du Tourisme et des Congrès de Paris* produces a monthly brochure called *Paris Sélection* that lists the month's *manifestations* (cultural events), spectacles, conventions, etc. You can receive it for an annual subscription fee of about 8 euros (free if the mailing address is abroad). A *passe musée* (museum pass), also available from the *Office du Tourisme*, gives you entrance to all the museums and monuments of Paris (including Versailles) and has the considerable advantage of allowing you to bypass the sometimes long waiting lines. It costs 10 euros for one day, 19 euros for three days, and 26 euros for five days.

Office du Tourisme et des Congrès de Paris
127 avenue des Champs-Elysées
75008 Paris
Tel.: 08–36–68–31–12
Fax: 01–49–52–53–00
www.paris-touristoffice.com
info@paris-touristoffice.com

Note that the *Office du Tourisme* has a voice-message service limited to 20 minutes per caller and which costs .34 euros per minute.

Calendar of Events

(For a more extensive and up-to-date listing of Paris Calendar Events, consult www.paris-anglo.com.)

January
Fashion shows (summer collection)
February
Bread and Pastry Exhibition
March
Palm Sunday, *Prix du Président de la République* at Auteuil race course, Bois de Boulogne
April
April–May: *Foire de Paris* (commercial exhibition ranging from houseware, travel, appliances, etc.) at Porte de Versailles
Early April–early October: *Son et Lumière* at les Invalides
First or second Sunday in April: Paris Marathon (foot race around Paris)
May
May–September: Illuminated Fountains at Versailles with Sound and Light shows
Mid-May–late June: Versailles Music and Drama Festival
Late May–early June: French Open Tennis Championships, Roland Garros Courts (Bois de Boulogne)
June
Early June: Paris Air Show, *Salon aéronautique* (odd years only), Le Bourget Airport
Early June–mid-July: Marais (4th *arrondissement*) Festival (music, drama, exhibitions)
June: a festival of music, drama, and dance at St-Denis
Mid-June: *Grand Steeplechase de Paris* at Auteuil race course, Bois de Boulogne
Mid-June: *Fête du Pont-Neuf* (booths and street performers on the bridge and in the Place Dauphine)
June 21: *Fête de la Musique* (Music Holiday)—Initiated under the auspices of then Culture Minister Jack Lang in the 1980s, the *Fête de la Musique* transforms the entire country into a venue for musical expression of all kinds. The streets of Paris are filled with people milling from square to square, bar to bar, listening to jazz, rap, soul, hip-hop, classical, and other groups. This is a joyous way of bringing in the summer (night of the solstice), and the holiday has caught on. Music groups and free open-air concerts throughout the city.
June 24: *Feux de la Saint-Jean* (fireworks) at Sacré Cœur
End of June: *Grand Prix de Paris,* Longchamp race course, Bois de Boulogne
July
Late May to early July depending on year: Festival de Saint Denis, Tel: 01–48–13–12–10. Classical music festival
July 14: *Fête nationale* (celebrations throughout the city and military display on the Champs-Elysées). The *Bals des pompiers* (street parties) happen the night before.
Late July: finish of the Tour de France cycle race on the Champs-Elysées.
Throughout July: Fashion shows (winter collection)

September
Fête de la Humanité, an international cultural fair, sponsored by the Communist daily newspaper, *L'Humanité,* with strong political overtones. Exhibits, international music, and food from around the world. Located in the northern suburb of La Courneuve
Festival de Montmartre
Late September–early December: *Festival d'Automne,* Tel: 01–42–96–12–27. Music, drama, ballet, exhibitions
October
First Sunday: *Prix de l'Arc de Triomphe* at Longchamp race course, Bois de Boulogne
Early October: Montmartre wine festival, Paris Motor Show at the Parc des Expositions (even years only)
November
November 11: Armistice Day ceremony at Arc de Triomphe.
Beaujolais Festival: when *le beaujolais nouveau* arrives, the party starts at midnight as the first bottle of the new harvest is allowed to be opened. People generally stop whatever they are doing and go for a glass at the nearest café or bar. For a week or so people talk about how bad or good or tasty or sour the *beaujolais nouveau* is. Bars are often decorated for the occasion and signs are on the tables and windows announcing that the stuff has arrived.
December
Christmas Eve: Midnight Mass at Notre-Dame.
Mass is also celebrated at American Cathedral, 23 avenue George V.

Climate

The word for weather, as in what it's doing out, is *le temps,* not to be confused with the same word for "time." The weather report is *la météo.*

Although the weather in Paris is seldom extremely hot or extremely cold, it is variable, since the city lies at the junction of marine and continental climates that have opposite characteristics. Autumn in Paris can be absolutely lovely, mild and somewhat sunny with a tinge of melancholy in the air. The foliage is nice but not always noticeable in the center of the city. Sweaters and light coats are needed. Similarly, the fall and winter can be, and often are, long and gray. The heavy grayness *(grisaille)* often contributes to drawn faces, sadness, and depressed moods. In the spring and autumn, temperatures average about 11° Celsius (52° Fahrenheit) with warm days and cool nights.

During the winter the average temperature is about 3° Celsius (37° Fahrenheit). The winters are wet, and warm rain gear and an umbrella are indispensable. In Paris there is rarely any snow, other than a few flakes in February, and there may be a strange and short barrage of hail once or twice a year. Nonetheless, winter coats or down jackets are necessary—the cold is damp and penetrating and often annoying. Ski jackets aren't usually worn in town, but students can get away with anything. Apartments are often inadequately insulated and can be damp.

Spring comes late, or winter seems to linger and fuses with summer. The blooming of the nubby, cut-back magnolia and horse chestnut trees along some of the boulevards is a pleasant sight. The leaves give off a sweet but strange fragrance that seems to be found only in Paris. April in Paris is often cold and rainy, and the chestnuts do not blossom until the last week of the month. It's a good idea to have an umbrella handy from November through June.

Summers in Paris can be rather hot and uncomfortable. The pollution gets thick and the air heavy. There are even "pollution alerts" in Paris when it's ill-advised to spend a lot of time in the streets. The tourists start arriving on Easter weekend, but the Parisians don't start leaving until July (see Vacation Time). Temperatures in the summer average about 20° Celsius (70° Fahrenheit) with some very warm days, especially in July and August.

A Few Weather Expressions

il fait beau	it's nice out
il ne fait pas beau	it's not very nice out
il fait mauvais	the weather is bad
ça caille	it's freezing (slang)
il pleut	it's raining
il fait froid	it's cold
il fait chaud	it's hot
il neige	it's snowing
il fait moche	it's ugly out

Average Temperature Range

Station	Altitude (m)	Annual	January (Temp. in C°)	July	Rainfall (mm)	Days rain
Lille	44	9	3.1	15.9	596	185
Lyon	200	11.1	4.2	19.7	973	186
Strasbourg	150	9.7	0.6	17.9	585	184
Brest	98	10.9	7.1	15.1	1,030	204
Paris	75	11.6	4.9	18.6	631	193
Bordeaux	47	12.4	6.6	19.6	801	184
Marseilles	4	14.8	8.4	23.4	498	79
Nice	5	15.1	9.3	22.3	576	59
Ajaccio	4	14.7	10.4	20.9	433	185

Temperatures

Converting Fahrenheit to Celsius:
Multiply Celsius temperature by 2 and add 32 for approximate conversion.

Fahrenheit	Celsius
0	-17.8
32 (freezing)	0
50	10
68 (room temperature)	20
77	25

86	30
98.6 (normal body temperature)	37
100.4	38
104	40

Paris Average Number of Rainy Days per Month followed by Millimeters of Rainfall and Average Number of Hours of Sunshine per Day

(To convert millimeters into inches, divide by 25. Ex: 55 mm = 2.2 inches)

	Rainy Days	Rainfall	Hours of Sunshine
January	10	55	2
February	9	45	3
March	7	30	5
April	6	40	6
May	8	50	7
June	9	50	8
July	8	55	8
Aug.	8	60	7
Sept.	8	50	6
Oct.	8	50	4
Nov.	8	50	2
Dec.	9	50	1

Geography

Départements: The division of France into ninety-five *départements* is a result of the Revolution and was accomplished in 1790. The three following principles were decisive in its formation: the size of each department was to be approximately 6,100 sq. kilometers; the seat was to be located strategically so that it could be reached in the period of one day on horseback from any point in the department; and the name was to refer to the department's provincial history and character.

France is also divided into twenty-two regions, which are less important for administrative purposes but should not be confused with the department names. The present organization of the regions dates from only 1960 and is the result of economic considerations.

Principal cities and départements. The numbers found after the name represent the codes for the department. These codes are used in the postal codes, on license plates, and other standardized nationwide printed application forms. People tend to refer to certain departments by their numbers. Paris and its surrounding six departments together make up the Ile de France.

ILE-DE-FRANCE			
Paris	75	Essonne	91
Seine-et-Marne	77	Hauts-de-Seine	92
Yvelines	78	Seine-St-Denis	93
		Val-de-Marne	94

Early Questions and Decisions

The best way to make any major international move is to anticipate and avoid the unnecessary traumas. And that best happens with preparation. As it is, moving to Paris will present hundreds of little and large surprises and a hefty dose of character-testing obstacles. So brace yourself. Both the planning stages and those first days will be thoroughly exciting and highly stimulating, but it is not going to be easy, and you will experience moments of intense doubt. This is wholly normal.

Don't assume anything. Take on a new innocence and learn to be humble enough to realize that although you may be an accomplished professional at home, when it comes to moving to—not visiting—France, the learning curve is steep. Your logic may not be theirs. In fact, it won't be. Not until you live in a foreign country do you realize how culturally influenced things that seemed universal (like logic) really are. "That's not logical," is not a valid complaint. Here, it may be logical.

An advantage in getting informed today is the wealth of resources on the Web. The Internet is perfect for making initial contacts and sharing information, stories, tips, and addresses. There are a number of excellent Web sites, chat rooms, and news groups for this purpose. With seventy-four million people visiting France each year and more than a hundred thousand permanent Anglo-American residents in Paris at all times, you should be able to kick up a few fruitful dialogues with fellow Francophiles. You should also check in at www.paris-anglo.com, where you'll find a full directory of Paris contacts and a lot of supplementary information and new updates to this guide. You can sign up for the free newsletter, *My Mercredi*, too, which I send out every other Wednesday. There are a host of other newsletters and publications that will help you as well: *Bonjour Paris*, *ParlerParis*, *ThinkParis*. Other sites to visit early include www.fgtousa.org, www.france tourism.com, and www.paris-touristoffice.com.

The obvious way to begin to figure out how to move to France is to contact the French government offices closest to your home.

French Consular Offices

For administrative, commercial, and legal issues concerning your travels to France, contact the French consular office nearest to you. The French government posts travel and administrative information on its official Web site, found at www.info-france-usa.org. Updated lists of addresses, phone numbers, and E-mail addresses are found here, and we've included the list on www.paris-anglo.com.

Maison de la France

(French Government Tourist Office)
The most complete and thorough source of basic travel information on Paris is the French Government Tourist Office, known as the *Maison de la France*. As of 1998, a phone center in Washington, D.C., fielding your questions and requests for brochures, has replaced the more personalized service travelers used to get. Receiving printed information can take up to a month, so start inquiring early. The direct line for the United States is (202) 659–7779. This is a toll call. Although their free booklet "Easy Reference Guide France" contains a great rundown of tour operators and travel agents in the United States specializing in France, it is more helpful for tourists and short-term visitors. Additionally, it mixes the small and personalized agencies with the huge and impersonal ones, the highly reputable with the unproven, and you'll end up not knowing who to contact. There is a list of companies and agencies here that handle housing issues and apartment rentals. You may decide to book a short-term solution to get you through the first month or two while looking for something more permanent and suitable, and to this end, the reference guide is a real asset.

To contact the *Maison de la France* offices in Chicago, Los Angeles, Miami, New York, Montreal, and London, consult www.paris-anglo.com.

The Alliance Française

The Alliance Française is a great source of cultural and linguistic information and overall support for Paris-bound travelers. It's also a sure way of both propelling you into the world of French culture before your Paris residence and maintaining your contact with your Parisian experience after returning. This century-old worldwide network is, according to its own brochure, "dedicated to promoting awareness, understanding and appreciation of the French language and culture."

Go to www.afusa.org for a list of its 144 chapters and French schools throughout the United States (sometimes just a contact person giving French classes in a small town). Or call or write to get on the Alliance Française mailing list: 2819 Ordway Street NW, Washington, DC 20008; (202) 6893000; Web site: www.info france-usa.org/culture/alliance.html.

Franco-American Chambers of Commerce

If your interest in Paris goes beyond the parameters of living and studying, and you're on your way to Paris for professional or commercial reasons, you may have a variety of specific questions relating to your mission. You may wish to search out potential business leads or local contacts. The Franco-American Chambers of Commerce, founded in 1896 to promote sound, strong relations between the United States and France, with its sixteen chapters in the United States, could be a key source of pretravel information.

Contact information for the Washington D.C. chapter of the Franco-American Chambers of Commerce office address is Franco-American Chambers of Commerce, 1730 Rhode Island Avenue NW, Suite 711, Washington, DC 20036; (202) 775–0256, Fax: (202) 785–4604. For a complete list of all chapters in the United States and related Web links, consult www.paris-anglo.com.

If You're Still Trying to Decide If Moving to France Is a Good Idea

Before you burn your bridges, think this through. Cross the bridge; don' burn it. There is a mammoth difference between visiting Paris over and over and loving each stay, and setting up shop. You could end up shooting holes in your love affair.

- If you're coming to study for a year or two, the legal and practical procedures are different from and less of an obstacle than those for the person moving to France to live and work open-endedly.

- If you've been transferred by your company for a measured stint of one or more years and know you'll be returning home, the steps and precautions again are distinct. You may be wildly excited about the opportunity to make this career move, or you may be upset that you have to leave suburban Connecticut or Michigan, or you may be glad and your accompanying spouse may be miserable, or vice versa. Get these feelings sorted out early.

- If you're coming with children, you may be worried about their schooling or terrified about the language.

- Many people who make the move simply want a change in their lives—a break from the monotony of their career, a split from a worn-out relationship, a means to get over the death of a loved one. Living in Paris can have as much to do with what you're leaving as with what you're finding.

- Cultural-minded folks are attracted to Paris because it's a good place to write or paint or take pictures or play music or think.

- Teachers and professors come for sabbatical, to conduct research, to get international experience, to further their knowledge in a field that relates to France, its culture, institutions, and traditions.

- Elderly people come to retire, to settle, to spend half their time in France and half somewhere else.

- And then, of course, there is a broad and mixed community of individuals who have fallen in love with a Parisian and have followed him or her to Paris, or have decided to stay here and remake their lives in this adopted home.

Whatever the reason, there are early decisions to make, and there are consequences to those decisions.

Three Pieces of Earnest Advice

1. Articulate your goals and expectations, write them down, and date the paper. On a weekly basis reread your statement and reevaluate it at each step of your preparations.
2. Make a plan for the move and a schedule that accompanies it.
3. If you're at all hesitant about uprooting yourself, give yourself a trial period of three months before making definitive and expensive plans. (You can take a leave of absence, sublet your apartment, etc., and give the move a preliminary try.)

Areas of Greatest Concern

1. Where do I/we live?
2. What's my/our legal status in France? Can I/we work legally? And can I/we support myself/ourselves in Paris?
3. What do I/we risk? What do I/we gain?

Housing *(Logements)*

One of your earliest concerns will be "Where do we live?" The issue of housing and accommodations is handled in depth in the Housing and Accommodations chapter of this guide. But to start you should begin to sound out and price some of the options that exist. Student housing, a room in a French family's apartment or house, an apartment rental, a furnished apartment rental, a suite in a residence-hotel, a hotel room, a house rental, a house or apartment purchase, a housing exchange.... Investigate some of the Paris housing sites on the Web to start.

Apartment Sites
    www.paris-anglo.com
    www.rentals-paris.com
    www.decircourt.com
    www.france-apartment.com
    www.locaflat.com
    www.paris-appartements-services.fr
    www.guestapartment.fr
    www.lamaison.fr
    www.homerental.fr

Early Legal Questions Concerning Your Status in France

A resident American lawyer in Paris, Samuel Okoshken, specializes in helping individuals and companies get legally settled. He has put together the following list of preliminary questions that you might be asking yourself already. These are organized according to five areas that generate the most frequently asked questions: obtaining visas, purchasing property, being able to work and starting a business, paying taxes, and handling inheritance and estates. Each of these areas is covered in greater depth elsewhere in this guide, but it's helpful to begin with an overview.

Obtaining a Visa

Americans and European Union members may enter and stay in France for up to three months as tourists without a special visa. But North Americans and other non-EU persons need visas in the following cases:

+ If you intend to remain in France on an extended touristic stay (i.e., a non-working visa)
+ If you are coming to study in France
+ If you are engaging in a self-employed activity (consultant, professional, artistic activity, selling agent, or other commercial activity)
+ If you are engaging in a corporate activity
+ If you will be working as an employee of a French company
+ If you will be working as an employee of a United States (or other foreign) company sent to work in France either for the local subsidiary or to create a subsidiary

If you fall into one of the above categories, you will need to know:

+ How do I go about applying for a visa?
+ Where is the visa application made?
+ What information do I need to furnish to the French government when applying for a visa?
+ Are there any United States treaty rules that may help me obtain a visa?
+ What will be the duration of the visa?
+ Is the visa renewable? Under what conditions?
+ What happens if I want to change my economic activity (change jobs, move from self-employed to employee status or vice versa, etc.)?
+ How does the visa assist or restrict me in making the switch?
+ What can be done to overcome these obstacles?
+ Can I do all this myself, or do I need professional help? And if yes, what should I budget for these services?

Purchasing Property In France

How to find housing, how to understand French apartments, and the procedures for renting are all covered in detail in the Housing and Accommodations chapter. If you'll be purchasing a house or an apartment in France, however, you'll need to be particularly prepared for the challenge. These are the steps and considerations you should take into account.

+ Engage a *notaire*. A *notaire* is a special breed of French lawyer (legal notary) who specializes in property transfers. No purchase in France can be done without one. The seller will be represented by a notary, and the buyer should be represented too. Since you're working outside of your first language, the need for representation is even more evident. *Question:* Should you use the seller's notary or engage your own?
+ Sign the purchase option *(promesse de vente)* and make a down payment. The *promesse de vente* is a binding agreement. *Question:* Is there a way to create a backdoor escape if you change your mind?
+ Close the transaction. The process from signature of the purchase option to

closing takes about three months. *Question:* Why so long? Is there anything you can do to speed it up?

+ Pay the purchase costs. *Question:* What are they? Who bears them? Is there any way to minimize them?

Other Questions to Consider

Collateral issues: Should you purchase the property in your own name? Should you use a corporation, trust, etc.? What are the pros and cons of each option?

When you become an owner what are your continuing obligations regarding (i) real estate taxes, (ii) occupancy taxes, (iii) income tax on rental income (if any), (iv) capital gains tax on eventual sale of the property, (v) possible annual 3 percent tax if ownership is by a foreign corporation, (vi) capital tax if the value of your property exceeds a threshold value, (vii) building charges.

How do you structure the purchase if you plan to buy with a spouse, friend, partner, etc.?

What are the tax ramifications in the United States for American citizens purchasing in France?

What happens to the property at your death?

What are the French wealth tax implications?

Must you be a legal resident of France to purchase French real estate?

Creating a Business in France

A description of the working culture and tips on job hunting in Paris are found in the Working in France chapter. Creating a business in France, though, requires much thought and understanding on a variety of levels—legal, fiscal, economic, practical, and cultural. Here are just some of the issues you must face:

+ Visa: If you will reside in France, you must obtain the appropriate visa to permit you to conduct your business activity.

+ Business structure: What is the appropriate structure or status for your business—self-employment, a corporation, a French-style S Corp (i.e., pass-through of profits and losses to shareholders), a branch of a U.S. or U.K. corporation, a nontaxable representation office, a partnership, an operation directly out of a foreign company, nonresident shareholders/managers, a non-profit organization, or other. Business factors, tax factors, and social security factors are key elements in the equation that will lead you to making the right choice.

+ Procedural steps: Registering as a self-employed person. Setting up a French company and registering with the appropriate authorities.

+ Costs: What are the costs of creating a legal business, acquiring an existing business or a business lease, two-year budget, and the like.

+ Subsidies for small businesses: Are there any fiscal or other subsidies for new businesses that can reduce your start-up costs or running costs?

+ Income tax: French income tax rules relating to business profits are similar to U.S. rules, but there are many significant differences that must be known beforehand so that grim reality does not hit you from behind.

+ Social charges: French social charges are so high that they are often the reason for a decision not to do business in France. What are they? Can they be avoided or minimized?

+ Other taxes and costs: What other business-related taxes and costs should you know about, such as doing-business tax, salary taxes, cost of acquiring business premises, V.A.T. (national sales tax), minimum corporate tax, and others.

+ U.S. or U.K. tax implications: How is your business income reported and taxed in the United States or United Kingdom (if you are an American or British citizen or tax resident)?

+ Changes in the business: What happens when you want to take in a partner? When you sell your business? If you die while owning the business or part of it?

+ Keeping books: Should you have an accountant and at what cost?

+ Regulated activities: Certain activities are regulated and restricted, such as tourism, the professions, etc. What are the entry-level problems? Can they be surmounted or mitigated? At what cost?

French Income Tax, Social Security Tax, Wealth Tax

Income Tax. Income tax affects most foreigners living in France. Here are some items to consider:

+ Are you a legal "resident" of France for income tax purposes?

+ All residents must file an annual French tax return.

+ A joint return must be filed by married persons.

+ U.S. investment income of American citizens is tax-free in France. So retirees with only U.S. investment income pay no French income tax whatsoever.

+ Income tax rates are progressive, ranging up to 64 percent (taking into account supplementary income taxes). However, marital status and family size have more impact on tax brackets than those factors do in the United States.

+ Capital gain rates are currently 26 percent.

+ Special deductions are available to workers (employees and self-employed) that help reduce the average tax rate.

+ U.S. Social Security benefits are tax free in France.

+ Planning opportunities are available to help maintain the French income-tax bite at a level that is often comparable to that in the United States.

+ The income tax is paid over three installments during the year (or in ten equal monthly installments if you elect to do so).

+ Americans living abroad must continue to file U.S. tax returns, but exemptions and tax credits by and large limit U.S. income tax to the tax due on U.S.-source income.

Social Security Tax. The French social security taxes are quite heavy. If you are working in France, whether as employee or self-employed, you are responsible for this tax. However, in certain cases, incoming employees and self-employed people may remain in the U.S. system for a period of up to five years for employees and two years for self-employed people. Special application must be made to the U.S. Social Security Administration to qualify for this important tax break.

Wealth Tax. The United States does not tax capital (except at death). The French do. The French capital tax (i.e., tax on net worth) applies to worldwide assets whose total net value exceeds 750,000 euros. Some important features to consider:

+ U.S. citizens are exempt from this tax (except on any French assets they may own) during the first five full years of their French residency.
+ Business assets, art, and antiques are exempt from the tax.
+ Principal residence is taxable but on 80 percent of its value.
+ Rates range from 0.55 percent to 1.8 percent.
+ This is an annual tax.

Part of the French wealth tax may be a deductible item in your United States income tax return.

Inheritance and Estate Taxes

The French laws of inheritance differ significantly from those in the United States Here are some important considerations in this legally complex area:
+ Children are favored over spouses. You cannot disinherit your children, not even children from a prior marriage!
+ If you are domiciled in France at your death, all of your assets, except for foreign real estate, are subject to the French inheritance rules.
+ Domicile is a question of fact and is not as easy to escape as many people believe.
+ Short-term corporate assignees are in general not considered domiciled in France.
+ The French inheritance rules may supersede contrary provisions in your wills and trusts, even if those documents are executed before you enter France.
+ Estate planning is essential for maximizing the share of your estate to which your spouse is entitled.

The French succession tax (estate tax) system is different from the U.S. estate tax. Some pertinent factors:
+ Rates vary according to the degree of kinship between the decedent and the heir. Children and spouses are taxed at much lower rates than aunts, uncles, and first cousins. Beyond first cousins, the tax rate is a flat 60 percent.
+ Americans are exempt from the French succession tax for the first five years in France and sometimes longer.
+ Americans are always exempt from French succession tax on U.S. real estate, U.S. business interests, and other small items.
+ The French succession tax is a credit against the U.S. estate tax.
+ French law does not allow a marital deduction (although a couple may be able to change their marital status to French community property, which results in the same thing).
+ The French system of gifts to children exists, but is quite different from the U.S. system.
+ Planning is required to harmonize estate tax treatment in the two countries, although perfect harmony is usually not possible.

An Early Tip from the U.S. Consulate in Paris

While living overseas, it is generally a good idea to have important documents and/or records at hand in case of an emergency or the need to leave. The U.S. Consulate in Paris suggests in its literature for American residents in France that you keep the following items readily available. Although this is an extensive list, keeping good photocopies of all important papers is a sound piece of advice.

1. Signed and notarized power of attorney executed by each spouse on behalf of the other spouse
2. Joint checking account
3. Current copy of will(s)
4. List of family members' Social Security numbers, bank account numbers, insurance policies, passport numbers and the dates of issuance
5. Medical records, prescriptions needed by family members, immunization records, eyeglass prescriptions
6. Up-to-date household inventory
7. Prior tax year records and other records necessary for filing the current year
8. List of credit card numbers (separate cards for each spouse is also a good idea)
9. Copies of birth and marriage certificates and passport biographical page
10. College and university diplomas
11. Employment records, résumés, and letters of recommendation
12. Children's school records
13. List of doctors, dentists, lawyers, and other professional providers of services
14. Mortgage records, deeds, bonds, etc.
15. Updated address books, both business and personal
16. Traveler's checks, bankbooks, checkbooks, cash—both U.S. and French currency
17. List of assets and liabilities

Summing Up Your Gains and Losses

Gains
• international experience
• exposure to a new culture
• new travel destinations
• increased knowledge and use of French
• escape from the routines of home

Losses
• interrupted career path
• distance from family and friends
• depleted savings
• stressed relationship with spouse/children

In our thinking, the gains far outweigh the losses, but it's healthy to think about the whole picture before you finalize your plans.

Legal and
Administrative Matters

Over the course of the last few years, *Paris Inside Out* has gathered, collected, and edited the comments of various professionals in Paris who specialize in helping English-speakers handle the legal and administrative requirements for living in France. Cross-cultural consultant Jean Taquet (qa@jeantaquet.com) must be thanked, as well as the versatile lawyer Daniel Laprés (lapres@easynet.fr). Daniel Laprés's Web site, www.lapres.com, is one of the best free sources of information in English on understanding the legal issues concerning living, working, and conducting business in France.

General Comments

The process of obtaining the right to enter and live in France often seems difficult, complex, and dehumanizing to Anglo-Saxons. The good news is that procedures are lightening up a bit and there has been some significant reform in untangling some of the red tape. But the tape is still red, and it's still pretty sticky.

A bit of historical explanation may help explain why the bureaucracy is labrynth-like. The French Revolution, which lasted from 1789 to 1804, resulted in the creation of a completely new society. Its main purpose was to fight the absolute power of the king and his aristocracy, and to establish government bodies that would ensure equality among the people and protect the nation and its people from oppression.

To this day the government scrupulously defends the rights of the people. To this end civil servants do not greet you informally and do not disclose their name, lest they evince some sort of preferential consideration, forbidden by the equality-of-treatment rule. That's the theory, in any case, whether or not the civil servants realize the historical origins of their nonresponsiveness or not!

In addition, government requests are based on irrefutable documents, the written word (as opposed to the say-so) being the most powerful tool of equality, despite the mountains of paperwork this might engender. To the foreigner and the Frenchman alike, French bureaucracy is admittedly heavy. And to make matters worse, the laws change often.

Regardless of who is in power, despite some shortened forms and the use of the Web, it is not getting easier for foreigners, especially non-EU citizens, to live and work in France. Laws concerning the legal status of individuals in mixed (French/non-French) marriages, multinational children, political refugees, etc., are in a state of flux. You'll sense the weight of the State as you are bounced around in pursuit of what seems to be an illogical succession of illogical documents for something called your dossier—a multiheaded animal you never quite seem to conquer until you grasp its logic by understanding which procedure you are going through and why. For reasons mentioned above, the French still have a love affair with paper, rubber stamps and fiscal stamps, signatures, and procedures—the last constantly being changed and modified and modernized, sometimes to your advantage, sometimes not, often only adding new confusion and always in the name of the well-being of the nation. As for whom this benefits in reality, no one is completely sure; the term in French is *l'intérêt général*, and you will hear it often.

For administrative matters, the French often require a *fiche d'état civil*, an official document proving an individual's identity and status by affirming their birth date, their parents' names, their marital status, etc. Like many documents issued by the government, it has a ninety-day validity and can be renewed by an in-person or written request to the city hall in the town or *arrondissement* of the individual's birth. The birth certificate remains at this city hall, which issues a temporary *extrait de naissance* as proof of birth. In some cases, the *fiche d'état civil* is no longer required. While Americans do not have an equivalent, the U.S. Consulate will issue U.S. citizens a convincing facsimile of the *fiche d'état civil*.

The French also carry a *carte d'identité* with them at all times. (A French student who learned that Americans didn't have national identity cards gasped, "How does anyone know who you really are?") The equivalent of this card needed by foreigners in France is the "residency title"—either the *carte de séjour* or the *carte de résident*.

The logic behind all immigration laws and regulations is that a country wants to control who comes in and, more important, who is coming in to stay. Like all countries, France and the United States of America have laws regulating this matter. Entering and even remaining in these countries can be relatively easy in certain situations, such as visiting as a tourist or having family ties in the country, and more complicated in others, such as pursuing a foreign education, taking a job, or establishing a business. United States law does not regulate the work environment to any great extent—for either the employee or the self-employed—so changing jobs, careers, or hierarchical levels has little or no effect on residency status. French law extensively codifies the status of the employee and places considerable obligations on the self-employed, in addition to strictly codifying the types of jobs that may be performed by the self-employed.

These layers of very complex laws make the French system almost impossible to understand without clear definitions of terms such as "living in France" and "working in France."

But first let's look at the short-term visitor. There is no reason to complicate your life if you can get by with an easier and quicker administrative procedure.

Entering France As a Short-Term Visitor

Entering France from North America, Western Europe, and Japan is an easy procedure. You just show up with a valid passport and all is dandy for a *séjour* (stay) of less than ninety workless days. European Union citizens don't even need a passport, just their national identity card. The United States signed a reciprocal agreement in 1989 (commemorating the French bicentennial) that lifted the requirement for preobtained tourist visas for French citizens visiting the United States—although on arrival EU nationals still must sign an application affirming their morality and innocence of all major offenses, international drug smuggling, crimes against humanity, and other egregious offenses.

For all other visitors to France, a tourist visa is needed, even for a short trip. Such a visa will be granted if the applicant can prove that the trip is being taken truly for the purposes of tourism, business, or a family visit. In addition the clerk at the issuing embassy must be convinced that the applicant has the funds and intention to make the trip back home (although proving such intention is nearly impossible).

Entering France As a Student, an Extended Visitor, or a Resident

Anyone who has lived in France can confirm that French bureaucracy is enough to provoke fits of rage. You have to learn to flow with the tide, to figure out the inner logic, and, when applicable, to use it to the ends that you're after. Don't panic. Everything administrative in France takes time, and most things, you will learn, are *en cours* (in process), which can be one of your greatest tools of defense. There are, nonetheless, a number of practical pointers that can ease you through the administrative labyrinth.

Because you're not just visiting France, your legal and administrative status takes on new proportions. If you have long-term intentions, you must face the reality of your choices. If you're self-sufficient and don't need to administratively establish your legal presence in France, you may choose to opt for the easy anonymity of tourist status, which means you circulate freely with only your passport. You cannot legally live or work in France. And in fact many foreigners who want to stay in France for more than three months but do not want to start the administrative process in motion for regularizing their long-term status simply take the train to Brussels or Geneva or London at the end of each three-month period to have their passports stamped and thus reinitiate another three-month period. This is feasible but somewhat impractical and of course not a real solution for those who think they might want to stay longer or hope to study or work legally in France. And local border authorities have in the last few years been on alert for people trying to use this technicality to subvert the law. However, if you don't need to work and you're sure you're only staying six to twelve months, this may be your best option. Tax experts will tell you that if you opt for this roundabout subterfuge, you may be legally responsible for filing a French tax return even if you didn't officially work in France. Tax implications come with physical presence in the country. This may be so, but for many individuals this is too close a reading of the law.

If you do hope to make Paris your home and you intend to work in France, and thus participate fully in French society, read on carefully. Your sojourn into the Kafkaesque caverns of French administration are about to begin. All foreigners residing in France for more than three months must have either a long-term visa *(visa de long séjour)* allowing them to do so, or a *carte de séjour*. (Until the age of eighteen minors may reside in France without a *carte de séjour* but they must still enter the country legally.) EU citizens, fortunately, have a relatively easy time obtaining their cards. For the rest of you, your greatest asset is your innocence, for if you know what is in store when you start the haul toward legality—*regularization*—you might not do it.

French Embassies and Consular Offices around the World

If you are not an EU citizen and you want to live, study, and/or work in France, the first step is to obtain a *visa de long séjour* (one year) or a student visa from a French consulate in your home country. Regulations, procedures, and requirements change frequently, so begin the process to legally reside in France with inquiries at the French consulate nearest you. Do this before coming to France, because in many cases procedures and visas must be obtained in your home country first, and you will be told to return home to set the process in motion. A complete list of French consulates worldwide *(Représentation diplomatique et consulaire)* can be obtained by writing to the *Ministère des affaires étrangères*, Centre des informations, 34 rue La Pérouse, 75116 Paris; Tel.: 01–43–17–60–79, Fax: 01–43–17–70–03; E-mail: mfe@diplomatie.fr; Minitel 3615 EXPATRIES (20 euros per minute). Updates can be found on the Web at www.expatries.org. You can also find a complete list of French embassies and consulates at www.paris-anglo.com.

Extended Visitor or Resident Visa Procedures

Request precise procedures at your local French consulate. If you want to come to France and do not intend to work but plan to write, research, work on translations, paint, play music, etc., the procedures are not very different from those for requesting a student *visa de long séjour*, except you will have to prove that you have sufficient funds on deposit available for the year. If you are applying with the intention of working, either for yourself or for a company, you'll need to satisfy other criteria. If you have been offered a job at any rank, your company will have to show why the company needs you and not a French national and prove that you are being hired at a minimum salary of about 4,000 euros per month ($4,000) in order to avoid the veto right of the state.

Private and Family Life

The category of status called Private and Family Life covers numerous situations, each carrying specific requirements. Essentially being married to or being the parent of a French national or someone in possession of a French *carte de séjour* or *carte de résident* may be your ticket to legality as well. The first two qualifying grounds are governed by the procedure known as *regroupement familial* (family reunification). For these categories of requests, the type of residency title granted *(carte de séjour or carte de résident)* depends on the situation of the person who was in France first. You may request a *carte de séjour* on the grounds that a spouse or a child holds one already, but this does not give you the right to work. On the other hand, marrying a French citizen enables a foreigner to get a *carte de résident* and French citizenship after that, both, of course, allowing you to work.

Persons who qualify for the private and family life status:

+ spouse and children of a foreigner carrying a *carte de séjour*
+ foreigners who have been in France since the age of six
+ foreigners born in France who can prove they have lived in France for at least eight continuous years and that, after the age of ten, they attended a French school for at least five years; on condition that the residency request be submitted between the ages of sixteen and twenty-one
+ foreigners married to French citizens (The spouse of a French citizen automatically and immediately receives a temporary *carte de séjour;* the government cannot deny this card on the grounds that the foreigner had no legal residency status before the wedding, but you must have entered the country legally. If the individual, however, is not yet in France, he or she is still required to request legal entry into France.)
+ the foreign mother or father of a French child, provided that she or he at least partially exercises parental authority over the child or that she or he finances the child's upbringing
+ foreigners who have lived in France for more than ten years (even as a clandestine/illegal immigrant) or for fifteen years in the case of foreigners who have been students in France
+ foreigners accorded the status of "stateless person," as well as their spouse and minor children if their marriage took place prior to the granting of residency status or if the marriage took place more than a year before the request
+ foreigners entitled to French worker's compensation benefits due to a work-related accident or illness with a minimum of 20 percent incapacity
+ foreigners living in France who require medical treatment that if not given would put their lives in jeopardy and that is not available in the country from which they come
+ foreigners accorded territorial asylum, as well as their spouse and children if the marriage took place prior to the granting of residency status or if the marriage took place more than a year before the request
+ foreigners who do not fit any of the above categories or those pertaining to family reunification, and who have such close family and/or personal ties with France that the refusal to grant a residency title would violate their rights to a personal and or family life

The Scientific Exchange

This category was created to lessen the difficulty previously experienced by foreign scientists coming to France to pursue research, teach at a university, or participate in related activities. In order to facilitate scientific exchange, the government has simplified the administrative procedures for these individuals, according them and their spouse and children a temporary *carte de séjour* provided their entry into France was legal.

To obtain this scientific exchange visa, you must be invited to France by an entity recognized by a research ministry, which initiates the request by sending you the appropriate documents. You then submit your request to the local French consulate, which notes your qualifications for the proposed activity and the proposed financial compensation, and verifies that you pose no national security threat to France. The consulate will then provide the list of other documents you'll need. The whole process must start with an invitation.

The request for your *carte de séjour* is made on your behalf by the French entity that issued the invitation. You will be notified of the date of your appointment at the *Préfecture de Police*. Keeping the appointment is all you'll need to do.

The Artistic and Cultural Exchange

As with the scientific exchange category, this new classification was created in order to facilitate exchange by simplifying the paperwork associated with requests for student or employee status. This residence title can be issued in two instances:

+ to the foreign artist, singer, writer, or other practitioner of the arts who has a work contract of more than three months' duration with a legitimate company or organization whose main purpose is artistic creation. The activity in question can be in-house or external. The residence permit carries the right to work and cannot be refused on grounds of the unemployment level in France. Examples of such individuals include a musician hired to play in an orchestra and an individual brought over to participate in a project funded by the French Ministry of Culture and overseen by several foundations.

+ to the foreign artist, singer, writer, or other practitioner of the arts who has signed a business agreement of more than three months' duration in order to participate in a cultural or artistic project of a company or organization whose main purpose is artistic creation. The activity in question can be in-house or external.

The residence-permit application procedure closely follows that governing the scientific exchange category. As these provisions are still quite recent and the interpretation of the law is not always consistent, individuals are strongly urged to consult their local French consulate for details.

The *Carte de Séjour*

Once in France you must proceed to obtain the *carte de séjour*. At the *préfecture* obtain a complete list of all necessary documents before making your request for the *carte de séjour*. This will minimize the amount of trips to the prefecture, the time spent in lines, the frustrations, etc. Sometimes it's hard getting your questions answered. Often to obtain one document on your list you have to provide six additional items, some of which you have already provided. Welcome to Gallic bureaucracy! Don't try to resist or change this way of thinking. In the end, remember, you're the one who will have changed. Your sensibility to procedures and protocol will be forever heightened. State employees handling these requests can be impatient, short-tempered, and seemingly spiteful. They are as stuck in the system as you. Remember to be as organized and efficient and as polite and pleasant as possible, even when you really want to scream. You might not get very far by charming the clerk, but you certainly will slow down the procedure if you create an adversary relationship. Nothing at all administrative can be done over the phone so don't even give it a thought. And don't ask for the clerk's name or to see the supervisor. French employees never give out their names, will rarely call over a supervisor, and will only be vexed by your attempt to overpower them. Don't get huffy; just learn how to maneuver, and be determined to persevere to the end.

And be prepared. Aside from your battery of papers, documents, certificates, photocopies, letters, receipts, statements, etc., always be equipped with stamped envelopes, pictures of yourself, bank statements, electric and gas bills (EDF/GDF—the only reliable and widely accepted proof of address in France), a stack of euro coins for photocopies, etc. (Make sure you keep copies of all major bills and receipts.) And remember, in France it's the written document that matters. Everything must have an official stamp *(tampon)* on it, and the more stamps there are, the more readily your documents will be received. Only the legal, stamped, and approved document in conformity with law and regulation has the weight of authority. This cannot be overstated as a cultural underpinning for French administrative life.

And, don't forget, as well prepared as you think you are for your administrative procedures, you will have to go back at least once or twice. *"C'est comme ça,"* and it's like that for everyone. In some cases your employer or university may have established regular inside contacts (*pistons*, as they're called in French) with the local authorities and will procure your papers for you. The system or practice of having a *piston* is inherent in the centralized bureaucracy. Don't get moralistic about this; if you have a good contact and are really in need of help, call your *piston*. But don't waste a favor on a small and banal matter. In other cases you'll be on your own. And you'll complain. But that's okay. The French complain all the time; it's built into the national charm. Soon, but not right away, you'll have the right to complain yourself.

Some contend that living legally in France is not as difficult as most foreigners tend to think. The key is learning the ropes fast. Problems arise only when people decide to remain in France after having entered as a visitor or tourist. The French are taking illegal immigration with increasing seriousness; most cases of severe legal action usually have been directed toward North Africans, black Africans, and Asians. The Bangladeshi vendors of nougat-coated peanuts in the métro are often rounded up. North Americans and Europeans are usually dealt with more leniently. Nonetheless, French employees of the state (*fonctionnaires*, a term you will hear a lot) don't appreciate broken laws, and the public at large has grown less tolerant of illegal foreigners in France; the key is being legal, or *en règle*.

Cartes de séjour for Non-EU Citizens

The French authorities issue two types of cards to foreigners, depending on their status: a *carte de séjour temporaire* and a *carte de résident*.

Cartes de séjours are issued to individuals of eighteen years of age and older. Parents of children below the age of eighteen should obtain a *visa de long séjour* for their children before coming to France.

Most foreigners coming to France for more than three months are issued a *carte de séjour temporaire*. This card is valid for up to one year, and it may be renewed. There is no fee for the initial card. Spouses of French citizens and parents of French-born children, however, are automatically entitled to the ten-year card, although the process may take a year or longer to complete.

Cartes de séjour for EU Citizens

EU nationals have the right to seek or take up residence and employment in France and to establish themselves in business and are not required to possess a work permit. On entry, if you are seeking employment, you have three months to obtain the *carte de séjour*. A contract of employment is a prerequisite, and the permit covers the duration of work contracts that are for less than a year. Apply for your *carte de séjour* at the (CRE) *Centre de Réception des Etrangers* or *préfecture de police* in your *arrondissement*. General telephone inquiries can be made at Tel.: 01–53–71–51–68. Spouses who are not EU citizens must apply for a visa at the nearest French consulate before traveling to France.

For Paris suburbs you'll have to report to the *préfecture* or *sous-préfecture de police* in the department in which you live.

After filling out a questionnaire and providing proof of a local address, you will be given an official notice of an appointment at the police *préfecture* for a date two to twelve weeks later. And the process is on its way! If it sounds easy, don't be fooled. It's a royal pain, but you can be assured that it's like that for everyone.

In Paris, the *préfecture* is centrally located:
Service des Étrangers
Préfecture de Police
1 rue de Lutèce (Place Louis Lépine)
75195 Paris RP (fourth *arrondissement*); Métro: Cité
Tel: 01–43–29–12–44 Ext. 4873
Hours: Monday through Thursday, 8:35 A.M. to 5:00 P.M.; Friday, 8:45 A.M. to 4:30 P.M.

Note the following list of Paris administrative reception centers. Try calling the above number to reconfirm which center you should report to.

If you live in the first through the seventh or the thirteenth through the fifteenth *arrondissements*, report to:
Centre de Réception des Etrangers du 14e
114–116 avenue du Maine
75014 Paris; Métro Montparnasse or Gaîté
If you live in the twelfth or twentieth *arrondissement:*
Centre de Réception des Etrangers du 12e
163 rue de Charenton

75012 Paris; Métro Reuilly Diderot
If you live in the eighth, ninth, tenth, sixteenth, or seventeenth *arrondissement:*
Centre de Réception des Etrangers du 17e
19–21 rue Truffaut
75017 Paris; Métro Clichy or La Fourche

Individuals living outside Paris should inquire at the local police station or at the *mairie* (town hall) about procedures for obtaining a *carte de séjour.* In some departments the *préfectures* have delegated to local officials the authority to process such applications; in others, applicants must deal directly with the *Direction de la Réglementation* of the *préfecture* or nearest *sous-préfecture.*

At certain times of the year, September and October, for example, lines at the *préfecture de police* in Paris can be four to five hours long. Curiously enough, arriving early is not always a solution, because everyone else might have had the same idea. While some individuals prefer arriving later in the afternoon (the *carte de séjour* office closes at 4:00 P.M.), there is no best bet. Bring a good book and some snacks, however, because even with the most well-devised strategy, lines are inevitable.

Students Applying for the *Carte de Séjour*

Students in possession of the student visa before arriving in France and enrolled in a university program or study-abroad program established in Paris may benefit from a group procedure that makes obtaining a *carte de séjour* a simpler routine. The only demands are that you comply with the basic physical examination required by the French government for the first card (not required for EU nationals) and pick up the card on the required date.

If you're a returning student living in Paris, you may submit requests for renewals via your university.

Legally enrolling at a university in France entails showing proof that you have entered France legally and have completed, or are in the process of completing, *carte de séjour* formalities. So don't take these instructions lightly. Listed below are the basic documents required by the *préfecture de police* when requesting a *carte de séjour.* This list is in no way definitive as *préfecture* requirements can undergo modifications and can vary from *département* to *département.*

If you arrive in France with the appropriate long-stay visa and plan to live in Paris, you should, within eight days of arrival, present yourself with your visa-stamped passport to the appropriate center *(centre d'accueil des étrangers)* as listed below, open from 8:45 A.M. to 4:30 P.M. daily except Saturdays, Sundays, and French holidays.

All non-EU students residing in Paris must report to
Centre de Réception des Etrangers du 19e
218 rue d'Aubervilliers (first floor)
75019 Paris
Métro: Porte de la Chapelle
EU students residing in Paris should report to
Centre de Réception des Etudiants
13 rue Miollis

75015 Paris
Métro: Cambronne or La Motte-Picquet

For the suburbs, you'll have to report to the *préfecture* or *sous-préfecture* of police in the *département* in which you live. The list of required documents and papers unfortunately may differ from *préfecture* to *préfecture*. Ask and ask again. When you're perfectly certain that you have it down pat, ask again.

At the center you take the initial step of filling out a questionnaire and providing proof of a local address. You will immediately be given an appointment at the *préfecture de police* for two to twelve weeks later.

Required Documents for Non-EU *Carte de Séjour* Applicants

To apply for a *carte de séjour*, the following basic documents must be submitted (others may be required in individual cases). Remember that laws, rules, regulations, and worst of all, interpretations of all of these are subject to change and modification at any time. Roll with the punches. Here are the pieces of paper you'll need:

+ Valid passport with the long-stay visa (and photocopy of passport title page and French visa page); for students, the *carte de séjour* will be a label stuck into the passport.
+ Three recent and identical black-and-white or color passport-type photographs (3.5 cm x 4.5 cm).
+ Proof of financial resources (applicable in all cases); the most acceptable proof of financial resources is a statement from the applicant's French bank showing account number and amount, or a letter from the French bank certifying that the applicant's account is regularly credited with a specified amount from an external source. In subsequent years you should keep receipts of bank transactions or bank statements from your French bank to prove that you have been receiving funds regularly from abroad to support yourself.
+ Medical certificate issued by a doctor approved by the French consulate or the results of a medical visit from the OMI *(Office des Migrations Internationales)*, which you will get once you have done the exam at the date requested by the *préfecture*. It is taken with you when you go to pick up your card, and thus it is extremely important that you do not miss this appointment.
+ Medical insurance. Bring along a full translation of your foreign medical insurance. If you have your own medical insurance, you must be able to prove that all medical expenses, hospitalization, and repatriation are included. Not only does the document have to be in French, it must be translated by an officially recognized translator or the Official Translation Office at 90 boulevard Sébastopol (Métro Réaumur-Sébastopol). No appointment is necessary and there is no fee for this service. The OMI exam costs 50 euros. Note that the medical exam you had for the visa requirement does not count in the *carte de séjour* requirement.
+ Proof of domicile in France (e.g., EDF/GDF—electric and gas bill in your name, or your rent contract, or a letter from the person who is housing you, a copy of their electric and gas bill, and a copy of their *carte d'identité française* or *carte de séjour*.

- Preregistration form *(certificat de scolarité)* for students or letter of admission to a school; the *préfecture de police* will require evidence that the student is a full-time student. Before issuing a student's *carte de séjour temporaire*, for example, the *préfecture* expects to see a preregistration form that clearly indicates the schedule of classes and the number of hours of study. The *préfecture* reports that twenty hours is the minimum weekly requirement for French-language studies; préfectoral authorities are not likely to automatically waive the twenty-hour requirement, especially if the student has already been in France for some time. Students who attend evening classes only or who are enrolled as auditors only *(auditeurs libres)* do not qualify for student status.
- Proof of health insurance coverage in France with specific mention of medical repatriation. This should be in French and clearly state the exact coverage for which the student is insured.

Other requirements:

- For an *au pair:* contract approved by French Ministry of Labor, 80 rue de la Croix Nivert, 75015 Paris, and preregistration form or letter of admission to a school.
- For a worker: contract with an employer.
- One self-addressed and stamped envelope (0,46 euros stamp).
- Some *préfectures* require birth certificates; others request originals as well as copies of all documents listed above.

Required Documents at the *Préfecture* for EU *Carte de Séjour* Applicants

The *carte de séjour* for an EU national gives the right to work for the period indicated on the card. It is also the official residence permit, and it should be carried at all times.

- Passport and three photocopies of passport
- Four passport-size photographs
- Two letters from employer (called *contrat d'engagement*) stating the duration of contract, qualifications, working hours
- Proof of residence *(attestation de domicile):* EDF-GDF bills in your name or in the owner's name and a letter attesting to your living at the said address and a photocopy of the owner's *carte d'identité* or *carte de séjour*
- *Fiche d'etat civil* (obtained at your embassy upon presentation of your original, long-form birth certificate)
- One self-addressed and stamped envelope (0,46 euros stamp)

The Receipt Issued to Both EU and Non-EU Applicants

The *carte de séjour* is not issued immediately, but you'll be given a receipt *(récépissé de demande de carte de séjour)*, which is evidence that an application has been made. Carry it until you receive your *carte de séjour*. This could take several months. Keep a photocopy in a safe place; it's your only proof. Yes, it's depressing: You provide all these great-looking original documents ,and all you get is a ratty stamped form that has been photocopied so many times that the type is blurry and crooked. But treasure it like gold, and photocopy it again. The card itself is computerized and plasticized with several layers of laminated watermark paper and covered with a high-security imprint to prevent falsification. This new card will enable the police to track your identity instantly and to limit the use of fake and stolen documents.

Applications for long-term validity French visas cannot be made in a third country, e.g., England or Belgium, unless the individual has been a resident there for one or more years.

It is not possible to come to France without a long-term visa and then apply within France for a residence permit. The French authorities will require such persons to return to their country of residence to apply for the appropriate visa.

If as the holder of a residence permit you move within France, you must inform the police department that has jurisdiction over your new place of residence within eight days. This is especially important if you are in the process of renewing your *carte de séjour*. The *préfecture de police* will not approve the application unless the change of address has been properly recorded.

Renewal of the *Carte de Séjour*

Your *carte de séjour* must never be allowed to expire or you will have to repeat all the above steps. Renewals are simple, but students must justify their student status of the past and current year. To renew you have to take the same documents listed above with the exception of the medical results. In addition students need a letter from a school or university attesting to their attendance and successful completion of courses, as well as a copy and the original of the *carte de séjour*.

To renew a *carte de séjour*, the holder again contacts one of the police centers to obtain an appointment at the *préfecture de police*. This initial step should be taken one month before the expiration date of a *carte de séjour temporaire* (two months for *cartes de résident*). If the *préfecture* is satisfied with the justification given by the applicant, the renewal process of the *carte de séjour temporaire* is approved.

Renewal of the *carte de séjour* costs 55 euros (25 euros for students) payable by government tax stamp that can be purchased at a tax office *(hôtel des impôts)* or, easier, in any *tabac* (tobacco shop). Sometimes they're out of stock, so you'll have to hunt down another. For renewal as a student, in addition to the required documents, you will have to produce proof of the amounts of money received from your home country during the previous year.

Carte de Résident

Anyone planning to stay in France for more than three years will eventually need a *carte de résident*. This card, created in 1984, permits its holders to live and work in France. It is valid for ten years and is automatically renewable. You can request the ten-year *carte de résident* if you have a *carte de séjour temporaire* and have been present in France for at least three years. Additionally, you need to prove that you have regular and sufficient revenue to support yourself and your dependents. This proof takes the form of a work contract or promise of contract.

Foreign students are considered to be a valuable asset to their country of origin, and for this reason the French government tends to discourage the awarding of the ten-year card to students who want to remain in France after their studies. Spouses of French citizens and parents of French-born children have in the past been able to obtain the ten-year card automatically. This is not easily the case any more because more jurisdiction has been placed in the hands of municipal mayors' offices. And in some cases the process to naturalize a child may take a year or two. Children of non-French parents who have been legally living and working in France for five or more years are entitled to request French nationality, but the process is long and the tightening of immigration laws has made it increasingly difficult.

There are other legal means of residing and working in France for both short- and long-term periods. For possibilities other than short-term, it is advised that you consult a lawyer.

Other Cases Requiring Extended-Stay Visitor Status

If you find yourself falling into one of the following cases, you definitely need an extended-stay visa and *carte de séjour*. Follow the procedures that have been outlined above.

✦ International-organization and embassy personnel and expatriates. These individuals are considered to be "on a mission" in France. They perform their tour of duty, then leave. All their legal relationships are with their home base, not with France. In these cases the residence permit is a *carte de séjour visiteur spécial*, and the employer usually takes care of the administrative paperwork.

✦ International-organization personnel. Individuals working for international organizations—such as UNESCO, OECD, UNICEF—are considered to be working on the territory and according to the rules of the organization, so the duration of the position is not an issue.

✦ Embassy personnel. Embassy personnel do not even work on French soil, since embassies and consulates are considered foreign territories. As with international organizations, the duration of the position is not an issue.

✦ Expatriates. Sent to France for a specific job for a limited time, expatriates remain employees of the foreign company. Although the activity involved is broader than that of a single mission, the concept is the same: The employee is not considered to be working in France. The foreign employer begins the administrative process by identifying the need for a specific job to be done in the company's French subsidiary and then asks the French government (via an embassy or consulate in the company's home location) to grant the employee the right to enter France and perform that job. The application file contains the work contract, the candidate's résumé, a description of the mission, and the intended expatriate-compensation package.

Businesspeople

✦ Creating or managing a branch office: While a branch office *(bureau de représentation)* is not an incorporated entity, it must be registered with the French government, as must its manager, who remains an employee of the mother company. This situation is very close to that of the expatriate. This is done at the *Bourse de Commerce.*

✢ Export (to France) of services: When a foreign company exports goods to France, the in-France presence of a company employee is not always necessary. Usually, however, when a service is being brought to France by a foreign company, someone has to go to France to deliver the service. And these people need legal status during their stay.

✢ Business trips: A business trip lasting less than three months conveniently falls into the tourism category.

✢ Research: Individuals may request permission to remain in France for six months to a year in order to research the feasibility of moving a business to France. The project, viewed as a sabbatical activity, needs to be solidly prepared and well presented and, as noted in the categories mentioned above, the applicants must prove that they have sufficient funds to support themselves during their stay, as well as health insurance covering all possible conditions and accidents.

French Nationality

If you've been in France long enough to request French nationality, you probably are able to fend for yourself without the help of this book; however, the lines can be absurdly long and the procedures are known to have led courageous people to the edge of sanity. At one *préfecture* recently it was observed that the line just to pick up the application folder—distributed at 14h to the first 100 in line each Tuesday—had formed at *7h.* Hmmm.

How to Obtain French Nationality by Naturalization

You can obtain French nationality if:

✢ your spouse is French and you have been married for at least one year.

✢ you were born in France and have lived in France for at least five consecutive years.

✢ your children are French and you have lived in France for at least five consecutive years.

✢ you have lived in France for more than five consecutive years.

Concerning Children born in France

✢ Children born in France of at least one French parent are French at birth.

✢ Children born in France of two foreign parents can become French if on their eighteenth birthday they have lived in France for at least five years since the age of eleven. Naturalization (of adults or children) may take up to two years.

Dual Nationality

U.S. law allows U.S. citizens to assume French nationality without losing American nationality but requires that they travel as Americans when in the United States.

Children born in France of at least one American parent may obtain U.S. citizenship when their birth is declared by their parents at the U.S. Embassy. The process requires an appointment with a consular officer, and the child must be presented in person.

Summing Up

The French have the reputation of living by the phrase "There is nothing that can be done"—and this reputation is often accurate when dealing with French administration and bureaucracy. You are practically obliged to do it the French way. So, grin and bear it, and learn the ropes. The best defense is to be resilient, patient, and persistent. With a forced smile, refuse to take no for an answer and do not give up. The system is made to be difficult; this is its built-in checks and balances. There are plenty of hairline cracks in the system, and the bureaucracy is run by individuals with varying degrees of formality when it comes to interpreting and applying the rules. A "No" today at one window may be a "Yes" tomorrow at the next one. Keep trying. Keep smiling. Cry before you yell. Get aggressive and the whole system comes crashing down on top of you. Recognize the power of the bureaucrat in front of you to stop you, to block you, to ruin your life ambitions, and show that you yield to it. They love feeling the power to crush you, so play on it. The ultimate bottom line is that you want your papers to be in order; you want to be able to live peacefully and legally in France; you want to be able to earn your living and be paid in full security and legality. To get there, you're going to have to be clever and motivated, with unlimited endurance. You will find a solution as long as you don't get discouraged. I once lowered myself to bringing a box of brownies to hand out to these powerful clerks. Yes, Betty Crocker bribes! Your understanding of the administrative culture combined with a mastering of the little nuances in the French language, and the ability to charm, please, beg, and wait will afford you your papers. And in obtaining them you will have passed the toughest obstacle course thrown at foreigners trying to legally survive and thrive in France. The rest will be gravy. If you still want to live and work in France after going through the administrative wringer, you're ready to be a true Parisian for life.

Travel and Tourism

When planning an extended stay in Paris—or possibly to stay forever—your concerns about airfare and travel connections are fewer than when planning a vacation. If you spend an extra hundred dollars to get to Paris, it's no big deal, especially when calculated over time. There are a few travel tips that you should consider, however:

+ If you're coming for a year or less and uncertain about your return plans, try to buy a ticket with an open return or one that allows you to change the date without out a penalty.
+ When moving overseas, you have lots to bring. Even when shipping your possessions ahead, you're likely to have a fair amount of luggage when you travel. Take a scheduled airline instead of a charter or excursion fare; the baggage allowance is far less restrictive. Students usually need to get all their stuff on the plane with them, so this tip may make the difference.
+ Don't be afraid of buying a one-way ticket if the price and schedule fit your needs. One-way return flights are easy to obtain in Paris for reasonable prices. If you plan to return for a major holiday like Thanksgiving, Christmas, Easter, or the summer vacations, reserve your round-trip, but don't pay for it yet. It's harder to find tickets at low fares at these times.
+ If you buy a round-trip ticket with an open or one-year validity and you plan on returning home for a holiday or break in between, consider buying a cheap round-trip ticket in Paris and saving the return portion of your initial ticket for your final return. This may save you money and stress.
+ Airplane tickets are now readily available for discount purchase on the Web, although in my experience most U.S.-based travel sites do not account for European travel or trips that begin in Europe.

Gateways in North America

There are 117 international airlines that regularly serve Paris, although most are not flying from your city. The following cities have nonstop service to and from Paris:

Atlanta, Boston, Charlotte, Chicago, Cincinnati, Dallas, Detroit, Houston, Los Angeles, Miami, Minneapolis/St. Paul, Montreal, New York, Newark, Philadelphia, Phoenix, Pittsburgh, San Diego, San Francisco, St. Louis, Toronto, Washington, D.C.

International Airlines with Flights to Paris

The following airlines offer direct, nonstop flights to and from eighteen North American gateway cities. This gives you possible connections you probably hadn't considered.

Air Canada	(800) 776–3000 (U.S.)
	(800) 268–7240 (Canada)
Air France	(800) 237–2747
American Airlines	(800) 433–7300
Canadian Airlines	(800) 665–1177
Continental Airlines	(800) 525–0280
Delta Air Lines	(800) 221–1212
Egyptair	(800) 334–6787
Icelandair	(800) 223–5500
Northwest Airlines	(800) 225–2525
Tower Air	(800) 348–6937
Trans World Airlines (TWA)	(800) 221–2000
United Airlines	(800) 241–6522
US Airways	(800) 428–4322

Register on the airlines' Web sites, and you'll systematically receive by E-mail the latest offers. Paris is often on the list. Open return tickets with a one-year validity are occasionally available.

Distances from Paris

(To convert kilometers into miles, multiply by 0.6.
For example, 1000 kilometers is 600 miles.)

Amsterdam: 504 km	Edinburgh: 867 km
Athens: 2,918 km	Florence: 878 km
Berlin: 1,054 km	Frankfurt: 465 km
Boston: 5,531 km	Geneva: 402 km
Brussels: 308 km	Helsinki: 1,894 km
Budapest: 1,257 km	Hong Kong: 9,982 km
Cairo: 3,210 km	Istanbul: 2,243 km
Chicago: 6,664 km	Kuwait: 4,403 km
Dublin: 854 km	Lisbon: 1,817 km

London: 414 km
Los Angeles: 9,107 km
Lyon: 460 km
Madrid: 1,316 km
Marseilles: 776 km
Mexico City: 9,194 km
Milan: 826 km
Miami: 7,361 km
Montreal: 5,525 km
Moscow: 2,851 km
Munich: 832 km
New York: 5,837 km
Oslo: 1,337 km

Prague: 1,035 km
Rio de Janeiro: 9,166 km
Rome: 1,388 km
San Francisco: 8,971 km
Stockholm: 1,549 km
Tel Aviv: 3,289 km
Tokyo: 9,998 km
Toronto: 6,015 km
Venice: 838 km
Vienna: 1,227 km
Warsaw: 1,044 km
Washington, D.C.: 6,164 km

Arriving in Paris by Air

Traveling to and from Paris is relatively easy from North America, all corners of Europe, and the rest of the world. More people visit Paris each year than any other foreign capital in the world—sixty-seven million people! Three to four million Americans visit the French capital. Paris is also a hub for international traffic to Africa, the Middle East, and Asia.

Most likely you'll be getting to Paris by plane. The two main international airports are Charles de Gaulle (also known as Roissy because it's located in the northern suburb by that name) and Orly, the older of the two, located twenty kilometers south of Paris. When being met at Charles de Gaulle or Orly, be sure to indicate which terminal you'll be arriving at. General airport information and message services can be obtained by calling 08–36–68–15–15 (Charles de Gaulle) or 01–49–75–15–15 (Orly).

Both airports are very well served by taxis, public buses, and commuter subway lines called the RER (see the Urban Transportation and Driving Chapter). Those first moments in a foreign airport are always filled with a rush of impressions—you'll immediately notice the aesthetics and details that reflect the local culture and attitudes. The culture's sense of style and aesthetics are present in the design and advertising. The cars and signs are new. A lot of people smoke, although this is slowly changing as signs and announcements remind travelers that smoking in the airport is forbidden. Taxis queue. Luggage carts are free. The racial and ethnic mix indigenous to France is different from that in London or Amsterdam. The vestiges of France's colonial history are present in the makeup of its people.

If you're flying into Paris from North America on a regularly scheduled flight, you'll most likely be arriving at Roissy in the early morning. The sounds of Roissy announcements and the strong wafts of espresso are details that you will pleasantly recognize upon each return.

If you need to change money right away, proceed either to the exchange office located on the arrival level near the exit or one of the ATMs. It's preferable that you do not change money in the airport; exchange rates are low, commissions are applied, and you'll waste time. (For detailed discussion of currency exchange and French banking practices, see Banking and Money.)

Roissy/Charles de Gaulle Airport (CDG)

Charles de Gaulle Airport is large, expansive, and modern, and not overly intimidating. There are three principal terminals: the older and circular Aérogare 1, which is devoted to long-distance international flights; Aérogare 2, newer and user-friendly, divided into six *halles*, or sections, 2A, 2B, 2C, 2D, 2E, and 2F, and dominated by Air France and other European airline flights; and Aérogare T9, which is principally used for charter flights, many of which serve Canada.

   Aérogare 1: As you disembark you'll follow the glass corridors and the crowd onto a long and bouncy moving sidewalk that carries you and your hand luggage toward the core of Aérogare 1 and the awaiting Immigrations and Passport Control lines. Non-EU citizens must fill out a simple yellow embarkation card, which you should do on the airplane to save you time and the aggravation of having to procure the form at the front of the line. Aérogare 1 is in the shape of a large circle with numbered satellites branching out from the core. The lines to get past the immigration inspector are often long and somewhat unruly. You will notice that the French—who love form—are not too concerned with order and are not keen on civic education. Thus, there will be some jockeying for position in the line. Follow the signs to the baggage claim area *(bagages)*.

Claiming your Luggage and Moving through Customs

Your luggage emerges from a lower level and tumbles out onto a circular conveyor belt rather quickly. First grab yourself a free luggage cart from the stacked line. There are usually plenty, but on days when lots of flights arrive at once, you may have a problem finding an available cart. If you are moving here for an extended period, you may be traveling with special luggage like animal cages, skis, oversized packages, bicycles, etc. These items are brought into this area by hand on a large cart, so keep an eye peeled. You may have to wait much longer for these.

   If your baggage is missing or damaged, there are counters within this area for reporting such. If your luggage is lost, call the Lost Luggage Service at 01–48–62–10–46. If your luggage is damaged, our experience is that trying to make claims on small damages is not worth it. A report will be made and you may be sent to a luggage repair shop in the middle of Paris to have your American Tourister restitched. This will be a waste of time. If there is substantial damage, file a form. You may be sent to the same shop for a replacement piece, or you may attempt to take this up with the airline upon returning.

   After passing through immigrations, nabbing one of the numerous and free baggage carts, and claiming your baggage, you proceed past the customs zone, where you are faced with the choice of whether or not to make a customs declaration. The two exits are side by side. Most likely you will have nothing to declare and will be able to pass freely without stopping through the exit marked in green *rien à declarer.* Americans are rarely bothered, but should you be carrying many large packages or computers or electronics in their original cartons or else huge and poorly made bundles held together with rope and tape, you could be asked to open them and be assessed for duty. If you already hold a French resident card (*carte de séjour*) in addition to your passport, you are subject to French law concerning imports.

Play this like a simple tourist; there is no need at this point to get slowed down explaining that you're moving here or staying for an extended period. Just ignore these men and keep walking. Do not slow down, hesitate, or make eye contact—that may give them the chance to stop you and make a spot check of your luggage. This doesn't happen too often, but people who are too hesitant or are lugging massive packages do get stopped. When moving past the customs area, we usually keep our passports out and take on a bored, indifferent look as a visual reminder that we should be left alone. In almost all cases you'll not even notice that you went through customs.

A word about arriving with a video camera or laptop computer: Occasionally visitors and residents suspected of bringing electronics into France are questioned, asked to produce proof of purchase, and sometimes assessed for value added tax (TVA). A photocopy of your sales receipt can help avoid this. In fact, it's a good idea to bring photocopies of all receipts from purchases of expensive equipment, computers, cameras, etc.

If you're coming into Paris from another EU country, there won't even be a passport or customs control. You will have cleared in your first country of entry, and you should consult that country's consulate in your home country before leaving to check if any customs regulations may affect your transiting. In the outer part of this circular terminal you'll see signs overhead in French and English for the numerous exits, parking, taxis, and buses.

Aérogare 2: The process of getting from the plane to the passport control and baggage claim area in Aérogare 2 is much simpler and faster than in Aérogare 1. The procedure is the same, but the lines are shorter and the luggage recovery tends to be quicker.

The Information Stand is immediately to your left as you exit. It is open from 6:00 A.M. to 11:00 P.M. Phone cards can be bought at the newspaper stand to your right and left. And there are six ATMs scattered around the six different halls should you need to get some cash quickly.

Aérogare T9: This terminal is primarily used for charter flights. It is served by taxis and the free airport interterminal shuttle bus, which also connects to the RER station at the airport.

The ADP (Aéroport de Paris) Information Stands
Information stands, marked in French *Renseignements*, provide lots of useful information and assistance in English. You probably have mapped out your arrival strategy already and won't need immediate assistance, but it's comforting that this excellent service is available. If you arrive in Paris without accommodations, you can find same-day hotel bookings here at up to 50 percent discount, a little known and very useful service.

Getting into Paris from Charles de Gaulle Airport Aérogare 1 or 2:
Unlike tourists, your Paris plans are long-term and you have not budgeted yourself for only a short stay. You'll probably be traveling with as much luggage as you could possibly carry with you, and this reduces your local transportation options.

If you don't have a lot of luggage, take the RER train. It's fast and reliable, and there are no traffic snarls.

If you do have a lot of luggage and you'd rather not incur the cost of a taxi, take the Air France bus into Paris or arrange for a pickup service. If your destination is near one of the Air France bus stops in Paris, you may prefer this option whether you have a lot of luggage or not. Otherwise, take a taxi.

RER (Paris's Fast Commuter Train Network)

This is the fastest and most reliable access into Paris from Charles de Gaulle Airport. Count on about forty minutes of travel time to central Paris. There is a direct access by foot to the RER station at the airport from Terminal 2. Follow the signs for RER. From Terminal 1 you need to take the free airport shuttle *(navette)* to the RER station, which is only five minutes away.

Trains run every fifteen to twenty minutes from 5:00 A.M. to 11:45 P.M. and cost 7 euros per person each way. Tip: Show up with exact change, and you can buy your ticket from a machine without standing in line. If you change money at the airport, make sure to ask for coins.

The RER stops in Paris at Gare du Nord, Châtelet–Les Halles, Cluny–La Sorbonne, Luxembourg, Port Royal, Denfert-Rochereau, and Cité Universitaire.

Above the platform you'll see a lighted sign indicating which train is the next to leave *(départ)* for Paris. The airport is the end of the line, so you can't possibly take the train the wrong way.

Air France Airport Bus

This is a very convenient and comfortable way to get in and out of town. It is accessible to everyone; do not be confused—you do not need an Air France plane ticket or be an Air France passenger to use the Air France airport bus service. From your terminal follow the well-marked signs for Buses to Paris. From Charles de Gaulle take either line No. 2 or line No. 4, depending where in Paris you'd like to be dropped off, Etoile/Porte Maillot or Gare de Lyon. All Air France buses are handicapped accessible and there is a baggage handler at each stop. You do not need to prepurchase tickets; you pay onboard. Children pay half price.

Line 2 leaves from Terminal 2 and stops at Palais des Congrès at the Porte Maillot and at the Charles de Gaulle–Etoile RER/Métro stop (avenue Carnot exit). Service runs from 5:40 A.M. to 11:00 P.M. Price: 9,50 euros per person each way/16 euros round-trip.

Line 4 leaves from Terminal 1 but stops at Terminal 2 before leaving for Paris's Gare de Lyon train station (Métro: Gare de Lyon, boulevard Diderot) and Gare Montparnasse (Métro: Montparnasse, rue Commandant Mouchotte). Buses run every thirty minutes from 7:00 A.M. to 9:00 P.M. Price: 11 euros per person each way/18,50 euros round-trip.

Line 5 is the same as Line 2 but leaves from Terminal 1.

Roissybus

This airport bus runs between Charles de Gaulle Airport Terminal 2 and the Opéra (rue Scribe in front of the American Express office at the Place de l'Opéra) daily every fifteen minutes between 6:00 A.M. and 8:00 P.M. and every twenty minutes between 8:00 P.M. and 11:00 P.M. Price: 7 euros. The information number is 01–48–62–22–80, but the English is even harder to understand than the French! They are also available on-line at www.adp.fr.

RATP Buses (Local City Buses)

Less known to out-of-town visitors, the RATP runs two lines between Paris and Roissy/Charles de Gaulle. These are the slowest and least convenient but cheapest form of public transportation between the city and the airport. Students and low-budget travelers with less baggage and plenty of time may opt for this service.

Bus Numbers 350 and 351 leave from the RER station and go to the Gare de l'Est and Place de la Nation, respectively.

Both make local stops, take one hour and ten minutes, and cost six métro tickets (5,70 euros if you buy a carnet of ten tickets at the ticket window in the RER station before leaving).

Taxis

Follow the signs for taxis and line up on the sidewalk as the next available taxi pulls up to the curb. Parisians do not share taxis and drivers do not appreciate your attempts to make a deal with the people in front or in back of you in line. Paris taxi drivers are not known for their loquaciousness or general friendliness. Few speak English. Some smoke. Others drive around with a dog in the front seat. Rip-offs are not common but nonetheless you should check that the meter starts only when you get in. You should have a rough idea of where you are going and not appear hopelessly dependent. You live here now! From Charles de Gaulle Airport to central Paris, count on 35 to 45 euros. You'll be charged a bit less than one euro extra for each piece of luggage. Tipping is really up to you, but most people add an extra 2 to 3 euros for an airport to Paris journey. Don't overtip. Count on an hour from the airport to the middle of Paris, depending on time of day and traffic.

Pickup Services/Shuttle

Aside from hotel services and limousines, there are several companies offering regular and reliable shuttle and/or pickup services: Airport Shuttle (The Blue Vans) or Paris Airports Service, or Parishuttle.

Airport Shuttle operates seven days a week, year-round. Simply reserve ahead by E-mail, stating your name, airport, flight number, and time of arrival. Upon landing, but before clearing customs or claiming baggage, you must call the toll-free number, 08–00–50–56–10, to let the driver know that you've arrived. This allows him to coordinate a reliable pickup. In normal circumstances you can expect to be at your hotel about an hour and a half after claiming your luggage. Their office number is: 01–30–11–11–90.

Parishuttle offers a comprehensive, upscale shuttle service to and from Paris's airports as well as excursions to major sights in and around Paris. The prices are slightly higher, but the comfort of the vehicles makes up for this. The toll-free number from the airport is: 08–00–63–34–40. The office number is 01–43–90–91–91, and the Web address is www.parishuttle.com.

You can reserve and pay for shuttle pickups on-line at www.paris-anglo.com.

Car Rental

If you must rent a car or need to pick up your rental, follow the sign for Car Rental (*Location de voiture*). It is a mistake to begin your new life in Paris behind the wheel. Avoid this. Your opinions of the place will become jaded quickly if you have to deal with traffic, gas prices, driving styles, parking, and tickets on your first days. If you'll be staying in the far suburbs, however, you may prefer a vehicle.

Inter-Airport Buses

Between Charles de Gaulle and Orly Airports, take the Air France Bus Line 3.

Count on an hour travel time. Price: 12,50 euros.

Air France Airport Bus service operates an information number in French and English: 01–41–56–89–00. You can also take the RER to Gare du Nord, change to the B line of the RER, take it south in the direction of Saint-Rémy-les-Chevreuse or Robinson and get off at Antony. From here take the Orlyval train to Orly Airport. The trip costs 16 euros (half price for children from four to ten).

Orly Airport

Orly Airport has two main terminals, Orly Sud and Orly Ouest. You'll most likely be arriving at Orly Sud. Both are equally served by ground transportation into Paris. If your luggage is lost, call 01–49–75–04–55.

Getting into Paris from Orly Airport (Sud and Ouest Terminals):
RER/Orlyval
Follow the signs for the RER/Orlyval. These trains are accessed directly from both terminals. The Orlyval is a fast, fully-automated train offering a connection service between Orly Airport and the RER (Line B) at a station called Antony. The trip takes thirty-two minutes to Châtelet in the center of Paris. *Tip:* Show up with euros, and, if possible, enough coins to be able to buy your ticket from a machine and not have to stand in line. Follow the well-marked signs for the RER/Orlyval train toward Paris. The train stops in Paris at Cité Universitaire, Denfert-Rochereau, Port-Royal, Luxembourg, Cluny–La Sorbonne, St-Michel/Notre-Dame, Châtelet–Les Halles, and Gare du Nord.

Orlyval runs every four to seven minutes between 6:00 A.M. and 10:30 P.M. Monday through Saturday, and between 7:00 A.M. and 11:00 P.M. on Sunday. Price, including uninterrupted use of the métro (*subway*): 11,50 euros per person each way, and half price for children between four and ten years old.

Air France Airport Bus
For description, see the Roissy/Charles de Gaulle Airport section earlier in this chapter. From your terminal follow the well-marked signs for Buses to Paris. From Orly Sud or Ouest, Line 1 takes you to Montparnasse (in front of the Hotel Meridien, 1 rue du Commandant-Mouchotte, Métro: Montparnasse) and the Air France Terminal at Invalides. The bus will also stop if you request it at Porte d'Orléans and Metro Duroc, but only for passengers that do not have luggage stowed underneath. All Air France buses are handicapped accessible, and there is a baggage handler at each stop. You do not need to prepurchase tickets; you pay onboard. Children pay half price.

Line 1 leaves Orly Sud and Ouest every twelve minutes between 6:00 A.M. and 11:00 P.M. and costs 9 euros per person each way. Round-trip costs 11,50 euros. A twenty-four-hour information service can be called at 01–41–56–89–00.

Orlybus
The RATP offers a regular Orly Airport bus service to the RER station at Denfert-Rochereau. You can get off at bus stops Jourdan Tombe Issoire and Alésia René Coty. Travel time is thirty minutes. Catch this bus at Porte H at Quai 4 in Orly Sud or Porte J on Niveau 0 in Orly Ouest. The service runs Monday through Friday every thirteen minutes from 6:00 A.M. to 11:30 P.M., and Saturday and Sun-

day every fifteen to twenty minutes from 6:00 A.M. to 11:30 P.M. Cost: 5 euros per person each way. Your *Paris Visite* five-zone pass (see Transportation section) is valid on this service. Tickets are purchased on the bus or at the ADP window in the airport. Many travelers use this service to Denfert-Rochereau and then take a taxi or jump on the métro to their final destination.

Taxis

Follow the signs for taxi and wait on line in the sidewalk as taxis pull up curbside. Expect to pay between 20 and 30 euros depending on your Paris location and the traffic, plus around one euro per piece of luggage. Be careful to check that the meter is started only when you get in. It's always good to have an idea in advance where the address that you're going to is situated and not to appear totally ignorant.

Car Rental

Follow signs for car rental *(Location Voiture)*.

Arriving in Paris by Train

If you're arriving by train, the sensation is very different. If you've never been to Paris before, pulling in under the metal-hooded roof of the Gare du Nord, Gare de Lyon, or Gare Saint-Lazare can be exciting. The smell, the pigeons, the cold echo all resonate with traces of a Europe that hasn't changed in half a century. The Gare Montparnasse has been recently overhauled and modernized so the feel reflects more of the new Europe. When you step down off the train, follow the crowds into the gare. There are usually baggage carts along the long *quais* (platforms), but you'll need a one or two euro coin to get them unlocked. Try to arrive with at least this one coin in your pocket. The coin is returned when you return the cart. Otherwise luggage hauling can be painful and difficult, because the distance from your train car to the station along the train platforms can be very long. Don't count on finding a porter. All Paris train stations have currency exchange points and information stands. Additionally, all stations are served by at least two subway lines. For a list of Paris train stations and the general directions they serve, along with reservation and ticket information, see the Urban Transportation and Driving Chapter. If you need to make a phone call, you'll note right away that Paris phone booths no longer use coins. If you haven't arrived with a *Télécarte* (see the Telecommunications and Media chapter), you'll need to buy one right away.

Upon arriving, again you have the choice of RER, métro, or taxi. Taxi lines at most stations can be frustratingly long around rush hour, which is about one hour later than its North American equivalent (6:00 P.M., or 18h). There are no "share a cab" options unless you strike up a friendly arrangement yourself, which is unlikely, in that Parisians aren't accustomed to becoming familiar too quickly, even if doing so is practical and cost-efficient. Drivers are not too happy having to make short hauls. Don't get depressed if your first encounter with a Paris taxi driver is marred by grumpiness. You're now a Parisian yourself, and *c'est comme ça!* Don't worry, you'll soon learn to complain too. Parisians love to complain. Don't take it personally or too seriously. Take your time.

Les gares / Train Stations

Paris has six main train stations, so make sure you know which station you're coming into and from which station you're departing.

For all stations: INFORMATION: Tel.: 08–36–35–35–35.

Recorded train times (French): Tel.: 08–36–67–68–69.

Here are the main stations:

Gare du Nord. 75010 Paris, Métro: Gare du Nord on Lines 4 and 5, RER B and D. Served by Bus Line Numbers 42, 43, 46, 47, and 48.

This enormous neoclassical train station, crowned with statues representing the larger cities of France, was designed by Jacques-Ignace Hittorf in 1863. As its name suggests, it serves destinations in the north of France. It is, as well, the departure point for the Eurostar (Brussels, London) and Thalys (Brussels, Amsterdam, Cologne, Düsseldorf) train lines.

Gare de l'Est. 75010 Paris, Métro: Gare de l'Est on Line Numbers 4, 5, and 7. Served by Bus Line Nos. 30, 31, 32, 38, and 39.

One of the more modest stations in Paris, it serves destinations in the east of France, such as Nancy, Reims, and Strasbourg, as well as Switzerland and Luxembourg. An enormous fresco by A. Herter illustrates French soldiers departing for the Grande Guerre, or Great War, as the French call World War I.

Gare Montparnasse. 75014/75015 Paris, Métro: Gare du Montparnasse on Line Numbers 4,6, 12, and 13. Served by Bus Line Numbers 91, 92, 94, 95, and 96.

This station lies beneath the 209-meter Tour de Montparnasse and serves destinations southwest of Paris, such as Poitiers, La Rochelle, Bordeaux, Toulouse, Biarritz, and Lourdes. Montparnasse has two sections. The TGV leaves from Montparnasse 2.

Gare d'Austerlitz. 75005 Paris, Métro: Gare d'Austerlitz on Line Numbers 5 and 10, RER C. Served by Bus Line Numbers 61 and 65.

Trains leaving from this station link Spain and Portugal with France.

Gare Saint-Lazare. 75008 Paris, Métro: Gare Saint-Lazare on Line Numbers 3, 12, and 13. Served by Bus Line Numbers 20, 21, 24, 26, 27, 28, 29, and 80.

This station has been called a "factory of dreams" because of its steel and glass architecture. It was designed by J. Litsch in 1885 and acts as the commuter hub of most of the suburbs to the west of Paris. Note the bronze sculpture of piled up battered suitcases in front of the station. It was here that thousands of homeless and uprooted eastern Europeans arrived at the end of the Second World War.

Gare de Lyon. 75012 Paris, Métro: Gare de Lyon on Line 1 and RER A. Served by Bus Line Numbers 20 and 63.

This station has been remodeled several times since its construction (1847–1852). It has had its present modern style since the arrival of the TGV *(train à grande vitesse)*, France's famous high-speed train. It serves destinations in the Midi (middle of France) and the Côte d'Azur, including, Dijon, Lyon, Montpellier, Marseilles, and Nice. It is also the departure point for the Artesia train line that links France and Italy (Torino in five-and-one-half hours, Milan in six hours fifty-one minutes).

The Famous TGV (*Train à Grande Vitesse*): This high-speed train has influenced recent demographic changes in France, allowing people who work in Paris to commute from the less crowded regions around the city. Travel on the TGV requires a ticket with reservation *(billet avec réservation)*. For more information and reservations call 08–36–35–35–35.

Train Reservations and Tickets

When arriving in Paris by train, you'll probably not need to buy a train ticket unless you are transferring to another French city. Any SNCF office, train station, or travel agent can sell you train tickets and reservations. The SNCF maintains an information phone line but you may spend a long time on hold and then the staff may not speak English or may get impatient if you ask too many questions. You can prepare for your train experiences in advance by going on-line with the French Railroad Web site at www.sncf.fr, or contact the Rail Europe Group in the United States at (800) 4–EURAIL.

Info: 01–53–90–20–20 (Ile-de-France regional trains)

Info: 08–36–35–35–35 (Grandes Lignes major destinations)

Lockers and Other Services

All the train stations have lockers called *consigne,* although due to the heightened security plan called *vigipirate,* many may be closed. Be equipped with euro coins. This will give you forty-eight hours of storage. Be sure to note the times that the *consigne* area is open with full access. Gare du Nord's area closes at 11:00 P.M. The stations also have a storage service for suitcases and larger items, although due to security measures regulations may change without notice. Never leave baggage unaccompanied. For security reasons, it will be carted off and blown up.

Taking the EuroStar

Getting between England and France is easy. The EuroStar brings Paris and London within three hours of each other via the 22-mile EuroTunnel (the Chunnel). The Paris-London service runs between the Gare du Nord and Waterloo Station every hour between 7:00 A.M. and 8:00 P.M. To make reservations in Paris, call 08–36–35–35–39.

Prices vary tremendously depending on promotions, dates, and times of travel. Full-price, one-way tickets cost around 220 euros first class and 135 euros in second class for adults. Youth fares for about 72 euros apply for passengers between age twelve and twenty-five and 59 euros for kids under age twelve. EuroStar offers a leisure round-trip fare of 315 euros in first class and 196 euros in second class for travelers spending a Saturday night on either side. If you travel on a weekday, be prepared for prices that are as high as or higher than a flight. Round-trip travel during the week costs about 415 euros! Keep your eyes open for specials.

The ride is generally comfortable and smooth, with the thirty-minute tunnel interlude passing by uneventfully. It just feels as if you're traveling at night. Multilingual EuroStar attendants decked out in navy blue and yellow scarves or ties are accommodating, and the onboard buffet car is convenient. The train has public phones as well. As of late 2001, all cars are nonsmoking.

Note: A TGV terminal at Charles de Gaulle Airport allows non-Paris-bound travelers heading north and southeast to avoid Paris altogether. Inquire. You can get to Lille and Brussels from the airport too.

Customs and Entry Regulations

The former European Economic Community (EEC or EC) is as of 1994 officially called the European Union (EU). No vaccinations are required to enter France from any EU country.

There is free trade between the fifteen European Union countries with no limit on what can be brought from one country to another. Customs control checks have increased, though, along the highways inside France near border areas. From non–European Union countries, if you are sixteen years or older, you have the right to bring in 200 cigarettes, 50 cigars, or 20 cigarillos. As for spirits, the limit is one liter of alcohol over 22 proof and two liters of alcohol under 22 proof per adult. Following the breakup of the Eastern bloc, the illegal importation of cut-rate caviar, especially from Poland, has been noticed and measures have been implemented to control this. The importation of abundant and inexpensive Eastern bloc fish has led to violent protesting and sabotage by French fishermen who are suffering. New goods or provisions originating outside the European Union for personal use are limited to 140 euros worth per person. There are few restrictions equivalent to the U.S. agricultural regulations concerning foods and plants. You can show up with a bunch of roses, a duffel bag full of bagels, or a pile of corned beef without any problems. Just don't head to the United States from France with fresh food; you risk confiscation and a fine.

Student Travel to Europe

If you are a student traveling to Paris from the United States or Canada, there are a number of reduced-rate travel possibilities available. Reduced rates are also possible for travelers under thirty. Council Travel, a division of the Council on International Educational Exchange (CIEE), issues international student and youth cards that allow substantial discounts on flights. Council is able to draw upon the expertise and resources of its travel divisions to support its educational activities and to provide the best travel arrangements for participants in its international programs. Each year, more than half a million travelers, predominantly students and young people, make their travel arrangements with Council's international network of retail travel agencies in the United States, France, Germany, and Great Britain. Services include mainly flights as well as air and train passes, accommodations, insurance, car rentals, and comprehensive travel arrangements for groups and individuals.

Through its Student and Youth Flight Services (SYFS), Council negotiates with airlines for substantially reduced student/youth fares on their regular flights. These fares are available through the council's own travel agencies, as well as through a network of student/youth travel agencies and organizations in many countries.

CIEE Contact Information

Council on International Educational Exchange
112ter rue Cardinet 75017

Tel. 01–58–57–20–40 or 01–53–76–04–00
E-mail: infofrance@ciee.org
Web site: www.ciee.org

Council on International Educational Exchange
633 Third Avenue
New York, NY 10017
Tel.: (212) 822–2600
Fax: (212) 822–2699
E-mail: info@ciee.org
Web site: www.ciee.org
For other CIEE Locations in the United States or around the world, contact the CIEE directly or search the www.paris-anglo.com web site.

If you are a student, a number of university programs are accustomed to making special travel arrangements for their incoming students from New York City and other cities in the United States at special group rates. Inquire with the program that interests you.

If you are coming from other parts of the world, you should consult local airline offices for information on youth and student reductions. Many national airlines offer reduced rates. Students may be required to show a certificate of student status completed by the registrar of their university: make inquiries well in advance of your departure date. University registrar's offices will usually certify the student status of any new student on the form provided by the airline, but it is your responsibility to send the form to the university in a timely fashion. Student air fare certificates are not transferable to other persons.

The national student associations of most European countries participate in an international network of student flights under the aegis of the Student Air Travel Association. Connections between Paris and cities in Europe, Africa, the Far East, and Australia do currently exist. The fares on SATA flights are normally 40 percent below commercial fares. More information is available from the national student association of your country of residence. These same offices can supply information on special student train and ship fares. For example, the Deutsche Bundesbahn offers a reduction to students traveling from Germany to Paris. The reduction applies only to the portion of the trip made in Germany. Applications, which must be certified by the University Registrar, are available in any German train station.

Remember, persons under age twenty-six are eligible for discounts of up to 50 percent on train travel in Europe.

Traveling in Europe

Train Travel and the Inter Rail card

The most advantageous and inexpensive way to travel extensively in Europe is with the Inter Rail card. This offers students (under age twenty-six) unlimited train travel in second class during one month from the date of the first part of the journey for the fixed sum of 365 euros. The Inter Rail Card is valid for all of western

Europe, Greece, Hungary, Romania, and Morocco. It gives a 50 percent reduction in the country of purchase. Other reductions are possible at certain times of the year for destinations more than 1000 kilometers from Paris. Information can be obtained from SNCF, Place 11 Novembre 1918, 75010 Paris; Tel.: 01–42–05–63–13, Minitel: 36–15 SNCF; www.sncf.fr

Principal Train Discounts

+ Carrissimo and Joker: youth fares, 12 to 25 years old, up to 50 percent.
+ Carte Kiwi and Joker: When traveling with children (even one child), discounts can go to 60 percent.
+ Carte Vermeil and Joker: senior citizen discounts for the over-60 age bracket.
+ Children under four years old ride free, but the child does not get a seat.
+ Animals: You pay half fare of a second-class ticket (or 4,50 euros if the animal is under 6 kilos and is carried in a bag measuring not more than 45 x 30 x 25 cms).

Aside from the ultra-modern TGV, the SNCF uses primarily two models of train cars. The older ones are divided into compartments of six moderately uncomfortable seats, while the newer ones are merely organized into rows of comfortably reclining seats. Trains are always divided into Second Class and First Class, Smoking and Nonsmoking. Most trains offer snacks and drinks and many are equipped with dining cars. Having your dinner on a train, elegantly seated at a table with linen tablecloth and real silverware can be a lot of fun, but be prepared to spend close to 23 euros per person for the meal. Otherwise, bring along your own provisions, especially a bottle of water.

The least expensive sleeping arrangement on a night train is the couchette, or six-bunk compartment. Depending who you get in your compartment, you may be able to sleep well or not at all. Be warned: Theft does exist in trains, even in first class. Though rare, the most remarkable thefts happen on trains going to or coming from Southern France and Italy, where entire cars have been gassed and robbed! We can offer no advice for these Mediterranean journeys, except that you may wish to take a gas mask with you. The overnight trains to Amsterdam, Copenhagen, Frankfurt, Venice, Athens, Rome, and Madrid can make for highly memorable experiences.

Each bunk comes with a blanket, a pillow, and a sleeping-bag shaped sheet that comes sealed in a plastic wrapper to ensure hygiene. When crossing international borders at night, the train conductor will keep your passport until morning to be able to show it to the border police. Customs inspectors have been reduced between EU countries, but spot checks and some drug checking does exist. This is totally normal—don't be alarmed.

Student Excursions

The following student organizations have planned domestic and international excursions at reasonable rates. Write or call for their programs and schedules. Traveling with French students can be an excellent way to meet new friends, improve your French, and see new parts of the world.

Bureau des Voyages de Jeunesse
20 rue Jean-Jacques Rousseau
75001 Paris
Tel.: 01–53–00–90–90
Fax: 01–53–00–90–91
(Spain, Greece, Tunisia, Turkey, Egypt, Sicily, West Indies)

Fédération Unie des Auberges de la Jeunesse
4 boulevard Jules Ferry
75011 Paris
Tel.: 01–43–57–02–60
(issues student hostel cards for all of Europe)

Usit Connect
12 rue Vivienne
75002 Paris
Tel.: 08–25–08–25–25
Fax: 01–44–55–32–61
(international travel and student IDs—English-speaking staff)

Voyageurs aux Etats-Unis et au Canada
55 rue Ste-Anne
75001 Paris
Tel.: 01–42–86–17–30

Bus/Coach Travel

There are some very cheap bus excursions from Paris to London, Amsterdam, and other European cities. In the days prior to the Islamic Revolution in Iran, there were weekly buses originating in London and passing through Paris on their way across Europe to Istanbul, Tehran, Kabul, and finally India. The route changed in the seventies, passing through Pakistan instead of Afghanistan on its way to India.
Bus information can be obtained from:
Eurolines (buses)
55 rue St-Jacques
75005 Paris
Tel.: 01–43–54–11–99
Fax: 01–43–54–80–58

Nouvelles Frontiers (bus trips)
13 avenue Opéra
75001 Paris
Tel.: 018–25–00–08–25

Crossing the Channel (La Manche)

Crossing the channel can be accomplished in numerous ways. Aside from the EuroStar train to London via the Eurotunnel (see above) there are several ferry companies offering crossing service for passengers and cars. Check for promotional offers, ports, and schedules.

EuroTunnel
140 boulevard Malesherbes
75015 Paris
Tel.: 01–43–18–62–22 (information and reservations)
Minitel: 36–15 Le Shuttle

Boats/Ferries
Brittany Ferries
Tel: 08-25–828–828
Hoverspeed (hydrofoil to United Kingdom)
135 rue Lafayette
75010 Paris
Tel.: 00–800–12–11–12–11
www.hoverspeed.com

P & O Lines
19 rue Mathurins
75009 Paris
Tel.: 08–20–01–00–20

Irish Ferries
8 rue Auber
75009 Paris
Tel.: 02–33–23–44–44
shamrock@wanadoo.fr

Flying to London

Flight fares to London have come down as the EuroStar has cut into the market. If you spend a Saturday night in the United Kingdom, you can find flights on Air France, British Air, and British Midland for under 150 euros round-trip. If you travel during the week, you'll be astonished by the rate jump: over 425 euros! The cut-rate solution at this point in time is Buzz, which belongs to KLM and operates between Charles de Gaulle Airport and London Stansted. You can book only on-line: www.buzzbookings.com. Other cut-rate airlines serve France too. See Ryanair and EasyJet, which offer Paris–London flights for as little as 27 euros.

Hitchhiking

It's rare to see people *faire du stop* (hitchhike) in Paris itself, but you may see hitchhikers *(autostoppeurs)* at the entrance ramps to the beltway around Paris called the *Périphérique*, especially at the Porte d'Orléans and Porte d'Italie, where the Autoroute du Sud feeds in. Hitchhiking is illegal on the autoroute ramps themselves. The Autoroute du Sud is essentially the only route to Lyon, Orléans, and the rest of central France *(Midi)* as well as to the south of France. Hitchhiking is not ill-advised but it tends to be slow—Europeans are cautious and slightly distrustful about letting strangers into their cars (or houses, for that matter). A much better solution exists in most European countries: an organized hitch-hiking agency that dispatches riders with drivers for a small fee. For 12 euros Allô-Stop will find you a seat in a car leaving for most destinations at around the same time you want to leave. Participation in the expenses for gas and tolls depends on the driver but tends to be standard.

Allô-Stop
8 rue Rochambeau
75009 Paris
Tel: 01–53–20–42–42

Annual Events in Paris

Of course there's plenty to see and do right in Paris, far too much to mention. But these annual Paris events might be of special interest.

Fête de l'Humanité: Sponsored by the Communist party each September in the northern suburb of La Courneuve, this massive festival features stands from Communist countries around the world. Great music, food, and crafts.

Fête de la Musique: This music festival was begun in the early eighties by the then–Minister of Culture, Jack Lang. On the evening of the summer solstice, every June 21, the longest day of the year, Paris and its suburbs generously celebrate music of all kinds with neighborhood concerts, dances, and free street bands. Not to be missed.

Foire du Trône: This mammoth amusement park can be found every spring at the Porte Dorée. Try it for kicks.

Banlieue Bleues: A fantastic month of blues and jazz concerts in a vast variety of spaces, halls, rooms, and buildings in the Seine St-Denis *département*, with world-class musicians such as B.B. King, Steve Lacy, Max Roach, Toots & The Maytals, and scores of others. The festival, which takes place each March, offers a one-price pass *(carte trombone)* for three concerts for 23 euros.

For the quintessential touristy experience—traveling on the Seine in a bateaux-mouche—head to Pont de l'Alma on the Right Bank (eighth *arrondissement*); Tel.: 01–42–25–96–10. Or try a ride on the Batobus, the Seine commuter boat at Porte Solférino in the seventh *arrondissement;* Tel.: 01–44–11–33–99.

If you're looking for a more unusual outing, an American-run outfit plans barge trips complete with hot-air balloon rides over Burgundy. There are also private chateaux visits, ballooning bed-and-breakfast weekends, and special TGV ballooning packages. Check with Fance Montgolfières at 8 Villa Hallé, 75014 Paris, Tel.: 01–40–47–61–04, Fax: 01–43–35–33–92.

A wonderful little day trip in the summer is an outing to Joinville, where the *guinguettes* are moored on the banks of the Marne, the wine flows freely, and the tango dancers move to the melodies of accordion music. Eat *moules* and *frites* and imagine you're in a Renoir painting. Call or write Chez Gégène, 162 quai Polangis, 94340 Joinville le Pont, Tel.: 01–48–83–29–43.

Excursions from Paris

Paris is a great place to live and work, but you'll appreciate it more if you leave it once in a while. Paris is a particularly endearing place to return to. And fortunately Paris is an excellent point of departure for international as well as domestic travel. The French travel considerably and spend sizable portions of their savings on travel. As residents or students in Paris, you'll undoubtedly want to capitalize on the fine opportunities to visit the diverse regions of France, as well as other European countries. For travel information of all sorts concerning Paris and its environs, consult the Office du Tourisme et des Congrès de Paris, 127 avenue des Champs-Elysées, 75008 Paris; Tel.: 08–36–68–31–12, Fax: 01–49–52–53–00; E-mail: info@Paris-touristoffice.com; Web site: www.Paris-touristoffice.com. There is a branch office in each major train station.

Other regions of France have their own information centers and travel offices in Paris. Regional information on rentals, hotels, sports facilities, gites (inexpensive, rural farmhouse and vacation rentals), festivals, etc., can be obtained at www.paris-anglo.com.

Paris is well connected to numerous locations around the Mediterranean as well as points in Africa. Reasonably priced charter flights are readily available to such destinations as Corsica, Greece, Canary Islands, Spain, Turkey, Tunisia, and Sicily. There has been a veritable proliferation of travel agencies specializing in cut-fair tickets to North America, Australia, and Asia. Here are a few suggestions:

Any Way
128 quai Jemmapes
75010 Paris
Tel.: 08–25–00–80–08

Blue Marble Travel
(organizes bicycle trips)
2 rue Dussoubs
75002 Paris
Tel.: 01–42–36–02–34
Fax: 01–42–21–14–77

Non-Stop USA
8 rue Berryer
75008 Paris
Tel.: 01-53-93-75-00
Fax: 01-45-62-02-10

Forum Voyage, USA
55 avenue Franklin D. Roosevelt
75008 Paris
Tel.: 01–45–61–04–75
Minitel: 36–14 FV

Go Voyages
22 rue Astorg
75008 Paris
Tel: 01–53–43–70–78
Minitel: 36–15 Go Voyages

Maison des Amériques
34 boulevard Sebastopol
75004 Paris
Tel.: 01–42–77–50–50

Nouvelles Frontières
13 avenue Opéra
75001 Paris
Tel.: 08–25–00–08–25
Minitel: 36–15 NF

Individual and Customized Tours

✦ **Essential France,** a French-run New York based company, organizes customized trips and tours of France with quality guides and an excellent price-quality value. www.essentialfrance.com. Contact: Magali Deur, Toll free: 1(866) 285–8758.

✦ **VAP** (www.voyageuraparis.com). Leaders in individual and chauffeur-driven tours for Paris, Normandy, and the Loire Valley.

✦ **Paris-Expat.** Cultural tours for small groups. www.paris-expat.com.

Tourist Offices

Paris, especially the area around l'Opéra, is filled with official tourist offices for European and far-off countries—excellent sources of information in preparation for excursions. Using www.pagesjaunes.fr or the Minitel, you can find all of these *"office de tourisme."* A partial list appears on www.paris-anglo.com.

Government:
What Embassies and Consulates Can and Cannot Do for You

Most of you will have little or nothing to do with your embassy while you are in Paris—other than picking up tax forms, renewing your passport, registering births and deaths, registering to vote by absentee ballot, checking on your Social Security benefits and the like. Your embassy, however, can be a tremendous source of additional, valuable information and guidance. The U.S. Embassy in Paris includes a Consular Section that provides extensive and detailed information at its Web site: www.amb-usa.fr. For non-USA cititzens requiring visas to the United States, there is a toll number with detailed information: 08–99–70–37–00.

Registering at Your Embassy or Consulate

Technically, U.S. citizens spending ninety days or longer in France are supposed to register at the U.S. consulate after arriving in France, but they have no legal obligation to do so, and many short- and long-term visitors never register. According to the embassy, "registration will make your presence and whereabouts known in case it is necessary to contact you in an emergency. No information on your whereabouts will be released without your authorization. When you register, be sure to bring your U.S. passport with you to the embassy or consulate. If your passport is lost or stolen, registration will also make replacement easier and faster." Registering can also be of assistance because it:

- ✛ establishes U.S. citizenship;
- ✛ expedites and simplifies the issuance of passports;
- ✛ simplifies the issuance of consular reports of birth abroad for children born to U.S. citizens; this is a vital step in establishing the U.S. citizenship of children born outside the United States;
- ✛ facilitates provision of benefits in the event of a registrant's death;

- facilitates assistance in personal emergencies such as accidents, arrest, or serious injury;
- expedites emergency evacuation in case of natural or other disasters, or life-threatening civil disturbances;
- makes it possible for children's passports to be renewed by mail;
- helps the embassy/consulate assist relatives more effectively and quickly if a registered citizen dies, or in the event of family emergencies.

It should take you no more that a few minutes to complete the registration card and have your passport verified. Give yourself an hour though. For additional information call 01–43–12–49–42 between 3:00 and 5:00 P.M. Monday through Friday. The U.S. Embassy Consular Section is at 2 rue St-Florentin 75001 Paris (Métro: Concorde); Tel.: 01–43–12–22–22; E-mail: citizeninfo@ state.gov; hours: 9:00 A.M. to 3:00 P.M. (except for notary service: 9:00 A.M. to noon) Monday through Friday except on French or American holidays.

The Office of American Services (OAS) at the embassy offers a host of other services to Americans in France (and French territories) that you should be aware of during your residence in Paris. These include:
- Issuance of U.S. passports
- Birth reports for children born in France of U.S. citizens
- Notary services for documents to be used in the United States or for documents to be used by U.S. citizens resident in France
- Assistance to U.S. citizens who are destitute, ill, incarcerated, or who have relatives who die in the Paris consular district. (For information about these services, you may consult the Minitel at 3614 code "Etats-Unis.")
- Lists of English-speaking doctors, dentists, and attorneys
- Travel advisories
- Information on absentee voting and selective service registration
- Claims for both veteran and Social Security benefits, and arrangements for the transfer of Social Security and other U.S. government benefits to beneficiaries residing abroad
- Information on procedures for obtaining a number of foreign public documents

There is a twenty-four-hour information line: 01–43–12–23–47. For emergencies during weekends and holidays, call the embassy switchboard and ask for the consular duty officer; tel: 01–43–12–22–22.

Passport Renewal

The Office of American Services renews, normally in one hour or two, expired U.S. passports that were issued less that twelve years ago. For passport renewal go to the passport office with the following items:
- Your most recent passport
- Two identical and recent photographs. They must be taken full face with a white or very light background and measure 5 cm by 5 cm (2 inches x 2 inches). Clarify to the photographer that the photos are specifically for a U.S. passport (photo requirements are different for French and other passports). Photo booth photographs are not acceptable. There is a while-you-wait photo shop on the rue de Rivoli near the consulate.

+ Fees in cash or traveler's checks. (The office has limited cash available, so bring exact change.) For adults age sixteen or older, the cost is $40, or 37 euros. For children under age sixteen, the cost is $25, or 23 euros. (All prices are subject to change.) You may also renew passports by mail and pay the fee by purchasing from a French post office a money order called a *mandat-lettre* (not a *mandat-carte*, or personal check, which the office is not permitted to accept).The *mandat-lettre* must be in the exact amount—no more or less. Parents or legal guardians registered with the embassy must send their own passport or a legible photocopy of it along with their children's application materials. Children age thirteen or older may sign their own application; parents must sign for younger children.

Lost/Stolen/Mutilated Passport:
The passport section is open to the general public from 9:00 A.M. to 3:00 P.M. without interruption Monday through Friday, except on French and American holidays. The Office of American Services can replace lost, stolen, or mutilated passports upon verification of your identity and your citizenship through the U.S. Department of State. Go to the passport office with the following items:
+ A police report substantiating loss or theft.
+ All available identification such as birth certificate, driver's license, photocopy of the missing passport, and expired passport. (If you have no ID, you might be able to bring along an American friend or relative with his or her passport to vouch for you.)
+ Two identical and recent photographs. See above for specifications.
+ Fees in cash or traveler's checks—no personal checks.

Special Consular Services

In addition to the regular consular services described above, the consulate provides a host of other services that include:

Welfare and Whereabouts

Should one of your family members become missing, the consular section can assist in locating the person. Keep in mind that once an individual is located, you will be notified of this only if that person has signed an authorization or given oral permission to a consular officer to waive the privacy act provisions.

In contacting the Office of American Services about these types of cases, have the name of the person you are looking for, their U.S. passport number, date and place of birth, travel plans, and the date when they entered France.

Visitation in Jail

Hopefully, we have included more here than you'll ever need to know, but . . . if you are arrested, you should ask the authorities to notify a U.S. consul in the American Citizens Services office. French government authorities are obliged to comply with your request. Consuls cannot get you out of jail (when you are in a foreign country, you are subject to its local laws), but they can work to protect your legitimate interests and ensure that you are not discriminated against.

Illness Services

Since many U.S. insurance policies do not cover expenses incurred overseas, travelers may wish to purchase special insurance covering medical care overseas before traveling to France. In France doctors and hospitals require payment upon completion of services rendered. The Office of American Services provides a limited list of English-speaking doctors but takes no responsibility for the professional competence of those doctors listed. See the Health and Insurance chapter. On the Internet www.paris-anglo.com includes it's own list, and it's a good place to ask others for recommendations of doctors.

Destitution

Americans who find themselves destitute in Paris may obtain money from relatives and friends in the United States in a variety of ways. One is through the U.S. Department of State's Overseas Citizens Services (OCS) office.

The Overseas Citizens Services office hours are 8:00 A.M. to 10:00 P.M. weekdays and 9:00 A.M. to 3:00 P.M. on Saturdays; Tel.: (202) 647–5225.

If you have a major credit card, you may telephone Western Union at 800–325–6000 or 800–325–4176. Remember, to call a U.S. 800 number from France you must change the 800 to 880 and your call will go through, but it is no longer toll-free.

Deaths of Americans in France

When an American dies abroad, a consular officer notifies the American's family and informs them about options and costs for disposition of remains. Costs for preparing and returning the body to the United States can be high and must be paid by the family. At times French laws and procedures can make returning a body to the United States a complex process. A consul prepares a report of death based on the French death certificate; this is then forwarded to the next of kin for use in estate and insurance matters. If you are in the United States at the time of notification of a U.S. national's death, it is suggested that you contact the Citizens Emergency Center at the Department of State in Washington, D.C., for assistance at (202) 647–5225.

Assistance in an Evacuation or Disaster

If you are caught up in a natural disaster, civil disturbance, or acts of terrorism, you should inform your relatives as soon as possible that you are safe, or contact a U.S. consul who will pass that message to your family through the Department of State. Be resourceful. U.S. officials will do everything they can to contact and advise you, but they must give priority to Americans who have been hurt or are in immediate danger.

Federal Benefits and Veterans' Services

The federal benefits unit provides assistance with Social Security and Department of Veterans Affairs benefits. All the latest details for this can be found at www.amb-usa.fr.

Social Security Applications

A first-time applicant must submit an original birth certificate as well as proof of U.S. citizenship. A parent may apply on behalf of a child under eighteen years of age, in which case the parent's identification must be verified by a passport or French *carte d'identite*. An original marriage and/or change of name certificate must be submitted in change of name cases. All first-time applicants eighteen years or older must appear in person at the embassy. To apply for replacement of Social Security cards, a U.S. passport is generally sufficient.

What Consular Officers Cannot Do for You

There is often confusion and frustration connected to the expectations citizens have of their consulates. There is a lot that your consulate cannot or will not do on your behalf. The diplomatic mission in a country, while committed to assisting its citizens abroad, has a larger geopolitical role to play, and often a local consulate will not jeopardize that role for the interests of one citizen.

The U.S. Consulate in Paris informs Americans that its consular officers cannot provide tourism or commercial services. They cannot perform the work of travel agencies, lawyers, information bureaus, banks, or the police. The consulate warns visitors that they should not expect help in finding jobs, getting residence or driving permits, interpretation services, missing luggage, or settling disputes with hotel and real estate businesses. The embassy is not authorized to replace lost, stolen, or expired driver's licenses; only the issuing office, the Department of Motor Vehicles in the driver's home state, can perform that service. "We can, however, tell you how to get help on such matters, and refer you to the more appropriate sources of assistance," they say.

The U.S. Consulate has assembled a very useful list of addresses needed to obtain the most commonly requested French public documents. Remember, you can do very little by telephone. You have to be prepared to get yourself to the office in question. Patience is highly recommended.

Obtaining Documents

Birth Certificates *(Extraits de Naissance)*

People born in France must obtain their birth certificate from the office of the mayor in the relevant town or arrondissement. Address inquiries to the mayor at the *Mairie* of the *arrondissement* in the appropriate section of Paris or of the town.

French people born in a foreign country must address requests to Ministère des Affaires Etrangères, Direction des Français à l'Etranger, Service Central de l'Etat-

Civil, 11 rue Maison Blanche, 44000 Nantes; Tel.: 02–51–77–30–30.

A request for a birth certificate must include the applicant's full name at the time of birth; the date and place of birth; father's full name; and mother's full name at the time of the applicant's birth, including maiden name.

The request must be accompanied by a self-addressed, stamped envelope. There is no charge for a copy of a birth certificate.

Death Certificate *(Acte de Décès)*

Death certificates are obtained from the office of the mayor where the death occurred. The request must include the full name of the deceased and the date and place where the death occurred.

Marriage Certificate *(Extrait d'Acte de Mariage)*

Marriage certificates are obtained from the office of the mayor of the town where the marriage took place. The request must include the date and place of the marriage and the full names of the two persons involved. It must be accompanied by a self-addressed, stamped envelope. There is no charge for a copy of a marriage certificate.

Divorce Certificate *(Extrait de Divorce)*

Divorce certificates are obtained from the office of the mayor where the marriage took place. The request must include the date of the divorce and the full names of the two persons involved. It must be accompanied by a self-addressed, stamped envelope.

Divorce Judgment *(Jugement de divorce)*

Divorce judgments are obtained from the Greffe du Tribunal Civil where the judgment was pronounced. Address your request to Monsieur le Greffier, Tribunal de Grande Instance, 4 boulevard du Palais, 75001 Paris, France; or to Monsieur le Greffier, Greffe du Tribunal Civil, in the appropriate town. The request must include the date of the divorce and the full names of the two persons involved. It must be accompanied by a self-addressed, stamped envelope. There is no charge for a divorce judgment.

Police Record *(Extrait du Casier Judiciaire)*

Police certificates can be obtained by any person, regardless of nationality, who has resided in France at any time after the age of fifteen. Police certificates can be obtained from Service du Casier Judiciaire, 107 rue du Landreau, 44079 Nantes Cedex; Tel.: 02–40–49–08–94.

Military Records

Military records for the army are obtained from Direction du Personnel Militaire de l'Armée de Terre, 14 rue St-Dominique, 75997 Paris Armées. Military records for the air force are obtained from Direction du Personnel Militaire de l'Armée de l'Air, 26 boulevard Victor, 75996 Paris Armées.

Legal Endorsement *(Apostille)*

The Hague Convention simplified the procedures regarding French documents destined for use in the United States. Both the United States and France are parties to the convention. Paris residents should go to the Palais de Justice, Service Apostille, Salle des pas perdus (Kiosque accueil), 6 boulevard du Palais, 75001 Paris; (Métro: Chatelet/St-Michel/Cité); Tel.: 01–44–32–51–37. Hours: 9:30 A.M. to noon and 2:30 to 4:00 P.M.

Notary Services

The Office of American Services performs notary services for those wishing to execute documents in the presence of a U.S. consular officer. The fee per document is $55, or 50,50 euros. Notary service is provided Monday through Friday between 9:00 A.M. and noon (closed on French and American holidays). Bring your passport or other photo ID (*carte d'identité* or driver's license).

Being Born in France

The report of births desk at the Office of American Services at the U.S. Consulate is open to the general public from 9:00 A.M. to 3:00 P.M. without interruption Monday through Friday, except on French and American holidays. For further details, call 01–43–12–49–42 between 2:00 and 6:00 P.M.

The Office of American Services can register the birth of children born abroad to U.S. citizens and help parents obtain a first passport and Social Security number for newborn children. The American parent must bring the child to the office with the following documents, either in the original or certified copy:

✦ The child's birth certificate issued by the local authorities at the place of birth. For births in France, request the *extrait de l'acte de naissance integral* from the *mairie*. Neither the *livret de famille* nor a *fiche individuelle d'état civil* can be accepted as a birth certificate.

✦ Evidence of the U.S. citizenship of the child's parent(s).

✦ The marriage certificate of the child's parents. If the marriage took place in France, bring the *livret de famille* as well. If either of the child's parents has been married before, evidence of termination of that marriage (such as an original or certified copy of the decree or dissolution or divorce or a death certificate) must be provided.

✦ If only one of the parents is a U.S. citizen, a statement by that parent listing the precise periods of his or her actual physical presence in France. The child's citizenship will depend on the length of the parent's presence in France.

✦ The completed forms that the OAS has sent you prior to the appointment.

✦ For the child's passport, two identical and recent photographs taken full face with a very light background measuring 5 cm by 5 cm.

✦ Fees in cash or traveler's checks—personal checks are not accepted. The report of birth fee is $40, or 37 euros. The first passport for a minor sixteen years or younger costs $40, or 37 euros. That is a total of $80, or 74 euros. Check for price changes beforehand.

To request an information packet or to make an appointment to record the birth of your child, call 01–43–12–46–71 (direct line) between 3:00 and 6:00 P.M. Monday through Thursday, or between 3:00 P.M. and 5:00 P.M. on Friday.

Getting Married in France

To get married in France, inquire both at your own consulate and at the *mairie* in the *arrondissement* in which you live. It will take a minimum of three weeks to satisfy the administrative requirement. If you or your partner are not *en règle* (in France legally), you may have difficulty marrying in France.

The following information is for the guidance of civilian American citizens contemplating marriage in France. United States military personnel should contact the legal officer of the defense attaché's office at the American Embassy in Paris at 01–43–12–46–96.

Although marriage statutes in the United States vary from state to state, a marriage performed in France under French law is generally recognized as valid throughout the United States. American diplomatic and consular officers do not have legal authority to perform marriages. Marriages cannot be performed within the embassy or within an American consular office in France.

To be legal all marriages must be performed by a French civil authority, i.e., an *officier de l'état civil*, before any religious ceremony takes place. In practice this means the mayor *(maire)*—or his legally authorized replacement, such as a deputy mayor *(adjoint)* or a city councilor *(conseiller municipal)*—of the town in which one of the parties has resided for at least forty days immediately preceding the marriage. If both of the parties to marriage meet the residence requirement but resided in different districts, the civil ceremony may take place in either district of residence. The forty-day residence requirement cannot be waived.

French law also requires the posting of marriage *bans* (announcements) at the appropriate *mairie* (town hall) no less than ten days preceding the date of marriage. The first publication of the ban can be made only at the end of thirty days of residence in France by one party to the marriage. Only in very exceptional cases can this requirement be waived by a French authority (the *procureur de la république* for the district in which the marriage will take place). A *mairie* may require that the complete marriage file be presented as much as ten or more days prior to the publication of banns. Contact your *mairie* to find out exactly what the waiting period is.

A religious ceremony may be performed after the civil ceremony. The minister, priest, rabbi, or other clergy member performing the religious ceremony will require the certificate of civil marriage *(certificat de célébration civile)* as proof that the civil ceremony has taken place.

Couples married in France automatically receive a *livret de famille*, a booklet that serves as an official record of the marriage, as well as of subsequent events in the family such as births, deaths, divorce, or name changes. The *livret de famille* is an official document. It is also possible to obtain a marriage certificate *(extrait d'acte de mariage)* by writing to the mairie where the marriage took place. You must indicate the date and place of the marriage and the full names (including wife's maiden name) of the two parties. If the certificate is to be mailed to an address in France, the request should be accompanied by a self-addressed, stamped envelope. If the certificate is to be mailed to a U.S. address, include a self-addressed envelope with a Universal Postal Union coupon to cover international postage costs.

Required Documents

It is important that you first learn the exact requirements of the city hall where the marriage will take place and find out if affidavits are acceptable. Most mairies in France require some or all of the following documents:

+ a valid U.S. passport or a French residence permit *(carte de séjour)*.
+ birth certificate *(extrait d'acte de naissance)* less than three months old. Some city halls accept an affidavit *(attestation tenant lieu de Fiche d'Etat-Civil)* executed before an American consular officer in France. (Because the information on American birth certificates differs from that provided on French birth certificates, individuals born in the United States must generally submit additional information about their origins.) The fee for this notary service (open from 9:00 A.M. to noon Monday through Friday) is $55, or 50,50 euros in cash per document. But some city halls require an original copy of your birth certificate less than three months old along with a sworn translation. You must obtain the translation from an official translator *(traducteur assermenté);* these are listed at every *mairie.* The Office of American Services also has a list. The embassy does not provide translation services.
+ A certificate of celibacy *(attestation tenant lieu de declaration en vue de mariage ou de non-remariage)* less than three months old. This attests that the person involved is not already married and can be in the form of an affidavit of marital status executed before an American consular officer in France. The fee for this service (open from 9:00 A.M. to noon Monday through Friday) is $55, 50,50 euros in cash per document. Again, keep in mind that some city halls do not accept affidavits and have special requirements.
+ An affidavit of law *(certificat de coutume).* Some *mairies* may request this in addition to the affidavit of marital status. The affidavit of law is a statement about U.S. marriage laws, certifying that the American citizen is free to contract marriage in France and that the marriage will be recognized in the United States. Only an attorney licensed to practice in both France and the United States may execute this document. The affidavit of law is prepared on the basis of the attorney's examination of the individual's documentation (divorce decree, death certificate of spouse, etc.), and verification and citation of the applicable marriage laws of the United States.
+ A medical certificate *(certificat médical prénuptial)* less than three months old attesting that the individual was given a prenuptial exam by a doctor. The marriage banns cannot be published until medical certificates have been submitted to the mairie. The certificates must be dated no earlier than two months before the publication of banns. Any qualified doctor can perform the medical examination.
  Individuals coming directly from the United States can be medically examined in the United States by a physician approved by the local French Consulate (usually a list of such physicians is furnished by the consulate). However, it should be noted that authorities in France require that the original certificate

be in the French language, or that an official translation notarized by a French consul in the United States be submitted with the original certificate in English. The two-month limitation of validity also applies.

✦ Proof of domicile *(justificatifs de domicile)*. Two proofs of residence in the city of marriage are required (e.g., electricity or telephone bills, rent receipts, etc.).

✦ *Certificat du notaire* (prenuptial agreement, if applicable). If the parties opt for a prenuptial contract governing their respective properties *(régime du mariage)*, the French notary preparing the contract will give the couple a certificate *(certificat du notaire)* that must be presented to the mairie as well.

Note: The way that the law is applied in France may vary from city hall to city hall. You may wish to consult others who have opted to marry in France. EU citizens generally have no administrative obstacles in getting married in France. Americans, however, who wish to be married in France because it's romantic, and do not reside in France, will find that this is a complicated idea. But, if you're determined, you'll find a way! Inquire at www.paris-anglo.com.

Recording Births in France

A government office in the hospital or clinic in which the child is born will handle the paperwork for declaring the birth of the child to the local *mairie*. You have two days following the birth of the child to go to the *mairie* yourself and sign the official birth certificate. You will be given copies, which you will need for French social security and school. Americans will also need this copy when requesting a birth certificate from the U.S. consular services. You should also request several *fiches d'état civil* at the same time, in that these are very useful for all sorts of administrative tasks, like passport requests. When recording the child's name on the forms in the hospital, indicate precisely how you want the name composed. If the parents are not married but the child is recognized by the father, the child automatically takes the father's last name. French law since the mid-1980s allows the child to take the name of both parents, but many administrators and clerks refuse to apply the law. Insist if you want the child to have both names. The U.S. consular office recognizes the child's name according to what is written on the French birth certificate. European countries differ greatly as to nationality laws and the naming of children. Germany, for example, recognizes only the mother's name if the parents are not married, even if the child is recognized by the father and takes the father's last name on the French birth certificate. American law grants U.S. citizenship to children born outside the United States as long as at least one parent is a U.S. citizen and can prove he or she was physically present in the United States for five years before the age of eighteen.

Selected Consulates and Embassies in Paris
(for a more complete list, please see www.paris-anglo.com)

Australia Embassy
4 rue Jean Rey
75724 Paris Cedex 15
Tel.: 01–40–59–33–00

Fax: 01–40–59–33–10
Visas: 01–40–59–33–06
Minitel: 36–14 AUSTRALIE
Web site: www.austgov.fr

Canada Embassy
35 avenue Montaigne
75008 Paris
Tel.: 01–44–43–29–00
Fax: 01–44–43–29–99
Visas: 01–44–43–29–16

Great Britain Embassy
35 rue du Faubourg Saint-Honoré
75008 Paris
Tel.: 01–44–51–31–00
Fax 2: 01–42–66–95–90
Fax: 01–40–07–03–65
Minitel: 36–15 GBRETAGNE

Great Britain Consulate
9 avenue Hoche
75008 Paris
Tel.: 01–42–66–38–10
Fax: 01–40–76–02–87

Ireland Embassy
4 rue Rude
75116 Paris
Tel.: 01–44–17–67–00
Minitel: 36–15 IRLANDE
Fax: 01–45–00–84–17

South Africa Embassy
59 Quai d'Orsay
75007 Paris
Tel.: 01–45–55–92–37
Fax: 01–47–53–99–70

United States of America Embassy
2 avenue Gabriel
75008 Paris
Tel.: 01–43–12–22–22
Fax: 01–43–12–21–72

United States of America
Consulate
2 rue Saint-Florentin
75001 Paris
Tel.: 01–43–12–22–22
Fax: 01–42–86–82–91

Cultural Awareness

Overview

Figuring out how French society works and how its people interact will undoubtedly take a fair amount of time. Think about your understanding of the society you live in—all those cumulative years spent learning to participate in a system with its multitude of unspoken rules, codes, and underlying assumptions. With an open mind you will broaden your knowledge of both French society and your own; you'll get sharper at knowing what people are saying when they're not talking. And don't forget that contemporary culture is like living tissue; it lives, dies, and changes. There is no way you can be up on the latest inside variations and cultural references, but these few basic observations should help you get oriented to the physical and psychic environment. Since all things are political in France, notes on the political arena come first.

The Political Arena

American political scientist and labor activist Larry Portis, who teaches at the Université de Clermond Ferrand, has contributed the following comments on French politics, the unions, and the press.

Ever since the French Revolution of 1789, France has been a place where political opinions are expressed so openly and frequently that they seem to be more a sport or amusement than anything else. Certainly the French differ from Americans, who are said to consider political debate in bad taste outside of electoral contests. French families relish gathering for Sunday dinner and shouting about their political differences. One of Voltaire's characters in *Candide* says "Wherever you go in France, you will find that their three chief occupations are making love, backbiting, and talking nonsense." This unflattering portrait could be attributed to the somewhat jaundiced view of what is often taken to be the superficiality of the French (and especially the Parisians), but the political intensity characterizing French culture results from the peculiar evolution of the society and governmental institutions.

It is generally known that the terms "right" and "left" in relation to politics stem from the seating arrangements of the first National Assembly created during the French Revolution. What is less understood is that a tradition of radical confrontation and extragovernmental means of political expression is not only rooted in social relations and political practice but remains entirely respectable to much of the population. The state bureaucracy may be considered a monolithic and virtually impregnable entity, but the French do not worship their institutions, laws, and constitution(s). Over the past two centuries they have had five republics, two imperial dictatorships, and several other experiments in constitution-building. Consider the remark of Charles Pasqua, former minister of the interior, responding to news that the high court had ruled his new law regulating immigration and naturalization to be not in conformity with the constitution. "Very well," he said, "the constitution is defective." His comment is representative of the spirit in which the French regard politics in general. In spite of the decline of some of the antiestablishment political parties and movements (especially the Communist Party), it is not difficult for the French to entertain at least the possibility of a significant restructuring of laws and institutions.

In recent years developments in French politics have revealed both how swiftly change can come and how some very basic attitudes tend to remain constant. When François Mitterrand, leader of the Socialist Party, won the presidential election in 1981 and immediately called for legislative elections that his party handily won, few were surprised or outraged that he launched an extensive program nationalizing banks and major corporations, raising the minimum wage, and legislating progressive reform of labor laws. By 1983 he and his party reversed themselves entirely, calling for incentives to private enterprise. When, in 1986, the right-wing parties won the legislative elections and Mitterrand was obliged to appoint a conservative prime minister, the new government promptly began privatizing state corporations and even part of the public television network. Such radical changes in public policy and institutional development were seemingly taken in stride by the French people, until, that is, one constituency felt threatened. An attempt to call into question the liberal system of universal entrance into universities quickly provoked one of the mass entrances of the French people into the arena that have punctuated French history. In a series of demonstrations, French students and their supporters filled the streets and forced the government to retract their plan. At one point there were a million demonstrators in the streets in Paris alone. In January 1994 popular reaction against a plan to increase public financing of private (Catholic) schools brought another million people into the streets (many of whom must have been the same ones). In November and December 1995, the plans of a moderately conservative government to reduce social expenditures and social security benefits sparked a quasi-general strike largely supported by all sectors of the population.

This readiness of the French people, whether of the right or the left, to take "direct action" means that French political life retains a special kind of volatility, the kind that produced the revolutions of 1789, 1830, 1848, and 1871, as well as more recent developments such as those connected with June 1936 and May 1968. The repercussions of the latter explosion are still reverberating, so profoundly did it change the attitudes and habits of the country. Since 1968, most of the French are less formal, more open, more conscious of living in an interdependent world where French culture is no longer the standard by which all others should be judged.

But French political life also revolves around the personalities of its most prominent representatives and leaders. The importance of the state is such that the "political class" of leaders is both highly respected and highly suspect. Respected because the omnipresence of state authority is still perceived with a kind of chauvinistic pride: The state is embodied in its representatives, in which most French people see themselves reflected. Suspect, because the omnipotence of the state is a permanent drag on individual initiatives. State representatives are resented for their privileges and their perceived tendency to profit individually from their offices at the expense of their constituencies.

As France enters into a new phase of European integration, French political leaders are more and more suspected of *affairisme*, of enriching themselves at the expense of the state. Over the past fifteen years, prominent members of all the major political parties have been investigated for fradulent campaign financing, diverting public funds toward private gain, and even assassination of potential whistle-blowers. President Jacques Chirac, for example, has been accused of a variety of illegal actions committed during the time he was mayor of Paris. Such charges, which may well be justified, are particularly important at the present time because of the insecurities generated by the new European Union. The French have always been proud of their cultural uniqueness, their intellectual authority, and their political sovereignty. All seem to be jeopardized at a time when globalization is rapidly reducing national differences in favor of an accelerating Americanization against which the only possible defense seems to be Europeanization. But both processes threaten to dilute the force of French distinctiveness. The malaise is also reflected in the sad affair of the contaminated blood stocks. Failure to treat or destroy AIDS-contaminated blood reserves by the national health service in the mid-1980s, it was charged, resulted in illness or death for hundreds of patients and was the direct responsibility of government decision makers.

More than ten years after the original accusations were made, a former prime minister (Laurent Fabius) and two of his cabinet ministers were tried. It was the first time in French history that such highly placed administrators were judged for the way they accomplished their official functions. But the trial did little to clear the air. On the contrary, the accused were brought before a special parliamentary court composed of members of the National Assembly. Since Fabius was acquitted by this tribunal of his peers, the feeling remains that justice has been again thwarted in favor of a political class that protects its own.

Such sentiments are also evident in the controversy over the status of Corsica. "The beautiful island" *(Ile de beauté)*, as it is called, was colonized by the French in the eighteenth century, but strong nationalist or regionalist sentiments remain. Since the mid-1970s terrorist bombings and assassinations have punctuated the life of the island, making it all the more risky for its legions of tourists. Strangely, the central government has never managed to subdue the rebellion, even after the prefect, the direct representative of the state, was assassinated in 1998. For many observers a mafialike smell hangs over the beautiful island, and over French politics.

The current president of the republic, Jacques Chirac, is unlikely to dispel suspicions. Evidence of illegal administrative practices engaged in when he was mayor of Paris continues to rise to the surface. Political cronies or relatives on the payroll who never worked, lists of voters whose only qualification was loyalty to the incumbent, choice lodging at bargain prices in Paris for himself and well-heeled collaborators (thanks to the municipal housing authority established to help needy households), illicit campaign financing, all this is known about the current president. But unlike the United States, there is no possibility of calling him to account, much less of impeachment. Chirac is so happily ensconced in his job, which consists mainly of diplomatic courtesy junkets (he has made dozens of trips to Japan in recent years, one of his favorite places) and solemn presidential pronouncements, that he has even been disavowed by a major part of the political party he founded.

As the century came to a close, personalities tended to dominate political life, at the expense of political parties. At this writing, the right-wing Jacques Chirac is still president, and the prime minister is still the socialist Lionel Jospin, thanks to the socialist party victory in the legislative elections of spring 1997. Jospin formed a government in collaboration with the Communist Party and the French Green Party. Seen in large perspective, therefore, France is governed by all political tendencies, excepting only the neo-fascist parties on the right and the revolutionary parties of the left. Jospin's leftist government has energetically carried out a political agenda inspired by the right-wing governments that preceded his, whereas Chirac, as president, has tried to embody the moral conscience of the French nation, in spite of his own tarnished record. The French people are perhaps understandably confused about where their leaders stand. The socialist government has attacked the system of national public education and has proposed overhauling the social security system along the lines proposed by the previous conservative government (a proposal that sparked the mass demonstrations of late 1995). With only mild protests from its communist partners, Jospin's government in only two years privatized more industries than the two previous right-wing governments. With only scattered protests from the supposedly pacifist Green Party, also part of the government, Jospin's socialists enthusiastically endorsed the American-led NATO offensive in the Balkans. In brief, in France, as in England and the United States, formerly progressive political formations decided to co-opt the programs of the conservative, business-oriented political parties in order to hang onto power. For French people, in spite of their traditional clarity, it is a perplexing situation. France's position in EU–U.S. trade disputes, the "War against Terror," and in an increasingly dangerous Middle East complicate further the perplexity.

Even at the extremes, political factionalization dominates. As the Communist Party appears to be in the terminal stage of its long and largely self-inflicted decline, the political left in France is drifting, vainly searching for a new identity. The political right is scarcely more healthy. Like the left, it is split into parties and factions. The two major parties are the RPR (Rally for the Republic) and the UDF (French Democratic Union). Even the neo-fascist National Front has now split into two parties, differing only in divided loyalties toward the movement's two major leaders. Jean-Marie Le Pen, ex-torturer during the Algerian War, retains the allegiance of the old guard; Bruno Mégret, a smoother operator representing a more respectable (in appearance at least) look, nevertheless advances the same solution to all economic and social woes: Ship immigrant workers back to where they came from. The only real exception to bitter infighting or disarray is the recent joining of forces of the two major revolutionary parties of the left: the Revolutionary Communist League (LCR) and Workers' Struggle (LO). This coalition stands to profit both from the divisiveness of parties tied to capitalist institutions and by the long-term economic restructuring caused by globalization.

Underlying all political reality in France is one central fact: economic contraction. Ordinary working people have suffered from declining real income and rising unemployment since the early 1980s. France is known for its powerful labor movement, and it could be expected that these conditions have elicited the kind of militant aggressiveness that contributed to the events of 1968. It is true that labor unions remain major players on the political scene. The most powerful is the CGT (General Federation of Labor). Created in 1895, it has gone through some important changes of orientation over the past century, but has always retained its character of working-class combativity.

Although the CGT has been linked informally to the Communist Party since World War II, the decline of that party and the dissolution of the USSR has rendered any such attachment irrelevant. An offshoot of the CGT is the CGT-FO formed in 1947, and most often called Force Ouvrière (Workers' Power) or simply FO. Although the FO is more oriented toward cooperation with employers and governments, its direction still reflects the Cold War ideological preoccupations that attended its birth. The fact that its split from the CGT was facilitated by money secretly provided by the United States Central Intelligence Agency has never helped its reputation, and now that the appeal to anti-communist sentiments seems baseless, FO's claim to be apolitical is even less convincing.

Another major union is the CFDT (French Democratic Labor Federation) formed in 1964. In the aftermath of 1968 it became the rising star of French unions, advocating autonomy from political parties and workers' self-management at the workplace. But its slavishness to the Socialist Party after the latter's electoral victory in 1981 has alienated masses of its members. In 1988 the CFDT even purged itself of its most militant (and critical) adherents.

On the whole French labor unions are declining in members and in their effectiveness. The deindustrialization of the economy, cumbersome union bureaucracies, and political entanglements have reduced their effectiveness and appeal. But this does not mean that the time of strikes, demonstrations, and other types of working-class direct action is over. For the past several years the most dramatic actions have been carried out by "coordinations" of employees who suspiciously avoid any type of union control over the organization of strikes and negotiations. The expertise and contacts of the unions are used, but their tendency to make secret deals with management and government has disqualified them in the eyes of the always critical French. The upshot is that continued and even intensified strike activity can be expected, something that the French tolerate as a normal course of events (although governments, especially on the right, would like to outlaw much of it, as has been done in the United States and in England). Strikes, demonstrations, and marches are an integral part of life in France, and any extended stay would be incomplete without attending a good-size demo. You may find it to be an inspiring experience. But don't forget to keep a very respectful distance between yourself and the riot police, the (in)famous CRS (Companies for Republican Security).

The Politics of the French Press

The newspapers in France generally reflect different political tendencies. The most well-known and respected newspaper remains *Le Monde.* With little advertising content, no photos, and straightforward, serious reporting and editorials, it is such an institution that students often carry it simply to enhance their image. Once moderately but ideologically leftist, its orientation is now centrist, close to that of the Socialist Party. Another major newspaper that has changed its perspective significantly is *Libération.* In the first years after May 1968, banning advertising from its pages, it expressed the idealism and alternative politics of the young rebels. It was, in fact, the first such paper in the world to be published daily. But since 1981 it has striven for respectability and has succeeded in becoming a profit-making enterprise with easy access to the corridors of power. More flamboyant in format and journalistic style than *Le Monde, Libération* is also critically socialist in orientation.

The major newspapers of the political right are *Le Figaro* (mornings) and *France Soir* (evenings). Both owned by publishing baron Robert Hersant, they go for the conservatively sensational and represent the traditional, bourgeois France that foreigners come for and (often) learn to detest. *Le Figaro* is thought to have the best want ads for real estate. A more politically bland, *USA Today* type of newspaper is *Le Parisien.*

In a class by itself is the hallowed *Canard Enchaîné*, a satirical paper of political opinion and commentary created in 1915 that hits the newsstands Wednesday mornings. Its biting humor is studded with exceedingly clever puns that will baffle the uninitiated or foreign reader (or the reader without extensive knowledge of French slang). But it is no joke. It is read by everyone who wants to know what is happening behind the scenes, especially by French politicians. The only French newspaper that specializes in investigative journalism, it has informants in the highest reaches of government and industry. Sued countless times, financially dependent on its sale (no advertising), *Canard Enchaîné* is a vestige of the French Enlightenment. It is a beacon of principled idealism in a politically murky French environment. A positive, new addition to the French press scene is *Courrier International,* a weekly composite of articles, commentary, and cartoons from the world press, translated into French.

The French Language

The Spoken Word

Speaking the language is absolutely essential for participating in the life of the society that surrounds you. In France this is particularly true. So much of French culture and so many French attitudes are present in the language—the verbal and facial expressions, the syntax, the vocabulary, the role of dialogue. You may find it difficult at first, especially when you realize that what you say and what you mean may not be the same thing. You may feel a sense of loss, because expressing yourself in another language means losing the comfort of the personality through which you have learned to define yourself. But making the effort will pay off in ways that are incalculably enriching—learning French will open your eyes to a different way of thinking and living in the world and enable you to share the concerns and feelings of the French.

The French in general like to talk, and the language in all its richness gains much of its melodic quality from the long and circular phrases needed to express what could be said in a word or two in English or German. This love of words and dialogue, though, is reserved for specific places and contexts . . . the café, the dinner table, the *table ronde*, the conference. You might notice that people don't talk very loudly in subways, buses, streets, or public places. This comes from the French distinction between public and private life. Personal life is private and is handled discreetly. The French will not openly talk about or be overheard discussing family matters, emotions, or money. With this silent backdrop it's not surprising that tourists seem remarkably loud and obnoxious.

On the other hand, the French can be highly vocal and overt when in the public mode—partaking in a *débat* (debate), *manifestation* (demonstration), or *grève* (strike), for example—and these are regular institutions in Parisian life. French intellectual life, which often carries over into the popular culture, tends to be characterized by obsessive analysis and verbal gymnastics. This is a phenomenon that applies mostly to political and social issues as opposed to personal or emotional ones. Often films shown on television are preceded and followed by a panel discussion or debate—even the mass-market entertainment films.

Learning to speak French doesn't mean that you'll be an effective communicator right away. Much of communicating in France is learning the social coding that accompanies the language (see the Working in France chapter). Whereas Anglo-Saxon culture emphasizes information, Francophone culture emphasizes form. Form is everything in France; the way you speak, the way you write, the way you dress, all impact the effect you'll have on French people.

The expressions and vocal sounds that French people make when reacting to situations differ from those you are accustomed to. The French often begin their response with a quick jerk or tilt of the head, followed by a curious ducklike sound made by pushing a bit of air through pursed lips. This is the French equivalent of hunched shoulders. The French also utter things such as, *berk!* for mild disgust, *tant pis* for what the heck, and a quick breathy version of *oui* for "yeah" or "sure."

The Written Word

To repeat, attention to form is primary. When it comes to written French, there are no short cuts; you must abide by the set forms for addressing someone or some problem, even in the most banal circumstances. Forms of *politesse* (politeness) may strike you as long-winded and even hypocritical, but their absence may very well be read as an insult. If you violate these rules, be prepared to be judged poorly. At best you'll get away with it because you're not French and you don't know better. One of the most revealing bits of ironic, written politeness is the line used to open formal letters announcing equally positive or dreadful news: *"Monsieur/Madame, j'ai l'honneur de vous annoncer que . . ."* and then it can go on to say that you've just been rejected from the university program you applied to or have been assessed an additional 1000 euros in back taxes, etc. Another such example is the French use of the verb inviter in official and formal letters. You could be invited to present yourself to the police to be arrested for arson as easily as you could be invited to an official function in your honor. In other contexts when someone invites you, it implies that the person doing the inviting will pay. If you invite someone, he or she is your guest and thus you pay. *C'est normal!* (Note that in written French there is always a space before punctuation—other than a period—at the end of a sentence, which is a typographical error in English. Additionally, the French use commas to join two sentences, whereas in English we use a semicolon to avoid a run-on sentence or comma splice.)

Although not a major point, you might like to know that French animals do not speak the same tongue as their American or British counterparts. French chickens go *"cocorico"* instead of "cock-a-doodle-do" (this is particularly noted as *cocorico* means "to crow," particularly in a proud sense, as *le coq* is the symbol of France); French dogs go *ouâ-ouâ* instead of "bow-wow"; and French cows go *meuh* instead of the highly American "moo." You can find out the others with newly made French friends, a sure party favorite. Another humorous but culturally revealing act of popular comparative linguistics is to discover the local equivalent of "Eenie meanie miney mo, catch a tiger by the toe. If he hollers let him go. Eenie meanie miney mo." The French say, *"Am stram gram, pic et pic et coligram, bourré bourré ratatam, am stram gram."*

Formules de politesse for Letter Writing

For formal letters addressed to someone you don't know well, here are two polite but neutral ways to close, roughly equivalent to the English "sincerely yours," "yours very truly," or "yours truly." Your best bet is to memorize one and use it to close all your letters of an official or administrative nature. Or purchase a small and inexpensive book called *La correspondance pratique,* by Jean-Yves Dournon (Livre de Poche), which, although a bit dated, provides models for all necessary forms of correspondence. Remember that *Monsieur* can be changed to *Madame.* When you're not sure whether the addressee is male or female, it's best to write *Madame, Monsieur,* instead of the more traditional *Messieurs,* which is now not highly appreciated by women.

—*Je vous prie de recevoir, Monsieur, l'assurance de mes sentiments distingués.*
—*Veuillez croire, Monsieur, en l'expression de mes sentiments les meilleurs.*

In writing to a superior (e.g., cover letters to possible employers, etc.):
—*Veuillez agréer, Monsieur, l'expression de ma respectueuse considération.*

For friends and parents:
—*N'oublie pas d'embrasser Jeanine pour moi.*
—*Meilleurs/Affectueux souvenirs*
—*Amicalement*

—Bien cordialement à vous/toi
—Grosses bises !
—Salut !

Note: The French have a high regard for the handwritten letter, hence the propensity of stationery and fountain-pen shops. In France you are judged by your handwriting. Telephone skills tend to be less than proficient, spotty at best, but the way the hand constructs words on a page in even the individual with the most basic level of education is taken seriously. And the skills are surprisingly high. You may find the French cursive formations of letters difficult to decipher, but this is no fault of the writer. Even the *clochard* (beggar)—now replaced by the more accurate and politically correct SDF *(sans domicile fixe)*—or down-and-out street person often takes the trouble to write out his story in chalk on the sidewalk or on a piece of cardboard. "I am fifty-six years old, unemployed, recently released from the hospital. Can't you help me?" Or the more direct and classic: *"J'ai faim. S.V.P."* When applying for a job or responding to a classified ad, it is always appropriate to reply with a handwritten letter, neatly formulated, beginning with your name and address, the city you're writing from, and the date. All official documents and contracts require that you close with *Lu et approuvé* (read and appoved) in your handwriting, followed by the date and your signature. In France a last will and testament will be considered invalid unless handwritten.

Handwriting is often analyzed professionally as an indicator of character and stability. Often the most inoffensive and slightest error will provoke the average French person to start all over or be faced with a possible rejection for a job. Don't send messy letters.

The letter plays an important role in France for a number of historic reasons. Whereas Americans often prefer the quickness and effectiveness of a telephone call, the French opt for the *courrier* (correspondence), especially in business, financial, and official matters. A letter creates a trace or proof of the exchange and everything done in France must be backed up by a signed piece of paper, as you will soon learn (if you haven't already). In areas where there could be legal or financial repercussions, get in the habit of sending *lettres recommandées avec accusé de réception* (registered letters with notice of receipt). This is the only real proof in France that a letter was sent and received. The French are menaces about this. The French are *méfiant* (distrustful) of the spoken word, banking everything on the signed contract, whereas the English sense of honor relies deeply on the spoken word and the handshake—the gentleman's agreement. So don't be overly casual when leaving a note for even the gas company, let alone your banker or the owner of the apartment you are renting. And, yes, penmanship counts a lot.

The typewriter seems to have been skipped over in the history of French communications. The French jumped from the handwritten page and carbon paper to the computer. Many young people in Paris own personal computers; the typewriter was a far rarer item in the French household. Not surprisingly, most French students cannot type and those who study at North American universities or business schools complain bitterly when required to type academic papers. French university professors never require that papers be typed.

"ça va"

Even if it is only from French 101 or some lightweight course in rudimentary français at night or summer school, chances are that you probably know that one great French catchall: *"Comment allez-vous ?"* or its familiar counterpart *"Comment ça va ?"* (How goes it?) simplified as *"ça va?"* But did anyone tell you that you can't just prance down the *pâté de maisons* (block) and sputter to complete strangers, *ça va ?* You just don't ask any random person how he or she is doing, the way you'd toss into the air a friendly or mechanical "Hi!" "Howdy!" "What's up?" "What's happening?" or "How ya doin'?" Make eye contact and ask a passerby how he is doing and in most cases the person will look behind him to see if you're addressing someone else, ignore you totally, or stop in his tracks with a perplexed glaze on his face, lower lip pursed, and inquire: *On se connaît ?* Have we met? Do we know each other?

The textbooks back home often forget in their first lessons on "Greetings" to discuss language as a function of culture. And face it, understanding a culture foreign to your own is precisely what's needed to assure a rewarding and meaningful *séjour* (stay) in your new country. The more you absorb about the social relations and interactions of the French and the cultural underpinnings of French society, the more you will not only enjoy being part of Parisian life but also begin to comprehend better your own culture and language. The world doesn't grow, but your conception of it does. So if you're ignored on Day One or you let yourself be influenced by the derogatory comments of cursory travelers who lambaste the French for alleged rudeness, arrogance, or chilliness, you're missing the much larger point and only widening cultural barriers.

A good rule of thumb is to suspend all judgments for at least a month! Admittedly there is a certain formality and pace of interchange deeply engrained in French culture (as witnessed in both verbal and written expression) that is at first going to separate the friendly and direct North American from his new environs. This is par for the course. It shouldn't be distressing; it's interesting! As North American or non-French students or newly arrived residents in Paris, an openness to your surroundings in a French—not North American—context will be your passport to an enriching and pleasurable time.

Two of the main exchanges with the familiar *ça va* reveal several important attitudes.

—*Ça va ?* the question, literally meaning "How goes it?" is often answered with itself, *Ça va !* meaning "It goes."

This makes for easy language learning, but what in fact does it mean? Everything lies in the intonation of the response. *Ça va* could reflect a great enthusiasm for life, a pang of desperate depression, or a plain moment of daily mediocrity. The nuances abound. So learn to listen for them and use them yourself. These are rich words.

—*Ça va ?* or the formal *Comment allez-vous ?* are often answered directly with the question *Et vous ?* (And you?)

The first few times you get involved in this interchange you are likely to get annoyed. Don't ignore me, that's not an answer, you'll want to complain. The repetition of the answer for the question simply demonstrates the French love of form, and often the French are too discreet to answer honestly. It's the asking of the question that counts, not the answer. There is nothing I can do if you aren't doing well; the best I can do is to ask you how you're doing. Soon you'll see that this little tidbit of dialogue is really very adorable and convenient.

Franglais

A note on franglais—or English borrowings into French. A law passed in 1994 limits the use of English in the French language. In the 1980s, there had been much to-do about finding French equivalent nouns for English technology that invaded the international marketplace. A prime example was *la balladeur* (from *se balladeur*, "to stroll") for the Walkman. The French care deeply about their language and linguistic influence in the world. Former Culture Minister Jack Lang often invited leading world intellectuals to Paris to discuss in French the state of international culture. The subsequent minister Jacques Toubon, mockingly called Mr. Allgood, whose ministry included the word *francophonie* in its title, battled under a fair amount of ridicule to preserve the language with legislation, finally enacted in 1994. Subsequent ministers have lightened up the attack, especially since the Internet and the high-tech world is so English-dominated and the French need to participate in these industries. The following words are just a few of the English terms commonly heard in everyday French life. They are pronounced as if they were French words.

best
best-seller
brainstorming
cash
checkup
chewing gum
copyright
design
designer
ferry
gadget—originally, in fact, a French word, from M. Gadget, who sold miniature Eiffel Towers at its inauguration

interview
jogging
label
listing
loft
mailing
marketing
must
OK
package
pickpocket
sandwich
shopping
standby

Greetings

Les Bises

When greeting someone they know, the French shake hands and/or give a quick succession of impersonal kisses on alternating cheeks called *les bises* (from *bisou*, or kiss). There are lots of nuances—often based on regional differences—that only experience can sort out. Some people give two kisses, some three, and others four. If there are six people in the room and you give four *bises* each, that calls for a lot of kissing. Remember, this is just a form of saying *bonjour*. The French are used to and comfortable with close personal contact. They are not bothered by human proximity or touching (though they don't often touch another's arm or shoulder to add emphasis, as North Americans tend to). In general they don't require the same distance Anglo-Saxons insist upon when talking. So get used to *les bises*. Even French people have cute little moments when two people are unsure if it'll be two, three, or four bises. Two is the most common, four is more classical; three is for those who want to be a bit different without abandoning tradition. People from the south of France and the younger generation tend to kiss more. *Les bises* are usually for men and women or women and women, but good male friends *font les bises* also. Start on the left cheek and don't really kiss, just touch cheeks and steer your lips inwards.

Handshakes are required when people greet each other whether for the first time or the zillionth time. When you arrive at work, for example, you shake hands with coworkers and say *bonjour*. It may seem highly repetitious, but it's a very pleasant way for people to acknowledge each other. The handshake or *les bises* are repeated when leaving. Every time you enter and exit a room you greet everyone present. Failure to say hello and good-bye is perceived as rude.

Farewells

What French people say to each other when they leave depends on how they leave and when they expect to see the other person next. Here is a brief list of possibilities and what they mean.

à tout à l'heure: "See you in a bit." This common phrase can refer to a moment in time slightly in the future, usually in an hour or two or later in the day, but it can also refer to a moment in the near past.

salut: This familiar and friendly way of saying hello or good-bye is said between good friends or people whom you can tell instantly are not hung up on old forms of protocol.

au revoir: your standard good-bye. Never wrong.

à tout de suite: You'll see the person in a matter of seconds or minutes, as in "I'll call you right back." It implies relative immediacy. A French person telling another person to wait a moment might say he won't be but *cinq minutes*. French people take this to be an acceptably short reference to the time they must wait even though the wait may not really be as long as five minutes; Anglo-Saxons indicating a short wait tend to exaggerate in the opposite direction, "I won't be a minute," or "Can you hold for five seconds?" Five minutes sounds too long.

ciao: This international phrase of dated Italian chicdom is still widely used everywhere. The French say *ciao* to people they know well and rather well.

à plus tard: See you later. You plan to see the other person again that day or night.

à demain: See you tomorrow.

à la prochaine: This means that you have no real plans, but you want to be positive and friendly, and thus say "Till the next time we see each other."

bonsoir: Good evening, used both when you greet someone or say good-bye. Polite.

bonne soirée: A friendlier version used when leaving in the late afternoon or early evening, wishing a good continuation of the evening and night.

bonne nuit: This is said before going to sleep. Good night. Not to be confused with bonsoir.

bonne continuation: This particularly French expression imparts your wish that the other person carry on whatever he or she is presently doing with continued pleasure and success.

bon courage: This is a farewell indicating that you are supportive of the task the other person has, be it something specific or just the act of continuing life.

bonne chance: A rather dramatic form of leaving someone while expressing wishes for general or specific success.

bonne journée: A generalized, good-hearted equivalent of "Have a nice day."

bonne après-midi: "Have a good afternoon." A more time-specific way of saying have a nice day.

bonne fin d'après-midi: This one is applicable when most of the afternoon is already over and you want to wish someone well for the part of the afternoon that's left.

dors bien: Sleep well. A cozy good night for kids, loved ones, and close friends. Dormez bien when addressing more than one person.

beaux rêves: Sweet dreams.

adieu: Classic good-bye for good. No longer used often, except for emphasis when you're really leaving and not coming back, or when you wish the other person would.

Going Out/Dating/Dining

The French almost always organize their social lives around a meal. This is true also for a lot of professional and commercial activities. So if you are asked out by a French person, count on a long and languorous dinner. If you're doing the asking, you should probably count on a meal too (your guest might be interested in or impressed by a meal indigenous to your culture). And remember a meal means a meal. You must be conscious of the form of the French meal: a first dish (even if it's a simple salad or a plate of healthy radishes with salt and bread and butter—yes, common), a main course, bread, salad (after the main course), cheese, dessert, and coffee. Younger people are less rigid but still most expect the meal to take this form. Often the cheese course gets skipped, but you should be prepared to offer one. And not just a block of Swiss or a wheel of Camembert; a nice selection of ripe cheeses is always appreciated, even by less traditional and younger folks. Also offer to change dishes from course to course, though more familiar guests are likely to accept the salad on the same plate as the main course. It's good to know these things.

It's very common to meet someone at a café at 20h or 20h30 (8:00 or 8:30 P.M.), have an *apéritif* (a kir or a glass of wine), and then proceed to dinner somewhere. A *kir royal* is delicious, but it's made with champagne and it'll put you back at least 5 euros. Learn the names of a few cafés that you like and that are convenient, so you'll be able to suggest a meeting point. I enjoy the Café Beaubourg next to the Pompidou Center, the Café Danton at Métro Odéon, the Café de l'Industrie near the Bastille, and the Café Dalou at Place de la Nation. Find your own.

Remember that usually, even among young people, the person who does the inviting also pays for the dinner. For the French this is highly normal. Going dutch is foreign. Often the guest will offer to pay the next time. *Je t'invite la prochaine fois.* You will almost never see French people dividing up a bill at the table. Sometimes they'll fight over who will pay, each wanting to pay, but the idea of determining who ordered what and the "did you have wine?" kind of thing is alien, and even distasteful. So be forewarned. Money still has a vulgar connotation.

The French also go to the movies a lot (see the Cinema/Film section in The Arts and Culture in Paris chapter).

If you're invited to someone's house in the evening, it's almost always going to be for dinner, unless it has been clearly stated otherwise. It's always appropriate to bring something, usually a good bottle of wine—never a *vin de table* (table wine) or inexpensive unknown wine. A well-wrapped bouquet of flowers, not the plain ones sold in the métro, is always appreciated. But don't show up empty-handed. As the economy weakens and people are more conscious of their budgets, more and more groups of friends are adopting the collective dinner or pot-luck concept, but if you're not sure of the folks, don't suggest such a thing to start. Dress slightly better than you think is appropriate. The French, even young people and students, tend to dress well when going out socially. Only in the last five years or so have people dared go out in the streets in sweatpants and sweatshirts, even for food shopping.

Sexuality

It's always very difficult and dangerous to generalize about how people think and act. In the area of sex this is particularly so, but a few comments might be useful. First, Parisians like to talk about sex. They love to verbalize fantasies, exhibitionist yearnings, private desires, etc. Sex is in the air. Sex is even in the Renault car commercials on TV. The popularity of sex as a subject doesn't necessarily translate into the act. It would be absurd to say, and hard to verify, that the French make love more than any other people, although they like to think they do. In fact, they're more driven by the pleasure of the act of seduction than by the results. As one French professor commented, "The French are caught in the nostalgia of the *coup de foudre*" (the crush). The film *La Discrète* captured perfectly the French obsession to seduce and dominate for no purpose other than to possess the soul of the other, to dominate verbally. The supreme art is the *combat verbal.* If you find yourself impatient with the relationships in contemporary French films, maybe this explains it.

Young French women, although not prudish, can be highly sentimental. Women are more jealous of other women than in Anglo-Saxon culture. There are fewer close female friendships, less of a notion of "the girls" going out together. (Careful not to use the word female, *femelle* in French; it refers exclusively to animals. Use *femme* as a noun and *féminin* as the adjective.) The French woman jealously guards her couple. The men, although not extremely macho, tend to embrace a fair number of Latin attitudes. The French concept of flirting—with the intention of picking up someone, is called *draguer* (to drag). This is actually closer to "chatting up" than to "picking up." It has a million variations and nuances and can be either flattering or annoying. Paris is at the northern edge of the Latin spirit. Male attitudes in general aren't as obviously macho as in Spain or Italy, but there are still attitudes here that might seem sexist to you. (Seventy-three percent of

French married men, one survey found, have mistresses or extramarital affairs, whereas 38 percent of married women have other lovers. What proportion of the 73 percent are seeing the 38 percent has never been established.)

On the whole it is fair to say that the French are less inhibited or uptight and have fewer hang-ups about sex, nudity, and human functions than Anglo-Saxons. Some French men, though, have preconceived notions about North American women, especially Californians, in terms of accessibility, openness, and wildness. These can be reinforced unknowingly because North Americans do tend to be more publicly expressive and open; however, in terms of attitudes, they are still more puritanical than the French. The French are quite comfortable with nudity and all that concerns the human body. The same ad in a London subway station with a clothed woman would show her topless in Paris. Topless advertising is not considered sexist by either women or men. *C'est beau* or *c'est normal.* Toplessness isn't even really considered nudity. In some boutiques you may see women try on blouses without stepping into a changing room; they may change from their swimsuit into street clothes on the beach. It is hard to watch French television for more than ten minutes without spotting a pair or two of bare breasts. No French shampoo commercial would be complete without a shot of a lovely women lathering up in the shower and a handsome man later enjoying her luscious hair. Aesthetics and sensuality, the textural surface of things, appeal to the French mentality.

Pornography doesn't come with the sick or dangerous edge that characterizes hard-core porn in American cities, and the French are not too judgmental about its existence. There are no Tipper Gores trying to clean up the streets and airwaves in Paris. The line between eroticism and pornography isn't clear in France, and no one is particularly interested in sharpening the line of distinction. Rather than battling against a male-dominated industry that has traditionally objectified them, women have responded with their own programming. Several *magazines de cul* (skin mags or, literally, "ass magazines") for women have appeared, including *Bagatelle.* And on the prime-time show *Méfiez Vous des Blondes,* TV sex star Amanda Lear, between highly erotic striptease dances, interviews stars on their greatest sexual fantasies. The live, cheesy phenomenon *Loft Story,* brought vulgar French TV down a notch.

The French don't judge public officials by their private lives and view sex scandals (like the one that nearly ruined Bill Clinton's political career) as absurdly silly and typically American. The talk of Clinton's extramarital relations only elevates the average French person's regard for him. Monica Lewinsky was by and large seen as a bimbo who couldn't keep a secret. Nonetheless, when her book came out in French, sales were brisk. The great French equivalent story was the late-president Mitterrand's second family; while married to Danielle he maintained a mistress with whom he had a daughter, Mazarine. After his death both "families" attended his funeral publicly. He loved them both and that, in France, is what counts.

Safe Sex

The movement for safe sex in France didn't get much further at first than sensuous television ads for the use of condoms. The French approach was not to scare the public with AIDS (called SIDA in France) but to convey the positive message that sex with condoms is beautiful and exciting, and thus an advantage. The ads themselves are pretty exciting. For Valentine's Day Yves St. Laurent once launched a designer condom associating condoms with lovers. The AIDS situation in France is much as it is in any Western country today, although perhaps young French people remain a bit more cavalier than elsewhere. Free public health centers provide confidential AIDS *depistages* (tests) and accurate information (see Health and Insurance). Generally there are fewer stigmas regarding health, sexuality, and illness in France than in Anglo-Saxon countries, but on the whole the situation isn't all that different. In the mid-nineties, to encourage young people to use condoms, a public health campaign made state-subsidized condoms available at all pharmacies for one franc each, a scheme called *tarif jeunes* or "youth price." The métros and TV were plastered with pictures of condoms and one franc coins. Condom sales have increased dramatically. The pharmacy at Charles de Gaulle airport limits sales to two per person to discourage travelers from hoarding at the low prices.

The *tarif jeunes* model is a basic condom distributed with clear, no-nonsense instructions. More affluent or demanding users prefer other brands, which run from five to ten euros for twelve. The French consumer report magazine, *50 Millions de Consommateurs*, ran a survey on condoms marketed in France; the Japanese-made Manix gained top kudos. Even six-year-old school kids know that condoms prevent unwanted babies and the spreading of AIDS. There is absolutely no stigma in France in going for a free AIDS test, and no impact whatsoever on your health insurance premiums, as there is in other countries.

The gay and lesbian communities in Paris, although more open and public now than ten years ago, are still somewhat discreet. The annual Gay Pride parade has gained momentum each year over the last five, and controversial new legislation that grants legal and fiscal equality to gay partners under new definitions of what constitutes a legally recognized couple has raised consciousness on the subject. On the rue Vielle du Temple and surrounding streets in the Marais, a large number of busy, gay nightspots and bookstores flourish. The gay community has a Paris magazine called *Gai Pied Hebdo*, 45 rue Sedaine, 75011 Paris, Tel.: 01–43–57–52–05 (which also has an SOS Ecoute Gaie phone line, Tel.: 01–48–06–19–11). It publishes a Minitel service at 3615 Gayguide and has a Web site (www.gaipied.fr) on which you can consult a continuously updated recreation guide. There are several other Minitel services catering to the gay community. *Fréquence Gaie* (FG) on 98.2 FM is a twenty-four-hour gay radio station, the only one in Europe. It hosts the only rave pre-party show featuring guest mixers live in the studio. The terrace on the Seine side of the Tuileries gardens at night is known as the *grand lieu du pickup* for their *rencontre éclair*, or flash meetings, where homosexual men can find quick and anonymous sex. The same is true along the quay of the Seine at night as well as in the Square Henri IV. Gay prostitution has found a home along the rue Ste-Anne and around Trocadéro. The highly acclaimed French film *Nuit Fauves* by Cyril Collard, who died of AIDS shortly after the film's success, heightened the gay-AIDS sensibility in France.

The rue St-Denis and parts of Pigalle have traditionally been the main turf for heterosexual prostitution in Paris. One recalls Henry Miller, *n'est-ce pas?* There has always been a romanticizing element to French prostitution, dating from the naturalism of Zola. There's almost a tradition of prostitutes that carries on, although the scene has clearly lost much of those associations, and the streets have become more dangerous with the increased presence of drugs and AIDS. Women, many who've originated in post-colonial Africa and the West Indies, stand out by their doors openly and, for the most part, unharassed day and night. Around 4:00 P.M. (16h) it's interesting to observe the undisturbed mixture of prostitutes coming out to work and school kids returning from school. This is indicative of a larger tolerance. Occasionally there will be police roundups and the prostitutes are each fined 310 euros, which is about the equivalent of one night's work. Other areas of dense prostitution have traditionally included the Bois de Boulogne, where prostitutes and dazzling Brazilian transvestites line the roadways peddling their wares to passing motorists. Due to the AIDS situation, the Bois has been closed to vehicular traffic at night. The Bois de Vincennes now finds itself dotted with white vans and small trucks; women lure passing male drivers for a quick visit in the back of these mobile bedrooms. Prostitution is not considered an illegal activity, but soliciting business in an aggressive manner is, so you won't see pimps doing this for the girls. The area around Métros Blanche and Clichy are also filled with prostitutes and pornography, with the rue Fontaine being noted for its transvestites. The *portes de Paris* around the edges of the city and the *axes rouges* or major arteries leading into town are usually dotted at night with women for hire. Cars stop to negotiate the deal and the women often get in and ride away (although they will usually refuse cars with more occupants than the driver). A surprising number of young women from Eastern Europe have ended up on Paris streets.

As for other possibilities in the spirit of great tolerance, or kinky perversion, depending on how you view it, couple swapping occurs at the Place Dauphine, and a number of *boîtes échangistes*, "swapping clubs," can be found in the first *arrondissement*. Le Triangle specializes in triples, as its name suggests; the entry charge is around 25 euros. One spectator reports alcoves for semidiscreet meetings and a boxing ring in the center. Another is called Adam's Club. Additionally, all sorts of sexual-oriented programming is found on the Minitel or in specialized press in magazine kiosks, but as one social observer remarked, "There is a deficiency in sexual communication in France today; the screen has replaced the body."

All this adds up to a culture attitudinally very different, perhaps, from what you're used to. Perhaps not?

Drinking

The legal drinking age is sixteen, but it is not enforced. You'll rarely get carded or turned away in a café, bar, or liquor store. You can buy whiskey along with your daily groceries in supermarkets, local shops, and even gas stations. As a positive, if somewhat counter-intuitive, consequence of this availability, public drunkenness by rowdy youths is not very prevalent. When people go out to a concert or club, they don't usually end up drunk, as is often true in an English, American, or Australian context; they listen to the music or talk. The need to let loose or partake in antisocial behavior is not as prevalent in France, largely because the culture is socially less repressed in general. It has been estimated that the average French person over twenty years old consumes an average of 53 grams (1.87 ounces) of pure alcohol per day, making him a participant in an impressive percentage: The French remain the world's heaviest consumers of alcohol per capita after the Luxembourgeois. Wine is still served with both lunch and dinner in many families, but the meal is no longer considered incomplete without it. Alcoholism in France is responsible for over 20,000 deaths a year, caused more by cheap red wine than hard alcohol, and it is a phenomenon that is vastly more common—or at least visible—in rural and slum areas.

Smoking

A very large portion of French society smokes cigarettes, more than 40 percent. Even French doctors smoke—to the tune of 30 percent! Antismoking consciousness is changing but painfully slowly. A bill limiting smoking in public places passed in 1992 polarized French society to some extent: the smokers vs. the nonsmokers. All cafés and restaurants must provide clearly marked sections for nonsmokers but people often smoke in nonsmoking sections and the restaurateur usually says/does little about it. Most cafés have complied by assigning the worst areas and back tables for this purpose. Some cafés have simply placed signs in the window announcing that theirs is a smokers' café, thereby discouraging the rare nonsmoker from ever entering. In practice most restaurants and cafés do not respect the law, reasonably claiming that they'd go out of business if they banned smoking. Smoking, like drinking, eating, or having sex, is integral to the French belief in the eminence of pleasure, plaisir; the act of pleasing and being pleased is essential to the French soul, and for many this still includes smoking. Smokers in France generally do not like being reminded of its evils. And many are intolerant of American intolerance of smokers.

Cigarettes can be purchased only in a *tabac* (tobacconist). They are not available in drug stores, gas stations, or department stores. Some cafés sell cigarettes as a service to their customers. They will cost up to 5 euros a pack in the cafés, 3 to 4 euros in the *tabacs*.

If you are a nonsmoker, be prepared for a lot of smoke and an overall indifference to the rights of nonsmokers. If the smoke has a pungent, unfamiliar odor, this is because in France hard-core smokers often consume the classic, blue-packed and filterless Gauloises or Gitanes, made of untoasted *(blonde)* tobacco. Also a number of people roll their own cigarettes. It's cheaper.

Smoking is now forbidden in the métro too, although this has yet to be fully enforced. Due to the outlawing of cigarette advertising in French publications, television, and cinemas, tobacco companies have launched huge and somewhat perverse campaigns to keep their names at the fore of smokers' lips. Camel has a travel agency. Marlboro offers its own line of clothes. Lucky Strikes, the naughtiest of the lot, plays on the reverse attractiveness of the banned, using the *warning le tabac nuit à la santé* (tobacco consumption is harmful to your health) as a marketing lure.

Drugs

Drug possession is a serious offense in France, and laws are particularly harsh on foreigners. Drug use isn't nearly as much of a social problem, though, as it is in the United States, England, Germany, or Holland; nor has it resulted in as desperate and widespread urban violence. Nonetheless, the area around Métro Stalingrad has become the most drug-exposed area in Paris with the arrival of crack. Crack dealers and users are concentrated in that district as are undercover police agents. A majority of crack and hard-drug users and addicts are French West Indian *(antillais)* and African, and the correlation between drugs, crime, and illegal immigration is an unfortunate one in that the police, special police (RG), and the Ministry of the Interior use drug control as a prime pretext for cracking down on foreigners.

Heroin use is relatively limited, with an estimated 30,000 addicts in Paris. Although French drug laws are nowhere as lenient as those in Holland, there was, until recently, a cinema in Paris where it was understood that marijuana smokers would not be bothered. And late at night in the métro as well as in certain bars and clubs, a whiff or two of the popular hash and tobacco mixture may come your way. But *attention!* If you want to remain in France without problems, think twice about breaking the law. It is ill-advised to buy drugs from anyone on the street. Crossing international borders with drugs is particularly unwise, especially when traveling from any island of southern latitude or returning from Amsterdam, as charter buses are often searched with the aid of police dogs.

Even at parties, smoking hash—marijuana is harder to find—can be met with disapproval. Cocaine use is not nearly as widespread as in North America. It is the drug of snobbery and trendiness, often found in the fast-lane parties of journalists, models, advertising executives, etc. It's the "baba cool" sign of superficial "in-ness."

Parties

Even among young people parties are rarely given without a specific occasion to celebrate. A party can be called a *fête, une soirée,* or *une boum.* To party can be referred to as *faire la bringue.* A *fête* is usually a celebration, such as a birthday or graduation. A *soirée* is a civilized evening party with not necessarily a lot of people. *Une boum* tends to be larger and louder, and is usually restricted to the high school crowd. Every city, however, has its limits for noise and rowdiness. Parisian law requires that on weeknights all noise stop after 22h, 10:00 P.M., and the police will likely come banging on the door if it doesn't. On weekends it's 1h, but once or twice a year, weekend festivities are allowed to go all night—as long as you inform the local police station and the neighbors as far in advance as possible. A surefire strategy to avoid problems with the neighbors is to start the party in the early afternoon, and have it wind down before 22h. Not very practical, admittedly. In any case, be sensitive about loud noise, blasting stereos, and the like in public places in Paris. Rowdy partying is not part of the French version of decadence and hedonism. They have their own, which you'll have to discover for yourself. Even the way you shut doors, talk in the stairwells of apartment buildings, and walk on parquet floors can lead to complaints. Be careful. Don't get off to a bad start with neighbors; it's hard to remedy bad relations.

Some sectors of Paris society have experienced a return to the adolescent habits and aesthetics of the formerly privileged class. Rallies or debutante *piplettes,* "coming-out parties," of the BCBG crowd *(bon chic bon genre)* or yuppies are being organized by parents in the bourgeois sixteenth *arrondissement.*

Common Abbreviations

Note that these are spoken and readily understood in daily Parisian conversation. Also note that for some odd reason the French love abbreviations.

Abbreviation	French	Explanation
A/R	aller-retour	round-trip
AV	à vendre	for sale
BD	bande desinée	comic strip
BHV	Bazar de l'Hôtel de Ville	a major department store
BN	Bibliothèque Nationale	a national library
BNP	Banque Nationale de Paris (Paribas)	a large bank chain
BP	boîte postale	post office box
CB	carte bleue	bank debit card associated with VISA
CGT	Confédération Générale de Travail	leftist trade union
CNR	Centre National de Recherche	national institute for research
CP	cour préparatoire	kindergarten
CCP	compte chèque postal	checking account offered by post office
CRS	Compagnie Républicaine de Sécurité	military police
CV	curriculum vitae	résumé
DEP	Diplôme des études approfondies	first diploma in doctoral prgram
EDF	Electricité de France	electric company of France
FISC	la fiscalité (les impôts)	tax collection bureau
FN	Front National	the extreme right political party
FR3	France 3	the third television channel
GDF	Gaz de France	the French gas company
HLM	Habitation à loyer modéré	subsidized housing
HT	Hors taxe	before sales tax
PC	petite ceinture	ring road around Paris within Périphérique
PCF	Parti communiste de France	Communist Party of France
PD	pédéraste	perjorative term for homosexual
PDG	président-directeur général	equivalent to CEO
PQ	papier cul	toilet paper
PS	Parti socialiste	Socialist Party
PV	procès verbal	parking tickets or fines

RA	Régie autonome des transports parisiens	Paris public transportation authority
RC	rez-de-chausée	ground floor
RDV	rendez-vous	rendezvous
RER	Reseau express régional	commuter train system
RF	République française	the French republic
RPR	Rassemblement pour la République	leading right-centrist party
SDF	Sans domicile fixe	the homeless
SECU	Sécurité Sociale	Social Secuity system
SIDA		AIDS
SMIC	salaire minimum inter professionnel de croissance	minimum wage
SNCF	Société nationale des chemins de fer	the national train system
SPA	Société pour la protection des animaux	animal protection league
TGV	train à grand de vitesse	ultrafast train
TP	trésor public	national treasury
TTC	toutes taxes comprises	sales tax included
TVA	taxe sur valeur ajoutée	value added tax/sales tax
UV	unité de valeur	university course credit
VF	version française	film dubbed in French
VO	version originale	film in original language with subtitles
WC	water closet	toilet

Children in Paris

Baby-sitters

The best bet for finding baby-sitters is through the bulletin boards in your local *boulangerie* and Monoprix or by asking your neighbors and friends. But Paris does have a number of highly reliable services that you may want to use.

The hourly rate for baby-sitters in Paris ranges from 5 to 7 euros (a bit higher for multiple kids and after midnight). The services listed here all promise that they provide carefully screened, bilingual baby-sitters, almost exclusively female university students.

Ababa

8 avenue du Maine, 75015 Paris; Tel.: 01–45–49–46–46
This service has around 500 available baby-sitters and has been in existence for nearly fifteen years. If you want to be sure to speak with someone in English, call after 4:00 P.M.

Price: For one or two children, 5,50 euros an hour with a two-hour minimum; 1 euro extra per additional child, plus a 10-euro agency fee. If you keep the baby-sitter later than 11:00 P.M., you'll need to pay her taxi fare. You pay the baby-sitter directly in euros. No credit cards.

Baby-sitting Service
4 rue Nationale, 92100 Boulogne, Billancourt / Tel.: 01–46–21–33–16, Fax: 01–46–21–16–05
Madame Marise Bloch's service has been providing baby-sitters since 1981. Her supply of about one-hundred young women includes English-speaking students. The hourly rate is 5,50 euros an hour with a 10 euros agency fee. No credit cards.

Special Parks for Kids

Cité des Sciences—Parc de la Villette/Musée de la Musique
211 avenue Jean Jaurès
75019 Paris
Métro: Porte de la Villette
Tel.: 01–40–03–75–03
The park has theme gardens for children, amateur musicians, workshops, a bike path, pony clubs, and a lot of green space (a rarity in Paris).

Jardin d'Acclimatation
Bois de Boulogne
75016 Paris
Métro: Sablons or Porte Maillot
Small train from the Porte de Maillot. A great playground, petting zoo, theater, and lake, with exotic plants. A highlight for kids.

Jardin des Enfants aux Halles (Labyrinth)
105 rue Rambuteau
75001 Paris
Tel.: 01–45–08–07–18
Métro: Chatelet–Les Halles (exit Rambuteau)
For prices and hours, call 01–45–08–07–18. Closed when it's raining.
A true Paris highlight for kids, the outdoor Labyrinth in the park at Les Halles is a wonderland of inventive and safe activities. Each hour a limited number of kids are allowed to move through a course of obstacles, illusions, doors, steps, tunnels, cliffs, slides, and more at their own pace while curious and envious parents watch from behind the gates. There is no better way to spend an hour on a Saturday morning with your kids in Paris than at the Labyrinth.

Jardin du Luxembourg
Between the rue Guynemer and le boulevard St-Michel
75006 Paris
Métro RER: Luxembourg
Free entrance.
Gardens for children, workshops, a bike path, a Guignol theater, pony clubs, tennis courts, miniature sailboats, basketball, and more!

Jardin Sauvage de Saint-Vincent
rue Saint-Vincent
75018 Paris
Métro: Lamarck-Caulaincourt
Tel.: 01–43–28–47–63
Open from April to October on Mondays
(during the school year) from 4:00 to 6:00 P.M.
Saturdays from 2:00 to 6:00 P.M.
An initiation into ecology and biology on Montmartre.

Parc Floral de Paris
Bois de Vincennes–Esplanade du Château
Route de la Pyramide
75012 Paris
Métro: Chateau de Vincennes
Tel.: 01–55-94-20-20, Fax: 01–43–41–97–02
Full price: 2 euros
Children under 10 years old: 1 euro
60 games for children.

Publications/Listings

For a listing of things to do with kids, check the *Paris Voice*, www.parisvoice.com
(free monthly community newspaper in English) or *Where Paris*, www.wheremag
azine.com (free monthly for tourists distributed in selected hotels).

Animals and Society

The French are highly indulgent with animals, children, and senior citizens, but
they clearly have a love affair with dogs. Paris alone counts 500,000 dogs, or 4,760
dogs per square kilometer, which by far exceeds the number of children. The colloquial French equivalent of "pooch" is *toutou* ("kitty" is *minou*). The most popular
dog name in France is Rex. Supermarkets sell fresh cuts of meats and animal
organs, like spleens *(rate)*, especially for pets. French dog owners are less obsessed
with the macho idea of "all-meat" and feed their dogs well-balanced meals that
include lots of vegetables. At the same time they are likely to offer your overweight
beagle a few sugar cubes at the zinc bar of the local café. *Vive les contradictions!*

Dogs are allowed in restaurants and most public places, although they must be
leashed in parks and "bagged" (concealed in a special bag or case designed for transporting animals) in the métro and on trains. For an assortment of dog bags, go to
La Samaritaine (Métro Sèvres Babylone), a popular department store. Unless you
are leasing a furnished apartment for a short period of time, there is no problem
renting apartments if you have pets. No extra fees. There are animal *auberges* for
vacation time, and numerous chic dog salons, where the poodles recline on mock
Louis XIV *fauteuils*. There are several taxi services for pets, as well as pet ambulances. In addition to many veterinarians throughout Paris, rue Maître Albert,
in the fifth *arrondissement*, houses an animal *dispensaire* for inexpensive veterinary

services. If you call *SOS Vétérinaires* (Tel.: 01–47–55–47–00), you can ask for emergency veterinary care contact information. The French SPA shelters homeless pets, many of which are abandoned along the autoroutes during vacation times. Beware—some are not healthy and not vaccinated. (*Société Protectrice des Animaux* (SPA), 39 boulevard Berthier, 75017 Paris, Tel.: 01–43–80–40–66; www.spa.asso.fr).

It is relatively easy to bring dogs and cats into France. Although a valid health certificate showing a recent rabies vaccination is required, chances are you won't have to show it at the airport when you arrive—but you may have to show it when you leave, so it's ill-advised to arrive without one. Technically, animals without proper certification can be deported or destroyed! If you're planning to pass through or visit the United Kingdom with a pet, be advised that a strict, six-month quarantine is enforced for animals, vaccinated or not! This can be a terribly cruel and costly surprise, so inquire first if you have any doubts.

Pets can travel on international airlines, in approved kennel cages, for the price of a piece of extra baggage. (The only airline that charges nothing for kennels is Air France.)

Some regulations should be carefully noted. Dogs under the age of three months and cats under six weeks are prohibited from international travel. You cannot bring more than three animals at one time, and only one can be a puppy or a kitten. Rabies vaccination certificates must state that the vaccine had been administered more than thirty days and less than one year prior to the date of departure. Birds are limited to two parrots and ten birds of small species with health certificates issued within five days of departure. All other animals require special import permits from the Ministry of Agriculture. Fortunately, the bottom line is that living and traveling in France with pets generally poses few problems and can even be an easy and agreeable way to make acquaintances quickly.

Bringing Fido to France

One dog-loving New Yorker-turned-Parisian, Justine Donato, adds her comments to Paris Inside Out*'s advice on bringing pets to Paris.*

Four years ago I had decided to put the wheels in motion and move to France from New York City. Preparation for the big move was slightly less daunting than I had imagined, but I was afraid that the biggest difficulty would be what meant most to me: my dog Henry.

At that time, Henry the Hungarian Vizsla was four years old and such a neurotic New Yorker that he could have been cast for a walk-on in a Woody Allen film. Naturally I was worried about his ability to handle the seven-hour-plus flight to Paris almost as much as I was worried about the rigors of French bureaucracy. My initial worry was unwarranted, though. For dogs (and cats) traveling from the United States, there is generally no quarantine and only two certificates are required: an International Anti-Rabies Vaccination Certificate and the more-official-looking "U.S. Interstate and International Certificate of Health Examination for Small Animals."

Due to the seriousness of rabies and the stringency with which the international authorities check all incoming domestic animals, organization on your part is key. Always call your veterinarian, your airline, and the nearest French Embassy to check on any possible changes in the laws regarding domestic animal transport to France. Now, assuming that the laws have not changed, make an appointment with your dog's vet no more than five days before your departure date. You are limited to bringing three animals into France, by the way, and only one may be a puppy under six months old. Your vet will do the standard check-up and issue you the two certificates. Remember that these certificates must be issued *no more than five days before your departure date.* Both certificates must include your vet's signature, address, and accreditation number. Your vet must stamp, sign, and list her license number along with the state in which she is licensed to practice. There are also rules regarding vaccination time periods depending on your dog's vaccination history. If your dog has just been given the rabies vaccine for the first time, it must have been done at least one month before and no longer than one year prior to your departure date. Also, any dog that falls under the category of "dangerous breed" may be prevented from entering France. In other words, check with your vet first if Fifi is an 80-pound pit bull.

Henry and I flew in mid-September and he was given a tranquilizer pill just before we boarded the plane, which worked amazingly well at keeping him calm. If your dog is less than ten pounds, he may be able to stay with you in the cabin. All other breeds must fly with the luggage where, depending on the season, it will either be very hot or very cold. Most airlines will not even allow animals to fly in the luggage area during the summer months simply because the temperatures are life-threateningly hot.

Upon landing at Charles de Gaulle Airport, I was happy to have found Henry (now "Henri") sitting quietly in his crate near a French Customs agent. Documentation in hand, the fear of French bureaucracy weighing heavily on me, I approached the customs agent. I was ignored as the vaccination dossier was taken from me and quickly reviewed. It was apparent that "Henri" was the star. There were hugs, kisses, and calls to the other agents to come and see this *"chien magnifique."* Henry was as ecstatic with the attention as I was with the French efficiency. And wouldn't you know it, he loves the French!

Caca on the Streets

The infamous problem of uncurbed dogs, which had given Paris a bad name for many years, has been somewhat rectified. You used to have to hop-skip-and-jump to avoid landing in a rude pile. The law states that you must curb your dog, directing him to do his *besoins* (needs) in the *caniveau* (gutter) off the curb—and there are even cute graphic reminders painted on certain sidewalks. The city has recently launched a clever and graphically pleasing poster campaign designed by famed illustrator Sempé to remind dog owners of their civic responsibilities. Now, in the nicer neighborhoods at least, the city cleans up in the form of a technician with a green designer suit on a converted motorcycle equipped with a high-powered vacuum cleaner. Much of the eyesore has been aspirated away. Since 1991 you can be fined on the spot for not curbing your dog, but as far as we know, this has never been enforced.

While on the subject, Paris has other ways of keeping itself clean. You may wonder why water gushes out of sewers and runs through the gutters so often—

even when it's not been raining. Paris street cleaners, mostly Africans in green municipal jumpsuits, open valves of clean (but undrinkable) water and direct the flow up- or downstreet by positioning soggy bolts of tied-up cloth. Then, with their green plastic-branched brooms, they sweep loose papers, *mégots* (cigarette butts), trash, and unclaimed dog doo into the moving stream, which drains into the city sewers and eventually into the Seine system for recycling. You can visit the impressive sewers *(les egouts de Paris)* daily at Pont de l'Alma (at Métro Alma-Marceau, then cross the bridge to the other side of the Seine) in the seventh arrondissement. Every address in Paris has an equivalent one underground. This complex, unlit network was extensively used by Resistance fighters during the Nazi cccupation. Now certain areas are lit for exhibitions.

For humans, Paris streets are equipped with automatic, self-disinfecting pay toilets. For 0,50 euros you gain access to a futuristic compartment where cleanliness and comfort are guaranteed.

The Emerging Urban Landscape

Since the mid-1990s the Paris area has experienced dramatic increases in both violent and nonviolent crime. Much of this occurs in the outer districts and suburbs, especially the Seine Saint-Denis *département*, where poorer and immigrant communities live in dense quarters or housing projects *(cités)*, each commonly referred to as *le zone.*

A number of well-made documentary films have captured this growing problem, the best known being *La Haine* (Hate). Much of the problem stems from the fact that young, French-born children of North African and sub-Saharan immigrants are faced with limited resources and an increasingly limited place in the social and economic environment. Compounded by high unemployment and rising frustration among middle-class French citizens, and the inadequate and ill-prepared law enforcement agencies, tensions in some areas have grown to alarming proportions. Although the Paris area still remains relatively safe, caution should be used when you travel alone, especially at night, to areas outside of Paris.

A Word on Graffiti

The streets and public places in Paris and its suburbs have experienced an explosion of artistic vandalism. Visitors notice quickly how extensive the graffiti markings are. The métro stations and cars are systematically hit by *"taggeurs"* who *"tag"* the walls, streets, and signage with their own urban language. The war is on between the RATP police and these individuals and gangs who express themselves with markers and spray paint. All this adds up to the reality that urban Paris is as socially complex as any large city in the world today.

Safety and Security

Safety is always relative to what you're used to. Although Paris is a big city and a degree of prudence and common sense should always be applied, it is fair to say that

Paris streets, day or night, are relatively safe. Although the city has taken on a harder tone over the last few years, there's little sense in even comparing the safety of Paris to that of any city in the United States. There are fewer dangerous weapons and drugs on Paris streets, and not many desperate and crazed individuals, despite increased numbers of homeless people and drug users. Nonetheless, one should always be careful and prudent. Incidents do occur. There are cases of muggings, theft, and attack. A bigger problem is learning how to remain streetwise while leaving at home that defensiveness that you were most likely, and for sound reason, brought up to maintain at all costs. You should not be frightened to take the métro. In the last few years there has been a significant increase of cases of theft and harassment in certain métro stations, especially late at night. Châtelet and Les Halles should be avoided late at night. Stalingrad can be pretty uninviting, as can Strasbourg St-Denis and République late at night. And it's true that certain *quartiers* can be a bit intimidating or less reassuring. Women may feel the harassment of being followed or catcalled by bothersome men or rude youths. As unpleasant as this may be, these encounters are in most cases harmless. Just ignore such advances and carry on. Of course it's never a bad idea, especially when going out at night into areas you're not familiar with, to have a friend or friends along. If you feel harassed or simply bothered by someone in the street or in a café or club, it's best to ignore them at first. If they persist, a clever retort works better than an insult. Try one of these: *"J'attends mon mari," "J'attends ma femme"* ("I'm waiting for my husband/wife") or, *"Est-ce que je vous ai donné la permission de me parler?"* ("Did I give you permission to talk to me?"). Make sure you have these mastered before you attempt them, however. Women should also be cautioned about making eye contact with strangers—North American friendliness can often be interpreted as a come-on. Common sense is the key. You need to be careful, as in all big cities, but not frightened. Paris is a city that has a relatively late social life and vibrant street/café life; it needs to be negotiated by foot.

Paris is dense; the space between people is often less than in cities in other countries. The social coding between individuals is different. The rules are not always the same. The body language is as distinct as the verbal language. For example, some women have complained that French men in clubs or discotheques become aggressive if they don't get their way after their graciously offered drinks have been accepted. As a rule, you should remember that Americans are more open, verbal, and casual than the French in initial social contacts. This difference can lead to misunderstandings that, although not usually unsafe, can be uncomfortable. Some discos attract individuals who want to pick up foreigners.

Areas of town that are known to be a bit less comforting to foreign students, especially women, include the area between Place Clichy and Barbès-Rochechouart, which delineates the Pigalle district. This area is filled with a lot of porno shops and single (and married) men. Being one of the poorer areas of Paris, there are a lot of immigrants, mostly Algerian, Moroccan, and West African. Although crime is higher here than in the chic parts of central Paris, these ethnic groups usually get an unfair reputation. There is nothing to be frightened about, but it's always good to have an idea about where you're going and to dress more conservatively in those areas.

Street people, the SDF formerly called *clochards* (bums), are for the most part harmless, despite their frequent drunkenness, desperate look, and sometimes angry-sounding comments. Some of the side streets near the Gare Montparnasse and the desolate back streets of the fourteenth arrondissement were known to be frequented by drug dealers. Now the drug zones are Stalingrad and the Gare de Lyon. More recently the eastern part of the Pont de Sèvres/Mairie de Montreuil Line has experienced some drug problems, especially Métro Oberkampf. The drug situation in Paris is a fraction of what it is in North American and other European cities but is growing steadily worse. Far more dangerous than anywhere in Paris are some of the stark concrete HLM complexes (administered subsidized housing) in the northern suburbs. There would be little reason for you to head out that way. Again try to avoid the larger métro stations such as Châtelet/Les Halles late at night, as they can be a refuge for late-night partiers of the slightly dubious type and generally a hangout for unsavory characters. The same goes for the area around Les Halles/Centre Pompidou—the rue St-Denis, a notorious sex shop/prostitution street, is not far away. But in any case, compared to any city in the United States where gangs loiter, Paris's worst is manageable.

Crime Statistics

Crime has increased dramatically in the Paris area, and although one still thinks of the city as relatively safe, one needs to apply caution like in all cities. Especially prevalent is the on-street theft of cell phones and purses and bags. Traveling home alone at night using certain métro lines and buses should be approached with caution. There are more youths commiting crimes against property and people now then ever before. The society at large and the police are not adapting too well to the situation, and politicians have been forced to add public safety *(sécurité)* as a key issue in current elections.

Officially, there were 100,000 homeless people and 19,000 street people in France. No one is certain how manyfold this has increased, but the increase in the homeless is substantial.

Crime is also directed at property and cars. House or apartment theft is called *cambriolage.* A great many apartment dwellers and home owners have steel-enforced doors called *portes blindées,* with five locking points—security that qualifies them for better theft insurance. You won't see grilled-over windows as you do in New York or nineteen locks per door, but you will see these heavy doors and peepholes. In many apartment buildings, there is a concierge, who adds to the safety. Most break-ins occur in August, when a large percentage of Parisians leave for holidays. Be suspicious of individuals who knock on your door offering services and wanting to check the inside of your apartment. This is an old trick for determining which apartments's are worth hitting. Thieves have an entire hieroglyphic language of codes that they leave for each other in chalk by the door or outside the apartment building.

Pickpockets

As in any big city, incidents occur. And the incidents of small-time crime in Paris have skyrocketed over the last few years. So without being afraid, be aware. There is some pickpocketing in the flea markets, in the métro, on buses, and in tourist areas like the Champs-Elysées and St-Michel. If you're careful with your possessions, you will have no problems. Be especially careful in the Barbès Station and on certain bus routes, where pickpockets are known to work in groups. One person drops something, and while you politely bend over to pick it up, another one empties your pocket or bag. Having your papers replaced at the *préfecture* is a real hassle. Be careful. Muggings are not very common, but they happen. Ironically, they seem to occur more frequently at night in the quiet, wealthy, and residential parts of the sixteenth or seventeenth arrondissements rather than in the seedier, more densely populated areas near Pigalle.

In the warm months there can be bands of immigrant children, often Romanian, falsely labeled gitans or gypsies, that hang out between Place de la Concorde and the Louvre. Their MO is to swarm around a confused tourist and pick him or her clean like sharks and the great fish in Hemingway's *Old Man and the Sea.* Although this practice has not been as acute as in the past, be careful with your wallet, passport, camera, and jewelry, especially in crowds during the summer. You could be targeted on the street, métro, or bus. To minimize problems, always try to look as if you know where you're going, even if you don't. Professional thieves can quickly spot foreign tourists who look like fair game. Keep your passport and money well concealed, never in your back pocket or backpack, which can be cut and easily emptied. It's not a bad idea to keep backup photocopies of all your documents—the replacement of papers is the most difficult and time-consuming aspect in cases of loss or theft. Some people prefer carrying photocopies and leaving the originals at home.

If someone from the street offers you a better exchange rate than the bank, refuse. Magicians earn money either pulling rabbits out of hats or switching the rolls of money they give to you. After the transaction, you will examine your impressive roll of money only to find two bills wrapped around a bulk of white paper. And legally you are helpless, since you were involved in an illicit transaction. Be especially careful these days; officials anticipate a steep increase in money-changing frauds with the introduction of the euro.

Lost or Stolen Property

If you have lost anything of importance or had it stolen, there are two things to do immediately. First go to the nearest police station and fill out a report *(déclaration de vol)*, which you will need in making an insurance claim. Second, pay a visit to your country's embassy and they will provide you with additional helpful instructions, including a means to replace your passport.

Reporting Crime

The U.S. Embassy offers explicit information on the procedures for reporting lost and stolen items and for handling other types of crime in Paris. Here are the essentials of what they say.

Lost and Found

The French police in Paris maintain a central Lost and Found *(Centre des Objets Trouvés de la Prefecture de Police de Paris)* located at 36 rue des Morillons, 75015 Paris, where you may go to verify whether your belongings were returned. Métro: Convention; hours: 8:30 A.M. to 5:00 P.M. daily, and until 8:00 P.M. Tuesdays and Thursdays. Tel.: 01–55–76–20–20.

What to Do First: Make a police report. All thefts and major losses should be reported to the police as soon as possible. Each of Paris's twenty districts (arrondissements) has three or four police stations *(commissariats);* train stations and the République Métro station also have one each. You should go to the one that has jurisdiction over the area where the theft or loss occurred unless you were robbed in the subway. In that case you can go to any police station, including the one located near the American Embassy, at 31 rue d'Anjou, 75008 Paris. The police will give you a *Recepisse de Declaration de Perte ou de Vol* (receipt for declaration of loss or theft). If you have lost your passport, identification documents, and other papers, as well as personal effects, you will receive separate receipts, one for your papers *(pièces d'identité)* and one for your valuables.

The report must be made in person. The police will not accept a report by telephone or from someone else on your behalf. Most police stations in Paris have English-speaking personnel; if you have difficulty making yourself understood, call the embassy's Office of American Services (Tel.: 01–43–12–45–18 or 01–43–12–45–01) for assistance in interpreting by telephone.

While it is unlikely that the thieves will be arrested as a result, it is important that you report thefts to the police. The police receipt is helpful and sometimes necessary in applying for the replacement of airline tickets, Eurail passes, passports, traveler's checks, etc. It is also useful for supporting insurance claims.

Airline Ticket: Report the loss or theft immediately to the Paris office of the airline. It is left to the discretion of each airline whether or not to replace a ticket. In any case replacement tickets are issued only after verification of the initial purchase of the ticket has been obtained from the airline's home office.

Air France, 119 avenue des Champs-Elysées, 75008 Paris;
Tel.: 01–42–99–21–01

American Airlines, 109 rue du Faubourg St-Honoré, 75008 Paris;
Tel.: 08–10–87–28–72

Continental Airlines, 92 avenue des Champs-Elysées, 75008 Paris;
Tel.: 01–42–99–09–09

Delta Air Lines, 119 avenue des Champs-Elysées, 75008 Paris;
Tel.: 08–00–35–40–80

Northwest Airlines, 16 rue Chauveau Legarde, 75008 Paris;
Tel.: 08–10–55–65–56

United Airlines, 55 boulevard Raspail, 92532 Levallois; Tel.: 08–10–62–62–62

US Airways, 23 bis rue Danjou, 92100 Boulogne Billancourt;
Tel.: 01–49–10–29–29

Replacing a Driver's License

The embassy is not authorized to replace expired, lost, or stolen U.S. driver's licenses. Only the issuing office (Department of Motor Vehicles) in the driver's home state can perform that service. If you have lost your driver's license or had it stolen in France, you should report it to the French police.

Replacing an International Student Card

Lost or stolen international student identity cards may be reissued in Paris by the CIEE, Council Travel Services, 112ter rue Cardinet 75017; Tel.: 01–58–57– 20–40 or 01–53–76–04–00; infofrance@ciee.org; www.ciee.org

Replacing a Eurail pass

If lost or stolen in France, a Eurail pass cannot be replaced. For information, contact French Railways Ltd., Service International, Gare de Paris Saint-Lazare, 13 rue d'Amsterdam, 75008 Paris; Tel.: 01–53–42–00–00. Office hours: 10:00 A.M. to 9:00 P.M., Monday through Saturday.

Replacing Credit Cards

Notify the Paris office of the issuing firm immediately.

American Express Company, 11 rue Scribe, 75009 Paris; 9:00 A.M. to 5:00 P.M.; Tel.: 01–47–77–72–00 Monday through Friday, twenty-four hours a day, every day for loss or theft of a card, Métro Station: Opéra

VISA, Tel.: 08–00–90–20–33 or 08–36–69–08–80 twenty-four hours a day for loss or theft

Diners Club de France, 50 rue Victoire, 75009 Paris; Tel.: 01–40–23–58–00; 9:00 A.M. to 6:00 P.M. Monday through Friday, 9:00 a.m. to 1:00 p.m. Saturday

MasterCard/Eurocard France, 16 rue Lecourbe, 75015 Paris; Tel.: 01–45–67–84–84; twenty-four-hour service seven days a week. To notify the bank in the United States, Tel.: 01–43–23–20–76. Toll-free number for MasterCard Global Service: 08–00–90–13–87.

If your card was issued by a French bank or La Poste, contact the issuing branch directly.

Replacing Traveler's Checks

American Express. Notify Amexco, Regional Refund Center, 11 rue Scribe, 75009 Paris; Tel.: 01–47–77–77–77. Office hours: 9:00 A.M. to 5:30 P.M. Monday through Friday. A toll-free number is available twenty-four hours a day: 08–00–90–86–00. For Amex members contact the travel incidents services at 01–47–77–70–00.

Bank of America. Theft or loss of Bank of America checks can be reported to Credit Commercial de France, 103 avenue des Champs-Elysees, 75008 Paris; Tel.: 01–40–70–70–40. Hours: Monday through Saturday, 9:00 A.M. to 8:00 P.M. and Sunday 10:00 A.M. to 6:00 P.M., Métro station: George V.

Barclays. In Paris call collect (415) 574–7111. You will reach the Visa travelers' services in the United States, which will give you appropriate instructions for refund. To call collect, dial 08–00–99–00–11 to get an AT&T operator. You can then proceed to Barclays, 21 rue Lafitte, 75009 Paris; Tel.: 08–00–90–62–48. Office hours: 9:00 A.M. to 4:30 P.M., Monday through Friday.

Citicorp. In Paris call Citiphone Banking at 01–49–05–49–05, twenty-four hours a day. Or go straight to Compagnie Generale de Banque Citibank, 125 avenue des Champs-Elysees, 75008 Paris. Office hours: 9:00 A.M. to 1:00 P.M. and 2:00 to 4:00 P.M., Monday through Friday.

Thomas Cook. Notify Thomas Cook, 8 rue Bellini, 75016 Paris; Tel.: 01–47–58–21–00. Hours: 9:00 A.M. to 5:30 P.M., Monday through Friday. If more convenient, you can report the loss or theft of your traveler's checks by calling collect the twenty-four-hour refund service at Thomas Cook, Peterborough, England; Tel.: 0800–90–83–30.

VISA. In Paris call 08–00–90–14–24 (toll-free) or call collect (415) 574–7111. To call collect, dial 08–00–99–00–11 for an AT&T operator.

Police, Law, and Authority

By law every person in France has a legal status and an identity card. North Americans—at least prior to September 11—often see the question of "papers" as a psychological hurdle, an invasion of privacy. The United States and Canada do not have national identity cards, unlike most countries in the world. Any policeman has the right to demand that you prove your identity at any time. No real reason or provocation is required. So it's advisable to carry your passport or *carte de séjour* with you at all times. If you're stopped *(contrôlé)* and you don't have identification or valid papers, say you're a tourist. Don't speak French; smile and be submissive. Show the agent *(officer, le flic* or *poulet* in slang)* that you respect his power, and in most cases you'll get a banal warning and be sent on your way with a polite salute. But you might have to provide identification within twenty-four hours or even be accompanied to the local police station. There is a lot of intimidation here. It's better to steer away from any unnecessary encounters with the police, especially in these security-heavy times.

There are several types of police in France. Basically, the *agent de police,* the local officer, is an employee of the Ministry of Interior. The *gendarmes,* the ones you see on the highways out of town and in the small towns, are connected to the Ministry of Defense. The police who ride around in gray-green armored vans and carry Plexiglas shields are the CRS *(Compagnies Républicaines de Sécurité),* the National Security Police. They are called in to enforce order and maintain security in situations of demonstrations, strikes, riots, protests, or upheaval. France experiences numerous national strikes and scores of organized *manifestations (manifs,* or demonstrations) each year. Be prepared to be inconvenienced. En masse, these guys are scary looking. In general, you'll find the police to be polite, formal, and mildly helpful. Not more. As already stated, you can be asked for seemingly no reason to *"présentez vos papiers"*—either your passport or your *carte de séjour.* You'll see systematic control points in the streets for drivers. From time to time, especially at moments when Paris is particularly vulnerable to terrorism, you'll see a lot of armed police in the métro stations as well. The RATP (the Paris public transportation authority) has recently hired supplementary private security police to answer the rise of crime in the métro. Although you may not be used to this, and may even be repulsed by the idea, don't be overly alarmed. Very recently there have been highly visible cases of arrested illegal immigrants, usually black Africans, handcuffed, being escorted to deportation planes at the airport.

Remember, in keeping with the Napoleonic Code, the burden of the proof is upon the accused. This system is being re-examined with the new *Présumption d'Innocence* law, but the general assumption still appplies. You're guilty until proven innocent. For instance, in the case of legal accusations, you can be detained twenty-four hours before you have the right to make a phone call. Yet this concept is just as applicable in numerous sectors of French life; everyday interactions with indi-viduals and administrators are mostly laced with an initial *méfiance* (mistrust). When dealing, for example, with the French tax authorities, even if you are certain that there has been an error, you're obliged to pay first. Justice will follow in due course; the system may be slow, but it is assumed to be right.

A Word on Terrorism

Terrorism has certainly changed the world in drastic ways in recent months. As early as the late 1980s, many visitors were highly concerned with the risks and fears of terrorist activities in Europe. Admittedly there was an atmosphere of uncertainty and distrust in Paris during the Gulf War. The street, cafés, and train stations were empty and mistrustful looks were cast at perfectly innocent Arab or Arab-looking individuals. Prior to that there was a short period in Paris in 1985 and early 1986 when an atmosphere of suspicion and terror permeated the air, following the bombings of a shopping complex on the Champs-Elysées and the popular work-ing-class department store Tati, near Montparnasse, in which innocent people were killed and maimed. And many still remember the terrorist attack on Goldenberg's Restaurant on the predominantly Jewish rue des Rosiers. Ironically, two Jews, two Moslems, and two Christians were killed in the blast and the event ultimately served to create a new feeling of interreligious solidarity in the community. These selected incidents aside, the actual risk of being subjected to any danger of this sort is highly remote and should not—at least for the moment—figure too prominently in your thinking about life in Paris.

The September 11 terrorist attacks on the United States have sent into motion a new wave of preventative actions in France called the *Vigipirate Plan.* Garbage cans are bolted shut and streets with embassies, schools, or public buildings are cor-doned off and parking is prohibited. Attitudinally, Parisians have reacted with great sympathy toward Americans, although many expressed moderate criticism of U.S. foreign policy as being related to the base causes of such barbarous acts.

Housing and Accommodations

Where To Live in Paris

Almost every district, or *arrondissement,* in Paris offers comfortable and pleasant housing options. And almost every corner of Paris is well served by public transportation. Where the métro leaves off, an easy bus route is found. The scale of the city is such that distances are never very great, and you may end up being just as happy (or happier) living in one of the outer arrondissements as you would be in the heart of the Latin Quarter. Most newcomers do not know the neighborhoods well enough to judge where they'd be most content. The charms of being close to the Seine in an old building are obvious, but there are lots of other factors to consider—like noise, distance to the métro, stairs, amenities for the children, parking, and of course price. This thumbnail sketch of each of the arrondissements should help you begin to figure out where you belong.

This brief description of each of Paris's twenty *arrondissements* and surrounding suburbs is highly subjective. Tastes and priorities differ widely. You may love the fact that your neighborhood is cluttered with great little Senegalese and Turkish restaurants. Someone else may feel more at home in the more upscale parts of the sixteenth arrondissement or in Neuilly. Others may hate those sedate, bourgeois back streets in the eighth and feel energized by the ethnic bustle of the eighteenth. It all depends on who you are and what you like.

Use a city map to locate these areas. Note that 75004 means Paris fourth *arrondissement,* etc.

Opéra: first, second, and ninth *arrondissements*
Les Halles: first
Le Marais: third and fourth
Ile Saint-Louis: fourth
Quartier Latin: fifth and sixth
Saint Germain: sixth

Champs de Mars/Invalides: seventh
Etoile/Faubourg St-Honoré: eighth
Bastille: eleventh, edge of twelfth
Chinatown: thirteenth
Parc Monceau: seventeenth
Montparnasse: sixth, fourteenth, and fifteenth
Victor Hugo/Palais de Chaillot: sixteenth
Montmartre: eighteenth
Belleville/Ménilmontant: nineteenth and twentieth

Paris by Arrondissements

Paris is orchestrated according to its *arrondissements*, from the French *arrondir* meaning "to make round," which are laid out in a loosely organized spiral numbered from the center outward. Each *arrondissement* is consequently divided into four neighborhoods, or as the French call them, quartiers, each of which is named for something specific to the neighborhood. There is quality housing with charm in every quartier, but a notion of each area might be helpful in deciding where to look and what to consider, especially when having to select a neighborhood sight unseen. One of your first purchases in Paris should be a small square red, blue, or black book called *Plan de Paris par Arrondissements*, which includes detailed maps, a street and métro index, and bus routes. It'll cost you around 15 euros. This is indispensable for finding your way around Paris. Trust this advice; you'll need a *Plan*. Carry it at all times. You keep this forever.

First—Central Paris, well connected by métro and bus. Tends to be pricey and very busy. Not a great place if you have a car. Châtelet is very congested, but very central. Les Halles, once chic and trendy, is now a bit overrun and seedy at night. The park at Palais-Royal is a bastion of undisturbed Parisian elegance and was the first "strip mall" in the country.

Second—Also central but in parts more commercial in the sense of wholesale outlets. Sentier is the core of Paris's garment district. You may find unusual places to live here but it's more the exception than the rule. The parts near the Opéra and Madeleine are very-high-rent districts and not especially inviting as far as daily Parisian neighborhood life. The streets between Les Halles and the Grands Boulevards are some of the oldest, truly Parisian, and enchanting you'll find. The rue Montorgeuil, the oldest market street in Paris, is worth a detour. Also contains the fashion-chic Place des Victoires, and banking and insurance districts. You won't get a lot of apartment for your money, but if you're single and have a job, you'll likely find something affordable and you'll appreciate the creative people in the area.

Third and Fourth—Very central with many lovely little streets, cafés, shops, etc. Congested, but worth it. This is the oldest (first) area of Paris. Expensive. The Marais has lots of living advantages. One of the most desirable areas of Paris, for those who insist on old buildings with character and multicultural exposure. Rue des Rosiers is the heart of the Jewish quarter and Gay Paris. Parking is dreadful. Buildings are very old, and are reasonably priced when the amenities are run-down or wildly priced when the facilities are renovated and modern. Great for singles and couples, kind of cramped for families. The two islands on the Seine are divine, but very expensive. Impossible for parking.

Fifth—Left Bank, the Latin Quarter, so called because the University students during the Middle Ages would speak to each other in Latin, even outside of class. This is where you get the intellectual, the chic, the classy, the cultural, and the commercial all mixed in. The areas down by St-Michel are tight and noisy, but you can't beat the location. The areas closer to the thirteenth are more residential, well connected to the center of Paris and very pleasant. The rue de Mouffetard is a favorite with expatriates because of its old-world charm and its quaint market, but the summer months are tourist packed. Around the Pantheon is expensive but exquisite. On the whole you can't go wrong in the fifth. Tends to be expensive, but great little finds, especially on studios and small one-bedrooms, are wholly possible.

Sixth—Left Bank, St-Germain-des-Prés, Odéon. This is for the stylish, wealthy, and artistic. The sabbatical taker working on a book, the retired shrink, the corporate family with more cultural and intellectual interests than others in the company, all find the St-Germain-des-Prés area ideal. Many bookshops, galleries, cinemas, upbeat cafés, restaurants, antiques shops, quaint hotels, and publishing houses, not to mention the Sorbonne and Jardin du Luxembourg. This is Paris's continued connection to ideas, thinkers, and the tradition of reading and writing. Between St-Germain and the Seine, prices are sky-high. The sixth extends to Montparnasse and to Duroc, including parts of St-Michel. Lots of wonderful little streets. Very desirable.

Seventh—Tends to be expensive, high-class, conservative, and residential. Also houses most of the government ministries, the Assemblée Nationale, and the Quai d'Orsay (Foreign Ministry). Not very lively at night, although very pleasant and pretty. The street behind Les Invalides, the avenue de Tourville, used to be the most expensive property in the French version of Monopoly. The Esplanade des Invalides offers sprawling lawns that are not off-limits for frisbee-playing and picnicking. The outdoor market on the rue Cler is particularly pleasant and filled with high-quality shops. The part near the fifteenth is a bit livelier, with decent cafés and restaurants.

Eighth—Right bank. Financial and corporate territory. The Golden Triangle. Champs-Elysées. Very high rents and a lot of pomp. Attracts wealthy residents from the Middle East, Asia, and Eastern Europe. Lots of motion and money and less of a neighborhood feel. But there are some surprisingly quaint and quiet streets as you venture away from the Champs-Elysées. The rue St-Honoré has to be a highlight for extravagant Sunday window-shopping, but does anyone really live there?

Ninth—This includes Pigalle and Clichy. More *populaire*, meaning working class. This can be fun, although living here requires that you're more streetwise. The area around Métro Blanche is famous for its funky collection of bars and nightlife with its diversely leaning regulars. Depends on particular street and apartment. Don't exclude this, especially singles and spunky couples. The circa ninth-century covered passageways wait to be discovered. The streets taking the names of foreign cities, north of the Gare St-Lazare, are pleasant, and you'll feel as if you're living in a city that hasn't changed for decades.

Tenth—There are some great spots near la République and along the St-Martin canal, although along the major boulevards and rue St-Denis an element of tackiness and sleaze is present. Lots of Turkish and North African restaurants, covered passages and bric-a-brac. Definitely worth checking out. Less expensive than nearby third and fourth arrondissments. The canal is good for joggers.

Eleventh—In the last ten years this district has emerged as perhaps the best combination of new in-places, with great apartments, artists' spaces, restaurants, and intriguing, centuries-old passageways. Not too far from things and still filled with great finds, but hurry. Close to the Bastille on one end and Nation on the other. The eleventh has a lot to offer without the pretensions of the Marais. Excellent for artists and folks into restaurants and lively, evolving neighborhoods. The newest neighborhoods to emerge include Menilmontant and Belleville. The eleventh comprises all sorts of styles, options, and aesthetics, and thus needs to be explored thoroughly before coming to a decision. If you're young, or think of yourself as young, and care about living in a lively and animated area where Parisians come to drink, dance, and make art, then this may be for you.

Twelfth—Close to the eleventh; up-and-coming around Bercy, the former wine market, and Gare de Lyon, areas that were rather run-down and depressed. Not the most beautiful district, but you may find more space for fewer euros here than elsewhere. Much of the *quartier* is populated with older and rather sedate, nondescript Parisians. If you're looking for a quiet place to blend in, the twelfth is fine. The area around Nation is pleasant and well connected by métro and RER. New construction in the district tends to be hideous, although the new Bercy business park flanking the Seine offers some of the most expensive and highly sought commercial properties in Europe. From Bercy, across the Seine, you can see the new Bibliothèque Nationale.

Thirteenth—The heart of Chinatown. Here you can find quaint streets with little houses next to horrible rows of Miami Beach–style high-rises. Some excellent, authentic Chinese restaurants, shops, and supermarkets, dominated by the ubiquitous Tang Brothers. The areas near the fifth are very desirable. The district is growing rapidly along the Seine and the Tolbiac Bridge area with the new Bibliothèque de France complex trasforming the scene and beginning to create new life along the river.

Fourteenth—Denfert, Montparnasse, Porte d'Orléans. On the major north–south axis. Many popular neighborhoods and great outdoor markets, particularly the one on the rue Daguerre. Without a doubt some of the best residential living in Paris. The area around the Parc Montsouris is lovely and quiet. Montparnasse itself is loud and congested, especially on weekend nights when out-of-towners and Parisians alike come here to eat, drink, consume crèpes, and see films. The streets around the Montparnasse Cemetery are quieter and nice to live on.

Fifteenth—Highly-sought-after residential district among Parisians, but you may find it dull and out of the way. Comfortable and not without its share of trees. The parts near the Seine host an unlikely outcrop of Japanese tourist hotels (to be avoided). The rue du Commerce captures the essence of daily Parisian family life. The streets around the avenue de La Motte–Piquet are particularly lovely, and there is genuine street life here with good cafés and markets.

Sixteenth—Etoile, Trocadéro, Passy, etc. Perhaps the most boring and bourgeois area of Paris, yet one of the wealthiest spots on earth. Studded with wonderful examples of architectural elegance. Many international students end up here, attracted by the nearby Champs-Elysées, a prestigious address, and safety (a mistake). The streets, although pretty, are dead quiet at night and there is nothing to do. Street life is absent except around the rue de Passy and Auteuil, where there is a real neighborhood feel and good shopping. Many lovely small museums and private streets. Don't even consider living on the Champs-Elysées. Walking down it a few times a year is plenty.

Seventeenth—The most schizophrenic district of Paris. Half is as bourgeois as the sixteenth, and the Parc Monceau is absolutely exquisite to stroll around. Living here throws you into a time warp consumed by nineteenth-century established wealth. The other half, near La Fourche, is *populaire*, real, and even funky with some tremendous back streets and apartments with character. A bit far from the heart of things, but this could be worth it if you want to really experience Paris life as it used to be. Prices vary dramatically.

Eighteenth—Kind of far from central districts, although this depends on proximity to a good métro line. More immigrants than elsewhere. Less expensive, so you definitely can get more for your money. Lots of things to discover. Encircles Montmartre. Some great markets—food, fabric, and bric-a-brac. Artists, Africans, working-class people, students, struggling actors, etc., all reside here amid historic sites from when the neighborhood was an artists' village.

Nineteenth—Probably the least known of all the Paris districts, mainly because it is so isolated. Not very convenient in most cases, but again, you may find a great space near a métro. Check it out. The Stalingrad area has become a bit tainted by druggies and dealers, so it shouldn't be a choice for expatriates with small kids, but there are real deals to be found in the nineteenth. You can find a much larger space here for the money. The area around La Villette offers a lot of advantages to families: more space, parks, and cultural attractions (especially the Parc de la Villette complex).

Twentieth—A lively mix of races and ethnic groups—Africans, Antilleans, etc. Some excellent work spaces and artists' *ateliers*. Less expensive than the middle of town, more working-class, and less prestigious, but it all depends on what you want. There are wonderful residential streets tucked in around the rue St-Blaise and the rue Vitruve.

Twenty-first—Not yet a reality, but discussion and some advanced advertising is already circulating. This district would include parts of the northeast quadrant of Paris around the canals near La Villette and Pantin where new neighborhoods are being carved.

A Word on the *Banlieues*

You may find yourself living in the Parisian suburbs *(banlieues)*, which can be either pleasant or grim, depending on your expectations and the actual town you're in. The contiguous suburbs, which are well served by métro and bus lines, are called the *proche-banlieue*. The most exclusive and desirable of these include Neuilly, Boulogne, and St-Cloud to the west, and St-Mandé and Vincennes to the east. The little towns in the Vallée de Chevreuse, served by the RER, are the most desirable southern banlieues. The towns to the north tend to be the poorest and what the French would describe as sad *(triste)*. The northern suburbs and scattered others have experienced increases in crime, drugs, and delinquency in public places and housing projects called *cités* or zones. Bands or gangs of bored youth called *les casseurs* (from *casser*, "to break") from these suburbs have on occasion invaded student and labor demonstrations and vandalized property, lit cars on fire, and looted sections of Paris.

The "red suburbs" *(banlieues rouges)* are municipalities with Communist city governments; they include Montreuil, Bagnolet, Bobigny, Kremlin-Bicêtre, and Malakoff. These communities, although not very different from the others, tend in theory to respond to the economic and cultural needs and interests of the working class. In Montreuil, which houses the headquarters for the CGT (powerful left-wing worker's union), there are large Arab and African communities and a huge and impressive constituency of working artists, designers, theater people, and writers. The town is conveniently located on the No. 9 métro line and has in the last ten years attracted many creative people and young families. Jean-Pierre Brard, Montreuil's dynamic deputy mayor, has set a tone for his town (the third largest in the region) as a place where multiculturism is celebrated and cultural policies are progressive. Montreuil hosts part of the annual Banlieue Bleues music festival, the largest children's book fair in France, a municipally subsidized art cinema, and a literary bookshop, as well as the only jazz club in the *département, Les Instants chavirés*. Apartments and work spaces here can be cheaper and more spacious than anywhere in Paris. Price controls help keep out speculators.

The more distant suburbs *(grandes banlieues)*, such as Versailles, and St-Germain-en-Laye to the west and Chantilly to the northeast, are popular with expatriates, and are served by RER and commuter trains. The eastern line of the RER has been extended to Marne la Vallée to better serve Disneyland Paris.

The choice to live in the suburbs is a highly personal one, depending on how important it is for you to be in the vicinity of Paris with its cafés and nightlife, and how important it is to have more space and even your own *jardin* (translated as garden, but really means yard). The suburbs tend to be quiet at night and provincial in feel, unless you're in one of the urban hot spots to the north of the city, known for increased tensions between disenchanted French and immigrant youths and an ill-equipped police force. With the many quiet and bucolic villages on the outskirts of Paris, there seems to be little difference in being 10 kilometers or 200 kilometers from the capital. Several Paris suburbs, nonetheless, offer very vibrant cultural programming such as the Banlieue Jazz and Banlieue Bleues Festivals in the Seine St-Denis, and the public theater in Bobigny.

The Chinatowns of Paris

The following article on Paris's Asian communities was written by Lucas Klein, a writer who recently moved to Paris after spending two years in China.

The Chinese word for most Chinatowns in North America is *tangrenjie*, literally the "street for Chinese people." In France, however, Chinese use the phrase *zhongguocheng*, which is much closer to the concept of a Chinese town. The history of Chinese people in France is a long and interesting one: The 2001 Nobel Prize for Literature went to Gao Xingjian, a Chinese transplanted to Paris, and both

Deng Xiaoping (PRC's paramount leader, 1979–97) and Zhou Enlai (Premier of PRC, 1949–76) spent formative years in France, no doubt honing their Marxist ideology with their student and factory-worker comrades while arranging meetings of the Chinese Communist Youth Group.

Chinese immigration to France continues to be strong to this day: Paris has three and a half Chinatowns, each of which has its own special characteristics and style. The image of Parisian Chinatowns is not too far removed from Chinatown as most Americans know it: Chinese characters in neon calligraphy hang in Hong Kong–style restaurants, open-air markets (much less a rarity in Europe than in the States) are stocked with exotic vegetables and meats, and women can buy imitation *qipao* (pronounced "chee-pow") in silk or rayon.

Distinct differences remain, however, between American and French Chinatowns: The Chinatowns based at Porte de Choisy, Belleville, Crimée, and Arts et Métiers are all much less kitschy than American Chinatowns tend to be. For instance, walking down Grant Avenue in San Francisco can be an experience as touristy as visiting the Eiffel Tower; the Chinatowns in Paris are much less orchestrated for the tourists than for the local Asian populations. Nonetheless, knowing some secrets of Chinatowns in Paris can make your life abroad all the easier.

Most of North America's Chinese population is Cantonese—that is, they come from Hong Kong or Guangdong (a region formerly anglicized as Canton) and speak a dialect unintelligible to speakers of Mandarin, the official dialect of both Taiwan and the People's Republic of China. The majority of Chinese in France come from Wenzhou (pronounced "wun-joe"), located south of Shanghai on the coast of the Pacific ocean. Their Wenzhou dialect is unique in China for having its own grammar, relatively unrelated to northern Mandarin dialects or to southern dialects such as Cantonese. Speakers of Mandarin need not worry, however; Paris's Chinese population also has many *émigrés* from Sichuan, Shanghai, Xi An, and Beijing. These days, moreover, nearly all Chinese people can speak Mandarin.

Many Wenzhou Chinese are—or were—illegal immigrants, though the vast majority of Chinese living in France have proper working permits. The Wenzhou Chinese are far from isolated in Paris's Chinatowns; indeed, many Wenzhou people work in Paris's Japanese restaurants, some of the best of which can be found in the sixth arrondissement, near the Luxembourg RER station on Rue Monsieur Le Prince. If you can speak Japanese, you may want to listen first before you assume that the person serving you sushi can understand Japanese.

Indeed, this is a minor problem confronting many Asians in France. Very often a French person, trying to be polite, will blunder by saying *arigatou* (thank you), or *sayonara* (good-bye), which are Japanese. Sometimes Asians themselves have this problem, as Chinatowns here are not only home to Chinese, but also to Vietnamese and Laotians. Restaurants in Chinatown (particularly at Porte de Choisy) often have Vietnamese and Chinese food together, and occasionally a Chinese person will order in Chinese to a Vietnamese waiter.

In fact, unless you are from Des Moines, where most Laotians in America have landed, or New Orleans, home to many of America's Vietnamese, you are likely not too familiar with Southeast Asian culture or cuisine, both of which have strong representation in Paris as a link to France's colonial past. One of the hidden treasures of Paris is the Vietnamese food—a beef-and-noodle soup specialty called *phö* is particularly popular—which is abundant in the Choisy Chinatown. In any kind of Asian restaurant in Paris, all the waiters will be able to speak French, and in some of the larger restaurants, they will likely be able to speak some English as well.

Though it is not in any of the aforementioned Chinatowns, the best Chinese restaurant that we have found—and this goes for all the Chinese we know in Paris—is a restaurant called, simply, Restaurant Chinois de Sichuan. Specializing in the spicy food of that region, it is always crowded with many Chinese people hungering for a taste of home. The restaurant is located near the Métro Strausbourg-St-Denis at 16 Boulevard de Strausbourg. You can call them at 01-40-18-56-37.

Something else of note is that while most of Paris rests on Sundays, making running errands a challenge, Chinatown bustles all weekend long (they get their rest Mondays, when the whole neighborhood seems to be asleep). The grocery stores in the Chinatowns, particularly the Tang Frères (a family with alleged underworld ties and a firm grip on the politics of the thirteenth *arrondissement* supermarket in Choisy), is particularly busy on Sunday, and while they stock ingredients for mostly Asian cuisine, Western staples (milk, butter, etc) are also readily available. There are several branches in Paris, including 48 avenue D'Ivry and 170–172 avenue de Choisy; open 9:00 A.M. to 7:00 P.M. Monday through Friday, 8:30 A.M. to 7:30 P.M. Saturday; 01-45-70-80-00.

A small bookstore, featuring mostly language-learning textbooks, can be found in the Belleville Chinatown, but the best Chinese language bookstore—full of Chinese language reading material from history to economics to popular literature, as well as French translations of Chinese literature or books on *qigong* or *fengshui*—is in the Choisy Chinatown, across the street from the middle school (collège), at 66 rue Baudricourt. Other common sights in any of the three and a half Chinatowns in Paris are real estate agencies *(agences d'immeubles)*, catering mostly to the Chinese-speaking population, and travel agencies, specializing in Asia but also able to book tickets anywhere. Chinese people pride themselves in being thrifty, so you can count on finding good deals on international calling cards in Chinatown as well.

For a basic rundown of the different Chinese communities in Paris, please refer to the list below:

+ Porte de Choisy: The largest of Paris's Chinatowns, as well as what most people tend to think of when they hear "Chinatown" in Paris—the neighborhood was shown briefly in the recent French comedy *Tanguy*—this area is accessible by bus (take either the PC1 or PC2) or by métro on Line 7. Both Chinese and Vietnamese live here, which results in restaurants of both styles, as well as restaurants specializing in both cultures' foods (for Vietnamese food, try the beef-noodle soup called *phō*, as well as the Vietnamese spring rolls with mint). Don't expect the cooking to be more authentic than in Chinese restaurants in North America; those familiar with authentic Chinese food will probably find the proportions small, the sauces a bit rich, and the spices dulled. Nonetheless, meals in all Chinatowns are known to be reasonably priced. This neighborhood is also full of clothing shops with both Chinese and Western styles, a bookstore with books in French translation, and many real estate and travel agencies. Some of Paris's tallest apartment buildings—with none too impressive architecture—can be found in this neighborhood. A Chinese Catholic church, as well as a

Franco-Chinese Friendship Association, can be found here. The McDonald's displays a menu in Chinese.

+ Belleville: Originally home to a large Arab population, many Wenzhou Chinese have been moving into Belleville in recent years, which is on the 10 and 2 métro Lines. Relatively small compared to the Choisy Chinatown, this strip nonetheless is home to great values: Jewelry shops sell merchandise at very low prices, and the fruit and vegetable markets are cheap, as well. A walk up the block leads to the Middle-Eastern neighborhood, but on the way one will pass the *Grand Restaurant Chinois de Belleville*, a banquet hall where Chinese newlyweds in Paris often celebrate their marriage. The Catholic church here has services in Mandarin, but the McDonald's does not have a menu in Chinese.

+ Crimée: Located on the northern end of métro Line 7, this small Chinese population has some of the standard fare for Chinese communities. Restaurants with Chinese cooking somewhat more authentic than in the above two Chinatowns can also be found, in addition to the standard clothing shops and travel agencies. Special to this neighborhood, however, is the weekly market, where a week's worth of fruits and vegetables can be bought for 15 euros. For another 15 euros, you're likely to have picked up a week's worth of meat.

+ Arts et Métiers: This is the so-called half Chinatown, which is almost an alleyway of quite fine Chinese restaurants lacking many of Chinatown's other trappings. Perhaps the best restaurant here is *Restaurant Chez Shen*, but all of these restaurants can be considered good quality food that Chinese people themselves will eat in, not only work in.

A word on Chinese culture in Paris: As in most American cities, Chinese culture at least on a surface level is enjoying a high vogue. Chinese men and women sit outside the Centre Pompidou and other tourist-heavy locations promising to write *"Votre prénom en Chinois"*—Your name in Chinese (most Chinese people find this calligraphy substandard, at best), and semi-meaningless Chinese characters pepper both Parisian clothing and skin. If you are planning on getting a Chinese character tattoo while in Paris, please note that the characters are written poorly or, worse, incorrectly more often than not; you ought to confer with someone who knows the language before getting tattooed. (Despite a rather intricate history involving tattoos, permanent inking of the skin is virtually nonexistent in China today, where tattoos are associated with criminals. Historically, Chinese criminals were tattooed with their crimes, so that even when let out of prison they would be known by their past transgressions, quite literally marked by their past.)

Housing Options

Below are some introductory comments from a resident real estate specialist on renting or buying property in Paris followed by a Q & A on housing.

Any way you look at it, spending time in Paris can be expensive, and the most costly item of all is lodging. Whether you are staying for only a few months or plan to settle for several years, it makes sense to take a few moments to map out a strategy.

For short-term stays there really is no problem. With more than 1,000 hotels, the Paris area can cover any short-term need, and in any style or price range. But the longer the stay, the more advanced planning is needed. Although there are many private dormitories and literally thousands of studio apartments, any foreign student will be competing with the normal French population of students who come to the capital for their university years. They have a jump on the situation, as an older sibling, other family members, or friends could have already opened the trail to that perfect flat. Be prepared to deal in French. It is also not rare to shell out a whole semester's rent at once, or at least to put up an equivalent amount in bank reserves to reassure your landlord that you won't get too homesick around Christmastime or Easter break. If you have been accepted to a school in Paris and receive a student visa, you should check out the housing office of your school early and often.

The next level of accommodation seeker is often that visitor or student awestruck by the beauty of Paris or nostalgic for a period of life once passed here. This person has the memory of a crisp, warm baguette lodged somewhere in the brain, with a whispering refrain of "*revient-me-voir*" that cannot be dislocated. It might be for a summer fling, it might be for a sabbatical, it might be for a midlife crisis or early retirement, but this person is determined to find a *pied-à-terre* or the mother of all Paris apartments to finally "live the Parisian life." Oh sure, there are business people transferred here too, often sulking at the "unfair" housing allowance equivalent and the miserable digs they have to move into compared to what they are leaving.

But whether you come on your own (enthralled) or come kicking and screaming, don't rush into buying real estate! If you are not staying for more than three years, my advice is to rent here in Paris and back at home (if you're a home owner). Keeping your house at home will give you a feeling of roots and belonging and make it easier to resettle if and when you go back. In most places, it's money in the bank, so to speak.

Why three years? With inflation in France almost nonexistent (between 1 percent and 1.5 percent) and with your closing costs averaging 6 to 8 percent of the purchase price, you need to keep the property at least four years in order to absorb the costs when you sell . . . if the market remains stable or rises over the period. If you will spend only two or three weeks a year here, you can finance your vacations with the closing cost money you didn't waste on buying! Then again, if you're in love (with Paris or a Parisian), you probably are not in an analytical mood. Just don't say you weren't warned.

Before leaping into the Paris real estate market, you should know that it is relatively volatile (like on the two coasts of the United States), so sometimes you win and sometimes you lose. The current Paris trend is toward a seller's market with firm or rising prices, less negotiating (if any), and fewer properties remaining on the market for any length of time (except for those proverbial overpriced dogs that nobody wants). This is not always the case elsewhere in France, where the rise and fall of the market is determined more by local or regional demand. In Paris the demand is international, and so are the prices.

Q: How can I get an idea of what to budget for renting or buying?

A: The ballpark price/square-meter formula is 14 euros—16 euros per month, before charges and local taxes *(droit au bail)*. You need to count on putting at least three months up front—first and last month, and at least one month's security. For buying the all-Paris average price per square meter is nearing 2500 euros and can go to 4500 euros or more for the very top-drawer, top-*quartier* type place.

Q: Please explain the value by square meter measure used in France.

A: It's basically the same idea as buying cheese or cabbages by the kilogram. It's an easy way to compare prices—especially for apartments—regardless of the upgrades, age, or improvements. Of course, my goat's cheese is made only from pure, mountain goat's milk, from goats fed on handpicked laurel leaves, and the cheese aged by three Franciscian monks who pray over it for at least ninety days before it goes to market. So, of course it is more expensive. You get the idea. The square meter price is a scientific way to strike a benchmark price, from which you may begin discussions.

Q: What are the main steps when buying an apartment in Paris?

A: Look and compare. Decide. Make an offer—*a promesse de vente* or *compromis*. The latter commits the seller, who promises to sell at a certain date and price, more than it does the buyer. If you are financing, you should have a contingency clause allowing time to secure financing. Apply for and procure financing. Then, you will need time for the *notaire(s)* to research title, get proof of financing, get settlement letters from existing banks, search liens, etc., and draw up the actual conveyance. Finally, close—usually in ninety days, but the closing can drag out to six months.

Q: Do I need a lawyer or can the real estate agent handle the transaction?

A: Real estate agents can handle everything but the closing. They know the local market values, can better negotiate, and can help get financing. But as in the United States, unless otherwise noted, the agent represents the seller. Each party will use a notary (buyer can use the seller's) to draw up the actual contract and handle all the legal aspects of the transaction.

Q: What are the costs? Any hidden ones?

A: Count on 6 to 8 percent of the sales price. This includes all transfer taxes, title search (the title insurance is covered by the notary's professional "Errors and Omissions" Insurance), other local and departmental taxes, and the notary's professional fees. There would also be loan application fees and some first-month interest from date of closing to the first monthly payment. Although not really a *hidden* cost, you need to be aware that in France property is sold *without* what we would consider as fixtures—lights, kitchen equipment, cabinets, even towel holders, mirrors, etc., in the bathrooms. You get bare walls with wires hanging out. Even the curtain rods and supports are considered personal property and are not sold with the apartment unless otherwise specified. All this adds up to a lot of extra cost.

Q: Is the culture of real estate shopping different in France than in the United States?

A: Not too much. If you are using an agent, it is really pretty similar, although the idea of quality service isn't at the same level. I've heard of agents not presenting an offer because it was after 7:00 P.M. and the agency was closing for a long holiday weekend.

Q: Any tips on how to get money to France?

A: A wire transfer, called Interbank Swift, is the best and cheapest way. But you need to have an account established here first.

Q: Any tips on how to judge good value in the Paris area?

A: The same as anywhere—location, location, location.

Q: Is there any printed information that people can easily access? Do big companies like Century 21 France have Web sites?

A: There are a number of sites, although you have to be careful about sorting out all that you read. There are relocation companies too that offer services. There is a well-known bookstore called Tissot that sells all the legal forms necessary for buying, selling, and renting property, starting businesses, paying taxes, and hiring people in France. Tissot, 19 rue Lagrange, 75005 Paris; Métro: Maubert-Mutualité; Tel.: 01–44–41–71–11, Fax: 01–44–41–71–00. They even have a mail-order service.

Q: Is it hard to get a mortgage in France?

A: It can be for outsiders. Proof of source of revenues (and the acceptance of same) is needed for the bank. Some banks have turned toward the mortgage market more than others—the Banque Transatlantique, for example.

Q: Aside from the economics, will foreign buyers be sorry if they purchase property in Paris?

A: Yes. But then, some of us don't like Paris . . . for daily living. So the disappointment will not be due to the purchase itself. I think there are better places to buy in France, but this is wholly personal.

Q: What taxes face apartment owners and renters?

A: There are two basic taxes that we could compare to U.S. property tax: the *taxe d'habitation*, which is paid by the person who has the right to live in the place on January 1 of each year, and the *taxe foncière*, which is paid by the owner of the place. If you are a renter, you will pay the habitation tax; if you own, you pay both, assuming that you live there. The *taxe d'habitation* extends to parking places and garage stalls too. These taxes are nearly equal in amount and come due near the end of the year.

Q: What steps should I take to find a rental apartment? Do I need an agent? Who pays the agent? And what are the fees?

A: An agent isn't totally necessary but can be very helpful in filling out leases, doing the inspections, transferring keys, explaining how things work, gaining a new friend in the *quartier*, giving tips on schools, transportation, shopping, restaurants, talking the old tenants into leaving (or selling you) the drapes or other fixtures . . . you get the idea. The agent's fee is in the range of one month's rent to 10 percent of the annual rent, and it is usually split fifty-fifty between lessor and lessee.

Q: Anything I should know about agents in Paris?

A: Not all agencies do rentals. And those that do often don't have a lot to propose. In the Paris area look for agencies that say *syndic, locations, administration de biens, gérance,* or *gestion.* Around the Alps and Lyon, they are called *regies.* These are property managers, and they would naturally have more to offer. Also scout several at a time and often. Things can change quickly and you aren't always at the "top of the agent's mind." So you have to remind him that you're still waiting.

Q: What are the most common complaints from Americans who want to buy or who have bought in Paris?

A: Agents don't stay in touch. I left my name and number and they never called back.

✦ Agents don't speak English and they act as if they don't care.

- It's so expensive for what you get.
- It takes so long to close.
- The sellers stripped the place of everything.

Going it Alone

If you're looking for housing on your own, local newspapers with classified announcements are key places, both for placing your ads and responding to others. Placing an ad may be more effective than simply replying to others. If you do, emphasize your Anglo-American side and any professional credentials you have, like professor of philosophy at Johns Hopkins University seeks . . . or graduate in art history is looking for . . . or former banker from San Francisco is interested in locating. . . . Landlords can be wary of foreigners but tend to like North Americans.

The following list of publications should be helpful. Read the classifieds daily and make your calls and property visits as early in the day as possible.

- *International Herald Tribune*
  6 bis rue Graviers, 92521 Neuilly-sur-Seine Cedex; Tel.: 01–41–43–93–00. Good source of high-end apartments. Be quick, and be prepared to have serious references.
- *Le Figaro*
  66 avenue Marceau, 75008 Paris; Tel.: 01–56–52–20–00. Good selection of rentals. You must be prepared to speak French when answering these ads.
- *France-Soir*
  45 avenue de Victor Hugo, 93300 Aubervilliers; Tel.: 01–53–56–86–00. Good selection of rentals. You must be prepared to speak French when answering these ads.
- *Paris Voice*
  7 rue Papillon, 75009 Paris; Tel.: 01–47-70-45-05. Community newspaper with a healthy selection of inexpensive classified ads.
- *France-USA Contacts (FUSAC)*
  26 rue Bénard, 75014 Paris; Tel.: 01–56–53–54–54. Well-read community advertising supplement. Apartments go fast because all the competition is watching these pages, too.
- *De Particulier à Particulier*
  40 rue Docteur Roux, 75015 Paris; Tel.: 01–40–56–33–33. Professional real estate agents are not allowed to advertise or respond to these ads. A very good source, especially if you're looking to buy.
- *La Centrale des Particuliers*
  17 avenue Villiers, 75017 Paris; Tel.: 08-26-88-10-00. Specializes in sales of automobiles but includes some housing.

Relocation Companies

Relocation companies provide services ranging from housing, auto registration, and immigration formalities to school enrollment, home decorating, and crosscultural training. When expatriates are sent by companies or organizations to work in France, often one of these relocation companies is contracted by the employer. If this is not done for you, you may find it helpful to contact one yourself. Inquire about services and prices in advance and make sure you receive a written agreement. The U.S. Embassy has prepared, as a service, a list of leading relocation services that have indicated a desire to work with English-speaking clients. It assumes no responsibility for the professional ability or integrity of the firms listed. We have included the most reputable establishments about which we have had the most favorable feedback.

- ✤ Cosmopolitan Services Unlimited, 64 boulevard Malesherbes, 75008 Paris; Tel.: 01–44–90–10–00, Fax: 01–44–90–10–10. Director: Joy Chezand
- ✤ Executive Relocations, 6 rue Copernic, 75116 Paris; Tel.: 01–47–55–60–29, Fax: 01–47–55–60–86
- ✤ Paris Welcome Service, 12 rue Helder, 75009 Paris; Tel.: 01–45–23–08–14
- ✤ Move-In, 4 rue de Gévaudan, Bat. D, Petite Montagne Sud, 91017 EVRY. Tel.: 01–69–11–82–75, Fax: 01 69 11 82 73.
- ✤ Crown Worldwide, Tel.: 01-45-73-66-00, paris@crownrelo.com

Street Signs and Addresses

Addresses in Paris may seem strange at first, but you'll learn the nuances rapidly. You can live on a *rue*, an *avenue*, a *boulevard*, an *impasse*, a *cour*, an *allée*, a *passage*, a *parc*, or a *chemin*. The street number may be a regular whole number like 34 or 7 or 178, but it may also have an extra bit, *bis*, or *ter*, which means that the house is attached or adjacent to the property that takes the whole number. Other aspects of the address: *bâtiment* (building name or number), *escalier* (stairway), *étage* (floor), *code* (door code), *à droite* (to the right), or *à gauche* (to the left). When visiting someone, always get as much of this information as possible. A Frenchman might tell you his address like this: *J'habite au 35, boulevard du Montparnasse, escalier C au fond de la cour, quatrième étage à gauche* (I live at 35, Boulevard de Montparnasse, stairway C, at the back of the courtyard, fourth floor, on the left). *Cedex* at the end of an address means mail for the address is kept at the post office. Most buildings have either a door code, which is activated at night, or a buzzer system outside the building, called an *interphone*. There will always be a button to activate the door, usually marked *porte*, and, on the inside, a lit button to turn on the timer for the lights in the stairwell. When going to someone's house, always ask if there is a door code, since many buildings now have them on all day and night and many people forget to inform their guests beforehand.

The availability of housing has lessened as the economy, which was softer in the early and mid-1990s, has improved. Prices rose steadily in the 1980s, then leveled out in the mid-1990s, and now have turned upward again. There are more buyers these days than sellers, but you should never feel pressured into taking an apartment you're not sure of or that seems too costly. You must see Paris apartments to begin understanding the local standards, the aesthetics, and the range of prices. Undoubtedly you'll have to reposition your expectations according to the local environment. What you'll lose in space, you'll gain in charm. You might have to sacrifice closets, but you'll get a rooftop view of central Paris. You may have to walk up four floors, but the seventeenth-century stairwell will distract you from your aching muscles.

Commercial space—sometimes even located inside appartment buildings—has become more readily available, with more than a million available square meters being empty in Paris. You can sometimes negotiate rents, commissions, fees, and perks, but generally the Parisians are not great negotiators and will often keep an apartment empty for a year rather than rent it at a lower rate. This is partly because it's difficult to get rid of a tenant. Owners always have the right to reclaim their apartments at the end of a lease (most apartments have a standard three-year lease) if it is for their own use or for a family member or if they want to sell it, but otherwise the tenant has the right to renew.

Whether you have a full lease or not, insist on a *quittance de loyer* (rent receipt) every month or quarter. This is your proof of payment and address.

Finding an Apartment

Probably the most frustrating aspect of living in Paris is the hassle of searching for a place to live. The options are numerous, from finding other people to live with to cloistering yourself in your own small room. The competition can be tough; those who rise early and call first have the best chance. The competition is at its worst during September and October, when the Parisians come back from a month of vacation and students need to find accommodations.

The simplest and cheapest way to find accommodations is to look for individuals who have apartments or rooms to rent. In some cases avoiding the agencies will save you a lot of paperwork, not to mention high commission fees. To recognize ads not placed by agencies, look for the words *propriétaire loue* (placed by the owner).

Those who yearn for the security of going by the book can make an appointment at the city hall of their district to receive free legal advice. This service, called AILAP, can be used to verify a contract or lease and the legitimacy of any other fees a landlord or landlady may mention after a lease has been signed. You can also rent the services of a *hussier de justice* (notary) from a real estate agency for about 30 euros an hour before you move into your new apartment. He will ensure that everything is done to the letter in only a couple of hours.

Here is a sample housing ad followed by a translated explanation: **17e ROME. 4p. cuis. bns. ref.nf. 960 44435111** (17th *arrondissement* near Métro Rome, 4 rooms, kitchen, bathroom, newly remodeled. 960 euros a month. Call 01–44–43–51–11).

Column Headings in the Newspaper

Immobilier	Real Estate
Achats et Ventes	Wanted/Offered for Sale
Location Offres/Demandes	Offered/Wanted to Rent
Meublé	Furnished
Vide	Unfurnished

Helpful Terms

agences s'abst.	no agencies
asc. (ascenseur)	elevator

bns. (bains)	bathrooms
bal. (balcon)	balcony
box	parking space
calme	quiet street, building
carac. (caractère)	with character (sometimes a euphemism for "needs work")
caution	security deposit
ch. (charges)	supplementary monthly fee in addition to rent for concierge, common-area upkeep, etc.
chb. (chambre)	bedroom
chambre de bonne	maid's room (now small, rentable rooms or studios)
chambre indépendante	independent room
charm.	charming (sometimes a euphemism for "needs work")
chauf. cent.	central heating
com.	agent's commission
cft. (confort)	"comfort"—i.e., private bath, carpeted rooms, equipped kitchen, etc.
coq. (coquette)	cute
cour	courtyard
cuis.	kitchen
cuisine eq. (equipée)	kitchen equipped with major appliances (not standard)
dche. (douche)	shower
et. el. (étage élevé)	upper floor
except.	exceptional
garçonnière	bachelor's apartment; small studio or room
grenier	attic, room under roof
imm.	building
imm. mod.	modern building
imm. nf.	new building
imm. p de t (pierre de taille)	cut-stone building
imm. rec.	new building
imm. anc.	old building
interméd.	agent
jar./jdn.	garden (yard)
kit.	kitchenette, not separate
living	living room
loue, je loue	I am offering for rent (i.e., no agency)
lux.	luxurious
loyer	the rent
m2 (mètre carré)	square meter (about 10 square feet)

moq. (moquette)	wall-to-wall carpeting
part à part (particulier à particulier)	private party to private party; no agency
p. (pièce)	rooms, not including bathroom
pierre de taille	cut-stone building (nicer than cement)
poss. (possibilité)	possibility of
pr. cpl.	couple preferred
poutres apparentes	beamed ceilings
rangements(s)	closet(s)
rav. (ravissant)	exquisite
ref. nf. (refait neuf)	newly remodeled
r. (rue)	street
slle. (salle)	large or formal room
salle de réception	large living room
salle à manger	formal dining room
salle d'eau	bathroom
salle de bains	bathroom with shower or tub (toilet in separate room)
ss. (sans)	without
stdg. (standing)	status or high-class building, fashionable address
gd. stdg., tr. gd. stdg.	deluxe studio, one-room apartment, usually with bath and kitchenette
s/ (sur)	on
tél	telephone
terr.	terrace
tcc (toutes charges comprises)	all charges included (see "charges")
w.c.	toilet, in room separate from bath and sink; water closet

There are also many bulletin boards scattered around Paris. Try the following for finding short- and long-term housing:

The American Church in Paris, 65 Quai d'Orsay, 75007 Paris, Métro: Alma-Marceau or Invalides. Open Monday through Saturday 10:30 A.M. to 10:00 P.M., Sunday, 10:00 A.M. to 7:30 P.M. Tel.: 01–45–56–09–50.

FUSAC (France-USA Contacts) Bulletin Board (Centre d'annonces et bureau), 26 rue Bénard, 75014 Paris; Métro: Pernety. Open Monday through Saturday 10:00 A.M. to 7:00 P.M., Saturday noon to 5:00 P.M.; Tel.: 01–56–53–54–54.

The American Cathedral, 23 avenue Georges V, 75008 Paris; Métro: Georges V, Alma-Marceau; Tel.: 01–53–23–84–00.

Shakespeare and Company, 37 rue de la Bûcherie, 75005 Paris; Métro: St-Michel. Open noon to midnight seven days a week.

Centre d'Information et de Documentation Jeunesse, 101 quai Branly, 75007 Paris; Métro: Alma-Marceau.

Many *laveries* (laundromats), *boulangeries* (bakeries), large grocery stores (Prisunic Leader-Price, Shopi, Monoprix, etc.), and gyms also have bulletin boards.

Short- and Long-term Housing Services

RayRoth
10 rue Nicolas Flamel
75004 Paris
Tel.: 01–48–87–13–37
Fax: 01–42–78–17–72 or 01–40–26–34–33
E-mail: lampard@worldnet.fr
A fine selection of very comfortable and tasteful furnished apartments in the Les Halles–Châtelet area. The two owners of the company, Ray and Roth, have an impeccable reputation for service. Highly recommended.

Rentals in Paris
Tel./Fax: (516) 977–3318
abby@rentals-paris.com
Upscale furnished apartments in the heart of Paris available for short-term rentals. Owner Glenn Cooper also manages apartments, so if you own a Paris property and need a property manager, contact him. Excellent service and very reliable.

De Circourt Associates
11 rue Royale
75008 Paris
Tel.: 01–43–12–98–00
Fax: 01–43–12–98–08
E-mail: circourt@easynet.fr
Selection of more than 10,000 short- and long-term executive rentals ranging from 1000 euros to 10000 euros a month. Claire De Circourt specializes in high quality service to English-speakers.

Locaflat
63 avenue de la Motte-Picquet
75015 Paris
Tel.: 01–43–06–78–79
Quality short-term rentals.

Apalachee Bay Residential Property
21 rue de Madrid
75008 Paris
Tel.: 01–42–94–13–13
Fax: 01–42–94–83–01
E-mail: info@apalachee.com
Web site: www.apalachee.com
Extensive range of selected furnished apartments.

France Appartements
97–99 avenue des Champs-Elysées
75008 Paris
Tel.: 01–56–89–31–00

Fax: 01–56–89–31–01
Web site: www.france-apartment.com
Selected furnished flats in the heart of Paris.

Capitale Partners
11 rue La Boétie
75008 Paris
Tel.: 01–42–68–35–60
Fax: 01–42–68–35–61
e-mail: capitalepartn@europost.org
Web site: www.capitalepartners.fr
Handpicked properties from studios to five-bedroom apartments.

Paris Appartements Services
69 rue d'Argout
75002 Paris
Tel.: 01–40–28–01–28
Fax: 01–40–28–92–01
Web site: www.Paris-appartements-services.fr
Short-term studio and one-bedroom rentals.

Other Apartment Rental Services

(Furnished and Unfurnished)
+ Apartment Living in Paris; Tel.: 01–45–67–27–90
+ My Flat in Paris; Tel.: 01–45–96–01–04
+ At Home in Paris; Tel.: 01–42–12–40–40, Fax: 01–42–12–40–48
+ A. B. M. Rent a Flat; Tel.: 01–45–67–04–04, Fax: 01–45–67–90–15
+ Servissimo; Tel.: 01–43–29–03–23, Fax: 01–43–28–53–43
+ Century 21 France. Check their website for their 700 offices in France.
  www.century21france.fr.

Warning

Some French real estate agents provide this warning to newcomers: "In France, real estate agencies are regulated by the law of January 2, 1970, which obliges them to possess a professional card marked *Transactions* and/or *Gestion* (administration), issued by the *prefecture*, a financial guarantee, and insurance covering their responsibility toward clients. A number of companies have no legal status to process furnished rentals. In order to prevent legal and financial risks, deal only with authorized real estate agencies. You can recognize them by their professional identity number, their financial guarantor, and their insurer, all of which must be indicated on their contracts and letterhead."

Types of Housing Contracts

+ Short-term furnished contracts can be for one year or less and are renewable at the option of the landlord.

+ Long-term unfurnished contracts are for three years and are hard for landlords to break without just cause. Both can be broken by the renter with one to three months' notice, depending on the contract.

Short-Term Apartment Rentals

If you are planning to stay in Paris for only several weeks or months, or you are on a preliminary trip to organize a more extended stay, you'll probably not want to stay in a hotel. One of your best options is the short-term apartment rentals that are available, especially when reserved well in advance. A leader in this type of housing is British advertising executive and housing aficionado Ray Lampard, whose small but top-rate collection of elegant apartments (called RayRoth) in central Paris are said to be the best in town.

"If you've stayed in your own apartment in Paris, you'll have a hard time going back to a hotel," Lampard says. The West Coast newsletter *Paris Notes* featured short-term apartment rentals and weighed the pros and cons of this living option. According to them: If you are staying less than a week, go to a hotel. For two weeks, a month, or longer, keep reading. If your main motivation is to save money, proceed carefully—savings depends on the number of people in your party and whether or not you cook at home. If you never cook, think again. On the other hand, if you're a family of four or five, two or more couples, or a small group of friends, the prospect of sharing a large seventeenth-century apartment with beamed ceilings and a view of Notre-Dame can be very tempting and ultimately more comfortable and economical than taking hotel rooms. If you fear that the scale and aesthetics of old Paris buildings, kitchens, bathrooms, etc., may be too alienating or too much of a hassle—or you've decided not to wash a single dish in Paris—you might prefer to consider this option for another trip. But then again, what better way to test whether you're cut out for Parisian life than by trying to live like a Parisian.

RayRoth's twenty or so centrally located apartments appear to be extremely well selected and impeccably maintained, chosen for both businesspeople and discriminating travelers. RayRoth focuses only on the "heart of Paris"—the Marais and the Châtelet–Les Halles area—from which you can walk to almost everything. With limited inventory, a highly loyal following, and a seven-day minimum, RayRoth's only downside is that the apartments fill up quickly. They require only a 25 percent refundable deposit and payment can be made by personal check in your own currency. Reserve as far in advance as possible.

U.S. Apartment Rental Services for Paris

Paris Notes named *Chez Vous* "Best American-based Paris Specialists" and commended *Paris Séjour Réservation* (PSR) for its supply of large apartments.

Chez Vous
1001 Bridgeway, Suite 245
Sausalito, CA 94965
Tel.: (415) 331–2535, Fax: (415) 331–5296

PSR
645 North Michigan Avenue, Suite 638
Chicago, IL 60611
Tel.: (312) 587–7707, Fax: (312) 587–9887
(Allows you to see what a Paris apartment looks like.)
Web site: www.qconline.com/parispsr/index.html

Property Management Companies
✤ France Homestyle; Tel.: (206) 325–0132; Fax: (206) 328–3673
✤ Paris Connection; Tel.: (954) 475–0615

On-line Housing Service (Housing in France)

The Paris-Anglophone Web site www.paris-anglo.com has initiated a housing listings database service, offering apartment rentals, purchases, and exchanges.

Housing Insurance

French law requires that anyone occupying space in France (an apartment, a maid's
room, a studio, or a room in someone else's home) be covered by property insurance. The landlord will assume that you have proof of this coverage. Renters are
responsible for any fire or water damage originating from their apartment—not just
for their premises, but for the entire building. This is so well known that your landlord may not ask for it, but you are legally liable so you must not overlook this.
More likely you will be asked to provide a photocopy of your policy each year to
the owner or agent.

A minimum legal liability policy covers damage by a renter to the owner's property. To be covered for your own property, you need a multirisk policy that covers
water damage, fire or explosion, and theft. In all claims cases, contact your insurance agent immediately by phone and by registered letter. In the case of theft you
will have to prove what was stolen. Receipts, inventories, guarantees, and photos
are very helpful.

Make sure you pay for your insurance on time, because it's hard to collect for
losses when a policy hasn't been paid. A *constat à l'amiable* is a form you fill out with
a neighbor if your apartment has damaged theirs. A copy is sent both to your insurance agent and to theirs. (Advantage Insurance has pre-prepared forms in English
for its prospective clients.)

For particularly wealthy homeowners, Chubb Insurance offers a personal asset
protection policy called Masterpiece, which is adapted for art collectors, antiques
buffs, etc., with replacement-value reimbursement, a rare feature in French insurance practices. In general, premiums are lower in France than in the United States,
but the services and reimbursements are also more limited.

Furnished/Unfurnished Apartments

When looking through rent ads, note whether the apartment is furnished *(meublé)*
or unfurnished. If you are staying for only a short time, a furnished place will be
much more suited to your needs, even though the rent may be higher. If you plan

to stay for a while, however, consider taking an unfurnished place, since you can most likely obtain a standard three-year lease *(un bail de trois ans)* and will want to get set up with your own stuff. The advantages of having a three-year lease include a set limitation on annual increases, the right to sublet for one year, and the right to break your contract if you give your landlord three months' notice by registered letter *(lettre recommandée avec accusé de réception).* On the other hand, you have the right to six months' notice from the landlord before having to move out, and the reasons for asking you to leave are limited by law.

When you do find an apartment, the *propriétaire* (landlord) will want a *caution* (security deposit) as well as some proof that you are financially able to pay the rent. A letter in French from a parent or sponsor stating financial support will normally suffice, but as the economy worsens, agencies are taking no risks and might insist on proof of income as much as four times the monthly rent, as well as a solid employment record. One executive employed at Disneyland Paris from the day it opened was denied an apartment by a major realty office in Vincennes because he'd been with the same employer for less than two years. Some of these agents can be quite unpleasant, even obnoxious. Don't lose your cool if you really want the apartment. Remember: Everything in France depends on the ability to *séduire* (charm). Yes, they'll make you feel like they're doing you a favor by taking your money. It'll baffle you why you, the customer, must be apologetic. Asking to see the supervisor is a sure way to lose the battle. Eat humble pie or move on.

If you do get the apartment, you will probably be asked to sign a lease. Under French law, minors (under eighteen) cannot sign contracts, so if you are under this age the landlord or his agent may insist that your parents or some responsible adult sign for you. If you sign a lease, ask for an *état des lieux* or an *inventaire détaillé* (detailed inventory) of the apartment's condition and its contents, and make two copies. This way the landlord can't hold you responsible for damage done to the apartment before you moved in. In any case, you should keep in mind that some landlords and almost no agencies will accept a guarantee of financial support from outside of France, since tracking down the tenants or their guarantors to pay for damages would be impossible.

The French Apartment

The aesthetics and functionality of Parisian apartments will undoubtedly differ from what you're used to. Sometimes these differences are absolutely enchanting; other times they are infuriating. Here's a quick tour of the Paris living space.

L'entrée (entryway)

Often the best apartments are in the most unlikely places, so don't be influenced by the building's streetside appearance; the grungiest looking building with a seedy stairwell may have a beautiful garden in the courtyard and an entirely different look behind the front door. On the other hand, a well-kept entranceway with bourgeois details, polished brass, etc., indicates immediately that the building is of "high standing," a term the French have borrowed. New laws permit old buildings to be gutted as long as the street facade remains unchanged. You'll come to see that the entranceway and stairwells of Paris buildings possess an aesthetic quality that is particularly Parisian—the worn, wooden steps, the old tile, the snaking banisters. What might at first feel old and seedy will grow on you, if you let it.

La cour

Most French urban structures are built in a square, around a courtyard. The Paris everyone can see is but a portion of what is there: Behind the average front door may be a formal garden complete with fountain and a stone-paved walkway leading to a private residence hidden behind the walls of the *bâtiment* (building) or parking lot. It may also be just a playground for the children of the *concierge* or a passageway to the back section of the building. Often it'll host a series of ateliers.

La concierge

The *concierge* in Paris, now very often a Portuguese or Spanish wife-and-husband team crammed into a tiny apartment in the entranceway of the better Parisian apartments, plays a unique role in daily French life. The *concierge* is the on-site representative of the organization or group of owners (*syndic*) in an apartment building. The *concierge* knows all, hears all, tells all, and is an essential person to get along with. Their principal tasks include shining the brass in the entranceway, distributing the mail in the building, cleaning the stairwells, doing minor repairs, carting out the garbage cans, receiving packages, etc. When you move in, and at Christmas, it is a good idea to tip your *concierge* as much as you can afford (20 euros is normal) and according to the amount of extra work you make for them. *Concierges* are very valuable allies and very powerful enemies. If problems arise over such things as noise after 10:00 P.M., your concierge can often prevent or instigate much unpleasantness.

Almost all buildings, even commercial and public ones, have live-in *concierges* or *gardiens*, who keep an eye on things. A 1948 law imposing rent controls limited the rapid improvement of buildings and thus helped maintain the institution, but with the increased installation of security systems, intercoms, and modern elevators, *concierges* are becoming redundant. More than 2,000 positions are eliminated each year in Paris.

Les toilettes (WC)

WC (pronounced as French VC) stands for water closet, and that's what it is, a closet-size space with a toilet. The WC (also called *le water*, pronounced as if the word were French) is often separate from the bathroom. Although this may seem odd at first, it's rather practical. The WC is colloquially referred to as *les chiottes* (the crapper). Don't use the word too lightly or in formal company. Other classic bathroom functions are performed in the *salle de bains*.

La salle de bains (bathroom)

You may be perplexed on your first trip to a French bathroom to find a little fixture called a *bidet*. Historically designed to serve aristocratic women as a hygienic aid, today the *bidet* can be used for lots of things, from relieving the pain of hemorrhoids, to hand-washing delicate clothing, bathing a baby, or soaking your feet.

Fresh water enters the fixture either through a vertical spray in the center of the bowl, through a flushing rim, or through a pivotal spout that delivers a horizontal stream. A drain stopper allows the *bidet* to be filled with water. New bathrooms often do not have these.

When it comes to a shower, expect anything. Although on the rise, showers are not as common in daily French life as baths. Consider yourself lucky if you end up with a large enough space in which to stand and lather up, let alone with a shower curtain. This seemingly essential bathroom fixture is not seen as essential by the French. Invariably a shower is taken via a metal hose running from the bathtub *(baignoire)* spout, and dexterity is a must to prevent splashing, especially since you will probably not have a place to hang the nozzle on the wall. Consider washing your hair with one hand as character building. In the older buildings you'll have to get used to tiny tubs, sitting tubs *(sabots)*, and other microscopic means of washing. It's all great fun. But remember to be careful. You are responsible for water damage to any and all floors below that stems from your apartment (see the Housing Insurance section earlier in this chapter). The bathroom sink is a *lavabo* (but a kitchen sink is an *évier*).

La Cuisine

Parisian kitchens tend to be an exercise in space utilization. They often have tiny but efficient appliances, especially refrigerators *(le frigo)* and gas stoves. Unfurnished apartments almost never come with appliances, and often don't even have kitchen cabinets. Get used to the *chaudière,* the hearth of the French home: the gas apparatus that heats on command the water for the kitchen and bathroom. Parisian kitchens are very often where you house your washing machine or dryer, if you have one. In recent years, most French households have caught on to dishwashers (although small) and microwave ovens. The king of French appliance stores is Darty, noted for its exceptional *service après vente* (after-sales service).

Renting a Room with a French Family

If you don't wish to, or can't afford to, rent an apartment, you can rent a room with a French family or, more often, an individual landlord. This housing arrangement usually consists of a private room with limited access to the kitchen, telephone, and bathroom facilities. Each situation offers varying degrees of privacy. Some landlords have more than one room to rent in their apartments, making it possible for two students to live together. Others have large rooms that can be shared by two people. There are varying degrees of comfort (private or shared bathroom, television, personal phone) and the price fluctuates accordingly. Landladies and couples are usually interested in some cultural or linguistic exchange, which can help the student ease into daily French life. This type of arrangement can often be made through university housing offices.

Chambre de bonne

The most inexpensive form of accommodations is usually a *chambre de bonne* or *chambre de service,* a converted maid's room on the top floor of middle- and upper-class apartment buildings. It often has a separate service entrance (a sixth- or seventh-floor walk-up). It is usually a small, mansard-ceilinged room with a sink and a hot plate. Shared shower and bathroom facilities are usually available in the hallway. Some landlords offer the use of the shower in their apartment. This doesn't sound too glamorous, but it can have its charm for a while. With simple accommodations you can focus more time and money on Paris itself. The view from a *chambre de bonne* can be memorable.

A new decree as of the end of January 2002 states that a *chambre de bonne* can be rented only if the area is at least 9 square meters, the ceiling is a minimum of 2.2 meters high, and the apartment has running water in the room. All *chambres de bonne* or *pièces mansardées* (attic apartments) not fitting these qualifications must be taken off the market or renovated per the decree.

Au Pair

Another alternative to finding an apartment is to look for an *au pair* position. *Au pair* arrangements are available primarily but not exclusively for female students. Duties usually include baby-sitting, housework, English lessons, mother's helper chores, picking up children at school, or any combination thereof in exchange for room and board and a small salary. It often entails some evening or weekend work. Students must generally have some knowledge of French and be willing to work a regular schedule. Agencies that arrange *au pair* positions require that students be at least eighteen years old and under thirty, have a valid student visa, and be enrolled in classes (usually French language courses). They ensure that students are given pocket money (not salary) of about 250 euros a month plus room and board in exchange for up to thirty hours a week of work. For full-time students with a heavy workload, it is wise to find *au pair* work for not more than ten to twenty hours a week. Be aware that *au pairs* are often treated as paid help rather than members of the family. The quality of this experience depends wholly on the household that you work in. Some experiences can be wonderful, especially when the host family is not only friendly, open, and instructive, but also has a country house in Normandy or Burgundy or asks you to accompany them on vacation to the Alps or Riviera.

During the school year a minimum stay of three months is required. The regular program stay is normally one year, but it can be extended to a maximum of eighteen months. A student may stay with more than one family during the *au pair* period, but the total stay cannot exceed eighteen months.

There are also summer *au pair* programs of one to three months. In these cases the requirement that the *au pair* take French courses is waived if the student has completed at least one year of college-level French studies.

Most families provide their *au pair* with a *carte orange*—a monthly pass valid for the métro, buses, and suburban trains—but they are not required to do so by the Ministry of Labor regulations.

The family must declare the *au pair* as *stagiaire aide familiale* to the French Social Security Administration and make the monthly contribution so the *au pair* will receive social security benefits in case of illness or accidents.

After arrival in France with a visa, the classic *au pair* must apply within eight days for a residence permit.

Along with a work contract, the classic *au pair* must present evidence of registration in a French language school (Alliance Française, the Sorbonne, etc.). Evening classes are not acceptable.

Having obtained an *au pair* position, the *au pair* returns to the *Service de la Main d'Oeuvre Etrangère* to receive a temporary work permit, which is normally valid for six months and is renewable.

The following agencies arrange *au pair* positions.

Accueil Familial des Jeunes Etrangers, 23 rue du Cherche-Midi, 75006 Paris, Métro: Sèvres-Babylone; Tel.: 01–42–22–50–34. Open Monday through Friday 10:00 A.M. to 4:00 P.M. and Saturday 10:00 A.M. to noon.

Inter Séjour, 179 rue de Courcelles, 75017 Paris; Tel.: 01–47–63–06–81. Open Monday through Friday 9:30 A.M. to 5:00 P.M.

Here are a few more places to try when looking for housing and/or au pair positions.

Alliance Française, 101 boulevard Raspail, 75006 Paris; Métro: Rennes, St-Placide; Tel.: 01–42–84–90–00. Open Monday through Friday 9:00 A.M. to 6:00 P.M. (For their students only.)

Institut Catholique, 21 rue d'Assas, 75006 Paris; Métro: Rennes; Tel.: 01–45–48–31–70. Open Monday through Friday 9:30 A.M. to 5:30 P.M. (closed noon to 2:30 P.M.), Saturday 9:30 to 11:30 A.M. Open year-round except Saturdays in July and August.

Foyer le Pont, 86 rue de Gergovie, 75014 Paris; Métro: Pernety; Tel.: 01–45–42–51–21. Open Monday through Thursday 10:00 A.M. to 6:45 P.M., closed noon to 2:00 P.M. and Friday 9:00 A.M. to noon. (Six-month students only. Financed by the German Government, the Foyer is open to others as well.)

Cité Universitaire

This lovely campus complex has rooms available at very reasonable rates in thirty different *maisons* (houses) for university students (under age thirty) studying in Paris. Architecture buffs might want to investigate the two houses designed by Le Corbusier: the Swiss Foundation and the Franco-Brazilian Foundation. Make sure to call or write far in advance of your arrival date if you are considering this option. Rooms go fast, and many can be booked only for a yearlong period. A single room goes for 14 euros per day, and 185 euros per month; monthly double room rates are 230 euros, depending on the *maison*. This could also be a good alternative to a hotel while you are looking for other accommodations—rooms are available to anyone with an international student identity card at 12 to 15 euros per night during the summer and in September before the beginning of the school year. Accommodations are usually provided in the maison of the country from which the student originates; some houses prefer graduate students only. A list of all the houses is available from the central office at the following address:

Cité Universitaire
19 boulevard Jourdan
75014 Paris
Tel.: 01–45–89–68–50

Or try contacting one of the following directly:

Fondation des Etats-Unis
Cité Universitaire
15 boulevard Jourdan
75690 Paris Cedex 14
Tel.: 01–53–80–68–80 (administration)
Tel.: 01–53–80–68–88 (students)

Maison des Etudiants du Canada
31 boulevard Jourdan
75014 Paris
Tel.: 01–40–78–67–00

Doing Laundry in Paris

Laundromats—those great American hangouts and Maytag meccas, those linty and egalitarian public spaces that would have thrilled de Tocqueville—are neither very numerous nor very complete in Paris, although there are signs of improvement. More and more laundromats are being created, but the laundromat concept has been slow to catch on. Parisians are unaccustomed to going out and doing laundry after hours, standing around with strangers while separating colors from whites, and folding underwear in public. It just isn't French.

Nonetheless, there are laundromats. But you have to seek them out and check out their hours and facilities. Bring a long novel—Parisian machines plow through lots of cycles; washers take an hour-plus and dryers eat up numerous 0,50 euros. The washing machines are calibrated by weight; the five- or six-kilo machines are the standard. The mega ten- or fifteen-kilo machines are for blankets, slipcovers, drapes, etc. They take either 1-euro coins or tokens (*jetons*), which are bought in machines for anywhere from 3 to 5 euros. Bring pockets of assorted change.

The common and traditional solution to dirty laundry in Paris is the local *blan-chisserie*, or laundry, which is usually combined with a *nettoyage à sec* (sometimes called *pressing*), or dry cleaners. These are relatively convenient but wildly expensive compared to North American and British standards. Rarely will you find a same-day or even next-day service (one chain, *5 à sec*, tries to accommodate). The white button-down shirt you were used to having cleaned and pressed in a day for a buck and a half will set you back either 3 euros if they send it out to some three- or four-day industrial service or 4 euros if they do it on the spot. If you opt for the industrial solution, be prepared to sacrifice a button here or there, or sometimes find that an unmatching button has been sewn on for you with unmatching thread.

When you pick your clothes up, you might be surprised at the way the garments are wrapped and folded in either plastic or brown paper. The laundry retains the wire hangers. Fortunately, your clothes will be newly creased when you open them at home. The contrarian *5 à sec* will give you hangers, actually charging more for folded and wrapped laundry.

Many Parisians have small washers in their apartments, usually in the kitchen or bathroom, because no space for bulky utilities had been anticipated in the master scheme of things Parisian. Dryers are rarer, and masses of Parisians are used to draping wet clothes over chairs, on clotheslines over the tub, and across radiators.

As for cleaning supplies, the French are addicted to their *eau de javel* (bleach), which they dilute and use to wash, disinfect, and bleach. Woolite is commonly found but pronounced *Wooleet*. To clean surfaces and especially floors, the French love their *serpillière*, an absorbent cleaning rag often wrapped around the head of a broom or mop.

Nestor Services, a dry-cleaning establishment that caters to the expatriate community, offers a pick-up and drop-off service at your home or office until 10:00 P.M. and advertises a rate of 2,30 euros per shirt for ten shirts. Tel.: 08–01–63–06–00.

Cleaning Lexicon

a stain	*une tache*
a sweater/pullover shirt	*un pull or pull-over*
an iron	*un fer à repasser*
button-down shirt	*une chemise*
cotton	*le coton*
hem	*un ourlet*
ironing board	*une planche à repasser*
jeans	*un jean*
laundry/dry cleaner	*une blanchisserie/ un pressing*
sewing shop	*une mercerie*
dye shop	*une teinturerie*
pants	*un pantalon*
socks	*une paire de chaussettes*
starch	*l'amidon*
to iron	*repasser*
to knit	*tricoter*
to sew	*coudre*
wool	*la laine*
zipper	*une fermeture éclair*

Hostels in Paris

Young travelers, students, and low-budget visitors may opt to stay in one of Paris's hostels *(auberge de jeunesse)*. This is another way of experiencing Paris, totally worth it if you have to do Paris on the cheap. MIJE *(Maisons Internationales de la Jeunesse et des Etudiants)* hostels are all centrally located and filled with historic atmosphere. Here is where to find hostels.

MIJE Fourcy
6 rue Fourcy
75004 Paris
Tel.: 01–42–74–23–45
Fax: 01–40–27–81–64
(Seventeenth-century aristocratic mansion)
Métro: Saint-Paul-Le Marais

Open: 7:00 A.M. to 1:00 A.M.
Dorm rooms: 20 euros (eighteen to thirty years old only)
Single rooms: 32 euros; doubles: 49 euros; triples: 22 euros per person.

BVJ (*Bureau des Voyages de la Jeunesse*) **Louvre**
20 rue Jean-Jacques Rousseau
75001 Paris
Tel.: 01–53–00–90–90
Fax: 01–53–00–90–91
Métro: Les Halles
Dorm rooms: 19 euros

BVJ Quartier Latin
44 rue des Bernardins
75005 Paris
Tel.: 01–43–29–34–80
Fax: 01–53–00–90–91
Métro: Maubert-Mutualité
Dorm rooms: 19 euros

Fédération Unie des Auberges de la Jeunesse
4 boulevard Jules Ferry
75011 Paris
Tel.: 01–43–57–43–28
Web site: www.fuaj.fr
Métro: La Chapelle

Ligue Française des Auberges de la Jeunesse
67 rue Vergniaud
75013 Paris.
Tel.: 01–44–16–78–78
Métro: Sèvres-Babylone

Comité National des Unions Chrétiennes de Jeunes Gens (YMCA)
Résidence Sienne
5 Place de Vénétie
75013 Paris
Tel.: 01–45–83–62–63
Métro: Porte de Choisy

Three Ducks Hostel
6 Place Etienne-Pernet
75015 Paris
Tel.: 01–48–42–77–77
Métro: Félix Faure
Open: 7:00 A.M. to 2:00 A.M. (Closed 11:00 A.M. to 5:00 P.M.)
Dorm rooms: 13,50–16,50 euros; double rooms: 16,50–19,50 euros

Young & Happy Hostel
80 rue Mouffetard
75005 Paris
Tel.: 01–47-07-47–07
Métro: Place Monge
Open: 8:00 A.M. to 11:00 A.M. and 5:00 P.M. to 2:00 A.M.
Dorm rooms: 16,50 euros, double rooms: 39 euros

Moving In

When you have found your apartment and are ready to move in, keep in mind that the electricity and gas will probably have been turned off. Contact your local EDF-GDF office *(Electricité de France/Gaz de France)* to reactivate the service. Bring proof of address—your rental agreement, for example. And make sure to take the meter readings as you move in to avoid being charged for the previous tenant's bills. You might need these to avoid paying for renters before or after you as well as proof in the case of dispute over the cost of electric and gas.

To obtain a telephone, call *renseignements téléphoniques* (information—dial 12) to find out at which France-Telecom office in your arrondissement you must make your request. The surest bet to have the service and number activated is to go in person. If you can bring the former tenant or at least his or her last bill with you, you might facilitate matters. Activation usually happens in one or two days. You may rent one of many snazzy models of phones or you may purchase your own. You will be offered a Minitel instead of a telephone directory. Take it; it's essential. If there is already a phone line, the landlord may insist that you list the number under your name, which is a smart move, since you would not want to pay for the previous tenant's calls, making your first bill an unpleasant surprise. If the phone is under the landlord's name (or a previous tenant's), your access to international or regional calls may be blocked. If you are sharing the apartment with others, it is best to restrict the phone to local calls. You can request a special service that gives you an access code from any phone. You dial 3610 and your code, followed by the number and the day. The call will appear on your bill.

It's best to reserve long-distance calls for your *télécarte* (see the Telecommunications and Media chapter), so you can gauge how much you are spending. It is more costly to telephone from France than from North America or Asia, although France Telecom rates have come way down and the call-back companies are offering services that are dirt cheap.

If you want an itemized bill of all calls *(une facture détaillée)* you must request this from the start. It's free. The bill (as well as all other utility bills) comes every two months, and you have two weeks to pay. Late bills are subject to a 10 percent penalty. And it's virtually impossible to contest items on the bill. Unlike in the United States, it's almost impossible to be credited for billing errors. Neither do you get credit for wrong numbers.

Before leaving, ask for a *relevé spécial* (special reading) of the electricity, gas, and telephone from the local EDF-GDF and Télécom agency listed on your bills. At the EDF-GDF center, your charges can be computed immediately from the meter readings, though the telephone company takes about one or two days. Don't forget to return your phone and Minitel, or you will be billed for them.

When You're Moving Home

Here's a simple schedule of events compiled by a Paris firm that moves thousands of expats.

Three months in advance
+ Get necessary passports, visas, work permits, international driver's licenses, etc.
+ Assemble necessary duty-free paperwork for your in-France purchases (unless moving within the EU).
+ Involve your children in the move through books, pamphlets, videocassettes, CD-ROMs, etc., about your destination as well as about moving in general.
+ Consider donating, or selling, the furniture and belongings you won't be taking with you.

Two months in advance
+ Inform/transfer/cancel, as appropriate: relatives and friends; electricity/gas, water, heating fuel, post office, phone line(s), fax lines(s), cellular phone(s), Internet connection(s), Minitel, Canal+/cable TV; income tax, *taxe d'habitation*, TV tax, bank(s), French social security, health care insurance; home/apartment lease, apartment owners' committee, concierge, home security service, subscriptions, memberships, school(s), etc.

One month in advance
+ Speak with your physician(s) about ongoing treatment instructions as well as medication renewals.
+ Do a value-per-item inventory of your belongings.
+ Ask your moving company about customs restrictions per your destination country on items such as wine and spirits, books, videocassettes, produce and plants, vehicles, arms, ivory, etc.
+ Check the electric voltage used at your destination and get appropriate adapters and transformers.
+ Get rugs, quilts, blankets cleaned.
+ Sort and tag per means of transport (land, sea, air) items to be moved.
+ Return borrowed items.

Moving day
+ Keep with you at all times your important personal move-related items such as your (and your children's) passports, visas, airline tickets, etc.
+ Do a final check in every corner of the house or apartment, including basement, garage, carport, attic, garden, etc., to make sure that all is in order and nothing will be left behind.
+ Relax, have a cup of coffee or tea, and let your mover take care of the rest!

Students Moving to Paris

Students coming for a semester or year most certainly will carry their possessions with them. This gets a bit complicated when the airlines limit you to either two bags or forty-four pounds. Carry your clothes and personal belongings, toiletries, medication, important papers, and your laptop. You may wish to ship your books and other heavy and nonfragile possessions via the mail, a shipping company, or as excess baggage. You can mail books to yourself in postal mail bags for under a dollar a pound, but this takes about three to four weeks, so allow sufficient time. If you declare a high value on the books, you risk being hit with a customs tax on the total.

The cost of books in Paris is high and the cost of shipping books by regular mail from overseas is prohibitive. Some students in France have made side trips to London to buy books, and recently some have discovered that book purchases on www.amazon.com via its U.K. service represents a great savings on postage.

Clothes in Paris are expensive too, so bring with you winter jackets and plenty of sweaters. For cheap clothes, you should get to know the good spots at the Paris flea markets. The Porte de Montreuil *Marché au puces* is particularly good for secondhand dress shirts, pants, and ties.

Picking a Moving or Shipping Company

All major moving companies work with correspondents in France. Call for estimates in your home city. You may also decide to request estimates directly from the French side and let them contact their agents closest to you. The U.S. Embassy in Paris provides a list of shipping companies that pick up and forward parcels and luggage to and from France. The moving industry is very competitive, and there are a lot of choices out there. Compare services and prices. For an annotated list, consult www.paris-anglo.com; here are a few of the most popular and reliable choices.

Grospiron International, Z.I. de Coudray, 30/32 avenue Albert Einstein, 93150 Blanc Mesnil; Tel.: 01–48–14–42–42, Fax: 01–48–14–42–40; info@grospiron.com.; www.grospiron.com.

Allied/Arthur Pierre, Z.I. du Petit Parc, 13 rue Fontenelles, 78920 Ecquevilly; Tel.: 01–34–75–92–92, Fax: 01–34–75–00–98.

Transeuro Desbordes, 42 route Principale du Port, 92 637 Gennevilliers Cedex; Tel.: 01–47–92–45–45; Fax: 01–47–92–50–50; www.desbordesinternational.com, www.transeuro.com.

Storage Facilities

Self-storage services and facilities in Paris have improved in the past few years.

Access Self-Storage, the leader in the field, has seven locations in the Paris area. Their spaces range from 2.25 to 80 square meters and are accessible from 7:00 A.M. to 8:00 P.M. Monday through Friday and from 9:00 A.M. to 1:00 P.M. on Saturdays. Rentals are made on a monthly basis. Large garages with twenty-four-hour access are available. Packing materials are sold on the premises, and moving vans and small trucks are rented at preferential prices to Access customers. Call their hotline at 01–53–01–90–00 for locations and details.

Another possibility is Les Docks du BHV, 56 quai Auguste Deshaies, 94200 Ivry Sur Seine; Tel.: 01–49–60–44–15; Fax: 01–46–70–75–04.

Shipping Excess Baggage

Homeship
62 rue St-Lazare
75009 Paris
Tel.: 01–48–65–21–61

Excess International
Tel.: 01–48–62–73–05
Fax: 01–48–62–73–01

Export Legalities

The following documents are required for the shipment of personal effects and furniture by someone moving from France. (Effects qualify as used household and personal effects when they have been owned and used for six months or more and are intended for personal use in the new place of residence.)

✦ Inventory declaration *(Inventaire-Declaration):* Three copies on plain paper (plus copies preferably in English for U.S. Customs). This inventory is a list of all personal effects and furniture, including automobiles, which comprises all household effects being exported. It must also include a sworn statement declaring that the articles listed on the inventory have been owned and used by the exporter for more than six months. (U.S. Customs requests that this inventory be as complete as possible, indicating the value and a description of all articles.)

✦ Change of residence certification *(Certificat de changement de domicile).* This can be obtained upon presentation of the laissez-passer from the income tax office below and one copy of the inventory declaration. North Americans living in Paris obtain this document from the Prefecture of Police, Services des Etrangers, 1 rue de Lutèce, 75004 Paris or from the local police prefecture, or town hall, for those living in the suburbs or in the provinces.

✦ Pass from the income tax office *(Laissez-passer des Contributions Directes).* This is obtained from the office of the Contributions Directes of the place of residence in France. This pass, in effect, should state that no outstanding tax payment is due in France. There are two types of passes:
1. *Certificat de Non-Imposition,* Form No. P234 (or a statement from the tax inspector) for a nontaxpayer, which states that the said party owes nothing in taxes.
2. *Bordereau de Situation,* Form No. P237 for a taxpayer, which states that there is no outstanding tax to be paid in France.

✦ For someone who has been employed in France, it is recommended that he or she obtain a letter from the employer stating that the employed person is leaving France after so many months or years of residence.

Restrictions

For the exportation of collectors' items or items that date back more than 100 years, there are long and expensive formalities to follow, including a *permis d'exportation* (export permit), which can be obtained from the Banque de France or the French Customs office.

In order to export a substantial quantity of alcoholic beverages, a permit is required from the tax office.

A certificate of origin is needed to export Champagnes and Cognacs.

Keys should be attached to all trunks and/or pieces of furniture and labeled should customs inspections need to be made.

Automobiles: If exporting a car, it should be listed on the inventory declaration for U.S. Customs, stating the year of manufacture, the original cost, the make and model, and whether it meets U.S. specifications.

Import Legalities

The documents listed below are required for the duty-free shipment of personal effects and furniture by someone moving to France. (Effects and furniture are considered as personal when they have been owned and used for six months or more [one year for an automobile] and are intended for personal use in the new place of residence.) French regulations require that the effects be shipped within a period of one year from the declared date on the stamped change of residence certification.

+ Change of residence certification *(Certificat de changement de domicile).* This can be obtained at the French consular post nearest the place of departure. This certification, which states the date of the change of residence, must be stamped at the French consular post.

+ Detailed inventory *(Inventaire Detaillé):* A list of all personal effects and furniture, including automobiles, which comprises all household effects being imported; to be dated and signed by the importer. This inventory should be as complete as possible, indicating the value in dollars and giving a description of all valuable properties, such as antiques, collection items, and cars. The inventory must also include a sworn statement declaring that the articles listed on the inventory have been owned and used by the importer (a) for at least six months for all personal effects, and furniture, and (b) for at least one year for automobiles, and that there are no outstanding U.S. taxes owed on the vehicle. This inventory should be in French.

Warning: The change of residence certification and the detailed inventory must be stamped at a French consular post. Failure to have this done results in considerable complications for the traveler once he has reached his destination in France.

Duty-Free Imports

The following household effects can be brought into France without paying duty: cats and dogs; stamp collections, provided they are for personal and not commercial use; tradesmen's hand tools; bicycles; sewing machines; personal computers;

automobiles; one television; and one radio. All televisions used in France are subject to a TV tax called the *redevance*. American-made televisions, however, must be drastically adapted to work in France, and the cost of this procedure is often higher than the cost of a new set.

The following are not considered duty-free: motors imported separately from vehicles or appliances; speed boats; pleasure craft (except canoes and kayaks); school, store, and office furniture; wine, alcoholic beverages, and spirits; trucks and utility vehicles; and raw materials.

There are also customs restrictions on the importation of various guns, ammunitions, and certain printed matter. Check with the nearest French consulate in the United States to obtain information about the specific restrictions on the importation of these objects.

Extra Note on Purchasing Property and Real Estate in France

+ Century 21 France lists its 700 offices in France at www.century21france.fr
+ International Living specializes in real estate for expatriates and retirees. Request their newletter at www.internationalliving.com.
+ www.paris-anglo.com offers a comprehensive real estate listings database for purchases and rentals.

Hotels

Paris has over one thousand hotels. Good resources/reservations include: www.france.com and www.citadine.com (residential hotels).

Health and Insurance

The French Health System

Although France has a highly impressive and widely democratic system of social-ized medicine, this might not undo the feelings of loneliness and despair if you fall sick in a foreign country where you are not sure where to turn for sympathy or help. This feeling is compounded, of course, if you are unsure about your language skills, so services in English have been included here. If you feel like braving the language barrier, you will find that almost any pharmacist is eager and willing to give you advice and maybe even recommend of a doctor around the corner. Pharmacists are even trained to know about the mushrooms you find in the woods and will offer free advice on the delicious and deadly. They play an essential intermediary role between doctor and patient. And pharmacies are not cluttered with all the non-medical goods found in North American and many British drugstores.

Prescription medication once came with two-part stickers (*vignettes*) on the packaging. One part was peeled off and stuck on the orange and white *feuille de soins* used for reimbursement from the *Sécurité Sociale*, the national health admin-istration reserved for salaried employees. Other sectors of professional activity have their own *caisse* (administration) handling the same coverage (see the Working in France chapter). Prescribed drugs have been traditionally reimbursed at 75 percent. This has changed somewhat with lower reimbursements on numerous medica-tions. The state is running out of cash. This stickering system was a bit cumber-some, old-fashioned, and costly, but it worked. It has now been replaced with a computerized system along with the introduction of a national Social Security card called the *Carte Vitale*, which has an imbedded computer chip that identifies each citizen and organizes medical reimbursements for doctors' visits, hospitalization, medication, and other healthcare services.

Don't be surprised, however, when you realize that treatment varies from what you are accustomed to. You may find yourself using methods you had never even conceived of at home. The French are keen on the use of suppositories, for example, for many different problems, including a cough. A lot of misunderstanding about French medical practices results from differences in aesthetics and style. French doctors' *cabinets* (offices) are surprisingly unclinical in feel, and doctors, particularly specialists, appear more like professors than physicians. Doctors' offices in France are not teeming with paramedical practitioners nor do they maintain extensive medical records. Children's medical records are maintained in a *carnet de santé* (health book) that accompanies the child throughout his life, beginning at birth. Prescriptions are given for tests at local laboratories. You must go for the tests and then pick up the results yourself. You pay for them and are subsequently reimbursed by the *Sécurité Sociale* if you pay contributions into the system. Very little lab work is done in doctors' offices, and the white-coat sterility associated with North American and Scandinavian medical facilities is virtually absent. You do not get the feeling of being dynamically treated; however, there is no denying that French medical procedures are wisely oriented toward prevention rather than intervention. Because the *Sécurité Sociale* reimburses most of the cost of visiting the doctor of their choice, people don't wait until they're seriously ill to see a doctor.

Don't be overly judgmental if the waiting room is drab, there is no air-conditioning, and the doctor examines you in an alcove of his study. Don't expect a nurse to be present during an OB-GYN exam either. A normal consultation should run from 20 euros to 23 euros. Many doctors don't require appointments and simply receive walk-ins during fixed hours. Specialists start at 30 euros per appointment (*consultation*) and may run up to 80 euros.

Hospitals

The American Hospital of Paris *(Hôpital Américain de Paris)* is a famous private hospital that employs British, American, Japanese, and French doctors on its staff and is partially bilingual. F. Scott Fitzgerald, among others, spent time here in the hospital's prerenovation days drying out. It is more expensive than the French hospitals but offers excellent healthcare with a style that you may recognize and appreciate. You can pay with dollars and major credit cards. Those covered by Blue Cross or Blue Shield have their hospitalization covered, provided they fill out the appropriate paperwork first. The hospital also offers its own hospitalization insurance, called the "Welcome Service."

The American Hospital of Paris
63 boulevard Victor Hugo
92202 Neuilly sur Seine Cedex
Tel.: 01–46–41–25–25
Fax: 01–46–24–49–38
82 bus (terminus)

Another hospital that employs English-speaking doctors and is noted for serving the anglophone community is:

Hertford British Hospital
3 rue Barbès

92300 Levallois Perret
Tel.: 01–46–39–22–22

Medical Practitioners

Practitioners in France are either *conventionné* (abiding by the social security system's schedule of fees) or *non conventionné* (charging higher rates). WICE (Women's Institute for Continuing Education) publishes a detailed booklet on healthcare in Paris, the best source on the subject. The American University of Paris's medical brochure recommends certain English-speaking doctors, but it's always wise to inquire of friends and colleagues.

The American Embassy also publishes a list of reputable doctors and medical specialists working in English in the Paris area, but it is simply a list of who is here and what they do and should not be taken as a recommendation. The www.paris-anglo.com Web site also provides a list.

Therapy/Counseling and Other Psychiatric Help

The American therapist Jill Bordais maintains a private practice in Paris and specializes in issues related to crosscultural relationships. Her monthly column in *Paris Voice* addresses many of the most commonly experienced problems. She also runs sessions for couples called Pairs. Check the directory in www.paris-anglo.com for full addresses.

Jill Bordais, Tel.: 01–43–54–79–25; E-mail: JABourdais@compuserve.com
Emmanuel Ansart, M.D., Tel.: 01–48–78–04–60
Barbara Cox, Tel.: 01–45–75–74–61
Elizabeth Leafy Feld, Tel.: 01–42–62–04–66
H.R.S. Nagpal, Tel.: 01–47–07–55–28
Sandra Pedevilla, Tel.: 01–45–07–29–75
Nancy Sadowsky, Tel.: 01–42–33–10–07
Joseph Shesko, Tel.: 01–43–47–19–72

Free AIDS-Testing Clinics

Centre de Dépistage Anonyme et Gratuit, Institut Alfred Fourier,
25 boulevard St-Jacques, 75014 Paris; Tel.: 01–40–78–26–56

Centre Medical de Belleville
5 allée Gabrielle d'Estées, 75020 Paris; Tel.: 01–42–01–54–00

Hôpital La Pitié Salpétrière
47 boulevard de l'Hôpital; 75013 Paris. Tel.: 01–42–16–10–53

Reproductive Health

A prescription is necessary for most contraceptive devices and drugs. There is no age limit. Male contraceptive condoms (*préservatifs*—not to be confused with the English "preservatives") and female contraceptive sponges *(ovules)* are available without prescription. Family-planning centers provide information on contraception. Le Planning Familial has centers at 10 rue Vivienne, 75002 Paris, Métro: Bourse (Tel.: 01–42–60–93–20), and at 94 boulevard Massena, 75013 Paris, Métro: Porte de Choisy (Tel.: 01–45–84– 28–25). Do-it-yourself pregnancy tests are available in pharmacies at a cost of about 20 euros. Ask for G-Test, Elle-Test, Predictor, or Clear Blue. When positive, these tests can be believed absolutely. When negative, they should be repeated five to seven days later. Abortions are legal in France. You may have heard of the male birth control pill. Like the Loch Ness Monster, one doctor commented, this pill shows its head in the press from time to time. It's still in the testing stages and is nowhere near the point of being put on the market.

Free, anonymous courses of treatment for venereal diseases are offered by the Institut Arthur Vernes, 36 rue d'Assas, 75006 Paris, Métro: Saint-Placide (Tel.: 01–45–44–87–64), open 8:00 A.M. to 3:00 P.M. Monday through Friday and 8:30 A.M. to noon Saturday; and by the Institut Alfred Fournier, 25 boulevard Saint-Jacques, 75014 Paris, Métro: Saint-Jacques (Tel.: 01–40–78–26–56).

Other Health-Related Services

For a more complete listing and updates, consult the directory in www.paris-anglo.com.

AIDS Support Group
American Church, 65 Quai d'Orsay, 75007 Paris; Tel.: 01–45–50–26–49

Alcoholics Anonymous
American Church, 65 Quai d'Orsay, 75007 Paris; Tel.: 01–46–34–59–65

Alcoholics Anonymous
American Cathedral, 23 avenue George V, 75008 Paris; Tel.: 01–47–20–17–92, (Saturdays at the American Hospital: 01–46–41–25–25)

American Women's Group (AWG)
32 rue Général Bertrand, 75007 Paris; Tel.: 01–42–73–28–72

British and Commonwealth Women's Association
8 rue Belloy, 75116 Paris; Tel.: 01–47–20–50–91

WICE (Women's Institute for Continuing Education)
20 boulevard Montparnasse, 75015 Paris; Tel.: 01–45–66–75–50
Offers courses (in English) in Career and Personal Development, Arts and Humanities, Living in France, Women's Support Group.

For more information regarding English-speaking medical personnel, a good resource is *Health Care Resources in Paris,* a comprehensive guide in English. Contact WICE at 01–45–66–75–50 to order a copy.

Pregnancy and Child Birth in Paris

As a foreigner, being pregnant in Paris and preparing for your *accouchement* (giving birth) can be both exciting and a bit scary. On the one hand, you should be very pleased that, attitudinally, Parisians are very open and accepting about such natural phenomena as pregnancy and giving birth. The *accouchement* is not seen as a medical or surgical intervention; nonetheless, most Parisian women give birth in hospital maternity *(maternité)* wards or private clinics, and a large percentage opt for the epidural *(péridurale)* procedure of painless but sensitized birthing. The *péridurale* procedure was devised by a Parisian doctor at La Pitié Hospital, the largest teaching hospital in France, located between the Gare d'Austerlitz and the Place d'Italie. Hospital aesthetics in Paris may not meet the visual expectations of visitors used to more clinically antiseptic environs. Because of state subsidies, less attention is given to the public relations and image of hospitals in France than in the United States. There are few frills in Paris hospitals—you usually have to bring your own soap and towels—and it is primarily for reasons of comfort and not medicine that many women have their babies in private clinics. Also, in clinics the postpartum stay can be up to ten days, whereas hospitals keep new mothers for four or five days, which in itself is substantially longer than in the United States.

The French usually have three or four sonograms *(echographies)* during a normal pregnancy, more than is usually prescribed in the United States and the United Kingdom. In France, of course, the state health coverage plan covers the cost completely.

Many women and their partners attend birthing classes run by midwives *(sages femmes)*, who are also reimbursed in part by the state. Almost all babies are delivered by midwives, except in the case of complications or cesareans. One absolutely wonderful place for birthing classes with highly trained and culturally sensitive midwives is the *Centre de préparation à la naissance* on the rue de la Roquette in the eleventh arrondissement.

Maternity leave is legally sixteen weeks, which many working women combine with their five weeks of paid vacation in order to stay home longer. Employers are used to this and do not stigmatize women employees who must go on maternity leaves. Their jobs are secure and they are paid fully during the leave. Some companies offer extended maternity leave to new mothers for a reduced pay.

Pharmacies

To match a prescription from home, be sure to have the following information, since finding the equivalent may be difficult: an up-to-date prescription with the medication's trade name, manufacturer, chemical name, and dosage. If you don't speak French, you may have an easier time if you go to an English or American pharmacy, since they are used to having to match prescriptions. The pharmacists, aside from speaking English, tend to be very helpful. For many prescription drugs you will be asked to give your address, which is noted in a register. This is normal.

Anglo-American Pharmacy (Swan)
6 rue de Castiglione
75001 Paris
Tel.: 01–42–60–72–96

Anglo-American Pharmacy (Cypel Evelyne)
37 avenue Marceau
75016 Paris
Tel.: 01–47–20–57–37

British and American Pharmacy
1 rue Auber
75009 Paris
Tel.: 01–47–42–49–40

British Pharmacy
62 avenue des Champs-Elysées
75008 Paris
Tel.: 01–43–59–22–52

Pharmacie des Champs (twenty-four-hour pharmacy)
84 avenue des Champs-Elysées (passage des Champs)
75008 Paris
Tel.: 01–45–62–02–41

Nights, Sundays, and holidays you can call the local *commissariat de police* for the address of the nearest open pharmacy and that of a doctor on duty. You can also check the door of a closed pharmacy for the address of the nearest open one.

If you cannot find a prescribed medication at a local pharmacy or you've been told that there is a *rupture de stock* (out of stock), try calling or visiting the *Pharmacie Centrale des Hôpitaux,* 7 rue Fer à Moulin, 75005 Paris; Tel.: 01–43–36–92–97, poste 299, Métro Gobelins, from 9:30 A.M. to 5:30 P.M. This is the central supplier for Paris hospitals.

Natural Medicine *(Médécine Douce)*

The French are great believers in traditional medicines. *Homéopathie* (homeopathic medicine) uses only herbs and other natural products in very carefully compounded mixtures whose composition is fixed by law. In many cafés, *infusions* (herbal teas) are served, largely for complaints such as nervousness, fatigue, weakness, etc. A few of the calming herbal teas available in most cafés are tilleul, camomille, menthe, and verveine. There are also a number of *fortifiants* (tonics, mild stimulants) available in pharmacies, as well as preparations for just about any common ailment. Pharmacies specializing in homeopathic medicine will be clearly marked and can be found throughout the city.

Health Insurance/*Assurance*

You'll need to find out the local ins and outs of insurance concerning your home or apartment, your car, and health coverage. These are complicated but essential elements of daily life. Even if your French is perfectly up to snuff, be prepared for alienation and confusion and perhaps exaggerated rates. For this reason, it's advisable to seek out an English-speaking agent. French insurance agents are not in the habit of fielding a lot of questions by phone or responding to a lot of questions in general, and gaining satisfaction with insurance claims can be a difficult and frustrating task. Like everything else administrative and legal in France, everyone begins with *méfiance* (distrust). The assumption is that everyone lies and cheats and thus it is the responsibility of the individual to prove his or her virtue and just cause. This attitude has a clear impact on the insurance industry, where you must prove with flawless documents that you really owned that Pentax camera that you claim was stolen or that the fireplace in your flat had been cleaned by a chimneysweep within a year before the fire that damaged the apartment on the floor above yours. As one insurance broker in Paris who had lived and worked in the United States says, "I prefer to work with Americans because in general they're more honest than the French. I'll commit myself to a car insurance policy on the phone because in almost all cases Americans will send in the check they promised."

In France insurance policies are renewed automatically each year. You can cancel them only with a written letter sent two months before the annual renewal date. Otherwise you'll be responsible to pay the next year's premium. If you are unhappy with your current broker or agent, you can replace him immediately by signing an *ordre de remplacement,* which entitles another broker to take over your policy as soon as the former one has received the letter. The commission will go to the first broker until the annual renewal date comes due, but the new agent will handle all claims in the interim.

In the early 1990s one insurance agency, Advantage Insurance, founded by Franco-American Vincent Kuhn and now run by Jacques Homo, emerged on the scene with the motto "Dedicated to Serving Americans in France." (No slight to British, Canadian, Australian, Irish, South African, etc., readers is intended.) Advantage Insurance has come to the fore in serving both the transient and long-term resident anglophone community. Advantage has demonstrated an understanding of the needs of newcomers. Its emphasis on service is not only helpful, it's unusual. Rarely in France will you feel that someone who is selling you something truly understands that by saving you money they gain your loyalty and repeated business. Advantage offers a full package of homeowner, theft, fire, water damage, and health insurance policies, and also answers questions on the phone, corresponds in English, and is willing to explain procedures and the *Conditions Générales and Particulières* of policies.

Advantage Insurance
57 rue du Faubourg Montmartre, 75009 Paris
Tel.: 01–53–20–03–33; Fax: 01–48–74–81–56
E-mail: advantage@easynet.fr
Web site: www.paris-anglo.com/advantage

For other specific insurance information, see the Auto Insurance section in the Urban Transportation and Driving chapter and the Housing Insurance Section in the Housing and Accommodations chapter.

More on Insurance

Before coming to France, you should find out whether or not you are insured overseas and in what instances. Certain firms will expect you to pay your bills in France and then reimburse you after you send them the receipt *(feuille de soins)*. It may take several weeks or more for the reimbursement to come through.

French law requires that students have complete medical coverage during their stay in France. Copies of official documents attesting to this fact are required when you request any visa from the French Consulate in your home country and by the *préfecture de police* when you apply for your *carte de séjour*. The law requires that the medical plan provide for the following coverage: hospitalization in Europe, short- and long-term outpatient treatment, visits to the doctor and dentist, laboratory expenses, pharmaceuticals, medical repatriation (transportation back to country of residence), and medical recommendation. Most national health plans in European Union countries meet these requirements. Many private plans in the United States and Canada do not. However, if you have substantial coverage by your health plan in North America (inquire for the United Kingdom and the rest of Europe) and can get a clause to include a provision for medical repatriation, you may meet the necessary coverage requirements. Several American university programs do provide a special student health insurance plan for students who require it. Students and non-students who are not covered by an employer but who legally reside in France can also take advantage of the French social security system (referred to in conversation as *la Sécu*) by paying the annual fee. Inquire at the office in your arrondissement.

Students who are covered by European National Health plans (e.g., French Social Security or British National Health), international organizations, or a particularly extensive private plan in North America may apply for an exemption. You must send a copy of your insurance policy to the administration or *bursar* of your program when paying the tuition fee to determine if your coverage meets exemption requirements. You will need official copies of your insurance policy translated into French to apply for your visa and your *carte de séjour*. In most cases exemptions must be approved prior to registration, or you may find yourself enrolled in your program's plan automatically.

The French social security medical coverage can be purchased at a rather reasonable rate if you are under age twenty-six. Above age twenty-six, however, the rates are about 1900 euros a year and cover you in France only. Additionally, the official reimbursement rates of the French social security are set at levels that still can leave you with a hefty bill. For the average doctor's visitation fee of 22 euros, you can expect a 70 percent reimbursement and 40 percent of the medication bill. This, of course, is only when you are not working and need to buy this coverage as if it were a private insurance; otherwise, the coverage is a right you have, which you pay for automatically as a percentage of your salary. When you see a specialist and pay 30 to 40 euros, you will still receive back only the 70 percent of the state-authorized fee. Citizens of EU countries covered by their own national health plans should file Form E 111 (the reciprocal health coverage agreement between European Union countries) with *Sécurité Sociale*.

Advantage Insurance offers several helpful health plans for those who don't qualify for the *Securité Sociale*, including an international package called the EEB

Medical Plan that in many cases is more advantageous than the official French coverage. This health insurance also meets the French requirements for visas and *carte de séjour* requests. It can be paid in U.S. dollars through checks drawn on American bank accounts and is available to anyone not living in his or her own country and not covered by the French health system. For Americans the *tarif confort* is recommended; it includes coverage in the United States and costs $2,350 per year if you're under age thirty and $2,750 per year if you're between thirty and forty (Over forty, inquire). For Europeans who do not travel to the United States and do not qualify for the French system, the *tarif basic* is suggested, with rates at $1,345 per year for those under age thirty and $1,645 per year for those between age thirty and forty.

Other Insurance Companies and Agents in Paris

The U.S. Embassy prepares a list of insurance companies that work in English. For a more complete list, consult www.paris-anglo.com or www.amb-usa.fr.

Medical Emergencies: Key Numbers

Police Secours: Tel.: 17.

Pompiers (Fire): Tel.: 18.

SAMU ambulances: Tel.: 15 or 01–45–67–50–50. Life-threatening situations; detailed information will be required by phone.

Burns (severe): Tel.: 01–58–41–26–49. Hôpital Cochin, 27 rue St-Jacques, 75005 Paris.

SOS Médecins: Tel.: 01–47–07–77–77. Twenty-four-hour emergency medical house calls—23 euros before 7:00 P.M., 46 euros afterward.

SOS Dentistes: Tel.: 01–43–37–51–00. Twenty-four-hour emergency dental help. Similar prices as previous listing.

Association des Urgences Médicales de Paris: Tel.: 01–53–94–94–94. Sends a doctor in an emergency.

Anti-Poison Center: Tel.: 01–40–05–48–48. Twenty-four-hour service.

SOS Pregnancy: Tel.: 01–45–84–55–91

SOS Rape: Tel.: 01–42–34–84–46

SOS Help: In English. Tel.: 01–47–23–80–80. Crisis hotline from 3:00 to 11:00 P.M.

SOS Help: In French. Tel.: 01–42–93–31–31

SOS Vétérinaire: Tel.: 01–47–55–47–00

Urban Transportation and Driving

The Métro and RER

The Paris Métro has been in existence since the turn of the twentieth century and gained its name from its first line, the Métropolitain. It plays an essential role in the life of the city and is filled with its own character, energy, and mythology. The system has fourteen lines that reach 368 stations, the newest being the Météore (Line 14), which opened in 1998 and runs between la Madeleine and the new Bibliothèque Nationale François Mitterrand in the thirteenth *arrondissement*. This rubber-wheeled and electronically driven subway is currently being expanded to link eighteen stations, including the original seven in central Paris. Some 5.5 million commuters use the system each day. You can get nearly everywhere in a relatively short period of time for a reasonable price in relative safety and security on the Paris métro. Don't be afraid of it. At times it gets a bit overcrowded, odoriferous, noisy, and confused, but on the whole the Paris subway system is among the best in the world. It'll be one of your greatest tools.

The major piece of métro news is the 2002 replacement of the classic magnetized tickets with the permanent scan-read tickets that you pass in front of a reader, like checking out groceries at the supermarket. This means no more tickets, just one that you stock with the desired value. Until the full switchover, however, the old-fashioned magnetic-strip tickets are still in use.

Whether you live in Paris or intend to commute by train from the suburbs, you should purchase a monthly pass, *une carte orange,* which allows unlimited travel within six specific price zones. This is one of Paris's greatest bargains. Avoid purchasing your card on the first day of the month because the lines can be brutal. Cards go on sale on the twentieth of each month, so think ahead. French employers often pay half of the price per month as an employee benefit. The circular zones are organized in concentric circles, with Paris-proper consisting of zones 1 and 2. The other six zones extend far into the suburbs. A single ride (a powder-blue magnetized ticket) costs 1,30 euros, a flat fee that allows you to go anywhere within the system. *Note*: Métro ticket prices increase by about 5 percent each summer. If not buying the *carte orange* or the weekly equivalent, *carte orange hebdomadaire* (13 euros), buy a *carnet* (value of ten individual trips) for 9,30 euros. This is a substantial saving over the purchase of individual tickets at 1,30 euros, but remember that a transfer between trains is free so long as you do not leave the station. The same card is also valid on Paris buses and the regional express trains (RER). The carte orange currently costs 43 euros for two zones; 56 euros for three zones, 70 euros for four zones, 85 euros for five zones, and 97 euros for six zones. This is a real bargain. The first time you purchase a card, you need a photograph of yourself, easily obtained from the instant photo booths located in many stations, and the orange card with plastic sleeve that you get at any métro station ticket window. A yearly *carte orange* ticket *(la carte intégrale)* is also available, as well as the *Carte Imagine "R"* for students. You are supposed to carry the magnetized ticket in a little slot in the sleeve and inscribe the number of the orange card onto the ticket. Failure to do either can cause you a fine upon verification by ticket checkers. The same is true for the lack of a picture. The card is strictly for the use of the person whose name and picture appear on the card. Periodically ticket checkers stake out métro stations and selected cars, usually at the beginning of the month, when some decide to rough it by not renewing their *carte orange* for the month.

One métro phenomenon you're likely to observe is gate hopping. A fair amount of people duck under or jump over the turnstiles either to avoid payment or because they are too lazy to get out their *cartes oranges*. RATP (Paris Public Transportation Authority) officials have reduced much of this by installing quick-moving stop gates that make cheating more difficult. Often people sneak in for free behind someone who has paid. So if someone pushes in behind you or asks to pass through the turnstile with you, don't be alarmed. If by some odd chance you get caught without a ticket, speak your mother tongue, play dumb and innocent, and when asked for your name and address, remember, you're from Oshkosh. If you are fined, though, you may be asked to pay from 17 to 50 euros on the spot for jumping over, sliding under, or riding without a valid ticket. If you cannot pay or refuse to pay immediately, the officer may either write you a ticket (PV, *procès verbal*), for which there is of course a supplementary fine, or threaten to take you to the police station. You are supposed to send in the payment. Two commonly patrolled stations are Franklin D. Roosevelt on the Champs-Elysées and the Bastille, where ticket checkers hide behind the ticket booths waiting for cheaters. Officers have had the color of their uniforms changed from military blue to khaki brown, a move designed to render their public image less aggressive. Plainclothes ticket checkers are now in service as well. According to its public relations director, the RATP is getting tougher on cheaters. So pay for your fare; it's a good deal and the embarrassment and hassle of being caught without a ticket isn't worth it.

Be aware of the last-métro phenomenon. For a city the size and complexity of Paris, it is surprising that the métro doesn't remain open all night. The métro runs till about 1:00 A.M., and you must keep this in mind if you want to get home the easiest and cheapest way. Be careful about catching the métro on one line but missing your transfer. If you miss the last métro you'll have to either find a taxi, walk, stay over, wait until the first train at 5:45 A.M., or find a stop for one of the late-night Noctambuses that leave Châtelet–Les Halles and branch out to the edges of Paris (see the Buses section in this chapter). Although the métro is safe, exercise caution when riding the métro alone late at night, and watch out for pickpockets during rush hour (a backpack is a fine invitation to pickpockets), especially in the Barbès and Concordes Stations.

If you ever do feel insecure or unsafe on the métro, climb in the car right behind the driver. There is a window into his cabin and you can watch the ride through the front windshield while being in the safest spot on the train. There has been an alarming rise in crime on the Paris public transportation system, especially on the RER outside of Paris, but riding any train during the day and early evening should pose no problem.

How to Use the Métro

The métro is easy to use, once you've mastered the symbols employed to indicate exits, transfers, and train directions. First of all, métro lines are named after their end points, e.g., the Porte de Clignancourt line is called Direction Porte de Clignancourt; the same line traveling in the opposite direction is called Direction Porte d'Orléans. Naturally it serves all the stations in between. Signs indicating direction are white. For transferring from one line to another, orange signs on the *quai* (platform) marked *correspondance* indicate the path to other *quais* and other directions. You can usually switch to a métro heading the opposite direction for free, though in some smaller stations there are separate turnstiles. Blue signs marked *sortie* point you in the direction of the exit; often you'll have a choice of exits, all emerging onto different streets or different sides of the street. When meeting friends at a métro station, make sure to specify which exit and whether you will meet underground or aboveground. In every big station you will find a *plan du quartier* (neighborhood map) on the platform, and all métro stops have maps at the ticket office exit, as well as Métro system, RER, and bus maps. When with a group, if one of you gets left behind, a good policy is to get off at the next stop and wait for your friend to arrive. Here is a list of métro lines and their respective directions:

Line 1	Château de Vincennes	La Défense
Line 2	Nation	Porte Dauphine
Line 3	Gallieni	Pont de Levallois-Bécon
Line 3bis	Porte des Lilas	Gambetta
Line 4	Porte de Clignancourt	Porte d'Orléans
Line 5	Bobigny-Pablo Picasso	Place d'Italie
Line 6	Nation	Charles de Gaulle-Etoile
Line 7	La Courneuve	Villejuif-Louis Aragon/Mairie d'Ivry
Line 7bis	Pré-St. Gervais	Louis Blanc
Line 8	Créteil Préfecture	Ballard
Line 9	Mairie de Montreuil	Pont de Sèvres
Line 10	Gare d'Austerlitz	Boulogne Pont de St-Cloud
Line 11	Mairie des Lilas	Châtelet
Line 12	Porte de la Chapelle	Mairie d'Issy

Line 13   Châtillon Montrouge   Gabriel Péri-Asnières/
                                          St-Denis Basilique
Line 14   Madeleine   Bibliothèque François
                                          Mitterand

A–Z on Using the Métro in Paris

Local writer and international moving specialist Shari Leslie Segall, who advises hundreds of Paris newcomers each year on the delights of the métro, has added this lighthearted piece on Paris's transportation system.

A—Accessibility: You've probably noticed that when the printed coordinates of a Parisian place of interest are given (a boutique, museum, restaurant, even a party-throwing private home), there is often a funny little symbol following the name, address, and phone number. The funny little symbol—a capital M with a "degree" sign after it (M°)—precedes yet another name, as in M° Pyramides or M° Ecole Militaire or M° Michel Bizot. This designates the métro stop nearest the destination in question, a practice affirming that the métro is everywhere and used by everyone but the most crowd-averse snobs.

B—Begging: On the rise in the métro and becoming worse seemingly weekly. Beggars boarding your car fall into three major categories: those who in a languorous, detached singsong recite their tale of woe; then, often accompanied by an inert baby or ragged child, pass the hat (or plastic cup, or listless hand); those who seek to sell little two-euro homegrown-by-the-homeless booklets about Parisian history or Provençal eateries or Pakistani zodiacs; and those who before passing the hat (or guitar case or callused hand) provide unsolicited entertainment (see E—Entertainment, below). Somehow, the French language seems ill-suited to the vocabulary of begging—like playing bluegrass on a Stradivarius.

C—Children: If you like the sound of their interrogative little voices, go out of your way to take the métro on a Wednesday. That's a day they're not in school. That's a day they are—accompanied by every permutation and combination of extended-family member—in every seat in every car on every métro on every line in the entirety of the mass transit network. Especially (sorry, Ministry of Culture) if the line goes anywhere near a McDonald's. Especially if the line goes anywhere near a McDonald's with a promotion going on. If you don't like the sound of their interrogative little voices, go out of your way not to take the métro on a Wednesday.

D—Dinner: As in what one is about to make for, or what one had last night for, or what one would have had last night for had one not worked too late to get to the supermarket, or what one had on the most memorable vacation of one's life several years ago due to the quality of the in-hotel dinners. One of the two main topics of conversation you will overhear on the métro. The other is soccer, especially of course around big-game times. You will hear little if anything about politics, religion, or, despite the tales the GIs brought back from World War II, sex.

E—Entertainment: (See B—Begging, above.) Unsolicited entertainment in the métro ranges anywhere from insultingly poor Jimi Hendrix imitations (sans guitar burnings) through accordion-enhanced re-creations of ethnic harvest-hymns to enchantingly elaborate puppet shows necessitating the transformation of the car into a makeshift stage complete with curtain, recorded Guignol-appropriate music, and a wood-and-cloth cast of thousands—or so it sounds. Entertainers are supposed to play on platforms only (i.e., not in cars) and only if authorized (via ID-badge license) by the *préfecture de police*. Virtually none of this is respected by the musicians or enforced by the authorities, leading some commuters to theorize that the potential enforcers possibly see themselves post-next-election in the shoes of the potential entertainers and don't want to unnecessarily rile their future coworkers.

F—Famous: Except for the newest of the new lines and stops—built within the late 1990s and accorded the obligatory millennium-resonant labels—almost every métro stop is named for a famous person, place, a thing. Even those named seemingly for the streets under which they run are named for a famous person, place, or thing, as the streets under which they run are named for a famous person, place, or thing. If you speak/read any French whatsoever, go into a good bookstore and ask for the book on the history of the métro stops. Each little paragraph or page reads like a novel. You'll learn more about the Battle of Austerlitz by researching the Gare d'Austerlitz stop than you did in all those high school geography, college history, and postgrad literature classes combined!

G—Garden: Speaking of newest of new lines and stops accorded the obligatory millennium-resonant labels, the Météore (as in "meteor"—as in not a famous person, place, or thing) line—No. 14—which opened in October 1998 and goes for the time being from Madeleine to Bibliothèque (the new national library in eastern Paris, last of François Mitterand's "Great Works") features stations that are a combination of Buck Rogers, Sir Terence Conran, and Salvador Dali. Dotted with little brass floor and wall plaques pairing familiar quotes with their authors, the Bibliothèque station looks in spots like a Roman forum, while the Gare de Lyon stop features a misty tropical garden from which parrots and toucans watch the métros flow by.

H—Happy: What most people on most métros don't look. The métro car has been referred to as "a cemetery on wheels." It is said that standing at the finish line of a marathon allows one to see the entire range of body types pass by in logical succession: first the *ectomorphs* (skinnies), then the *mesomorphs* (mediumies), then the *endomorphs* (you guessed it). Same with the métro and the entire range of unhappiness: Riding Line 6, for instance, which goes from the Arc de Triomphe's glamorous Place de l'Etoile—perceived, even if inaccurately, as the geographical center of Paris—to the working-class Place de la Nation—almost as far east as you can get without being out of town—allows one to see the entire range of social classes enter and exit in logical succession, according to the real estate value and ethnicity of the neighborhood under which one is rolling. But elevated social status apparently does not a happy commuter make.

I—Identity Papers: Checked—usually on the platforms or near the turnstiles by members of the constabulary or by roving bands of green-suited transport-company workers or both—during periods coinciding with terrorist attacks, immigrant-phobic political campaigns, and the publication of newspaper articles about the increase in urban violence. If a Chanel-suited Caucasian female adult with a briefcase, and a baggy-jeaned North African male adolescent with a boom-box approach a turnstile at the same time, you can guess whose papers will be requested.

J—Junction: Don't worry about not getting a seat in a crowded métro car: just look at the easy-to-decipher métro line map above the doors. In the mornings you'll certainly be able to figure out where the commuters will soon be getting off *en masse:* stops along the Champs-Elysées and major boulevards, certainly near principal commercial and business areas, around points where significant numbers of workers are needed to serve significant numbers of tourists. In the evenings check which upcoming stop is served by other métro lines—especially multiple other métro lines—especially multiple other métro lines taking people out into the lower-rent suburbs, where many commuters with families live. You can be sure that at these times at these junctions the car will disgorge as a chemical-treated blocked drain.

K—Karma: The force that we hope will in a future life bring back as one of their former passengers all the sadistic métro drivers who stop in the tunnel between stations for no fathomable reason, who announce that a standstill will last "just a few minutes" when they mean "until I decide it's time to get going again," and who close the doors just as we are approaching them.

L—Logo: Look hard at the relatively new (as of mid-1990s) RATP (see R—RATP, below) logo emblazoned on the sides of métro cars and buses (as well as printed onto tickets, route maps, transport-system brochures); it is one of the most ingenious emblems ever designed. (No wonder the French win international graphic arts awards year after year!) What seems at first a squiggly line through a circle appears before your eyes to morph into the profile of a woman. It's supposed to. But the trick here is to know that the double-duty squiggly line is more or less the shape of, and thus represents, the Seine, performing visual magic like those sketches of Grecian urns in your college psychology textbooks, which before your eyes used to morph into the profiles of a two women. Amazing!

M—Métro: Ever wonder what it means, where the word comes from? Métro-politain. An adjective describing the kind of rail system it is.

N—Name: In addition to being designated by number (which denotes the order in which they were built, with Line 1 being the logical first, as it follows along the Champs-Elysées and delineates what is now the longest urban axis in the world), métro lines are named for the stops that anchor them, i.e., the first and last stops of the line. People with a penchant for thoroughness will say, for example, "That's near Line 8: Balard–Créteil."

O—Open: As in doors. Just when you get used to the fact that the doors of the métro car do not open automatically but have to be activated by you, you happen upon one of the spiffy new Line 1 trains or venture onto the Météore line (see G—Garden, above) and find yourself desperately foraging for the button to push or the lever to flip while the "Sesame" occurs in spite of your good offices. Then it all happens in reverse, as you stand there on, for instance, an old Line 12 (Mairie d'Issy–Porte de la Chapelle) train awaiting the electronic intervention that never comes . . . and your train leaves the station without your having gotten off.

P—Plaque: A secret. A hermetically sealed secret. The best-kept secret in Paris. I shouldn't even tell you. But I will. When you're on Line 1 in the direction of La Défense, the minute the train pulls away from the Bastille stop *en route* to the Saint-Paul stop, start looking at the wall across the tracks. (Conversely, when you're on Line 1 in the direction of Château de Vincennes, the minute the train pulls away from the Saint-Paul stop en route to the Bastille stop, start looking at the wall on your side of the tracks.) Within about thirty seconds or so, you will see a beige marble plaque whose gold letters tell you that this—here—right here—right where this very plaque is whizzing past you (or vice versa) in this very tunnel—is where the original Bastille—as in prison—as in French Revolution—as in built in 1370 and stormed in 1789—right where this little quadrangle of signage is, is where the original Bastille really stood. (That column now out in La Place de la Bastille is, of course, a placeholder.) Wow. The experience catapults you into another dimension. You could take that train every hour of every day for the rest of your life, and catch that split-second glimpse of enlightenment, and never tire of the thrilling awe it inspires.

Q—Queer . . . Quirky . . . Quasi-insane: What you are deemed (and for which you are brutally gawked at) by the natives if you board a métro car wearing, partaking of, participating in, or carrying any of the following: running shoes, running or bicycle clothing, food or drink, loud conversation (especially if not about dinner or soccer [see D—Dinner, above]), a foreign newspaper. Extraordinarily tall, beautiful, and/or ugly individuals have a hard time of it too. And if one or the other happens to be wearing running shoes and/or eating a sandwich, the stare level approaches the unbearable.

R—RATP: You'll see it on everything that has to do with the Paris public-transportation system (tickets, brochures, maps, equipment, Web site: www.ratp.fr), so you might as well know what it stands for and means: *Régie Autonome de Transports Parisiens*—the Paris public-transportation system.

S—Shopping: Due to their size and the number of lines feeding into them (to which in fact their size is due), some of the major métro stations have become veritable emporia. If you play your logistics right, you could gorge on grapes from the vendors in the République station, chomp a chocolate chip cookie from the subterranean snack bar at Porte Maillot, select a scarf at Franklin Roosevelt, purchase a paper at Opéra, get your pictures processed at Charles de Gaulle/Etoile, and, at La Défense—the mother of all agoras—have your hair cut, buy a bouquet, check out some CDs, and decorate your den—all on one unlimited-transfer ticket!

T—Tickets: Speaking of tickets, the RATP (See? It helps to know what it means.) offers a wide range of possibilities: individual tickets (the most expensive, thus least recommended, way to go unless you are planning during your total time in Paris to set foot on only one sole solitary single member of the entire transport fleet); packets of ten (ask for *un carnet, s'il vous plaît*); daily/weekly/yearly passes; and passes that allow you to leave town and hop onto all manner of vehicle within exotic transportation networks throughout the Paris suburbs and beyond. Since many of these passes are geared toward tourists, much of the info about them—posted on ticket-counter windows and available in station-based printed matter—is available in English.

U—Underground: What a pleasant surprise! Not every métro line stays underground from one end to the other. Line 6, for example, treats riders to a view of the Seine when the train crosses it in the east (between the Bercy and Quai de la Gare Stations) and in the west (between the Bir-Hakeim and Passy Stations). So don't bury yourself too deeply in that newspaper you bought at Opéra (see S—Shopping, above)—you might miss something!

V—Vacation: Leave us not kid ourselves—when we are on vacation, the métro drivers are too. In other words, don't believe everything you read on a schedule.

From about July to early September (in other words, when the kids are not in school), trains run less frequently, but the schedule rectifiers are on vacation as well, so you should leave a couple more minutes if you're budgeting underground time to get to an appointment.

W—Wait: Speaking of waiting, François Truffaut was not the only one concerned with the last métro. They do not run all night. You can learn about hours of operation, which differ slightly from line to line, by reading notices on platform walls (poster-size sheets bearing the informational equivalent of *War and Peace* printed in characters the size of dust particles), glancing at ceiling-suspended electronic readouts (only in the most recently built stations) or asking the nice ticket seller (unless you're holding up a huge line, ticket sellers do seem to be nicer and nicer these days).

X—X-rated: If you are squeamish about your children sighting an occasional graphic-art breast or buttock, you might want to stay not only out of the métro but also maybe out of the nation! As already noted, the French are among the world champs in graphic design (see L—Logo, above), and the advertising posters lining the platforms (as well as on bus shelters, sides of street-level newspaper kiosks, and basically any appropriate—the operative word here is "appropriate"—public surface) turn an underground ride into a visual celebration. But yes, in order to sell those heartwarming telephone services, tummy-warming mashed potatoes, and, let's say, bikini-warming beaches, our Gallic cousins do not refrain from showing the hearts, tummies, and bikinis—and their neighboring anatomical parts—for which all this warming is promised. Several years ago an ad campaign was mounted in which each week, in the same position in the same ad, the same woman appeared minus yet one more article of clothing, the ad's caption being nothing more than a plea to "Watch This Space!" (presumably for the eventual pitch for the product, whose nature was not made known until the woman was in near–Garden of Eden state).

Y—Yesteryear: Until very recently there existed the second-best-kept secret in Paris (see P—Plaque, above): a little beautiful museum, tucked away in bucolic (well, at least near the Bois de Vincennes) Saint-Mandé, where tired old brass-and-wood métro cars (some from the century-old birth of the métro itself) and geriatric leather-seated trolleys could be visited, boarded, and, most important, "listened to" as they implicitly told of the frock-coated men in Vandykes and the bustled women in bonnets who sat in their glazed wicker seats en route to—where? A dance hall in Montmartre where Zola found his Nana? Until recently—about five minutes ago—because that is when the phone call for address confirmation was met with the saddening news that the museum will be closed for several years because of a change of venue. Watch this space.

Z—Zoo: Early Sunday morning on the métro. Very early Sunday morning on the métro. In an otherwise dead-empty car are some half-asleep beings in jackets that smell of smoke en route to clean up the Saturday-night refuse left behind by the other half-asleep beings in jackets that smell of smoke. Or alcohol. Or the gastrointestinal results of much smoke and alcohol. Not a pretty sight. Or smell. If you have to get someplace very early Sunday morning in Paris, if at all possible, walk.

The RER *(Réseau Express Régional)*

The RER system (also run by the RATP) is the high speed city-suburb network that in a short amount of time can zoom you across the city, out to Versailles or Saint-Germain-en-Laye, and even to Disneyland Paris. The aesthetics are very different from those of the métro. The stations are vast tunnels with deep platforms, and the trains are fast and silent. While the métros approach each platform from your left, the RER trains approach from your right. There are four lines (A, B, C, D), each of which forks into numerous directions. The RER and métro lines connect at various points, and even though the RER is not designed for short distances, it makes traveling longer distances across the city or from city to suburb incredibly easy and efficient. Key junction *(correspondances)* stations are Châtelet/Les Halles, Nation, Etoile, Invalides, Gare de Lyon, Gare du Nord, Saint-Michel/Notre-Dame, and Auber. Don't confuse Charles de Gaulle/Etoile, where the Arc de Triomphe is located with Charles de Gaulle/Roissy, the site of the airport. On the platform there are lit panels indicating the precise direction and list of stations the next train will be serving. All trains stop at all Paris stations on that line. At Nation and Etoile be careful not to mount a train on the correct line but on the wrong branch, or you'll have to circle back and pay another fare. You can go to the Château de Vincennes métro stop with the same one ticket, but to get off the RER at Vincennes you need an additional fare. Ticket checkers often stake out the Vincennes RER station catching hoards of violators in their net. Also note that on those lit panels the name of the train and the time of arrival are posted. The trains have funny four-letter names which are written in lights on the front of the first car. And some trains are longer than others. The stopping point for both Train Long and Train Court is indicated by fixed signs suspended over the platforms at the points where the *tête* (head) and *queue* (tail) of the train will stop. This is important in that you could be waiting for a train on the correct platform but 100 meters behind or in front of the train.

There is normally one first-class car on the RER trains for which you must pay a premium on your ticket. There is absolutely no advantage.

RER A1	Saint-Germain en Laye	RER A2	Boissy Saint-Léger
RER A3	Cergy-le-Haut	RER A4	Marne La Vallée/ Disneyland Paris
RER A5	Poissy		
RER B2	Robinson	RER B3	Roissy-Aéroport Charles de Gaulle
RER B4	Saint-Rémy -lès -Chevreuse	RER B5	Mitry-Claye
RER C1	Montigny-Beauchamp	RER C2	Chemin d'Antony
RER C3	Argenteuil	RER C4	Dourdan-la-Forêt
RER C5	Versailles-Rive Gauche	RER C6	Saint-Martin d'Etampes
RER C7	Saint-Quentin-en-Yvelines	RER C8	Versailles Chantiers
RER D1	Orry-la-Ville Coye	RER D2	Melun
RER D4	Malesherbes		

Buses

The sign of a real Parisian is the mastery of the bus system. Many new residents take a long time before attempting to use buses. The Parisian bus system is excellent, although its efficiency suffers from the generally congested traffic situation and, like the métro, from frequent strikes. The bus does have the advantage of allowing you to see more of the city than by traveling underground by métro. And there are still some lines with buses that have open, trolleylike back sections. Aside from the pollution, these are fun. *Paris par arrondissements* (street-map book sold at newspaper kiosks and train stations) has maps of individual bus routes. Stops are indicated on maps inside the métro, at bus stops, and in the buses themseles, with major stops in large black letters on the side of each bus. Buses use the same tickets as the métro. Formerly these were canceled or punched (*oblitérés*) in the machine located at the front of the bus, but by now all buses have replaced these machines with electronic readers. Don't cancel your *carte orange*, or it won't work in the subway! Just flash it by the driver. The driver also sells individual tickets, which must be inserted into the machine upon boarding and are good only on the bus. If you do not have a *carte orange*, traveling long distances on the bus may cost you more than one ticket if you travel through additional sections. Inquire of the driver if in doubt. When standing at a bus stop, signal the driver if you want to be picked up. Inside the bus there are red stop–request buttons located on the aisle posts. Several lines have incorporated new vehicles that you can enter via the middle doors without showing your card to the driver, but ticket-reading machines are placed at back entrances as well. The driver still prefers when card holders enter the main door and show their cards.

Most buses, whose numbers are indicated at stops by black numbers on a white circle, run every day of the year. Buses whose emblem is a white number on a black circle generally run only Monday through Saturday except holidays. For specific times of first and last buses, check the schedules at the bus stops.

When the number on the front of the bus has a slash through it, the bus runs through only part of the route. This short-range service usually happens only at rush hours and on certain routes. If you're a late-nighter, familiarize yourself with the Noctambuses, which leave the Châtelet-Hôtel de Ville area (avenue Victoria) every hour from 1:30 to 5:30 A.M. for 5 euros and traverse Paris in every direction. The mob scene to get on these can be intimidating, but the service is safe and reliable. Here's a complete list of night buses, all marked with the sign of a black owl in a yellow circle:

A: Bezonq Grand Cerf
B: Gare d'Argenteuil
C: Epinay-sur-Seine/Place René Clair
D: Pierrefitte Stains
E: Alnay-sous-Bois/Garonor
F: Gare de Chelles, Gournay
G: Noisy-Le-Grand/Mont d'Est
H: Gare de Nogent/Le Perreux
I: Porte d'Italie/Pyramide de Juvisy
J: Massy Palaiseau

K:	Clamart/Georges Pompidou
L:	Eglise de L'Hay-les-Roses
M:	Sucy-Bonneuil
P:	Gargis Sarcelles/Aubervilliers-Pantin/Quatre-Chemins
R:	Chevilly-Larue/Rungis Marché International
S:	Porte d'Orléans/Clamart
T:	Pont de Neuilly/Nanterre
V:	Sevran Livry/Mairie de Pantin

The Balabus (so called from the French *se balader*, to stroll) is a specially routed bus that for a simple fare takes you past the most important sites of Paris. This is a very good way to see Paris and to orient yourself to the city by yourself or with friends for next to nothing. The route begins and ends at the Gare de Lyon and the Grande Arche de la Défense every Sunday afternoon from mid-April to late September. Even longtime residents should cash in on this prime opportunity to relax and take in a visual reminder that they live in one of the most beautiful cities in the world.

For more information, stop in at the information stand in the concourse of the Châtelet/RER station or at RATP headquarters:

RATP Info
54 quai de la Rapée
75012 Paris
Tel.: 01–44–68–20–20 or 08–36–68–77–14
(information in French, 0,34 euros/min)
Info Flash: 08–10–03–04–05
Minitel: 3615 RATP (0,20 euros/min)
Web site: www.ratp.fr

Taxis

In general Paris taxis are readily available and reasonably priced. However, finding a taxi in Paris is different from finding one in, for example, New York. Paris taxi drivers frequently do not feel obliged to stop for you. When you do get them to stop, if your destination doesn't appeal to the driver, he will tell you so and drive off. Although relatively orderly, taxi stands can be competitive scenes—stand your ground. When ordering a taxi between 6:00 and 9:00 P.M., don't be surprised to find 3 to 5 euros already on the meter. French taxis, when ordered, start counting from the moment they set out to fetch you. It's always a better idea to find the number of the taxi stand closest to where you live, work, or usually need taxis. The system of lit bulbs on the roof of taxis indicates if the taxi is in service, is already carrying a fare, or is available. Hailing a cab midblock is practically unheard of. When the taxi crosses the *Périphérique* into the suburbs, the driver presses a button on the meter, changing it over to Fare B (day) or C (evening), a higher rate. The *Périphérique* itself though is considered Paris and the meter should indicate so. The lit display on the back ledge of taxis indicates how many hours and minutes that particular driver has been on duty that day. Taxis drivers are legally limited to a ten-hour day and are heavily fined if they exceed this limit.

Paris taxis now have a 5-euro minimum fare. It costs an extra euro when taking a taxi from a train station. It costs an extra euro per suitcase or luggage that weighs over five kilos. Don't overtip, but remember that it costs the driver about 7 per cent of social charges on the fare.

Taxi Stands

Here are the main taxi services you can always call:
+ Taxi Bleu   01–42–61–67–60
+ Taxi G7   01–47–39–47–39
For a list of taxi stands by *arrondissement*, consult www.paris-anglo.com.

Cars/Driving

Newcomers to Paris most likely will neither need a car nor want one, but still there are a number of things you might want to know regarding cars, driving, and parking in France. Young people in France tend not to be as obsessed with cars as are their contemporaries in many other countries, certainly in the United States. This may be because obtaining a driver's license in France is costlier, the price of vehicles higher, and the necessary paperwork cumbersome. When you consider that every driver in France has obligatorily gone through driving school, you may be surprised at the amount of tailgating, passing on the right, and cheating on left turns you'll see in daily traffic. On the other hand, cars are often marketed in France as objects of luxury, style, design, pleasure, seduction, desire, and grace, and less as practical vehicles for families and their pets. Some French students have old cars—traditionally the 1968 style, weak but brave and charming *Deux Chevaux*—but this is certainly no longer the rule; the models have gotten better.

The attitudes you may witness among drivers should tip you off to a lot of things. Although the French are fast and aggressive, relatively few acts of real meanness or violence occur in traffic. The largest difference between French and American urban drivers is a question of morality or principle. If you're waiting on a long line to make a left turn, undoubtedly some feisty guy in a Renault 25 or Espace van will barrel past you through the oncoming lane, zoom to the front of the line, and steal the light. In the United States, the United Kingdom, or Germany, this would cause instant anger because it's a violation and it's unfair. In France drivers might show discontent too but not out of moral outrage; they'd envy him or at least not fault him for making the most of an opportunity. Opportunism, in general, isn't seen negatively. Other drivers would be angry because he pulled ahead and they were left in the dust, not because he demonstrated a lack of respect for society and its rules. At the risk of overgeneralizing, when the French can profit for their own gain and get away with it, they tend to do it. Higher principles are reserved for higher matters than daily traffic.

Parisian drivers use humorous facial and hand gestures. They speed up at yellow lights and breeze past slow cars or jaywalkers, but they rarely hit anyone. Pedestrians usually stroll across streets with an indifferent gaze.

The *priorité à droit* (yield right-of-way) is often seen as a peculiarity by North Americans, who find this rule awkward and dangerous. Remember that anyone coming from your right in almost all situations has the right-of-way. Sometimes a car will pull out onto a busy road from a tiny side street. You must yield unless there is a sign that tells you otherwise. Often drivers take unfair advantage of this and swing far to the right and loop around to make left turns or merge onto another road. The *priorité à droite* is so engrained in the Parisian mind-set that people tend to follow it even when walking. For British drivers and pedestrians, the right-hand system will take a bit of getting used to. As will the lack of outward, public politeness.

In France the law requires that seat belts be worn by all passengers. Failure to do so can result in a 40-euro fine for the driver and 140 euros for any passenger. Although this law is a good safety measure, it sometimes can be employed as a pretext for the police to stop cars at random to check identity papers. The law also states that you must carry your *permis de conduire* (driver's license), *carte grise* (registration papers), and *certificat d'assurance* (insurance papers) at all times. Failure to present these can mean stiff fines, up to 150 euros. *Brûler un feu rouge* (running a red light) is a serious offense that will cost you a minimum of 300 euros and perhaps an afternoon in court. Crossing a solid white line is also seen as a major fault. U-turns are illegal. You can be stopped, remember, for no reason at all other than a check of your identity. Hide your indignation, or be prepared for some sort of fine for an infraction of some sort. Driving without a license can result in a fine of 1500 euros.

Driver's Licenses

EU nationals with valid driver's licenses from their respective countries have no problems receiving a French driver's *permis*. Apply at your local police station or town hall.

The following information for U.S. citizens driving in France was provided by the Paris *Préfecture de Police* via the Office of American Services at the U.S. Consulate. French regulations distinguish between persons in France on short tourist or business trips (less than ninety days) and those who are here as long-term residents.

If you are a temporary visitor to France, you may drive with a valid U.S. or international driver's license. If a U.S. license is used, the French government recommends but does not require that it be accompanied by an officially recognized French translation.

If you are a resident of France (holder of a *carte de séjour* or *carte de résidence*), you may drive in France with a valid U.S. (not international) license for a one-year recognition period, beginning on the date of validity of the first *carte de séjour*. The license must be accompanied by a translation made by a sworn (official) translator *(traducteur assermenté)*.

Persons with valid driver's licenses from the states of Pennsylvania, Kansas, Illinois, South Carolina, Michigan, Kentucky, and New Hampshire may directly exchange their state driver's licenses for French permits through a reciprocity agreement (legislation is pending to make this possible for other states as well). The licenses must have been issued prior to the holder's first entry into France as a resident, however. If you have a license from one of these states, you must apply for your French *permis de conduire* at least three months before the expiration of the one-year recognition period. Beyond this delay, the exchange will not be possible.

To apply, go to the *Préfecture de Police*, ground floor, at 7 boulevard Palais, 75004 Paris, between 8:30 A.M. and 5 P.M. Monday through Friday; Tel.: 01–53–71–53–71.

Applicants with licenses from all states must take the written *(Code de la Route)* and driving portions of the French licensing examination. All applicants must furnish the following documents:

- completed application form
- U.S. driver's license with sworn translation in French
- *carte de séjour* with photocopy of both sides
- two passport-size photographs
- proof of current address
- 25 euros in cash or check

In France almost everyone applies for a license through an *école de conduite* (driving school); private companies practically have a monopoly on the market. Almost no one succeeds in getting a license as a *candidat libre* (independent applicant). New laws require you to show up at the road test with a duo-control car, which needs to be rented from a driving school. Thus with the required twenty hours of classroom and road time, getting your license is time consuming and costly (450 to 900 euros). For the first year though, your national or state driver's license, along with an international driver's license, will suffice. This license can be obtained at AAA offices throughout the United States for $20 or by contacting AAA at 1000 AAA Drive, Heathrow, FL 32746-5063. It's not possible to obtain one in France.

For more precise information on driving in France and driving lessons, contact the legendary but costly English-speaking Fehrenbach Driving School, 53 boulevard Henri Sellier, 92150 Suresnes; Tel.: 01–45–06–31–17. For a list of driving schools with English-speaking teachers, call or write the Office of American Services at the U.S. consulate.

Replacing Expired, Lost, or Stolen Licenses

Foreign embassies are not authorized to replace expired, lost, or stolen driver's licenses. If you have lost your driver's license or had it stolen in France, immediately report it to the commissariat of police having jurisdiction over the area where the loss or the theft occurred. The commissariat will issue a *Récépissé de Déclaration de Perte ou de Vol de Pièces d'Identité* (Acknowledgment of Declaration of Loss or Theft of Identity Documents). This *récépissé* will generally cover the lack of a driver's license for a few weeks while a replacement is being obtained. The *récépissé* is good for this purpose only in France. In the case of U.S. residents, if the U.S. citizen's home state requires a sworn affidavit or a notarized application for a replacement license, the embassy's Office of American Services can notarize the application from 9:00 A.M. to 12:30 P.M. Monday through Friday, French and U.S. holidays excepted. Keep in mind that since September 11, replacing a U.S. driver's license by mail has become very difficult.

Purchasing a Car

When purchasing a used car, you need to bring the *carte grise*, the French car registration papers of the seller (on which he has written *"Vendu"* and signed and dated it), to the *préfecture* in your *arrondissement* or *département*. You also need to obtain, at the police station or town hall of the arrondissement where the car has been pre-viously registered, a *lettre de non-gage*, verifying that there are no liens or outstand-ing debts on the car. Cars over five years old must undergo an annual technical inspection *(contrôle technique)* and receive a *certificat d'inspection*, which can be obtained for 45 euros from certified service stations by no later than five years to the day from the date the vehicle first appeared in circulation. License plates *(plaques d'immatriculation)* must be changed by the new buyer within forty-eight hours after the new registration has been issued. New plates are stamped out at many service stations for under 25 euros while you wait. When buying a new car let the dealer guide you—he'll most likely obtain the *carte grise* for you.

Annual Registration Sticker

Registration stickers *(Vignettes)* were traditionally purchased in November at any *tabac* in the department in which the car is registered, upon presentation of the *carte grise*. They were renewed annually and affixed to the inside lower right-hand cor-ner of the windshield. In 2000 this tax was abolished and, for the time being, has not been reinstated.

Auto Insurance

An unlimited third-party liability insurance policy is compulsory for all automo-biles entering France. Whether the owner accompanies the automobile or not, the vehicle must be insured. As proof of insurance, the owner must present an interna-tional motor insurance card (green if the policy is purchased in France) showing that the vehicle is insured in France. A temporary policy is available from the vehi-cle insurance department of the French customs office *(la douane)* at the point of entry (border crossing or seaport). These policies have a validity of eight, fifteen, or thirty days. Those who wish longer-term or additional insurance should check with their embassy for a list of English-speaking companies.

Often you'll be told that if you can prove that you've been insured for two years, you can benefit from a French insurer's discount. This is wrong. Even if you've been insured for one year, you should qualify for a discount. You absolutely must obtain proof of previous insurance elsewhere. Try to have your former insurance agent at home send you a letter affirming your insurance record. The further back you can go, the better. The motor vehicle department of the state in which you lived can also issue a "no collision accident letter," which may suffice when the insurance agency cannot be reached. In France ask previous insurers for a *relevé d'informa-tions*. Each year of insurance with no claim entitles you to an additional 5 percent discount. This discount is extremely important if you'd like to save on insurance premiums. For salaried employees, the best rates for cars bought in France may be obtained from the MACIF and MAAF, two large insurance cooperatives, but don't expect snappy service, and don't plan on communicating by telephone. The rates may be low, but the frills are missing. In the case of stolen cars, you may be obliged to wait sixty days or more before your claim is settled, and the cost of a car rental in the interim is not included.

If you are considering the purchase of a car in France, the following list should be of interest. These vehicles are difficult and very expensive to insure because of their statistical chances of being stolen and/or of provoking accidents.

Ford Escort Cabriolet, Honda Accord Berline, Opel Corsa Berline, Opel Kadett 2000, Peugeot 205, Peugeot 405 MI, Renault Super 5, Renault Clio Baccara, Renault 19-16S, Renault 21 Baccara, Renault 25 Turbo, Renault Cherokee, Seat Ibiza, Volkswagen Travelling, Volkswagen Golf.

Documentation of Motor Vehicles

Foreign-registered automobiles entering France by road or ferry are not normally documented by French Customs at the point of entry. Vehicles shipped to France are treated differently. The shipping company is issued a *déclaration d'admission* by French Customs at the seaport and this is delivered to the owner with the car.

The French Customs office decides if foreign license plates can be used in France or if French plates *(plaques d'immatriculation)* are required. In general, cars imported for less than three months can keep their foreign plates; those brought in for more than three months need French plates. After having cleared their vehicles through a French port of entry, foreigners who plan to reside temporarily or permanently in France should consult the local customs office to establish the legality of their vehicles. In Paris the address is: Bureau de Paris-Douane, Tourisme-véhicules, 1 boulevard Ney, 75018 Paris; Tel.: 01–53–35–92–00.

In addition to license plates, imported automobiles should have a nationality sticker (F for France) mounted near the rear license plate. These stickers (usually an adhesive plastic disk) can be purchased at most auto accessory stores.

Once an imported vehicle has been processed through French Customs, the most practical way to register it and get license plates is to apply to: Automobile Club de l'Ile de France, 6 Place de la Concorde, 75008 Paris; Tel.: 01–40–55–43–00. The automobile club has offices or representatives in most cities and larger towns in France, but motorists outside of Paris should contact the regional offices in major cities to document their vehicles.

For information on sales and transfers of ownership, consult the embassy of your home country, which has printed material available on request.

If you want to bring a car to France from the United States or from another country, you'll need to apply for a French registration card *(carte grise)* for the car. This card is required to obtain theft insurance in France. Some agents will take your money for a full-risk policy, but no company will ever pay you if a car without a *carte grise* is stolen. So if the car is worth insuring against theft, you must go through the steps.

First of all, be prepared to suffer. At the end of all the administrative rigmarole and fees, you may wonder if it was worth bringing the car into the country. But if you want to proceed, here's how to do it. If you enter France from an EU country, you do not need to clear customs at the border. Proceed to your destination. First stop is the tax office *(centre des impôts)*, for a tax clearance form. On cars more than five years old, there is no value added tax or duty to pay. Newer cars are subject to a tax. Then you must go to your local *prefecture de police* for a *"dossier de demande d'immatriculation."* You will be asked to fill out numerous forms and will be required to provide the previous registration, the car title, Form 846A, your identification card or passport, a tax stamp for 30 euros, and an *attestation de conformité,* which affirms that the make and model of your car complies with French conformity laws. To obtain this you must find a dealer or importer of that make of car and have him verify your car's conformity. The fee may range from several hundred euros to several thousand, depending on the make and whether or not the car needs changes to meet French conformity. Assuming your car easily meets conformity, you will receive a letter from the state requesting that you produce the car and all the paperwork at a control center in Gonesse, a dreary urban suburb north of Paris. Be prepared to wait. You might be asked to return to the dealer to change a number of small or not so small items on your car. This can happen several times, until they are satisfied. Finally you will receive a letter informing you that you are entitled to a French *carte grise*, which will be issued within the next six to twenty-four months! The *carte grise* comes with an annual fee as well, depending on the size of the engine. Wouldn't it have been better to have bought a car locally?

Practical Advice against Auto Theft

Three hundred thousand cars are stolen in Paris each year. Don't tempt thieves.

+ Don't leave anything in the car, particularly valuable objects and papers.
+ Never leave your *carte grise* or insurance papers in the car. It makes it easy for the thief to resell the car.
+ Use the steering lock.
+ Remove the radio/cassette if possible (most new cars come with radio fronts, of no interest to thieves).
+ Engrave the windows with the license plate number of your car. This makes the resale more difficult.
+ Install an alarm.

For more specific information ask for Advantage's prepared Auto Policy Pack.

Advantage Insurance
57 rue du Faubourg Montmartre, 75009 Paris
Tel.: 01–53–20–03–33, Fax: 01–48–74–81–56
E-mail: advantage@easynet.fr
Web site: www.paris-anglo.com/advantage

Car Rentals

To rent a car in France you must be at least twenty-one years old and hold a valid driver's license (for at least one year). A major credit card facilitates matters. To rent a vehicle for moving and transporting goods, ask for an *utilitaire*.

ADA (Centrale de Réservation)
Tel.: 01–48–78–18–08 (08–36–68–40–02, recorded information, 0,34 euros/min)
Minitel: 3615 ADA (0,34 euros/min)

Autorent
Tel.: 01–45–54–22–45
Fax: 01–45–54–39–69
E-mail: autorent@wanadoo.fr

Avis Location de Voitures S.A.
Tel.: 01–44–18–10–50 (reservations and information),
08–02–05–05–05 (a special toll-number, 0,12 euros/min)

Budget
Tel.: 01–42–46–16–33; 08–00–10–00–01 (reservations, toll-free)
Minitel: 3615 Budget (0,20 euros/min)
Web site: www.EasyCar.com
Budget rentals by Internet only.

Europcar (National)
Tel.: 01–42–16–80–80, 08–03–35–23–52 (national and international
reservations; 0,15 euros/min)
Web site: www.europcar.com

Hertz France S.A.
Tel.: 01–44–18–10–50 (reservations and information)
Web site: www.hertz.com

Parking

Parking in Paris can be a nightmare. There are just too many cars in Paris for the amount of space. Throughout most of central Paris, on-street, paid parking is the rule. Instead of parking meters, Paris has adopted a system whereby you purchase a paper ticket from a parking meter machine on the block where you've parked, indicating the time you have paid for. You leave this on the dashboard. The flock of women in blue coats that parade up and down the avenue writing tickets can rarely be charmed. They're called *pervenches* (periwinkles) after the color of their coats (they used to be called *aubergines,* eggplants). The basic parking ticket is 12 euros, which skyrockets to 35 euros if unpaid after three months. Parking in an illegal spot is an automatic 35 euros, which becomes 77 euros if unpaid, later to jump to 170 euros, etc.

At the same time, the style of Paris parking is somewhat chaotic. You'll habitually see cars pulled up on sidewalks, over curbs, and into other seemingly illegal spaces. This is especially true at night in the Latin Quarter and around Montparnasse, where cars park along the center of the boulevard du Montparnasse. Parisian drivers, who often leave parked cars in neutral *(point mort),* also have the odd habit of pushing cars forward or backward with their bumpers to make room for their vehicle. One Japanese student observed this and gasped, "In Japan that'd be considered an accident."

If you get towed, call the police in the neighborhood in which you've parked for the address of the tow yard *(fourrière).* Be prepared to pay in cash or by French check. Some take *carte bleue* (Visa and MasterCard). Bring your *carte grise* and your identification.

Curiously, there is a tradition in France that all parking fines are waived by the new administration after each presidential election, so if elections are coming up within a year, you might want to hold out on paying; otherwise, you'd better pay promptly to avoid the accumulation of penalties. Parking tickets are paid by check or by purchasing a revenue stamp, again in the *tabac*. Stick half on the return portion of the ticket and retain the other for your records. If you receive a note in the mail and a bill for the penalty on unpaid tickets, you can no longer pay with a stamp; you must send a check to or visit the public treasury. Payment schedules can be negotiated. With the increase of greater European cooperation, tickets given to other EU cars are forwarded for collection in those respective countries.

If you want to utilize the reduced parking rate for local residents indicated on parking meters, go to the town hall *(mairie)* of your arrondissement with proof that you reside there, and they will issue you a resident permit in a little plastic pouch which you adhere to the right-hand corner of your windshield. There is a place to put your meter receipts next to your residence permit. There are also parking-meter subscription cards usable like the *télécartes*. Inquire at your local city hall.

Note that French drivers are taught to leave their cars parked in neutral, whereas Americans learn to leave a parked car in gear so that it can't roll.

Traffic Patterns

Traffic in and around Paris is often heavily congested. The Périphérique (the ring road that encircles the city) is particularly affected, especially in the mornings and late afternoons. Paris rush hours tend to be nearly constant. The areas around the Porte d'Orléans, Porte d'Italie, Porte de Bagnolet, Porte de la Chapelle, and Porte Maillot can be particularly clogged up. Traffic jams are called *bouchons* (from boucher, to clog), and backed-up traffic is called *un embouteillage*, bottleneck. Friday afternoons getting out of Paris are agonizing and Sunday evenings are miserable getting back.

Since France is so centralized, the French are preprogrammed, and schedules are set so that everyone travels at the same time and usually in the same directions. The school vacation periods for the entire country are divided into three zones with shared sets of dates. In winter departure for winter sports resorts in the Alps and Pyrénées causes major and predictable bottlenecks. The same phenomenon occurs at the Easter break and of course in the summer. For traffic information weather conditions, and recommended alternative routes, consult 3615 Bison Futé on the Minitel.

Motorcycles *(Motos)*

Paris hosts a proliferation of motorcycles, scooters, *mobylettes,* and other motorized two-wheelers. Most of Paris's internal message and delivery messengers *(coursiers)* move this way.

If you see a rambling mass of motorcycles on a Friday night, don't be alarmed. There's a long tradition in Paris of motorcyclists gathering at 11:00 P.M. at the Bastille and making a giant tour *en masse* along the *grands boulevards.*

A special driver's license is not needed for scooters and mopeds, although helmets are required. These vehicles run on a special gas/oil mixture called *gasoil.*

Bicycles

Riding your bike in Paris can be a hazardous but exhilarating experience—existential even. While the narrow bike lanes painted onto some streets between the bus/taxis lane on the right and the car lane to the left are merely an ignored concept in the minds of Paris drivers, advancements have been made with the new mayor's addition of many bike lanes throughout the city. Helmets, although required, are practically never worn but are highly recommended. Although sports cyclists are respected in France, and the Tour de France holds an important place in the average French person's view of the world, Parisian drivers are not the most respectful to recreational bicycle riders. The traffic circles at the Bastille, Nation, Etoile, and Concorde require an Indiana Jones sense of daring.

But getting around Paris on bike, especially in the spring and summer, is lovely and practical. The SNCF (national railroad) rents bikes in most train stations around France for a modest fee; it is also equipped to take on your bike on most trains. One particularly nice bike trip from Paris in the summer is to follow the Marne River along its banks. For bike rentals and repairs, look in the Sports and Recreation chapter or on www.paris-anglo.com. Some people go to Amsterdam to buy excellent and sturdy used bikes and bring them back by train.

Auto Parts/Used Parts

If you have a car and feel like doing some mechanics or bodywork yourself, you might have need for a junkyard (*la casse*). You can find a strange stretch of urban sprawl specializing in used and wrecked automobiles along the N7 (National 7), heading south from Porte d'Italie in the towns of Vitry and Villejuif. Here, on both sides of the road, you'll find ugly heaps of cars of all makes and years, gutted, stripped, and available for your perusal for just that missing seat belt or wing window or smashed fender or carburetor. Bring your own tools and always bargain down the prices. You'll see a part of Paris that they don't show you in the travel brochures, and for just this reason, you might want to take a weird stroll through the land of the stripped chassis.

As for taking your vehicle in for work at a dealer or garage, you might need some vocabulary specific for the task. Be wary of little added gems on your bill like petites *fournitures,* which sounds like joints and washers and stuff like that, but is really just an invented way to add 3 percent to your bill. The garages all try this and always get away with it.

Lexicon

battery	*la batterie*
brakes	*les freins*
chassis	*la carrosserie*
clutch	*l'embrayage*
gasoline	*le carburant*
gear box	*la boîte de vitesses*
fender	*le pare-choc*
hood	*le capote*

horn	*le klaxon*
neutral	*le point mort*
seat	*le siège*
seat belt	*la ceinture (de sécurité)*
steering wheel	*le volant*
tires	*les pneus*
trunk or boot	*le coffre*
windshield	*le pare-brise*
windshield wiper	*l'essuie glaces*

Driving Schools

Most driving schools in the Paris area do not have English-speaking instructors, though you can find a number of institutes that do staff English-speaking teachers with variable fluency. For a full list of driving schools claiming to have English-speaking staff, consult www.paris-anglo.com.

Fehrenbach Driving School (for English-speakers only)
53 boulevard Henri-Sellier
92150 Suresnes
Tel.: 01–45–06–31–17

Banking and Money

The Euro Arrived! Adieu the Franc.

The introduction of the European single currency, the euro, in January 1999 was a dramatic event in the world of money and banking. The January 1, 2002, total conversion to the euro coins and bills has been a radical change to contemporary life. The currencies of twelve countries—France, Germany, Greece, Italy, Spain, Belgium, the Netherlands, Luxembourg, Portugal, Ireland, Austria, and Finland — is exclusively the euro. No one has been able to spend or accept franc currency since February 17, 2002, and only banks were able to accept francs until June 30, 2002. Although the transition has occurred without much turbulence, people still talk in francs at times, some machines are still being retooled, and the psychological adaptation to what sounds and seems expensive and cheap is still a reality. We are still in a period of transition, so expect some minor confusion throughout 2002 and 2003.

The euro's introduction has prodded French banks to begin offering more complete services for international customers at competitive prices. Your reactions and experiences with French and international banks in France will vary depending on what you're accustomed to. Remember one thing—France has never really been a service-oriented society. Things do not run around the operating principle that the customer is always right. Although money and financial gain play an important role in France, as in all Western societies, the French are unwilling to sacrifice everything for the sake of profit and rarely discuss money at social gatherings. A shopkeeper may refuse to stay open slightly after closing time, even to make a sale. Businesses often don't stay open at lunch time, much less answer phones then. Real estate brokers and automobile salespeople will wait for you to call back. French law states that all employers must give employees two days off in a row, meaning that many small businesses, who do not have extra staff, are closed Mondays as well as Sundays. All this can be both enchanting and annoying. Learn to be enchanted—

the quality of daily life wins out over the inconvenience of less aggressive commercial practices. Take the longer meal.

You will probably not have a personal, first-name-basis relationship with your banker. He or she will not close each transaction with a drippy but sincere "Have a Nice Day." If you receive moderately polite and efficient service in a bank, consider yourself lucky. And don't expect toaster ovens or Walkmans for opening an account! Patience is not a commodity found in abundance when the thick Plexiglas *guichet* (window) service is involved. No one in any particular branch of any bank will ever have the authority to credit your account one cent without first passing on your written request to *la direction* (management) of the bank. All operations, complaints, modifications, and verifications are slow and tedious; they should be avoided whenever possible. It is a good idea to get yourself known by at least two bank employees at your branch. That way when one is *en vacances* (on vacation) you still have a chance of better service if needed. This will save you time and reduce aggravation—bank operations run more smoothly when you're recognized and don't have to provide identification each time.

Over the last five years, France has become highly *informatisée* (computerized) in everything from banking to dating. ATMs *(Guichets automatiques)* abound. Between the Carte Bleue bank payment card, the Minitel, and the Internet, the private citizen in France has access to all sectors of commercial life. This computerization comes as much from the French love of form (or systems and structures) and aesthetics (or style) as from a search for greater efficiency. So service in France is improving in business as less and less is required from human interaction.

In the last few years, some banks have understood that customer service is the way to go. Barclays Bank, which in the mid-1990s opened up branches all over and confronted the French banking system head-on, tried to offer interest-bearing checking accounts, something French banks had never done and French customers had never demanded. But the French authorities clamped down on this, and Barclays ended up shutting many branches. With the euro, banking products are obliged to become more unified and consumer-oriented. French consumers never demand anything; they accept. This stems from an old-world mentality that is so grateful for and content with the luxury of individual freedom and the availability of goods that price and service are inconsequential. Americans take the first two for granted; only price and service matter. French consumers haven't yet discovered the power of their pocketbooks to the extent that Americans have.

Everyone has a horror story about dealing with French banks. One American businessman nearly went out of business in 1992 when his local branch of the Crédit Lyonnais neglected to deposit a large foreign check for four weeks because the document needed a 4 FF (0,60 euros) *timbre fiscal* (tax stamp) to make the required transaction. By the time the customer complained, the payor of the check, an international company, had gone bankrupt and the American in Paris had lost U.S. $35,000 due to the bank's incompetence. Stories like this are not all that uncommon. Young banking personnel are often narrowly trained clerks. The BNP/Paribas have recently decided not to accept cash transactions after noon. I recall one twenty-year-old teller sending an eighty-year-old man back out onto the street because he wanted to deposit 500 euros into his account. Scandalous treatment!

Stay on top of your bank, court a personal relationship with at least two different bankers if you're doing business in France, and scream like crazy if—make that *when*—they foul up.

As for daily banking you'll probably have a few early questions: How do I change money? How can I receive money from abroad? What do I need to open a bank account? Which banks are the best for students? Where can I cash traveler's checks? And what about credit cards in France? These are all answered in the pages to come.

A society's relationship to money reveals much about that society. If you're coming from the United States, where banking (except currency conversion in small banks) is a relatively easy and flexible activity, you may be frustrated at first when attempting even simple transactions. In France the banks are a highly regulated industry. The state has played an increasingly present role in matters of banking since 1983, when Mitterrand nationalized the industry (although the trend is reversing now, with the privatization of some large banks—some of the same ones he nationalized). A handful of huge and omnipresent banks have hundreds of branches all over the Paris area and in a majority of towns in the provinces. The largest French banks, and thus the ones with the most branch offices, are Crédit Agricole, BNP-Paribas, Crédit Lyonnais, and Société Générale. In 1993 the BNP reverted from being a state bank to being a private bank in a move to privatization that also included the Banque Hervet and petroleum giant ELF. These banks are the most visible and the easiest to work with concerning overseas transfers, but they don't necessarily provide better service than the smaller banks.

When selecting a bank, first consider the branch's location in terms of convenience to your home, place of work, or school. In fact you'd better choose a bank close to your home or work, because banks will often not accept new accounts otherwise.

Here are a few key banks well-adapted for foreigners, where you'll be able to change money and ask questions. Insist on service. If you're displeased, go elsewhere; there are plenty of banks and almost as many answers to your questions as there are banks. Don't forget that in France the post office *(La Poste)* also serves as the largest banking facility in the country, issuing checking, savings, and money-management accounts that are often advantageous in that you pay less income taxes on interest. One reason *La Poste* is popular is that every post office is a branch, the hours extend from 8:00 A.M. to 7:00 P.M. (till noon on Saturdays), and every transaction is confirmed with a receipt by mail. This makes for easy bookkeeping. One snag: La Poste often requires that its banking customers have resident status.

American Express International
11 rue Scribe, 75009 Paris; Tel.: 01–47–77–77–07.
Travel agency, exchange service, reception of clients' mail, and issuing of traveler's checks. Open 9:00 A.M. to 5:00 P.M. Monday through Saturday for clients' mail, currency exchange and traveler's checks and 9:00 A.M. to 5:30 P.M. Monday through Friday for travel agency. In cases of stolen credit cards during hours of closure, call 01–47–77–72–00. For lost traveler's checks, call toll-free 08–00–90–86–00. American Express green card holders can write checks off their

accounts up to $1,000 per week; for those with gold cards, the limit is at least $2,000 per week.

Crédit Commercial de France (CCF)
103 avenue des Champs-Elysées
75008 Paris
Métro: George-V
Hours: 8:45 A.M. to 8:00 P.M. Monday through Friday
Tel.: 01–40–70–27–22

Banque Nationale de Paris (BNP) / Paribas
2 Place de l'Opéra at rue du Quatre Septembre
75002 Paris
Tel.: 08–02–35–57–41
Métro: Opéra
24-hour VISA automatic cash machine and automatic changer for foreign notes.

Barclays Bank (two locations)
24 bis avenue de l'Opéra
75001 Paris
Métro: Opéra
Hours: 9:15 A.M. to 2:30 P.M. Monday through Friday
6 Rond-Point des Champs-Elysées
75008 Paris
Tel.: 01–44–95–13–80
Métro: Champs-Elysées–Clemenceau
Barclay checks only, and traveler's checks. 1,20 euro commission on checks up to £100.

Citibank
125 avenue des Champs-Elysées
75008 Paris
Tel.: 01–53–23–33–60
Hours: 10:00 A.M. to 6:45 P.M. Monday through Friday
One automatic currency exchange machine and four ATMs.

Banking hours: generally 9:00 A.M. to 4:40 P.M. (9h00 to 16h30) or 5:00 p.m. (17h00) on weekdays. Some banks have begun to open on Saturday, but beware: Depending on the bank, this might mean they are now closed on Monday. Foreign banks close at 4:00 P.M. (16h00). The currency exchange, and some smaller bank branches, close for lunch, although this is gradually changing in tourist areas.

Foreign currency exchange: Open nightly on weekdays until 8:00 P.M. (20h00) at the Gare St-Lazare and the Gare de L'Est, every day at the Gare du Nord and Gare de Lyon until 9:00 P.M. (21h00) and 11:00 P.M. (23h00), respectively. Many banks also have exchange windows, usually open during select hours (rarely during lunch). The Crédit Commercial de France, 103 avenue des Champs-Elysées, is open on Saturdays from 8h30 to 20h00. Exchange rates and commissions vary greatly in France, so don't be too hasty. A couple years ago I noticed an instance of a branch of the BRED bank offering 8.05 FF per English pound with a 25 FF fee while the post office across the street paid 8.39 FF with no fee whatsoever. Some major post offices do offer a foreign exchange service, and because they are slow to change their rates day to day, when official rates drop you can actually gain by using their service. Many branches of banks do not handle foreign currency exchange; those in tourist areas often stick a handwritten note in the window: no change.

In the nineties many private exchange services opened all over the city. Exact Change has seventeen key locations, English-speaking tellers, and competitive rates. These services are usually reliable in terms of rates and commission and advantageous in terms of hours. Another popular one, Chequepoint (Head Office, 150 avenue des Champs-Elysées), accepts Eurocheques and personal checks drawn on British bank accounts. You can almost always negotiate a slightly better exchange rate with these walk-up change bureaus, especially if you're changing large sums. If they won't budge, go elsewhere. Be wary of individual money changers: Numerous travelers and students have reported being victims of short-change artists. Some have even ended up with fists full of worthless, outdated Polish zloty.

Opening an Account

There has been some inconsistency regarding the procedures for foreigners for opening accounts in France. Rules, regulations, and formalities vary greatly not only from bank to bank but also within branches of the same bank. As a student or new resident, the way you're handled is highly discretionary. It's to your advantage to present yourself well and convey stability, respectability, and the certainty and regularity of deposits. If you hit a small snag, don't fight or lose sleep; try another branch, or another bank—there are plenty.

In most cases, you'll be asked for a *carte de séjour* and proof of address. However, even this varies. One Société Générale manager stated confidently, "Just a passport will do." The BNP/Paribas, although one of the larger banks, tends to require a lot of paperwork. The Société Générale may ask for fewer documents to begin with but tends to be cautious in issuing checkbooks and Carte Bleue bank payment cards. Some of the smaller banks, like BRED and the Crédit du Nord, may prove to be the easiest for opening up accounts and may offer more or better services, but have fewer branch offices. Many banks will let you open accounts only if you live or work in the neighborhood of the branch. Friends have reported that at one BNP/Paribas branch they were told that they had to maintain a 3000 euro minimum in the account at all times. A certified letter from an American banker testifying that they had $100,000 on deposit in the United States didn't help.

For your first two years in France you will be entitled to a *compte non-résident* (non-resident account) unless you are from an EU country. Previously this type of account limited you to making deposits from outside of France. These regulations have been dropped. So essentially there is no difference between a *compte non-résident* and a *compte résident* for deposits up to 7500 euros. For higher amounts, make an appointment with your bank. Within France you can withdraw and deposit funds of any currency without limit. Although it's easy to deposit foreign-currency checks and cash, hefty and seemingly illogical fees and commissions, as well as TVA (sales tax) on the fees and commissions, may be debited from your account and a delay of up to four weeks may occur before payment is completed. In most cases you'll receive your *chéquier* (checkbook) in two to three weeks, and, if you request one, your Carte Bleue bank payment card. Cards must be picked up in person, while checkbooks may be sent to you via registered mail at your expense. When you leave France, you might want to maintain your account since after two years you'll qualify for a *compte résident*. This is easier than starting everything over should you decide to return, and it's an easy way to settle bills that arrive later. This makes home accounting easy.

Immo'Poste is a postal banking product in which savings investments reap immediate tax deductions. *Audioposte* is a service that provides twenty-four-hour access to your CCP—*compte chèques postal*—balance by phone.

Checking Accounts

Although eclipsed by the Carte Bleue as the most used form of payment, the personal check still plays a vast role in daily French life. You will most certainly want to get yourself *un compte chèques* (a checking account) and *carnet de chèques* or *chéquier* (checkbook), because paying by check is a widely accepted and easy form of handling your affairs in France. Everywhere from restaurants to gas stations, the personal check is readily accepted. You can even pay for your monthly métro pass with a check. All stores accept checks. The post office accepts checks, too. You will often, but not systematically, be asked to show some form of identification when you pay by check. The widespread acceptance of checks stems from the fact that checks in France are not negotiable or even cashable as they are in the United States, Canada, and, to a great extent, the United Kingdom. Most checks in France are *barrés*, meaning they have two lines or bars preprinted across the front, signifying that the check cannot be signed and reendorsed for payment to a third party. All checks must therefore be deposited into the bank account of the person whose name appears on the face of the check. So be wary of accepting a personal check from someone if you do not have a bank account yourself. You will not be able to go to the payor's bank and cash the check. It must be deposited. This means that all payments by check are officially recorded and thus are easily tracked by bank inspectors, accountants, and eventually the *fisc* (tax collectors). Most salaries in France are paid directly into the employee's bank account via electronic bank transfer *(virement)*. Similarly, bank mortgages, utility payments, telephone bills, etc., can be deducted automatically from the recipient's account upon request of the payor. A printed form at the top of your monthly statement—*relevé d'identité bancaire* (R.I.B.)—gives all the codes of your account, bank, and branch. These are demanded of you when payment is to be wired directly into your account. This obviously limits the mobility of money in French society, but it also seriously restricts the degree of fraud and the frequency of bounced or bad checks (*chèque en bois*—wooden check). It can be difficult to stop payment on a check and French law is unrelenting concerning writers of bad checks, although as the economy tightens more and more bad checks are in circulation. The strictest penalty for writing bad checks is being declared to the national Banque de France, where your name goes on a list of people not allowed to have checking accounts in France.

Savings Accounts

Un compte d'épargne sur livret (savings account) can also be opened. Most banks will pay modest interest on funds left in savings accounts for extended periods. Depending on your bank, your current balance may be noted on a receipt or in *le livret* (passbook) after each deposit or withdrawal—or this task may be left to you. Many people also have a P.E.L. *(Plan d'Epargne Logement)*, a government-subsidized interest package offering low-interest-bearing savings accounts designed to accrue credits toward a future low-interest loan. These funds must be used exclusively for the purchase of a house or apartment or for a home improvement project. Minimum monthly deposits of 50 euros for at least five years are required to benefit from this account. *La Poste* also offers beneficial savings plans. The private bank Cortal has attempted to compete with the commercial banks, which offer little or no interest, by offering safe and attractive banking products that function like a money market account based on French treasury bills. Cortal, 131 avenue Charles de Gaulle, 92571 Neuilly sur Seine; Tel.: 08–00–10–15–20.

Banque Transatlantique

One bank in Paris has specialized in serving French citizens abroad since the nineteenth century. Today the Banque Transatlantique caters to expatriates moving to France with financial, investment, property, and tax services. Contact: 26 avenue Franklin D. Roosevelt, 75008 Paris; Tel.: 01–56–88–77–77; E-mail: contact@ transat.fr.

Credit Cards

In France the *Carte Bleue* (CB) offered by each bank has become an institution in daily life. The French attraction for computerized systems has been married to this centralized form of payment. The CB (part of both the VISA and Master-Card/Eurocard network) is widely accepted, although it is not really a credit card; it's a debit card. Purchases and automatic cash withdrawals are automatically deducted from your checking account on a fixed date of the month. Thus you do not really get true credit. You do not receive a monthly credit card statement, although a given month's purchases and withdrawals will appear on your checking account statement. You can run up large debits as long as you continue to maintain a positive balance. You do not have a credit line other than the overdraft limit permitted by your bank. The idea of real credit, which permits people to live painlessly beyond their means, is still rather foreign in Europe.

The main advantage of the *Carte Bleue* is its surprisingly wide acceptance. You can use your card at any ATM regardless of which bank the card belongs to, although the withdrawal limits vary. You can pay your tolls on the autoroute with your CB; you can pay for all your supermarket purchases with your CB; you can stick your CB into a ticket machine in selected métro stations to buy your monthly *carte orange;* you can purchase a museum admission ticket in the lobby of the Louvre.

CB cards now contain not only a magnetic strip that permits users to draw up to 275 euros (amount depends on bank) per week in cash from any bank's automatic teller machines, but also a microchip containing your four digit access code

(PIN—Personal Identification Number). This system has eliminated the need for customers to sign bills, since most restaurants, gas stations, hotels, etc., now have portable, cordless machines that read the chip and check it against the number the customer punches in. (CB cards sometimes malfunction due to static buildup and need to be rubbed with a clean cloth; also, keep the card away from keys, métro tickets, cell phones, and other credit cards, which have their own magnetic strips.)

ATMs will often be marked with stickers indicating they are part of the Plus, Cirrus, and NYCE ATM networks and American banks often tell customers that their American cards will work in France. This is not always the case, however. The cards are not always compatible. Sometimes it takes stops at several ATMs before you find one that will accept your U.S. card, and sometimes you just can't find one. It can be a bit of a crapshoot. ATM cards issued in France will work in many other ATMs around Europe, however.

The most important detail to remember is to come equipped with your four-digit PIN code. Without it you'll not be able to use a French ATM with a "foreign" card.

French ATMs that carry the American Express "Express Cash" logo will work with Amex cards. And the Amex card issued by Air France affords you miles on the airline's Frequence Plus program.

All major credit card companies are represented in France. Here are phone numbers in case of lost or stolen cards:

American Express
Tel.: 01–47–77–70–07

Diners Club de France
Tel.: 08–-20–82–04– (Info)

Eurocard (MasterCard)
Tel.: 01–45–67–53–53
Tel. lost cards: 01–45–67–84–84

Carte Bleue (Visa)
Tel.: 01–42–33–24–12

Transferring Funds from Abroad: Getting Cash Fast

One of the most important questions you may face is: "How can I get money quickly from home?" Despite assurances made by many issuing banks in other countries, the majority of money orders and interbank checks and *all* personal checks must normally be cleared through the issuing bank before they can be credited to your account. This can take weeks. Other quicker possibilities include:

✛ Wire transfer: The sender can wire money directly to a French euro account, specifying the bank name, branch name, address, account number, and, where possible, the routing code—this normally takes forty-eight hours. Always note the *agence* (branch) number and *clé R.I.B.* (bank code). Having money wired to your Paris bank account can be done quickly if the issuing bank is directly affiliated with the receiving bank and the money does not have to go through intermediaries. Money wired from the Société Générale in New York, for example, will go directly into your account in a Paris branch of the Société Générale if the branch name and account number are specified. If you plan to receive a regular transfer of funds over a period of time, and if the issuing bank is not directly affiliated with your bank in Paris, the transfer can take as long as four weeks, so it is a good idea to ask your home bank if it is affiliated with a French bank before you choose the French bank where you open an account. Most banks have a funds-transfer system called SWIFT, but it doesn't always live up to its name. Although the actual transfer takes one day, some banks may take a day to send the order from one branch to a larger one, and then another to process the transfer. When weekends and holidays interfere, money can be slowed down tremendously. Foreign-fund checks deposited into a French bank account can take weeks to clear and cost you high fees. It's usually better to group small foreign-fund checks and deposit them together. A small sum like $10 or £10 might cost you more to deposit! Contrary to popular belief, Eurochèques in either euros or foreign currency will cost you at least 5 euros per check, plus the commission and exchange charge and TVA sales tax on these.

✦ American Express. If you don't have an account in France, a wire transfer can be made through American Express—one of the most rapid systems. A Moneygram allows you to send or receive cash instantly, the minimum being $100 and the maximum being $7,500. The American Express Bank on the Champs-Elysées is not for currency exchange. At the 11 rue Scribe, 75009 Paris, you can draw French cash against your American Express card.

✦ Western Union Worldwide Money Transfer. You can send money to any of Western Union's 19,000 agents from the United States, and Canada. In theory, you can charge this transfer by phone to your VISA or MasterCard, seven days a week. In the United States call (800) 325–6000. A trick: Call from Paris and send yourself money against your credit card, 01–43–54–46–12. Travelers report that no Paris office has been able to confirm the credit card debit service.

✦ Bank checks in euros. Have the sender purchase a bank check drawn in euros at your Paris bank's foreign branch and send it to you through the mail or courier service. (Be careful: This is like cash. Payment cannot be stopped.)

✦ Thomas Cook Moneygram: Friends or relatives can call (800) 543–4080 to obtain the address of the local Moneygram office. They then go to that office with cash or Visa, MasterCard, or Discover credit card. The money will be in Paris at one of the Thomas Cook offices within the hour. Call 01–42–96–26–78 to find the one closest to you and its hours of operation.

Telecommunications
and Media

France's sophistication in communications is impressive; the telecommunications field is one of the most dynamic areas of French industry. The post office *(la poste),* formerly PTT *(Postes, Téléphones, Télégraphes),* has been separated administratively from France Telecom, the nationalized telephone company, in an effort to increase efficiency. As with other French industrial giants, France Telecom has been partially privatized, with individuals able to purchase shares. France has worked hard to link new technology and *la vie quotidienne* (daily life). Well before computers became a household appliance anywhere in the world, France brought was what then the latest technological developments into the home via the Minitel, an on-line computer and screen that is at once a telephone book, a reservation network, and a research library, as well as a home-shopping tool, a means of direct written communication with other Minitel users, and a computer and video linkup. Use of the Minitel as a fax, printer, modem, etc., is possible as well. Minitels can be obtained free from the France Telecom office in your arrondissement. (See the Minitel section in this chapter.)

The Public Telephone Booth and the *Télécarte*

Over the last several years most public coin-operated phone booths *(cabine téléphonique)* have been replaced by a new type of booth that accepts only cards, called *télécartes.* These are sold in post offices and *tabac* (cafés licensed to sell cigarettes, etc.) in units of 50 or 120 for 8 euros and 15 euros, respectively. Buy one right away; they're very practical! You can use them to call anywhere in the world as long as you have enough units left on the card. Each call-unit costs 0,06 euros and is automatically deducted from the card's microchip *(puce)* at a rate that depends on where and when you're calling. You can change *télécartes* in the middle of a call.

It's getting virtually impossible to find a public phone that takes coins. If you find yourself caught without a *télécarte*, try a café, bar, or the lobby of a small hotel; many of them either have coin-operated phones or let you use their desk phones and then charge you afterward for the call.

In the 1960s and 1970s, some broken phones allowed free unlimited international calls to go through undetected; when word got around, at all hours of the night lines would fill up with foreign students waiting to call family and friends. These wonderful little finds have all but disappeared with the *télécarte*.

To use *télécarte* phones, pick up the receiver, slide in the card, arrow facing up and forward, close the *volet* (sliding hatch, if there is one), wait for a dial tone, and make your call. In booths with sliding hatches, after hanging up wait about five seconds: The hatch will open and a beep will sound, reminding you not to forget your card; in nonhatch phones just remove your card after you've hung up.

Télécartes have become collectors' items in France, much like baseball cards in America. The card with the Van Gogh portrait has been very popular, as are the cards commemorating the 1998 World Soccer Cup. Hundreds of private companies have paid France Telecom for the right to advertise on the face of these cards. Collectors and traders—a vast number of them, curiously, African and West Indian—hang around the cluster of *cabines téléphoniques* in the concourse of the Châtelet/Les Halles Métro/RER station dealing these cards. In the outdoor postage-stamp market at the Rond Point des Champs-Elysées (Métro Franklin Roosevelt), collectors and vendors trade, buy, and sell *télécartes* with the seriousness and intensity of dealers in fine art.

01 and 1

In Paris all local calls begin with 01. When dialing the same number from outside of France, drop the 0. When dialing Paris from another part of France, use the 01 prefix. The numbers for the rest of France begin with 02, 03, 04, and 05; cellular phone numbers begin with 06. Toll-free numbers begin with 08–00 (other 08 numbers will cost you more than 0,30 euros a minute!).

Number Prefixes

For telephoning purposes, France has been divided into five regions, each with its corresponding phone prefix, as below. A detailed, color-coded map indicating area and corresponding phone prefix can be found in the front of the Yellow Pages or on a pocket-sized laminated card available at France Telecom offices (try post offices and phone stores as well, although once the initial batch of these cards was distributed, they were not always reordered).

✛ Paris and its close suburbs: 01 plus eight-digit number
(When calling from outside France: 33–1 plus eight-digit number)

✛ Northwest (Normandy, Brittany): 02 plus eight-digit number
(When calling from outside France: 33–2 plus eight-digit number)

✛ North and Northeast (Lille, Strasbourg): 03 plus eight-digit number
(When calling from outside France: 33–3 plus eight-digit number)

+ Southeast (Nice, Marseille): 04 plus eight-digit number
  (When calling from outside France: 33–4 plus eight-digit number)
+ Southwest (Bordeaux, Toulouse): 05 plus eight-digit number
  (When calling from outside France: 33–5 plus eight-digit number).
+ Calls from France to outside the country are preceded by 00.

Rates

France Telecom's rates have been radically reduced over the past several years, reversing a situation that had made French rates prohibitively higher than those offered by U.S. companies, and reflecting great efforts on the part of the phone company to both increase service and cut rates. France Telecom now offers several money-saving "calling plans," making international dialing all the more affordable. Nonetheless, if you get cut off or experience disturbing interference on the line, don't count on asking the operator for credit—it's not an option.

For the latest rates consult www.francetelecom.fr. The site has an English translation.

Calling from Home

+ To the United States and Canada
  1:00–7:00 P.M.: 0,30 euros/minute TTC (toutes taxes comprises—including tax)
  7:00–1:00 P.M.: 0,24 euros TTC/minute
+ To the United Kingdom
  8:00 A.M.–7:00 P.M.: 0,28 euros TTC/minute
  7:00–1:00 P.M.: 0,22 euros TTC/minute

Using a *Télécarte*

+ To the United States and Canada
  8:00 A.M.–7:00 P.M.: 1 unit is used up every 14 seconds
  7:00 P.M.–8:00 A.M.: 1 unit is used up every 17 seconds
+ To the United Kingdom
  8:00 A.M.–7:00 P.M.: 1 unit is used up every 19 seconds
  7:00 P.M.–8:00 A.M.: 1 unit is used up every 23 seconds

The American telephone giants along with an outcrop of smaller and ambitious outfits have been investing heavily for what AT&T calls "expatriate accounts." You can compare and choose. From France, to call the United States collect or to use a phone company's calling card, dial:
  AT&T Direct-Dial Service: 08–00–99–00–11
  MCI Direct-Dial Service: 08–00–99–00–19
  Sprint Direct-Dial Service: 08–00–99–00–87
France Telecom offers its own *Carte France Telecom* (formerly *Carte Pastel*) for direct dialing to France from overseas or within France. In case of loss or theft of the Carte France Telecom, call toll free (*numéro vert*)
+ from within France 08–00–10–20–40.

From outside France there is a different number for each country (see below for some examples). You call the number and the computerized prompt asks you to punch either one or zero. Calling collect, punch zero, ask for PCV (*payez chez vous,* a collect call), then give the following number: 03–83–80–09–10.
+ from the United States: 1–800–537–2623
+ from Canada: 1–800–000–4033
+ from the United Kingdom: 0–500–890–033

Cegetel 7

Cegetel 7 is France Telecom's domestic competition for stationary telephone lines. The service does not require a subscription. You simply sign up for the service and then precede your calls with the number 7. The rates and other services are advantageous. For their rates and conditions, call 08–05–77–79–99. The same company manages AOL and Compuserve in France.

Call Back and Alternative Companies

A few of the newer, smaller, and potentially more economical services advertise regularly in Paris. While their rates may be attractive, they often stipulate minimums or require certain other conditions. Check them out first.

Global Access (Telegroup)

This group has grown quickly in France, with a number of agents selling the same service and vying for your business. The group's customer service toll-free line is 08–00–01–00–11. An American named Jack runs one agency and targets American clients, offering periodic promotional deals for calls to the United States. His number is 01–39–07–01–01. If you're confused and need to reach the head office in France, call 08–00–33–39–99.

Big Fone Co

This one advertises at 58 centimes a minute to the United States and 68 centimes to Canada twenty-four hours a day, seven days a week. Call for details: 01–47–70–34–43.

Long-Distance Phone Cards

Another option on cheap calls home are phone cards, such as offered by PTI Com + and other companies. Available in many small shops and *tabacs*—try Chinatown if you can't find them anywhere else—these cards offer great rates on international calls (a 15,24-euro card can give you 700 minutes for a France–United States call). Different cards are available for different countries/continents. Dial-up service is available in nine languages. Do not use these as *télécartes*, however: a local call is drastically more expensive.

Cordless Phones

Brands not accredited by France Telecom tend to have less-secure frequency-protection systems. At the beginning of the nineties there were numerous cases of pirated calls and large unexpected phone bills, especially to Turkey, Pakistan, and the Philippines, due to people breaking into unprotected frequency bands on cordless telephones and dialing away at the subscriber's expense. France Telecom has not reimbursed users who had nonapproved cordless phones and claims no responsibility despite a class-action suit brought against France Telecom by angry citizens with inflated bills.

There is a company offering free incoming cell phone calls in France when you buy their phone card. Tel.: (800) 858–4289 or visit www.paris-anglo.com.

Cell Phones

Paris now enjoys, or is plagued by, more telephone stores than beauty salons. The deals change weekly, the technology changes monthly, and your mind will change almost as fast. Paris streets are teeming with Parisians with cute little cell phones glued to their ears; everyone from construction workers to the corporate president today wouldn't think of leaving home without one. In France today you have essentially three major choices of cellular telephone service, France Telecom's Orange, Bouygues Telecom, and SFR. For detailed information on which service best suits you and the most up-to-date prices, here are the key players. Ask at any telephone store for prices, conditions, and extent of coverage.

+ France Telecom (Orange): 10–14 for private lines; 10–16 for professional lines
+ Bouygues Telecom: 08–01–63–06–30
+ SFR (Cegetel): 08-05-77-77-77 individuals, 08–05–80–58–05 companies 95 percent coverage, 100 percent in all towns with 20,000 people or more.

All three offer nonsubscription services as well. You buy the phone and stock the chip with credit with your Visa or MasterCard. As you make calls you use up the credit and restock it as you go.

Note that most cell phones bought in the United States or the United Kingdom will not work in France. New worldwide cellular systems are expected in the near future, and at least one company has already begun offering inserts that will allow phones to work in countries where they previously didn't.

France Telecom also offers a host of paging services, including OLA totem and Tam-tam, popular with young people, which find you and leave written messages on a belt-clip screen. Nearly all French cell phones these days come equipped with text-messaging capabilities.

Getting Directory Information

Directory assistance can be obtained by dialing 12 on your telephone; it costs 0,69 euros for one to three inquiries at a time.

By Minitel the same service is accessible by dialing 36–11; there is no cost for the first three minutes.

For international directory assistance dial 00–33–12 plus the country code if the country code is of more than one digit; if the country code is only one digit, dial 00–33–12 plus the country code plus 1. (For the United States this would be 00–33–12–11.) The cost is 1,70 euros TTC from a home phone and fifteen units from a phone booth. To get international directory assistance at no cost, call the access number for one of the American phone companies and then dial the area code followed by 555–1212.

For international directory assistance by Minitel, dial 36–17 then follow the prompt. The cost for this service is posted on the Minitel screen.

France Telecom Key Numbers

France Telecom sales office: 10–14
France Telecom customer service: 10–13
France Telecom business sales office: 10–16
France Telecom business customer service: 10–15
National directory assistance (up to three requests per call): 12
National directory assistance (more than three requests): 36–92
Telegrams: 36–55
Programmable wake-up calls: 36–88
Operator-assisted call, international: 00–33 plus country code
International directory assistance: 00–33–12 plus country code (for the United States, Canada, and countries whose codes start with 1, dial 11 instead of 1).
To find out who has tried to call you when you were out, dail 31–31

Carte France Telecom Calling Cards:
Direct dial call: 36–10; Operator-assisted call: 36–50; to report the loss or theft of your Carte France Telecom, call toll free: 08–00–10–20–40.

Country Codes Most Often Dialed

For consistently updated information on country and city codes, consult www.francetelecom.fr. Click on the word "Go" to access the English pages and

then select How to Call Another Country. *Note:* Dial 00 before the country code.

Algeria: 213
American Virgin Islands: 1809
Angola: 244
Antilles: 599
Argentina: 54
Australia: 61
Austria: 43
Azores: 351
Bahamas: 1809
Bahrain: 973
Bangladesh: 880

Belgium: 32
Belize: 501
Benin: 229
Bermuda: 1809
Bolivia: 591
Botswana: 267
Brazil: 55
British Virgin Islands: 1809
Brunei: 673
Bulgaria: 359
Burkina Faso: 226
Burma: 95
Burundi: 257
Cameroon: 237

Canada: 1
Cap Vert: 238
Cayman Islands: 1809
Central African Republic: 236
Chad: 235
Chile: 56
China: 86
Colombia: 57
Comoros: 269
Congo: 242
Congo (formerly Zaire): 243
Cook: 682
Costa Rica: 506
Croatia: 38
Cuba: 53
Cyprus: 357
Czech Republic: 42
Denmark: 45
Djibouti: 253
Dominican Republic: 1809
Ecuador: 593
Egypt: 20
El Salvador: 503
Ethiopia: 251
Falkland Islands: 500
Faroe Islands: 298
Fiji: 679
Finland: 358
Gabon: 241
Gambia: 220
Germany: 49
Ghana: 238
Gibraltar: 35
Greece: 30
Greenland: 299
Grenada: 1809
Guadeloupe: 590
Guam: 671
Guatemala: 502
Guinea: 224
Guinea-Bissau: 245
Guinea Equatorial: 240
Guyana: 592
Haiti: 509
Honduras: 504
Hong Kong: 852
Hungary: 36

Iceland: 354
India: 91
Indonesia: 62
Iran: 98
Iraq: 964
Ireland: 353
Israel: 972
Italy: 39
Ivory Coast: 225
Jamaica: 1809
Japan: 81
Jordan: 962
Kenya: 254
Korea: 82
Kuwait: 965
Laos: 856
Lesotho: 266
Lebanon: 961
Liberia: 231
Libya: 218
Liechtenstein: 41
Luxembourg: 352
Macao: 853
Madagascar: 261
Madeira: 351
Malaysia: 60
Malawi: 265
Maldives: 960
Mali: 223
Malta: 356
Martinique: 596
Mauritania: 222
Mauritius Island: 230
Mexico: 52
Monaco: 93
Mongolia: 976
Montserrat: 1809
Morocco: 212
Mozambique: 258
Namibia: 264
Nauru Islands: 674
Nepal: 977
Netherlands: 31
New Zealand: 64
Nicaragua: 505
Niger: 227
Nigeria: 234

Norfolk Island: 6723
Norway: 47
Oman: 968
Pakistan: 92
Panama: 507
Papua/New Guinea: 675
Paraguay: 595
Peru: 51
Philippines: 63
Poland: 48
Portugal: 351
Puerto Rico: 1809
Qatar: 974
Romania: 40
Russia: 7
Rwanda: 250
Samoa U.S.: 684
Samoa Western: 685
San Marino: 39
São Tomé e Principe: 239
Saudi Arabia: 966
Senegal: 221
Seychelles: 248
Sierra Leone: 232
Singapore: 65
Solomon Islands: 677
Somalia: 252
South Africa: 27
Spain: 349
Sri Lanka: 94

St. Helene and Ascension: 247
St. Kitts: 1809
St. Lucia: 1809
St. Vincent: 1809
Sudan: 249
Surinam: 597
Swaziland: 268
Sweden: 46
Switzerland: 41
Syria: 963
Taiwan: 886
Tanzania: 255
Thailand: 66
Togo: 228
Tonga: 676
Trinidad and Tobago: 1809
Tunisia: 216
Turks and Caicos Islands: 1809
Turkey: 90
Uganda: 256
United Arab Emirates: 971
United Kingdom: 44
Uruguay: 598
United States: 1
Vatican City: 39
Venezuela: 58
Vietnam: 84
Yemen: 969
Zambia: 260
Zimbabwe: 263

City Codes Most Often Dialed

Note: Dial 00 before country code. To find other city codes, dial 00–33–12 and then the country code.

Amsterdam: 31–20
Athens: 30–1
Auckland: 64–9
Beijing: 86–1
Berlin: 49–30
Bombay: 91–22
Boston: 1–617
Brussels: 32–2
Budapest: 36–1
Cairo: 20–2
Casablanca: 212–2

Chicago: 1–312
Copenhagen: 45
Dublin: 353–1
Edinburgh: 44–131
Frankfurt: 49–69
Glasgow: 44–141
Hamburg: 49–40
Helsinki: 358–0
Istanbul: 90–212
Jerusalem: 972–2
Johannesburg: 27–11

Kyoto: 81–75
Lisbon: 351–1
London: 44–171 or 44–181
Los Angeles: 1–213 or 1–818 or
    1–310
Luxembourg: 352
Madrid: 349–1
Manchester: 44–161
Melbourne: 61–3
Mexico City: 52–5
Miami: 1–305
Milan: 39–2
Montreal: 1–514
Moscow: 7–095 or 502
Munich: 49–89
New York: 1–212

Oslo: 47–2
Prague: 42–2
Rio de Janeiro: 55–21
Rome: 39–6
San Francisco: 1–415
Shanghai: 86–21
St. Petersburg: 7–812
Sydney: 61–2
Tel Aviv: 972–3
Tokyo: 81–33 or 81–35
Toronto: 1–416
Tunis: 216–1
Vancouver: 1–604
Warsaw: 48–2
Washington, D.C.: 1–202

A Note on Call Waiting
When you telephone someone who is already on the phone, instead of a busy signal you will often get a recorded message from France Telecom stating: *Veuillez patienter. Votre correspondant est en ligne. Nous lui indiquons votre appel par un signal sonore.* (Translation: "Please wait. Your party is on the line. We will inform him or her of your call with a tone.") Lots of people misunderstand this recorded message and hang up. Don't.

Telephone Skills in French

Those first few calls can be traumatic. It's especially difficult to integrate your French into dialogue when you cannot see the other person and can't rely on gestures or facial expressions. Here are a few simple telephone dialogue patterns for the uninitiated:

How to ask for someone:
—*Bonjour, est-ce que je peux parler avec . . . ?* (Hello, can I speak with . . . ?)
—*Bonjour, puis-je parler avec . . . ?* *(*Hello, may I speak with . . . ?)
—*Bonjour, est-ce que Monsieur (Mademoiselle, Madame) . . . est là ?* (Hello, is Mr. (Miss, Mrs.) . . . there?)

Answering the telephone:
—*Allô* (Hello.)
—*Ne quittez pas.* (Don't hang up, or, hang on.)
Other useful dialogue:
—*Il/Elle n'est pas là.* (He/she is not here.)
—*Vous vous êtes trompé de numéro.* (You have the wrong number.)
—*Qui est à l'appareil ?* (Who's calling?)
—*Est-ce que je peux laisser un message ?* (Can I leave a message?)
—*C'est (your name) à l'appareil.* (It's . . . calling.)
—*Comment ça s'écrit?* (How is that spelled?)

—*Je suis désolé(e)*. (I'm sorry.)
—*Répétez, s'il vous plaît.* (Please repeat that.)
—*Lentement, s'il vous plaît.* (Slowly, please.)

Minitel

The Minitel is a small, on-line computer with multi-services that can be connected to any French telephone line and can be accessed internationally via modem hookup. The basic telephone directory service (which has virtually replaced the telephone book in France) is available free of charge for the first three minutes to anyone possessing a Minitel and telephone; simply dial 3611. Other services, such as banking, shopping, financial information, ticket reservations, etc., each with different access numbers and codes, are charged by the minute directly to your bimonthly telephone bill. Prices vary for different services, ranging from 0.06 euros a minute to half a euro, with some highly specialized services costing much more. Rates are listed at the beginning of the connection. So be careful with this fascinating, seductive, and vastly useful tool and toy.

Today, much of the Minitel's appeal has been replaced by the Web, so much of its initial use has become obsolete. For many services, however, it remains faster and more convenient and ultimately more local. You can also access the Minitel on-line (you have to download software and pay a service fee) at www.i-minitel.com.

The Agoris 55 is a fax machine that sits on the Minitel and prints from the Minitel. For more info on the Minitelnet, access 3623 MNET on the Minitel or go to www.francetelecom.fr.

Throughout Paris you will see a strange host of billboards advertising Minitel services. These begin with the access numbers plus a usually catchy code, the most embarrassing one for Anglo-Saxons being 36–15 CUM, a service for singles to meet, talk, play, seduce, sometimes marry. The 2,000-plus porn-oriented services, better known as *messageries roses,* generated some controversy; the state has tried to limit "unhealthy" use of the Minitel while it reaps the huge financial benefits of electronic quasiporn. Minitel services had mushroomed over the last few years, but have recently begun to peter out as the French have discovered the Internet. Telephone numbers starting with 08–36 are often special-rate services, games, contests, and pay-for-information lines, such as when you call the SNCF (national railway system). Many television shows have 0836 services for viewers wishing to call in and place orders. Rates can be as steep as 1,50 euros per minute.

User's Instructions

To use the Minitel, turn on the unit, dial the code number on your telephone, wait for the faxlike tone, type in the rest of the code on the Minitel (what you type in appears on the screen), and then press *Connexion fin* on the keyboard. Now you're on-line. The rest should be self-evident. To break the connection and stop the billing clock, but not erase the information on the screen, touch *Connexion fin.*

France Telecom now has a very complete print guide for the Minitel, called the *Annuaire Minitel,* available at France Telecom offices. The newspaper *Libération* publishes a minidirectory from time to time as well. You can consult the guide to services when connected to the Minitel, but that costs. Here is a sampling of some of the more useful services and their access codes. The price of each service per minute is displayed on your monitor as you sign on. A more complete list and direct links are availble a www.paris-anglo.com.

Minitel List
3615 AF Air France information.
3615 AIRTEL National and international airline schedules and airfares.
3615 BHV Information, bargains, services, and job offers of the department store Bazar de l'Hôtel de Ville.
3615 DICO The first dictionaries available by Minitel: spelling, synonyms, conjugations.
3614 ED Administrative and emergency phone numbers and addresses.
3614 EMS Chronopost—the fast mail service of the post office.
3617 FAX In order to send a message by fax, type in the fax number and the correspondent, then the message. For a fee, via Minitel, it will arrive by fax.
3615 FLORITEL Send some flowers—to anywhere in France. Prices range from 15 euros to 250 euros, plus 5 euros delivery charge.
3615 FNAC A listing of all existing CDs, but no listing of which are available on the market, and no way to order them.
3615 GAULT Listing of 2,500 selected Paris restaurants with Henri Gault's opinions on the best ones.
3615 HORAV Airport guide: parking, services, hotels. Flight departure and arrival times.
3615 ITOUR National directory of tourist bureaus by region, department, and town.
3615 LIBE American and international news in English direct from *USA Today*.
3615 LOCAT Looking for an apartment? Find one through classifieds and agencies on the Minitel.
3615 PARISCOPE This allows you to reserve your seat at a movie theater.
3615 RANDO Guide of walking trips in France. List of maps and guides.
3615 RATP This connection is helpful in determining the best means of transport (métro, bus) to use and how long it will take you. About four minutes is average for this inquiry.
3616 SEALINK Times and prices for ferries to England and Ireland.
3616 SITU A comprehensive service offering the best route on all Paris area public transportation. You put in where you're going and it tells you how to get there.
3615 SNCF If you indicate the station of arrival and departure and the chosen date of your journey, this service of the national railroad offers all the possibilities of travel. For instance you can reserve your ticket and pick it up later at either an SNCF window or a travel agency, on the condition of having kept the reference number that the Minitel provides. The catch? This service is always blocked up during rush hour; the average time to reserve two tickets from Paris to Marseille is about six minutes.
3615 TMK This service allows you to order your groceries via Minitel and have them delivered to your door the same day—for a 10-euro charge if your purchase is

less than 200 euros, or the next day for 7 euros. Order before 10:00 A.M. if you want delivery the same day, and after 10:00 A.M. to choose the day you want delivery.

3617 VAE This new service, *ventes aux enchères*, is a complete listing of merchandise being sold off at auction following the bankruptcies and liquidations of companies.

France Telecom Services

In keeping with the times, France Telecom has continued to introduce a host of new services and products. France Telecom has also invested heavily in up-to-the-minute telephones, fax and answering machines, and portable telephones. You can request these features for free or nominal fees by visiting your France Telecom office, dialing 3614 on your Minitel, or calling 1014 on your telephone *(agence commerciale)*. You should also note that the way the French telephone company has undergone a face-lift; it has changed its corporate image in France and around the world to that of an international leader in the telecommunications industry. The logo was modernized in the mid-1990s and then refreshed again when the company added on Orange, its cellular-phone branch. Here are some services and products, though many more are constantly being added.

Facturation détaillée (itemized bill). Otherwise you'll just receive a bill for the total. Bills come every two months and you have ten days to pay or risk a 10 percent fine.

Signal d'appel (call waiting). By touching the key on your phone marked R and then 2, you can put one call on hold while you take an incoming call.

Conversation à trois (conference call). Press R then 3 to call and be connected to two numbers at once.

Transfert d'appel (call forwarding). By using the star and pound keys, you can program your phone to transfer your incoming calls automatically to another number, and back again, at your command (detailed instructions are provided when you sign up for this service).

Orange is France Telecom's mobile phone service or GSM (Global System for Mobile Communication). The portable phone units are manufactured by several firms, notably the Swedish Erikson. The service, marketed under the trade name of Cellway, is rapidly expanding its area of use. Although Orange did not initially work outside of Europe, the service now does function in numerous countries, and there are imminent plans for a wholly international mobile telephone.

Mémophone (Voice Mail). Dial 3672 for an explanation on how to set up this useful voice-mail service.

Numeris. This is one of France Telecom's most sophisticated telecommunications technologies. Numeris is designed primarily for commercial concerns to transfer data bases, high fidelity sound, and video imaging from computer to computer through the telephone system. The implications of this technology are vast in that any phone line with this service and hardware can function as a computer terminal, video or film set, or recording studio.

Other services include Caller ID identification, 3131 (Call Return System, what Americans might know as Star-69), Automatic Ring Back, and a host of discount plans and services.

Internet High Speed Connection Providers

France Telecom's Wanadoo and the ADSL Modem

France Telecom also runs the largest Internet service provider in France, called Wanadoo, with 36 percent of the French market, providing both dial-up service and an unlimited high-speed Internet access via your phone line on something called an ADSL modem.

Wanadoo offers a number of options ranging from three to thirty hours of on-line time per month. Forfait libre @ccès, for example, gives you twenty hours of surf time per month to up to three ISP numbers. Malicio Nuit allows you to surf between 10:00 P.M. and 8:00 A.M. for half price.

The ADSL high-speed solution comes in a "Pack Modem" and activation may take up to a week. You are obliged to purchase the modem for around 150 euros and then are billed a monthly fee for access to the tune of about 45 euros a month. With this service you get up to five E-mail addresses, 24/7 customer support, and 30 minutes of telephone support. Many people swear that France Telecom's ADSL is the best high-speed option available in France today.

For further information on France Telecom's services, including Wanadoo and Orange, you can pick up their English language brochure at any of the forty offices in Paris (or dozens in the *banlieues*) or call the *Numéro Vert* at 08–00–36–47–75 for English-speaking customer service. For more information, connect to www.paris.francetelecom.fr/anglo.

Other Providers

In competition with France Telecom's high-speed phone lines, NOOS (formerly Lyonnais des Eaux) offers high-speed Internet, television, and telephone cable connections for businesses and individuals in Paris. To contact NOOS, call 08–00–11–41–14. There are others, like UBC, which provides a cable service called CHELLO, but many people have complained about the lack of or lousy customer service.

The Post Office *(La Poste)*

Although the French postal service has been rated tenth among those of the twelve European Union countries, you will probably be both impressed and frustrated by your experiences concerning the mail. One of the latest public relations slogans for *La Poste* was *"Pas de problème."* First, you will have to get used to longer lines than you're probably accustomed to. The French post office performs so many functions that sending a simple letter sometimes gets caught in the shuffle of all the rest. *La Poste* handles long-distance telephone calls, telegrams, an express-mail system called *Chronopost,* the entire array of letter and package possibilities, plus numerous financial and banking services such as savings accounts, money market investments, cable or wire transfers of funds, payment of telephone bills, distribution of major mail-order catalogues, retirement plans, checking accounts, tax consulting, investment plans, housing funds, mortgages, and more. *La Poste* is in direct competition with commercial banks. Of eight windows *(guichets)* open in an average post office, sometimes only two or three will be equipped for sending letters or packages (these windows are marked *Envoi de lettres et paquets* or *Toutes opérations*), but it is becoming much more frequent to have other windows open for more services. If you plan to ask a lot of questions across that awful pane of Plexiglas, don't expect to be treated like a human. You must sound apologetic if you are asking for something unusual like the price of a postcard to Mexico or an extra form for customs. Watch the price display carefully; it's not unknown for postal workers to make mistakes. Clearly mark your letters *par avion* if you want to send them airmail. For small packages and heavy letters, always request service économique. You'll save money and not lose too much time. (This is a service whereby your mail goes by air, but not necessarily on that very day's flight.) Don't expect to borrow tape, paper, string, etc. If you are displeased, don't yell, just ask for the *inspecteur*. You may or may not get to speak to him or her, but it's your only chance at satisfaction short of writing to the ministry for *La Poste*. Some of the older and bigger post offices are being or have been renovated, the very pleasant results including the disappearance of the above-mentioned Plexiglas and the introduction of a take-a-number system, which seems to shorten the wait.

La Poste
Hours: Monday through Friday 8h–19h (8:00 A.M. to 7:00 P.M.),
Saturday 8h–12h (8:00 A.M. to noon)
Don't show up three minutes before closing time. Chances are you won't be allowed in.
The Main Post Office (open twenty-four hours a day, seven days a week)
52 rue du Louvre
75001 Paris
Tel.: 01–40–28–76–00
Métro: Louvre or Etienne Marcel

Postal Products and Services:

Lettres: All letters should be marked *lettre* to ensure that they go first class. Your basic letter in France costs 0,46 euros. It's the same price for letters to all of the European Union countries. *Aérograms* are 0,76 euros for the whole world. The basic ten-gram airmail letter to North America and the Middle East is 0,67 euros. The price for postcards is the same. The French often send postcards in envelopes, a habit that seems bizarre to North Americans. In any case, they usually put the same postage on a postcard as a letter, in that it then goes as fast as a letter. Since postal rates change periodically, it's a good idea, upon arrival, to request a rate sheet from your local post office.

Lettre recommandée sans avis de réception (registered letter without return receipt): The French use this rather expensive means (2,82 euros for up to twenty grams within France) not so much for security as to have proof that a particular letter, document, bill, or administrative measure was executed and received. Post offices tend to be cheap with the forms so you often have to wait to get to the front of the line to fill in your registered letter form (as opposed to having piles of them at a customer service desk). When picking up a registered letter or package (and don't delay too long to collect it—it's not unusual for *La Poste* to be temporarily unable to find things), you must bring (in person) your *avis* (notice) plus picture identification. If you want someone else to fetch it for you, you must file a form ahead of time or send that person with their identification card plus yours (though you will likely still need to sign a form). The post office will hold a registered letter (or package) for only fifteen days, so be careful when leaving town on vacation to have someone pick up your important mail with a *procuration* (signed proxy). Otherwise you will find that registered letters and packages have been returned to the sender, and, in most cases, the post office will not be able to tell you who the sender was. Very annoying.

Lettre recommandée avec accusé de réception (return receipt requested): Use this if you want proof that your letter was in fact received on a certain date. This costs 4,04 euros for up to twenty grams within France. *Note:* There is no such thing as insuring your letters or parcels; however, items sent *recommandé*—if lost, stolen, or damaged—can be reimbursed at up to 115 euros. But you will never meet anyone who has ever collected.

Service économique, formerly, pli non urgent (PNU) (Third class mail): This is cheaper but can be slower, especially for items mailed near the end of the week (PNU items do not travel on weekends). The package will travel by air but not necessarily on the first plane out. The *tarif economique* is designated by its new green sticker. It is advisable for air-mail packages overseas and for sending books.

Colissimo: Packages require more work to send in France than in many other countries. First of all, they need to be packaged in a special wrap, so you are better off just buying the ready-made boxes at the post office. Also first-class letters and small packages are limited to 2 kilos (4.4 pounds). Books and larger packages are limited to 5 kilos (11 pounds). For heavier items you are obliged to take your wares to a special window at the main post office of any arrondissement or the Central Post Office at 52 rue du Louvre in the first arrondissement, Métro Louvre or Etienne Marcel. This post office, it should be noted, is the only twenty-four-hour seven-days-a-week postal facility in Paris. This is useful when you have applications and other materials that need to be postmarked by a particular date. Inquire about special postal sacs for sending books, and *classe économique* for cheaper air-mail service.

Chronopost International: Chronopost is the French post office's express mail service. Letters sent to North America by Chronopost arrive in forty-eight hours, guaranteed. Packages of up to thirty kilos can also be sent by Chronopost. A letter will cost you about 30 euros. Minitel provides information on everything you ever wanted to know about Chronopost—3614 EMS. Items sent via U.S. International Express Mail arrive in France via Chronopost and can be delivered to a post-office box, whereas Federal Express or DHL parcels cannot. Service is valid for 190 countries.

Poste restante: If you find yourself in France without a reliable address, you can always receive mail by having it sent to the post office of your choice marked with your name and *poste restante.* Other options include the American Express Office (11 rue Scribe 75009 Paris; Métro: Opéra; Tel.: 01–47–77–77–07) or Western Union. *Poste restante* costs 0,21 euros for a newspaper, 0,43 euros for other objects.

Distingo: For domestic French mail, this prestamped oversized envelope is designed for express mail up to 250 grams and costs 3,05 euros for small format and 3,80 euros for large format.

Postéclair: The post office offers this fax service. Within France expect to pay 2,30 euros for the first page and 1,98 euros for each additional page. For New York, it's 6,86 euros for the first page and 3,8 euros for each additional page. It's expensive, but at least you always have a way to fax something.

Lexicon

cedex	special post office handling for company mail
la/le destinataire	addressee
l'aérogramme	aerogram
par avion or poste aérienne	airmail
le carnet de timbres	book of ten stamps
le changement d'adresse	change of address
le timbre philatélique	commemorative or collector stamp
le guichet	counter window
la déclaration de douane	customs declaration
la distribution	delivery
la réexpédition	forwarding
la poste restante	general delivery
la réclamation	inquiry, claim (for insurance, etc.)
assuré	insured
le facteur	letter carrier
le courrier	mail
la boîte aux lettres	mailbox
le paquet or le colis	package
le bureau de poste	post office
boîte postale (B.P.)	post-office box
le mandat	money order
l'imprimé	printed matter or a printed form
le récépissé	receipt for official document
une lettre recommandée	registered letter
l'avis de réception	return receipt
sans avis de réception	without return receipt
l'expéditeur	sender
la dimension	size
par express	special delivery
la carte postale	prestamped post card pré-affranchie
le poids	weight
emballage	mailing box

Media

Television

French television has progressively loosened up and expanded over the last five years. Some would argue that the quality has diminished. The arrival of cable and satellite too has changed the face of what's seen on the tube in France. For example, CNN, Sky, BBC, Eurovision, MTV, and other networks are now available. Not so long ago there was no programming before noon so that kids wouldn't be fixed to TV sets. And there were few programs after midnight. This is still true of several of the channels.

There are five French television stations and one subscriber station currently available to Parisian viewers. TF1 is privately owned; France 2 (formerly Antenne 2), which is state-owned, shares much of its programming with France 3 (formerly FR 3), which is also state-owned but more regionally oriented than France 2. The subscriber station, Canal Plus, is on channel 4 and can be viewed only with a decoder that comes with the subscription. Canal Plus is particularly useful for those interested in catching Monday Night Football, World Boxing matches, and NBA play-offs. The films are often worthwhile but more than often B-class. Some daytime programs on Canal Plus are *transmitted en clair* (unscrambled). One of these is the 7:00 or 8:00 A.M. (depending on the season) transmission of Peter Jennings *ABC Nightly News* from the previous evening, subtitled for French viewers. It can be fun to watch your shifting perceptions of American life and media as you live overseas and begin to see the world from a wider, more international perspective.

La Cinquième, channel 5, a highly commercial station, went belly-up a few years back, and, fortunately, has been replaced with a station providing by far the best quality cultural programming in Europe, *Arté. Arté* is a joint venture between France and Germany that includes funding and input from a host of sources. While documentaries are mostly in French and/or German, sometimes you'll find programs in English, Russian, or some other language. Although not watched by too many folks, *Arté* offers the viewer an idea of how television can be used with creative intelligence. M6 is on channel 6 and is harder to *capter* (receive/tune in).

French television programming has lost some of its didactic edge and has taken on some of the worst aspects of American television, such as the taste for violence (American cops in Los Angeles and Miami are rather well known in France). The French viewing public has become increasingly consumer motivated. *Wheel of Fortune* is a favorite. French game shows are derivitive of those of American television of the 1970s, although far more sexist in their blatant objectification of women, not inconsistent with French culture in general.

On subjects that do not have a bearing on French government, French television documentary news can be excellent; cultural reporting is extensive, and panel discussions and interviews are frequent and lively. Subjects are afforded time and people are allowed to speak at length. On the other hand, don't count on any of the channels to bring you tenacious, investigative reporting on politically hot issues. Although there has been traditionally little editorial criticism of the government, a new wave of investigative journalism in France is beginning to emerge, despite what has been a general public tolerance for not knowing. The American fundamental belief that the public has the right to know everything instantly is just beginning to make sense here. And French viewers tend to be critical of the American obsession with news as a commercial product. In defense of French television, it is refreshing to have the prime minister or defense minister, or even Président Chirac, as the guest on the nightly news, live. French politicians are more candid and less packaged, less reduced to sound bites.

Here are a few more notes on the various stations: TF1 has been privately owned for only a handful of years. The programming is solid but a bit conservative.

The news reporting seems a bit less riveted to the government line. Some good films. France 2 is more liberal and more progressive in its programming. It programs many special events, interviews, and cultural happenings. There is an excellent film series on Friday nights in VO *(version originale)*—often in English. This follows Bernard Rapp's literary talk show, *Jamais sans mon livre*, the follow-up to *Apostrophe*, which famed Bernard Pivot gave up in 1991 to initiate his *Bouillon de Culture*. France 3, sharing much of its programming with France 2, adds a lot of regional broadcasts, news, and documentaries, and also does some excellent environmental programming. It has improved substantially in the last few years. France 3 also has a fine film series in VO on Sunday nights. *Canal Plus* shows a lot of films, many of which are second-rate. It also provides a fair amount of American sports coverage otherwise unavailable in France. *Arté* offers high-quality programming. Excellent documentaries with a tendency to focus on twentieth-century German history. Free in France, but available only by cable subscription in Germany. If you're fed up with American TV, this will refresh you. M6 has a lot of entertainment, show biz, and video clips. Some good programming here, despite the lack of promotion and general low visibility.

Cable reaches almost all of Paris now. There are two cable companies exclusively for France. Each town decided whether, first, it would accept cable installations and, second, which company would be awarded the contract. Generally cable costs each user around 25 euros a month plus a one-time *frais de dossier* of 80 euros, the great French catch-all fee to gouge the public. You can argue it, but they'll think you're nuts and won't budge. Some people have opted for the satellite dish *(antenne parabolique)* instead. One place you may contact to receive cable is Canal Cable, at 01–46–48–93–00. There are also TPS (Tel.: 08–99–70–79–07) and Canal Satellite (satellite reception). Noos, which provides internet, television, and telephone service by cable can be reached at 08–00–11–41–14.

Video/TV

If you buy a television or VCR in France, don't forget that you can receive only French channels. A United States or British video player usually will not work with a French set, which is in the SECAM standard. Britain and the rest of Europe use PAL, while North America and Japan use NTSC. Multisystem video players and recorders *(magnétoscopes)* are scarce and expensive, although the prices are coming down. The FNAC carries both a multisystem video and TV. Some North Americans opt for two VCRs and two TV sets. Many multisystems can play only on those NTSC videos recorded in SP (standard play).

French law requires a special annual users tax *(la redevance)* for TV and video owners. Electronics stores were obliged to report all sales to the government, so quick-witted and laissez-faire consumers paid in cash and gave fictitious addresses; although the tax rate has come down some, you will still probably find yourself with around 90 euros to pay each year. Prerecorded video films are readily available but expensive, with few in English. This is changing with DVD format. New video services in Paris are springing up all the time (check the local papers), including a self-pick system developed by Cinébank that functions like an ATM for videos. The FNAC's service stores, found in almost every neighborhood, now offer a service that converts and copies videos from and into all standards; while prices for this used to be prohibitive, they are coming down.

French Radio

A true sign of an integrated newcomer is the mastering of what's on the local radio. To this end, we've compiled an overview of the French radio environment: the major stations, their call numbers, and some popular programming.

In the 1970s French radio bands were strictly controlled. The airwaves were certainly not free. Numerous unofficial pirate stations were hidden around the city. Now most radio broadcasts come from one centralized building complex in the sixteenth arrondissement called the *Maison de la Radio*. When Mitterrand came into power in 1981, radio in France was deregulated.

Scores of little radio stations sprang up at once. Many represented ethnic groups, alternative attitudes, or regions. The result was a glut on the airwaves; it became difficult to pick up clear signals except for those of the huge and powerful commercial radio stations such as RTL, Radio Luxembourg, Radio Monte Carlo, NRJ (pronounced Energy), and a few others. So new rules were clamped on. Things have leveled out now, but the airwaves are packed tight. Radio programming can be quite original in France, and if you are used to having to turn the dial to hear a different style of music, you may be pleasantly surprised to hear—on the same station—a Chopin nocturne followed by John Coltrane followed by Led Zeppelin. It seems that to the French, either quality transcends the bounds of style or the art of the smooth segue is still to be learned.

The irreverent expatriate DJ from New Jersey, Bart Plantenga, whose show *Wreck This Mess* has been heard on the feisty Radio Libertaire, writes: "Paris radio is more open and unpredictable in general than American or British radio. Just spin the dial and one gets an amazing variety of sound. But Paris radio is formatting fast. Their station IDs are very inventive, often better than the music they play. While in America there is lots of talk about nothing, in Paris there is too much talk about significance. The French like to talk about music. That's why you'll hear five minutes of music and then ten minutes of discussion about it. Perhaps that's why jazz is popular."

Black Sifichi, poet, performer, and DJ at Radio Nova, has updated Plantenga's extensive list and included some addresses for on-line radio in France.

Paris's Major FM Radio Stations
(* State-owned radio/national FM radio)
87.8 *France Inter
French variety and cultural chandelier chats (intellectual chats—a three-minute Leon Redbone song commands a fifteen-minute panel discussion). Unadventurous forays into culture Muzak from this state-run station. Worth tuning in for *Là-bas si j'y suis*, an original program in the early afternoon. Also Zoom, from 10:00 to 11:00 A.M. Evenings (after 8:00 P.M.) are given over to French songs and later on to Anglo-Saxon music.

88.2 Génération—Paris Jazz
Shared station playing all kinds of music, rock, jazz, rap, soul, groove, hip-hop, etc.

Decent stuff, depending on the show. Unique dedication to listener call-ins. Best: Rough Cuts, Saturdays, 9:00 to 10:00 P.M.

88.6 France Méditerranée—Soleil
From 6:00 A.M. to 3:00 P.M., modern Arabic songs and music, also French and Mediterranean music, news from Arab countries in French and in Arabic, and BBC news in French. There is film and theater discussion (on Mondays and Fridays at 10:30 A.M.), and time is also given to horsey talk (the races etc.).

89.0 *RFI 1 (Radio France Internationale)
Rather good world news, interviews with musicians, writers, and other leading or emerging lights from all over the planet.

89.4 Radio Libertaire
The Anarchist Federation's Voice Without Master. Eclectic embrace of world's disinherited and disaffected. Some of Paris's best blues, jazz, and alternative information. Interesting: L. Diouf's adopted *Wreck This Mess*, Tuesday, 12:30 to 2:30 P.M.

90.0 TSF
News, politics, general interest, and interviews. Between kitsch and excellent in choice of music.

90.4 Nostalgie
A continual stroll down memory lane. Only oldies. Piaf to Eddy Mitchell. Something like H.G. Wells's *The Time Machine* with hits. Hear your favorite old songs in French.

90.9 Chante France
Similar to its neighbor Chérie, this station plays only music that is sung. Everything in French song from Juliette Greco to Francis Cabrel.

91.3 *Chérie FM
Modern and syrupy French and international tunes, light stuff—"Honey, can you turn on the FM?"—*l'amour toujours l'amour.*

91.7/92.1 *France Musique
Though this state-run station is devoted mainly to classical (Friday night concert at 8:30 P.M. and Sunday mornings at 11:00 A.M.), it wanders into jazz, ethnic, and experimental sounds. Monday through Friday at 6:00 P.M. (also 11:00 P.M. on Friday) two programs devoted to jazz.

92.6 Media Tropical
Truly one of the cream. Joyous black and equatorial music that is eclectic and human. Great creole-juju-mambo-salsa-zulu-ethno-pop-reggae-R&B bubbling stew. Ads aimed at the West Indian populace of Paris and its suburbs—concerts, clubs, restaurants, etc.

93.1 Radio Aligre—Radio Pays
Radio Aligre: multicultural radio, morning literary programs at 8:45, acid jazz around 5:00 P.M.; *Planet Claire* Wednesdays 7:30 to 9:00 P.M., and *Helter Skelter* on Saturday evenings. Radio Pays: pluricultural, into cultural minorities: Breton, Basque, Alsatian, Provençale, Languedocien, etc.

93.5 / 93.9 *France Culture
France Culture (perhaps the only station in the world exclusively concerned with culture) broadcasts serious cultural topics twenty-four hours a day uninterrupted by advertising. Heated debates (everyone talks at once, *bien sûr*), programs on history, music, literature, theater, also special documentaries. Very in-depth. *Les Nuits Magnetiques*, 11:00 P.M. daily!

94.5 Horizon FM
The pop future as seen from the cyber-souls of E.T. fans, Ninja Turtles, and Lara Croft.

94.8 Judaiques FM—Radio J
Rue des Rosiers en direct. Music, culture, and news aimed at Paris's Jewish community.

95.2 Paris 95.2
This is the station that is played in Paris's métro stations. Middle-of-the-road pop.

95.6 Radio Courtoisie
This station is national-Catholic and interview-heavy (and we mean heavy). Extreme right-wing politics.

96 *Skyrock
This giant describes itself as "chewing gum for the ears." Chain-talking DJs vaccinated with phonographic needles whack off crappy, headless recordings programmed by the record companies.

96.4 BFM
A *cocktail d'infos* with stock market updates accompanied by classical music.

96.9 Voltage FM
The Strumpf station. Cheap adolescent techno-music. Sounds like a children's party. Very teeny-bopper-commercial.

97.4 Rire et Chansons
French comedy and joke station. They must have a thousand hours of laugh tracks. Light music leaning toward nostalgia. Another must for the taxi driver stuck in a traffic jam.

97.8 ADO
The hip-hop and rap station! Soul and New Jack, too. Something like WBLS in

New York City. Recently captured a large portion of the radio Nova crowd. Let's talk about grafs, skateboards, streetgear, and poppin'.

98.2 Radio F.G.
The gay and lesbian, techno and house station of Paris. Dance, Dance, Dance. Excellent lineup of DJs. Nightclubbing, fashion, theater, and art information and recommendations. Also daily: *Afternoon House* with emcee Adrian (American) 2:00 to 6:00 P.M. and *Global Techno Magazine* with Jean-Yves Leloup, 7:30 to 9:00 P.M.

98.6 Alfa
Is schmaltzy sentimentality a universal affliction? French with a Portuguese accent.

99 Radio Latina
Solid and adventurous jazz daily like Cecil Taylor compositions actually allowed to stretch and explore. Latin culture (Spain, Portugal, Italy, France) is the specialty. Very up-tempo, percussive, and bright. International news, tourism, and food talk.

99.5 Radio France Maghreb
Traditional and modern Arabic music, news, and chat shows.

99.9 Sport O'FM
Light music, French and international games, culture and politics: the TF1 on the FM dial.

100.3 *NRJ
Energy! This giant boasts five million listeners because of its national presence with ninety transmitters and its fast-food and music taste. A fair selection of pop, house, and rock. Hits, hits, and more hits.

101.1 Radio Classique
Commercial-free, twenty-four-hour-a-day classical music. One exception is the financial news, Monday through Friday 7:00 to 8:30 A.M. Classical, nothing but classical.

100.7 Radio Notre Dame
As you can imagine, a radio station with a very faithful listenership.

101.5 Radio Nova
Everything from rap, love-funk, house-dub to zulu and latino. Easiest station to pop on anytime. Whizzes you around the five continents. Highly seductive DJ, Pikaboo, daily 5:00 to 8:00 P.M. for club and concert info. Also: Black Sifichi's Sub Para Dub, Tuesdays 10:00 to 11:00 p.m. The weekend offers a solid selection of international mixes such as Gilles Peterson's two-hour-long *World Wide*.

101.9 *Fun Radio
Noisy like your worst pinball nightmare on speed. Pop without pulp. Bump without bang. *Note Lovin' Fun*, the most listened-to program on FM, at 6:45 P.M.

102.3 Oui FM
Overrated computer-generated rock format. Trendy guitars and a bit of self-serious rock news.

102.7 *Radio Montmartre—MFM
French popular songs, complete with accordion, cocked beret, baguette, and indispensable string of onions. The ratatouille for the Paris region.

103.1 *RMC
Traditional recipe. Music, news. Sounds like the television. (See RTL)

103.5 *Europe 2
The younger clone of Europe 1.

103.9 *RFM
International variety, rock, golden oldies.

104.3 *RTL
News bulletins on the hour, every hour. The concept here is accessible, popular, and lively—in short, close to millions of hearts nationwide. Inane advertising. Nothing really interesting or surprising.

104.7 *Europe 1
News, soft rock, festival coverage, almanacs, and DJ-hosted variety and entertainment programming. Very informal tone. Not unlike RTL.

105.1 *FIP
Almost nonstop music, no ads; pop, folk, country, classical, exotica, and, above all, jazz (every night *Jazz à FIP* at 7:30) all wonderfully put together on this twenty-five-year-old station. Traffic bulletins for the Paris region and weather. Sexy suave voices given to satire.

105.5 *France Infos—RTL 2
Around-the-clock, state-run, nationwide news. Broadcasts in all French cities, albeit on different frequencies. Almost as up-to-the-minute as a wire service. Good to tune in to for latest headlines and reports, but not for extended listening.

106.3 Fréquence Paris Plurielle
Paris's Afro station: Plays a mix of African, Caribbean, reggae, and black American music with African news. Commercial-free, cultural programs, music, art, items of interest.

106.7 Beur FM
Marrakech sur Seine. Beur FM puts out modern Maghreb music with conversation that switches from French to Arabic. Exotic commercials (marabouts, calling cards, mutton, couscous, etc. . . .), local call-ins, psychotherapy, and community discussion.

107.1 Radio Bleue
All jazz! With no commercials! Tune in, stay cool.

107.5 Africa N°1
Transmitted from Libraville in Gabon: news, music, jazz. Worthwhile tuning into for news (African news of course).

For news and information in English, you can tune into a range of international English-language news services, each with its particular ideology. One American professor in Paris used to claim that there was only one way to learn what's really happening in the world: listen to BBC World Service, Voice of America, Radio Tirana (Albania) English Service, and Radio Moscow English Service, and average them out. With the new evolution of the world political order, this system needs revamping. In any case it's both revealing and amusing tuning into alternative sources of information. To get the BBC World Service, you need to be able to receive shortwave. The frequency moves around depending on the time of day but from 7:00 A.M. to 9:00 P.M. you'll most likely find it at 12095 KHz. It's always a pleasure hearing the hour strike on Big Ben and then hearing the world news from London. BBC Radio 4, serving mostly the northwest part of France, is found on long wave 198 KHz; BBC Europe is on middle wave 648 KHz. To receive BBC Worldwide program (BBC's international news), write or phone BBC Bush House, PO Box 769, Strand, London WC2B 4PH UK; Tel.: (00) 44–71–257–2211. The Paris office does not field inquiries.

A selection of French stations can also be listened to live and direct via the Internet if you're on-line. Most stations use RealTime Audio, which you can download free of charge.

We recommend that you start your audio visit with the Radio France site: It will save a lot of time as they have five stations in one address!

*Radio France (National)	www.radio-france.fr
*Chérie FM (National)	www.cherie.fm
*Europe 1 (National)	www.europe1.fr
*Europe 2 (National)	www.europe2.fr
France Culture (National)	www.radio-france.fr
*France Info (National)	www.radio-france.fr
*France Inter (National)	www.radio-france.fr
*Fun Radio (National)	www.funradio.fr
*Le Mouv' (National)	www.lemouv.radio-france.fr
*NRJ (National)	www.nrj.fr
*Radio Campus (Lille)	www-radio-campus.univ-lille1.fr
*Radio FG (Paris)	www.radiofg.com
Radio Latina (Paris)	www.latina.fr
*Radio Nova (Paris)	www.novaplanet.com
RTL (National)	www.rtlradio.com
*BFM (Paris)	www.radiobfm.com
*Radio in English	www.radioinenglish.com

* Can be heard live and direct with RealTime Audio

The following are the long-wave and middle-wave stations that can be heard in Paris.

162	kHz	France Inter
183	kHz	Europe 1
216	kHz	RMC
234	kHz	RTL
738	kHz	RFI 2
864	kHz	Radio Bleue
963	kHz	Radio Sorbonne
1467	kHz	RMC–TWR
6175	kHz	RFI

English-Language Radio

RadioInEnglish is "FM Radio, Web community and cool events" for English speakers in Paris. Radio fiend William Stearns has coordinated a balance of music, news, and announcements for the international community of Paris, in English. Interviews with colorful locals and world-class artists. He promises "a good dose of drop-dead fun." The station, which is housed at an existing French FM station, publishes its new and evolving program at www.radioinenglish.com.

The Press

Dailies

For a foreign city, Paris has a healthy variety of permanently self-rejuvenating English-language publications, and of course a complete foreign press corps of correspondents. All the major press organizations, publications, and networks represented in Paris are listed in an excellent publication called *Média-Sid* put out by the offices of the prime minister. It can be ordered for 20 euros from La Documentation française, 29 quai Voltaire, 75344 Paris Cedex 7, Tel.: 01–40–15–70–70. Here is a descriptive listing of what's being published regularly here in English:

International Herald Tribune: Daily newspaper written and compiled by local staff with much content from its owners, the *New York Times* and *Washington Post,* or occasionally with content from other American leading papers, published six days a week in eleven printing plants, catering primarily to the international business community in 181 countries; 1,50 euros at the kiosk. A special three-month subscription for students or teachers in France is available. Call to inquire.

Special daily features in addition to regular features include:

Monday: Technology, sports, international recruitment.

Tuesday: International stock markets, fashion.

Wednesday: Media, performing arts reviews and features.

Thursday: Health and science.

Friday: Leisure section, film reviews, travel.

Saturday/Sunday (combined issue): Economic scene with The Money Report, Fine Arts, featuring Souren Melikian's articles.

International Herald Tribune
6 bis rue des Graviers
92521 Neuilly sur Seine Cedex
Tel.: 01–41–43–93–00, Fax: 01–41–43–92–10
Web site: www.iht.com
Editor: David Ignatius
Managing Editor: Robert McCartney

The Financial Times is a London-based international financial paper, many of whose European commercial and editorial activities are carried out in its Paris office. Extensive international coverage. Excellent cultural pages on the weekend.
The Financial Times
40 rue Boétie
75008 Paris
Tel.: 01–53–76–82–50 (commercial), 01–53–76–82–56 (editorial)
Fax: 01–53–76–82–53
Web site: www.ft.com
Manager: Ben Keeley

Wall Street Journal Europe, published daily out of Brussels, specializes in financial and economic news with a focus on European news and money markets.
Wall Street Journal Europe
3 rue du Faubourg Saint-Honoré
75008 Paris
Tel.: 01–40–17–18–19, Fax: 01–42–23–96–13

USA Today: The international edition is coordinated in London. This four-color daily brings American news, sports, and events to Europe. No Paris editorial office.
USA Today International
17 rue Tronchet
75008 Paris
Tel.: 01–42–66–08–61, Fax: 01–42–66–08–74

Free Press

Paris Voice: This monthly community-oriented free newspaper has a circulation of 50,000-plus. Cultural news, features, and local color. Published since the late 1970s by community leader, blues guitarist, and professor of photography Bob Bishop. Inexpensive and effective classified advertising.
Paris Voice
7 rue Papillon
75009 Paris
Tel.: 01–47–70–45–05
Fax: 01–47–70–47–72
E-mail: parisvoice@easynet.fr
Editor/Publisher: Bob Bishop
Web site: www.parisvoice.com

Time Out publishes a quarterly magazine of Paris information, events, and addresses.

Time Out
100 rue du Faubourg Saint-Antoine
75012 Paris
Tel.: 01–44–87–00–45
Fax: 01–44–73–90–60
E-mail: timeoutp@francenet.fr
Managing Director: Karen Albrecht

Where Paris publishes a monthly magazine distributed in some 50,000 of Paris's best hotel rooms. Topical articles and well-researched dining and entertainment listings.

Where Paris
13 rue Royale
75008 Paris
Tel.: 01-43-12–56–56
Fax: 01-43-12–56–57
Publisher: Kay Rolland
Editor: Amy Serafin

France-USA Contacts (FUSAC): A thick and ubiquitous semimonthly publication of display and classified advertisements and useful tips targeted at the English-language community. The ads reflect the commercial anglophone presence in Paris.

France-USA Contacts (FUSAC)
26 rue Bénard
75014 Paris
Tel.: 01–56–53–54–54
Fax: 01–56–53–54–55
Métro: Pernety
Editor: John Vanden Bos

Irish Eyes. This monthly magazine focuses on the Irish community in France and its commercial and cultural activities.

Irish Eyes
2 rue Laitières
94300 Vincennes
Tel.: 01–41–74–93–03
Fax: 01–41–74–94–67
Editor: Hilary Staunton

Publications/Newsletters

Paris organizations and clubs often publish newsletters for their members and the public. Here are some that could be helpful to newcomers. (For full addresses and phone numbers, see the Anglo-American Clubs and Organizations chapter.)

AAWE (Association of American Wives of Europeans)
American Chamber of Commerce

AWG (American Women's Group)
BCWA (British and Commonwealth Women's Association)
France-Amérique
Franco-British Chamber of Commerce and Industry
Message Mother Support Group
PAN (Paris Alumni Network)
WICE (Continuing Education organization and classes)

Literary and Art Journals

See the Arts and Culture in Paris chapter.

Other English-language Press Represented in France

W.H. Smith and Brentano's are good sources for purchasing English and American magazines and newspapers. (See the discussion on bookstores in the Arts and Culture in Paris chapter).

For a list of English-language radio, TV stations, and print press represented in France, consult www.paris-anglo.com.

Computers in Paris

Not long ago, lugging your Mac or PC to Paris posed all sorts of practical and technical hassles. First there was the obvious drag of carting cumbersome cartons through airports and train stations, not to mention the concern about customs. Then there was the obstacle posed by the different electric current, requiring bulky transformer hookups. Almost all of these problems have been cleared up.

Almost all new computers today are made with built-in auto-switching electrical currents, so that with a simple adapter plug you can plug your computer into any electrical socket in Europe, Japan, or North America. Make sure, though, that your computer has this before you plug in and fry your machine. One American writer inquired at his Apple outlet in Boston before coming to Paris and was informed that he could just plug his Mac into any French wall. False information, and he had to find a friend flying back to the States to carry the computer back for repair. So check this out thoroughly.

If your computer—or answering machine, or fax machine, etc.—is not equipped for 220 volts/50 cycle electricity, do not sweat. Just march over to the basement of the BHV (Métro: Hôtel de Ville) or another store that carries transformers and adapter plugs and buy a transformer to convert the 220 volts to the 110 volts that your machine requires. Then turn it on.

Another major computer dilemma in the past has been the huge gap in prices between France and the United States. American prices have been radically lower for both computers and software. Recently the gap has closed considerably for hardware, to the point where it no longer makes sense to buy a computer in the United States to carry to France, let alone a printer. Software, however, continues to be cheaper in the United States. French distributors have a smaller market and are faced with the costly need to localize the product, translate the program, and complete the process of Frenchification of the application. As a result, software in the United States may be as little as 30 percent of the cost in France. One American computer programmer in Paris admitted that he often orders software from the United States with a credit card, has it sent to an American address, and then forwarded to him in Paris via Federal Express, declared as a NCV (No Commerical Value) Document. This is a dollar-savings subterfuge that circumvents the trade restrictions on products licensed to irate French distributors, who have paid hefty sums for exclusive rights.

There are many Apple dealers *(concessionnaires)* in the Paris area and loads of PC outlets. Most sales contracts entitle the owner of a computer to international guarantees and service from approved dealers worldwide. For Apple computer technical service, call 08–03–08–96–59; for commercial service, dial 08–03–08–60–88. Or visit the Web site, www.apple.fr. In France, like in most places, the Mac/PC dichotomy is pretty much the same: 95 percent PC and 5 percent Mac, but if you eliminate professional and industrial users, accountants, banks, etc., the split is nearly fifty-fifty. The creative world, however—artists, designers, publishers, journalists, advertising agencies, etc—is heavily invested in Apple computers. If you hope to rely on a local computer *concessionnaire* for service, it's a good idea to become a paying client. The dealers most open to anglophone customers advertise in the local anglophone publications. They are also more sensitive to your technical questions regarding software in English as opposed to French. Be aware that keyboards on French computers are organized in the AZERTY configuration, not the QWERTY, English configuration. American keyboards can be obtained in Paris, and almost all computers have systems that allow the switching of keyboard systems internally.

Most major software companies have user hotline assistance numbers for products such as Microsoft Word and Excel. Most don't require an identification number indicating when and where you bought the program. Sometimes, however, it's ultimately easier and faster to call a service number in the United States. You can make helpful contacts at the annual Apple Expo at La Défense each September, the largest MacWorld fair in Europe, as well as at the InfoMart, which is a permanent fair held in the CNIT building, also at La Défense.

In general France is highly sensitized to electronics and computerized information transfer, to a great extent due to the Minitel, which has completely revolutionized daily French life and will go down in history as one of the great achievements of the Socialists. You can hook up your computer to your Minitel so that your screen becomes the Minitel screen and then access all the services available on Minitel and download anything you want, converting data into word processing files, and conversing, ordering, and researching on your computer the way you would on a Minitel. Access to the Minitel is now built into many of the Internet provider services. You can also buy/download software that gives your computer access to the Minitel.

Computer Stores

Call around town to find the best place for computer sales and service for your needs. Check the local English-language community press for specials and new services. When you are in the market for a computer, printer, scanner, digital camera, etc., it is generally a good idea to start your search by checking out the choices at the FNAC. The personnel is well informed, the selections are broad, and the prices are about as good as you'll find anywhere in Paris.

FNAC Micro Informatique
71 boulevard St-Germain
75005 Paris
Tel.: 01–44–41–31–56
Hewlett-Packard and IBM Maintenance
Tel.: 01–44–49–02–22

IC International Computers
26 rue Renard
75004 Paris
Tel.: 01–44–78–26–26

Foire Surcouf
139 avenue Daumesnil 75012
Tel.: 01–53–33–20–00
Fax: 01–53–33–21–01
Mail order: 01–53–33–20–61
After sale service: 01–53–33–20–03

Surcouf has become a Paris phenomenon. This computer and office supply bazaar is the largest of its kind in Paris. Stand after stand of the latest technology fills the aisles of this high-tech supermarket. The prices are low for Paris. *Warning:* Don't count on much customer-oriented service. Don't expect to get a human being on the telephone. If you know precisely what you want and know what is a good price for it, you may decide to make your purchase here. But if you're likely to need post-purchase support, think again. www.surcouf.fr.

The Internet

France has continued to lag behind North America and other countries in the number of individuals and businesses with Internet connections. But what started out as a very sluggish beginning for France in the on-line explosion has speeded up as more businesses are understanding and using this communications tool. The irony, of course, is that France was way ahead of other Western nations from a technical point of view, with the introduction of the on-line Minitel and the ubiquitous smart cards *(carte aux puces)*. The Internet's anglo dominance and on-line payment via credit cards have contributed to the French government's hesitancy to open the floodgates, and unless you have an ADSL connection, prices can be very high. French university students are still limited in their access to connected machines at their institutions, although this is changing quickly. The percentage of people in France who own a PC is still below 20 percent, so Internet use is understandably low as well. The removal of barriers between work time and leisure and between the workplace and personal space has been more problematic to the French culture than for North Americans. The French cherish their leisure time, and resent intrusions into it.

E-mailing

(pronounced—and sometimes spelled—in French "le mél")
In terms of number of users, France is still behind the United States and other Internet-advanced countries, but the gap is closing. Use of the Internet is on a sharp rise in France. If it's important for you to access your E-mail or get on-line from Paris, you can do so without excessive problems. The larger hotels have business centers with Internet connections. The city has a handful of cybercafés from where you can send and receive E-mail. (See below.)

On-line traffic is particularly heavy in the late afternoons in Paris and depending on your connection and modem, your experience may be painfully slow.

AOL Customers

Check before leaving home with AOL on how to set the dial-up setting on your computer in Paris. For questions, problems, etc., while in Paris you can visit the AOL Web site (www.france.aol.com) or E-mail them at franceweb@aol.com. You can also call a customer service agent in Paris at 08–26–01–00–16 (Monday through Saturday, 9:00 A.M. to 10:00 P.M.).

(*Note:* The operators will assure you they can speak English but will respond in English only if you are hopeless in French. Expect a 5,34 euros/hour surcharge to your stateside AOL account.)

Compuserve

Set the dial-up setting on your computer to dial in Paris. To check by telephone the local access node, call 03–21–13–49–47. Otherwise, try setting your modem to dial up 01–41–02–03–04 or 01–70–70–01–70.

Lexicon

battery	*la pile*
black and white	*noir et blanc*
bromide/camera ready	*la bromure*
cancel	*annuler*
cartridge	*la cartouche*
character	*le font*
chooser	*le sélecteur*
clock	*l'horloge*
color	*la couleur*
computer	*l'ordinateur*
control panel	*le tableau de bord*
disk	*la disquette*
document	*le fichier*
file	*le dossier*
film	*le typon*
hard drive	*le disque dur*
hide	*masquer*
keyboard	*le clavier*
layout program	*le logiciel de mise en page*

laser	*le laser*
memory	*la mémoire*
modem	*le modem*
mouse	*la souris*
outputting	*le flashage*
plugged in	*branché*
printer	*l'imprimante*
program	*le logiciel*
scanner	*le scanner*
screen	*l'écran*
size	*la taille*
sound	*le son*
spreadsheet	*le tableur*
to copy	*copier*
to cut	*couper*
to find	*chercher*
to format	*formater*
to paste	*coller*
to print	*imprimer*
to save	*sauvegarder*
trash can	*la corbeille*
to turn off	*éteindre*
to turn on	*allumer*
typeface	*la police (de caractères)*
word processing	*traitement de texte*

Access Providers

The number in France has grown to more than 200 Internet access providers, each offering its own dial-up and other business connections. Aside from AOL and Compuserve, the most popular providers are Club-Internet (www.club-internet.fr) and France Telecom's Wanadoo (www.wanadoo.fr), both offering several months of free connections with a subscription. The commercial side of the on-line world changes so frequently that you should double-check with several providers before committing to one. Check with your access provider before traveling to find out if they have an access node in France or how to access your mail. The site www.paris-anglo.com lists Paris access providers.

Cyber Cafés/Web Bars

Web Bars

Paris has its dose of Web bars that could be helpful for travelers wishing to send or download E-mail. Numerous hotels now have business centers that allow you to send and fetch your E-mail and use the Internet for a fee. Here are your cyber café/Web bar choices in Paris. For word processing on Macs or PCs, call ahead.

Web Bar	Telephone Number	Métro
EasyEverything 8 rue Harpe 75005	01–55–42–12–13	St-Michel
EasyEverything 15 rue Rome	01–44–70–76–00	Rome
Cyber Cube 5 rue Mignon 75006	01–53–10–30–50	Odéon
Web Bar 32 rue de Picardie 75003	01–42–72–66–55	Temple, République
Multimèdia 4 rue du 4 Septembre 75002	01–42–60–40–81	Bourse
Café Orbital 13 rue de Médicis 75006	01–43–25–76–77	Odéon
Café Cox 15 rue des Archives 75004	01–42–72–08–00	Hôtel de Ville

Computer and Computer Time Rentals
Consult *Fusac* and the *Paris Voice* for listings.

Working in France

The Work Culture

An astounding number of English-speakers dream of living in Paris, and, after housing, the most troublesome concern in making this a reality is legal employment. The last five years have shown us that when the workplace, especially the high-tech workplace, needs skilled "anglophone" employees, they get them and figure out the legalities after. Hundreds of Web and IT individuals have managed to land good jobs with French firms, start-ups and others, and manage the formalities in a variety of legal and quasi-legal ways. On the whole if you really want to be in Paris, and you're persistent, you'll find work. But it may not be easy, and it might take a while. If you show up without a job, make sure you have budgeted yourself amply to sustain the burdensome days with no income.

The working environment in France is radically different from that in the United States, or the United Kingdom, or, for that matter, Germany or Japan. It takes a good long time to figure out how people think and communicate before they say or do anything. You just have to know. Americans tend to be too direct, bold, and to the point for French employers. The French care more about the individual's ability to integrate, to work well with others, to respect protocol, to grow patiently with the job. In that the French enjoy greater job security, they can concentrate on building long-term structures. They are less in a hurry to make money, although a new breed of young French managers has been influenced by the American model and seems to be attempting to get everything at once. The French understand profit and the accumulation of wealth, but they are less comfortable showing wealth; there is still something vulgar about money in the French mind-set.

The French also prefer to maintain a sense of formality among employees and management, even after having worked many years together. People *vouvoyer* (use the formal *vous* in address) each other for what may seem like forever. Use *vous*.

One American journal editor finally told the printer that he had worked with for seven years that he could *tutoyer* him (use the informal *tu*). Politely the Frenchman agreed, but continued to *vouvoyer* his client for another two years.

Remember, the French are in love with form. Don't be too loud, gregarious, or familiar too quickly. Business is done at a culturally recognized pace. One American metals dealer from Boston was stunned when he took along an experienced translator friend to help him sort out a nasty snag in a deal with the director of a large French importer. The American had one hour to resolve the problem and catch his plane at Charles de Gaulle Airport. The first thirty minutes of the meeting were devoted to chatter about the director's summer house in the Loire, wine, his son's interest in studying in the United States, and other assorted blabber. Only when the director was comfortable and a rapport had been established did the conversation turn to the details of the metal shipment. The director proposed a compromise slightly better than what the American had expected. Everyone shook hands, conversation returned to the Loire for a minute, then proper good-byes were exchanged, and the American made his plane with fifteen minutes to spare. The key was to respect the local cadence. Always wait for the other to start in on the serious stuff. The French, at best, will understand your eagerness and directness because you're Anglo-Saxon, but they will not really like it.

Laws and procedures can always be learned by reading books and hiring professionals. It's the atmosphere in the workplace, the underlying attitudes about life, work, money, etc., that requires personal knowledge and experience.

Getting Help

The following comments were compiled with the consultation of Jean Taquet (qa@jean taquet.com), a French jurist and associate member of the Delaware Bar Association. Paris Inside Out also consulted the Web site of Canadian lawyer and Paris resident Daniel Laprés, www.lapres.net.

France's attraction not only as a place to visit but also as a country in which to live and work continues to mount, especially among English speakers. North Americans especially continue to be drawn by the quality and style of life as well as by Paris's commercial ripeness in certain sectors. Citizens of Britain and Ireland arrive with both the ability to work legally in France and the desire to benefit from its culturally rich environment. As the new Europe continues to develop, more and more companies send their executives and their families to live and work in foreign countries, while, ironically, more and more French businesspeople head to English-speaking countries to gain experience and fortune. Over the last few years, the number of tourists coming to France has increased, and the number of companies relocating executives to France has continued to grow (although many opt for the less-expensive Ireland and eastern Europe). Likewise, there has been a braindrain from France with entrepreneurs and new companies setting up shop elsewhere in Europe. It was recently reported that more than 40,000 French people in the high-tech industry now work in Silicon Valley. There are fewer statistics on the number who have returned following the bottoming out of the dotcom craze.

Being able to work successfully in France requires a certain number of legal steps as well as an understanding of the local work culture. Traditions that once limited mobility in the French workplace have broken down to a certain degree, and a receptivity to new commercial ideas and marketing strategies has increasingly grown. The Internet certainly gave the French workplace a boost for a while, but then dropped off like elsewhere. One lasting effect of the high-tech revolution and the dominance of the United States in the on-line world is that talented young Americans have found it easier to find Paris-based employment than arriving Americans would have in the past—regardless of their legal status in the country.

Economic indicators fluctuate everywhere in the world. At low moments, there is constant talk in France of the *reprise* (economic upturn). This was especially true when official unemployment peaked at 11 percent, accompanied by high prices and relatively stagnant economic growth. Paris streets and métros subsequently began to host not only panhandlers but also the ubiquitous homeless (SDF—*sans domicile fixe*). While the city is still relatively safe, the patches of despair associated with large American cities have encroached on the French capital and especially its outer districts and suburbs. In assessing the economic environment, this is a sign not to be ignored. English speakers tend to be more fortunate in that many sectors of the French economy need to work in English or maintain an English component.

Although a new generation of MBA-driven French professionals either are trying to work differently in France or are opting to work elsewhere, the French traditionally tend to be less mobile in their careers in general; in a tight economy they are even more reluctant to change or to risk. At the moment the financial security of a salary is more important in France than the quest for a raise in pay. Young people in particular feel insecure and threatened by the economic uncertainty of the future. Banks are not lending as they once had, and on the whole it is not the easiest time to launch new entrepreneurial projects. Recent legislation in France reduced the workweek from 39 hours to 35 hours in an attempt to prompt new hirings.

Working in France and the U.S. Embassy

The U.S. Embassy does not intercede with the French authorities on behalf of Americans seeking visa exemptions and work permits. Its publications caution Americans hoping to enter the French labor market that it is very difficult to find employment, either temporary or permanent, in France. To be able to work in France, Americans, except for those in a privileged situation, must have arranged employment approved by the French Ministry of Labor and have obtained a long-stay visa as a worker before entering France.

Americans who disregard the visa requirement and apply in France for a work permit are required to leave the country to obtain the appropriate visa at a French consular office in the United States.

Americans should not come to France in the expectation of being able to find a job and to regularize their status after arrival. These expectations are unlikely to be fulfilled and personal hardship may result. Most foreigners are not eligible for French social security and unemployment benefits. In some cases individuals may have difficulties with the French authorities and may face expulsion.

Since July 1974 there has been a virtual freeze on the employment of nationals of all countries other than nationals of member countries of the European Union.

Unemployment in France has been over the three million mark since 1993, and French laws and regulations governing immigration and employment in France are being enforced with increasing rigor.

A few categories of Americans in France are in a privileged position in regard to employment: bearers of *carte de résident* who have resided in France in that category for ten years; spouses of French citizens; and students who have studied in France two of the preceding years and who have a parent with four years of residence in France. Most Americans, however, do not fall into any of the privileged categories.

The only other Americans who have any chance for full-time employment in France are highly skilled technicians and qualified managerial personnel. Some students can qualify for part-time *au pair* employment, and other students can qualify for part-time or summer employment. There are also some voluntary collective work programs.

The U.S. Embassy has no information on employment opportunities with private firms in France. As a rule American firms with overseas operations keep their American staff to a minimum and the employment of Americans is normally arranged in the United States, not in France. Americans interested in working in France should contact the domestic employment or personnel offices of U.S. firms.

The entire French system has been set up so that the government keeps as much control as possible over who gets the right to become an employee; even the French employer does not have the final say as to who can be hired. Foreigners wishing to work in France must obtain both the authorization to live in France and the authorization to work in France. These two authorizations are issued by different entities. In order for the foreigner's right to work to be even considered by the authorities, the employer must prove that there is no one in France who can do the job in question.

To work legally in France affords you a great amount of social benefits and a national insurance coverage that protects you in case of illness, hospitalization, and, of course, unemployment, whether you're laid off or fired. The law even stipulates that all working people are entitled to five weeks of paid vacation. This coverage—typical in Europe where socialized public services are the rule—is a great provider of security, but is expensive to both the employer and the employee. Large withholdings are retained from your monthly salary by the employer and paid to the state. The employer contributes about 40 percent of your base salary to the state as well. These costs are called the *charges sociales.* They must be paid in all forms of legal employment. Failure to do so leaves both the employee and employer legally vulnerable.

In general working in France could be defined as being "engaged in an activity or task that brings financial compensation on a regular basis." French law addresses five categories of worker, only the first two of which are afforded the right not only to cross the French border but also to enter the French social benefits system; the other three are kept outside the French system even though they remain on French soil. These five are the employee, the self-employed, the expatriate, the creator or representative of a corporation, and the exporter to France.

The employee *(salarié).* An employee works for a company for a monthly salary. Salaries in France are always calculated on a monthly basis. If you are paid as an employee, you do not have the right to invoice someone else for your services. Your employer pays your social charges and you are entitled to numerous legal benefits. It is difficult for a non-EU person to obtain this status unless he is being sought by a company who offers a work contract with a salary of at least 3600 euros per month, or already holds a ten-year *carte de séjour* or *carte de résident* with the right to work. Salaried people receive a monthly *fiche de paie*, or payslip, that details earnings and deductions. Salary is most often deposited directly to your bank account electronically on the day of the month stipulated by contract. Very few people in France are paid regularly by check (checks in France cannot be cashed; they can only be deposited into the account of the person named on the check). When the French government needs to raise more cash, it creates and implements new withholdings from salaries.

The self-employed *(travailleur indépendant)*. A person legally in France with a *carte de séjour* (see Legal and Administrative Matters) can request status as a *travailleur indépendant* (self-employed person). Those in this category are usually writers, translators, consultants, members of professions that don't work permanently for one company, etc. Students are not eligible. Workers with this status must pay monthly sums to the URSSAF (the social security administration for self-employed individuals) or to one of the other agencies *(Caisses)* that administer the *sécurité sociale*. The key is that working people pay into the social security system. Authors, for example, pay into an administration called the AGESSA, musicians pay into the SACEM, artists contribute to the *Maison des Arts*, and journalists pay their charges to the *Syndic des Journalistes*. Most self-employed persons, however, go through URSSAF *(Union pour le Recouvrement des Cotisation de Sécurité Sociale et d'Allocations Familiales)*. The URSSAF fees for the first two years are around 100 euros per trimester; 5.4 percent of your invoiced earnings after that.

URSSAF, 10 rue Faubourg Montmartre, 75009 Paris; Tel.: 01–53–34–75–75, Fax: 01–53–34–75–76. The main address for the entire Paris area is: 3 rue Franklin, 93518 Montreuil Cedex; Tel.: 01–49–20–10–10. You may consult www.parisrp. urssaf.fr for help—in French only. (*Note:* It is not advised to go to URSSAF yourself if you do not speak French or tend to be short of patience.)

Although this may seem like an expensive option in the beginning, it gives you the ability to work legally and benefit from the social insurance coverage offered in France. Also, as a *travailleur indépendant* you'll increase your employment chances in that employers are not obliged to pay the high social charges for employing you nor are they locked into a potentially expensive permanence.

To get paid, you simply bill your client for your services. Your need to include and pay TVA (value added tax) depends on your activity. Inquire with URSSAF or your local tax office.

Nearly every expatriate you meet will have a story on how he or she managed to maneuver through the system. This is particularly true with the self-employed. There are no absolutes when it comes to working in France; you have to get out there and ask questions, supply documents, and ride with the tide. You'll be told one thing one day, another thing the next. Don't despair; give 'em what they want or pick a new strategy. The system is oppressive, but porous.

The expatriate. To qualify as an expatriate worker under French law, you must be employed by a foreign employer for whom you are performing a job in France for a specified, limited time. There must be an existing subsidiary of the company that welcomes the expatriate where he or she will perform the job.

The creator or representative of a corporation. To fall into this category, the business activity in question must be incorporated as such; an entity with bylaws must be created; and shareholders must own the corporation. If the owner of the shares is another corporation—French or foreign—then the owned corporation is a subsidiary. If the owners of the corporation are individuals residing in France, the owned corporation is a normal corporation. Opening a liaison office representing a foreign corporation also requires official registration.

The exporter to France. In this category the goods or services in question are located in a foreign country; they are needed by a French client who will pay to have them come to France; and billing will be made from and payment made to the foreign country.

A Word on Holiday Time

Remember that all employees in France are legally entitled to five weeks of paid vacation. Most people take three or four weeks in the summer and one or two weeks in the winter. This is a right, not a privilege. The new thirty-five-hour work week has had an impact on vacation time; some companies have given employees more days off and maintained the 39 hour week. Others have compromised.

Small businesses and shops usually close for three or four weeks in the summer, usually August. You'll see signs on shop windows indicating the reopening date.

Part-time Student Employment

North American and other foreign students in France can, under certain conditions, obtain a temporary work permit *(autorisation provisoire de travail)* for part-time *(mi-temps)* work during the summer vacation months or during the regular school year. Students at any school that does not provide French social security medical-care coverage of students are not eligible, however. (Such schools include The Alliance Française, the Institut Catholique, and the Sorbonne's Cours de Civilisation Française.)

Part-time work during the school year is limited to a maximum of twenty hours per week, and during the summer vacation, a maximum of thirty-nine hours per week. During the last trimester of each academic year the French government issues instructions governing part-time employment from June 1 of the current year through May 31 of the following year.

The following categories of foreign students can be considered for summer employment if they have completed one year of study in France: students pursuing higher (university) studies; students, sixteen years and older, in secondary and technical schools *(collèges* and *lycées);* and students aged fourteen and fifteen (light work only). Summer work cannot exceed three months and must fall within the time frame of June 1 to October 31, except for a maximum of fifteen days each for the Christmas and Easter holidays. The work period for students aged fourteen and fifteen is limited to one-half of their school vacation time.

Part-time employment during the academic year is restricted to foreign students attending French universities and other institutions of higher learning. A student must submit his or her current card *(carte d'étudiant)* in order to be eligible. Secondary and technical-school students are not eligible.

Temporary work permits are usually given to students who do not have sufficient private resources to pursue their studies. Recipients of grants and those who have sufficient means are not authorized to have temporary work permits. Students wishing to work part-time during the school year must, in addition to the usual documents, submit a letter justifying the need to work as a student.

The part-time work must fall within the academic year. The temporary work permit is valid for three months and may be renewed upon presentation of evidence of continuing studies.

Foreigners attending French universities in Paris should apply at:
Ministère du Travail
Service de la Main d'Oeuvre Etrangère
210 quai Jemappes
75010 Paris
Tel.: 01–44–84–42–86
Hours: 9:30–11:30 A.M. and 1:30–4:30 P.M.
Métro: Pantin.

Along with the documents required, you'll need a letter from an employer stating your name and address, the position or job description, number of hours to be worked, wages, place of work, and length of employment.

You will probably also be required to prove that you are not a French *boursier* (French state scholarship recipient). Pick up a waiver form at CNOUS, 6 rue Jean Calvin, Fifth arrondissement; Métro Censier. Open 1:30–4:00 P.M.

Three-month work permits are also issued to students at CIEE at 1 Place de l'Odéon, 75006 Paris, for the fee of 145 euros. In that regulations and fees are subject to change, it is wise to always verify latest information. Anne-Cécile Menuelle is in charge of the Work in France program there.

The Work in France program has been state-approved since 1990 and is designed to help foreign students work legally while completing their studies in France. To qualify you must be a full-time student with a student card, an international student card (ISIC), and a passport.

The program costs 275 euros and allows you to work in France for up to three months. Students benefit from the CIEE's database of job leads and housing options. Once you locate an available job that interests you, you go to the CIEE office to pick up your work permit.

You can sign up for this program either in Paris upon arrival or at Council offices in the United States or Canada.

Other Situations That May Grant Working Status

A number of situations may—or may not—afford you the right to work in France. Local municipal authorities have considerable discretion, and so what might work for one may fail for another. Here is a short list of conditions that may help give

you the right to work in France (these are not all automatic; you must inquire in each case):
- ✛ marriage to a French national
- ✛ being an accompanying family member of someone eligible to work in France
- ✛ being a short-term transferee from a foreign company with offices in France
- ✛ having a French or French-nationalized child
- ✛ marriage to a British Commonwealth national
- ✛ marriage to an EU national

All the above categories for being in France carry some right to work within one of the legal definitions of work. In order to request the proper title and its concomitant rights, it is crucial to identify, in official terms, the nature of the work to be done in France. We understand that for many of you, work means work, but in France, where categories are made up of subcategories, and subcategories consist of branches, and each branch has its rules and exceptions, work may mean any one of a score of things. Never stop with a simple answer. Search for the next possible question.

Finding Work in France

A nonresident foreigner's prospect of being hired under the first category of worker, as a salaried person, is slim but not impossible. The potential employer must first identify the position to be filled, draft a job description, submit this information to the national unemployment administration, and advertise the position in the newspapers. Only if an appropriate candidate cannot be found in France can outside applications be considered. If a suitable foreign candidate is found, the employer confirms the job offer by writing a letter stating that the employee will be hired on the condition that a residence permit will be granted by the government. This launches the work papers authorization process.

The employer must submit a host of forms in order to process authorization to hire you, including a draft of a limited-period work contract, a promise to pay, a housing questionnaire, a questionnaire regarding specific information about you, and a letter explaining the reason(s) you are being offered the job. These requirements should be taken very seriously. The government can and often does refuse residency to individuals whose salary would be less than 3645 euros per month, which is a substantial salary in France.

If both work and residence in France are authorized, you will be contacted about a medical exam. For this you'll need a copy of your birth certificate, a résumé, and professional references from previous employers.

If you are already in France but do not yet have the right to work, the employer must submit a signed work contract covering at least one year, a promise to pay a required fee, and a housing questionnaire.

In both these instances, the government can reject the application if it deems unemployment too high in the field or region in question, even though the foreigner has been offered the job and is well qualified to perform it. The foreigner has the right to file another request regarding another job. In theory, for positions paying a salary of 3645 euros or more a month as such positions are usually management level, for which foreign recruitment is more common, the law prevents the DDTE administration from issuing a veto.

If you are interested in becoming a self-employed worker in France, be aware that permission to move into France in order to set up as a self-employed individual is rarely if ever granted. It is better to request a research/sabbatical visitor-visa, enter France, prove (at least on paper) that you can run a successful business in France, and then request a change of status.

If you already have legal status in France and want to be self-employed, you must first prove the seriousness of your intentions by showing that you will generate enough revenue to support yourself. At the same time you must determine that the profession you want to practice is not regulated by the French government or one of its semipublic entities. Many positions and professions in France require a specific, professional diploma, such as plumbers, electricians, mechanics, day-care workers, fitness trainers, etc.). Other professions, such as lawyers, CPAs, pharmacists, architects, etc., require by law a "recognition by peers." If there is no specific regulation governing the position or profession in which you are seeking to establish yourself, you can start the process of registering with the French government to become *un travailleur indépendant.* If your profession requires a professional certificate, then you must inquire further into the procedures for obtaining such a certificate. Most foreigners usually find picking another activity less discouraging.

In cases where self-employment is the only legal option for remaining in France but where it is difficult or impossible to fit the related residence-permit requirements, individuals sometimes incorporate in their home country—especially as incorporation is often quite easy in Anglo-Saxon systems—with the intention of doing business in France. This is not the best solution in all instances, however, since obtaining the right to perform the work your corporation has been set up to do may still be difficult or outright illegal in France.

Anyone wishing to set up a business in France should be aware that the French legal system puts salesmen, craftsmen, and farmers in a class of their own for different and sometimes contradictory reasons: While centuries-old traditional French thinking holds that sales/businesspeople are not to be trusted and that the general population must be protected from them, the same thinking highly regards farmers and craftsmen and thus deems them in need of specific legal protection.

Going back to the days of Louis XIV, selling (buying to resell), running an industry (transforming raw materials into salable products), and transporting people/products were activities performed by "unworthy" individuals, who did not have "proper" status (as did aristocrats) or proper education (as did craftsmen). Colbert, Louis XIV's most famous minister, codified these activities in such a way as to set them apart and create extra liability for them. The first and most important of these makes a commerçant (merchant, trader) personally responsible for the debts of a business or company. Second, in a partnership of two or more *commerçants,* creditors can ask that business debts be paid in full by any one of the partners (again, from personal assets if need be). Third, a special court system has been established for *commerçants.* Finally, merchants are required by law to register with the state so that the government knows precisely who is engaged in such activity.

Although modern France has a more positive view of the business world, the rules governing this world have remained just about the same. A special card is required for individuals who run a business that falls within one of the above three categories (salesmen, craftsmen, farmers); managers (*gérants*) of small French corporations; all the partners of an SNC (*Société en Nom Collectif*—i.e., a partnership); and the CEO and senior executives of a SA (*Société anonyme*—larger corporation with seven or more shareholders and a minimum of 38.000 euros of initial capital).

The ten-year *carte de résident* affords a foreigner the right to do business in France without requesting the above-mentioned special card for merchants. But you need one or the other: the ten-year *carte de résident* or the *carte commerçant*. Many foreigners wishing to start a company in France avoid this regulation by simply hiring a French person to become the company's *gérant* (legally responsible person) with either a minority share of the company (often a symbolic one share) or a salary or fee. This applies to EU citizens as well as to those of several other countries as noted in the law (mainly other Western countries and some former French colonies).

There are a number of requirements for a *carte commerçant*. The applicant must:
+ be at least eighteen years of age
+ have no criminal record
+ not have been forbidden to do business by a court decision in France
+ not have another job incompatible with being in business
+ not have filed for bankruptcy in France
+ possess the higher-education degrees required for the proposed business in question
+ possess a certain level of proficiency in the French language, especially as concerns the retail sector

It is generally understood as well that the business must be proved to be sound and profitable enough to sustain the family of the person requesting the card, that the creation of the new business should not produce unfair competition in its area of activity, and that the applicant must be fit for the job of creating and running the business.

Though it is difficult to anticipate official response to some of the more vague criteria regarding the application, it is highly recommended that a detailed business plan be prepared proving that all requirements for the *carte* can be met and leaving as little as possible open to interpretation by the government. Be neat and well organized and you should be fine. Invest in a folder for your papers.

Doing business or forming a company in France is potentially complicated— for assistance, consult as many experienced professionals as you can find and spend as little as possible until you're sure you know how to proceed. Contact the Foreign Commercial Service of the U.S. Embassy at 2 avenue Gabriel, 75382 Paris Cedex 08; Tel.: 01–43–12–23–83, Fax: 01–43–12–21–72 and see what they say. (Note, though, that their commercial library is no longer open to the public.)

Additional information and support can be obtained from the American Chamber of Commerce in France, although their services have been reduced over the past few years. You can contact them via E-mail: amchamfrance@amcham france.org. The chamber publishes a business directory and a newsletter called *Commerce in France.*

For a list of lawyers, see the print directory *Paris Anglophone* on the Web site www.paris-anglo.com. The following North American lawyers are often consulted in the community:

Samuel Okoshken, 51 avenue Montaigne, 75008 Paris; Tel.: 01–44–13–69–50; Fax: 01–45–63–24–96. Has correspondents in the United States.

Stephanie Simonard, 16 avenue Georges V, 75008 Paris; Tel.: 01–53–23–94–20, Fax: 01–40–70–16–08.

Daniel Laprés, 81 rue Faisanderie, 75016 Paris; Tel.: 01–45–04–62–52, Fax: 01–45–44–64–45. Immigration lawyer from Montréal, specialist in North American, European, and Asian international law. E-mail: Lapres@easynet.fr, Web site: www.lapres.net.

John Fredenberger, 109 avenue Henri Martin, 75116 Paris; Tel.: 01–45–04–10–10, Fax: 01–45–04–49–67.

The British Consulate gives these law firms as capable of assisting British citizens:

Wise and Mercer, 203 bis boulevard St-Germain, 75007 Paris; Tel.: 01–42–22–07–94

Herbert Smith & Co., 20 rue Quentin Bauchart, 75008 Paris; Tel.: 01–53–57–70–70

Ask enough questions to make sure the lawyer you have consulted understands your precise needs and your budgetary restrictions. The range of legal advice concerning legal status in France and means of setting up a business in France varies greatly depending on the experience and preference of the lawyer you consult. Find out your options before you commit. And ask for a written estimate (*devis*) before you start. If you have the time and the energy, you can handle many of the administrative procedures yourself (initial searches can be made on the Minitel, etc.). You can also receive free or low-cost legal counsel at your city hall one evening a week. Trade unions and professional organizations also provide legal assistance to their members.

The cost of creating an infrastructure for a business in France is higher than in the United States or United Kingdom, and it is easy to start off with a great idea, lots of energy and enthusiasm, and a bit of money, only to get discouraged fast by the red tape and the cost of retaining a lawyer and accountant. Think this through before you jump into the deep end. For really small businesses, a nonprofit may be a better option. Lawyers and accountants rarely suggest this, but it often makes sense for activities of a cultural, educational, or scientific nature for which distribution of profits is not essential.

There are three types of companies in France, plus the nonprofits.

✦ SARL *(Société à responsabilité limitée)* This is the equivalent of "incorporated" in the United States or "limited" in Britain. It is the easiest to establish and most common corporate structure in France. It requires an initial capitalization of a minimum of 7600 euros, which is deposited at a bank by the shareholders in the name of the company and cannot be touched until the company is officially registered and receives its papers of incorporation (or K-Bis). The company will receive an official number that must appear on its letterhead, along with the amount of the capitalization and the legal address. There must be at least two shareholders *(associés)* but not more than fifty. The legally responsible person for the company is the *gérant*, who, among other legal, administrative, and fiscal responsibilities, must keep the register of the official minutes of the company's meetings of shareholders. The *gérant* must have a *carte de commerçant*, a ten-year *carte de séjour,* or be an EU national. If you don't fit into these categories, you'll have to hire a *gérant* for your company. Lawyers bill from 1500 euros to 3800 euros to set up a SARL.

⚜ SA *(Société anonyme)* is a larger corporation with a minimum capitalization of 38.000 euros. It carries more weight with banks. It must have a least seven shareholders and a board of directors, and more serious accounting and auditing is required annually. Companies with numerous employees often opt for the SA.

⚜ EURL *(Entreprise unipersonnelle à responsabilité limitée)* is essentially a SARL with one shareholder. For an independent or a freelancing individual, this solution may make sense, in that personal assets are free from risk (although banks are increasingly requiring personal guarantees on loans made to EURLs). There are major tax implications on this and other company formations, so careful discussion should precede all decisions to incorporate in France.

⚜ An *association de loi de 1901* is not a company, but a nonprofit organization, created legally for a clearly described reason, usually cultural, artistic, or humanitarian, but not necessarily. The legal, administrative, and fiscal tasks of setting up and running an association are reasonable, although the size and budget of the association determine everything. The American University of Paris is a nonprofit organization with more than 150 employees. An association cannot make profit, but it can buy and sell, hire employees, invest earnings, etc. If your project contributes to the cultural, educational, or scientific life of France, and your intentions don't go further than being able to make the project come alive with an honest salary for yourself and your collaborators, an association is the easiest, cheapest, safest, and least frustrating legal structure available to you in France. On the other hand, an association gains its working capital from its members, and membership by law is open. Members vote. Banks may be less keen on lending capital to associations. If you need major funding and need to maintain a business profile, the association won't do. On the third hand, if you hope to receive subsidies or funding from the Ministry of Culture or one of its organs, you need a nonprofit organization, thus an association.

Your business will need an accountant. In France a certified public accountant is an *expert comptable.* A *comptable* is a simple accountant, and someone who just does the *comptabilité* is a bookkeeper. Companies almost always hire an *expert comptable* (chartered accountant) or a *cabinet d'expert comptable* (accountant firm). Individuals may or may not do so, depending on the size and complexity of their earnings and holdings. If you do set up a business in France, make sure that the accounting side is established from day one. It is imperative that books are kept impeccably according to French accounting principles. There will be no reasoning with an accountant later as to why the books were kept in some other fashion, and he or she will spend countless hours (at 60 to 90 euros an hour) getting every centime to match up with a scrap of paper, receipt, bank statement, invoice. You may have to spend fifteen hundred euros to make fifty euros fit into these books.

So find out how to keep your accounts straight *à la française.* At times, it'll feel like you are working for your accountant. Don't throw anything away and when purchasing goods or services always ask for a receipt *(reçu* or *fiche* or *facture)* in the name of your company and showing the TVA. As of 1992 the French have allowed the recovery of TVA on business-related restaurant bills. You'll need a proper receipt, though; your credit card slip is not an acceptable accounting document in France. The act of recovering *(récouperer)* TVA in general is a national pastime. Although the advantage of working *au noire* (under the table) or undeclared *(non-declaré)* or buying something without a *facture* is the TVA savings (19.6 percent), such practices are highly illegal. A lot of small businesses cheat here, but be forewarned: TVA is serious business in France. Don't ignore it unless you want to end up out of business, facing a severe penalty, and losing your right to live and work in France. And ignorance is no excuse. You're wrong until you can prove yourself right.

Setting Up Your Company in the U.K.

A number of savvy business people in Paris have opted to set up their companies not in France, but in the United Kingdom, which is part of the European Union, but enjoys far less red tape and requires no initial capital. Some of these administratively-based U.K. companies or individuals working from within an incorporated structure carry out their activities in France but invoice from the United Kingdom. Others prefer to register with the Bourse de Commerce in Paris as a *filiale succursale* or *office de representation* in France. When asked why she registered her U.K. company in France, one American businesswoman replied, "I like to sleep well."

David Adams specializes in helping to set up companies in the United Kingdom and provides a full service, including hosting and British accounting. Savings are great. The company gets set up quickly. The tax and charges may be lower. An interesting alternative.

To contact Adams, Tel.: 01–41–09–15–97, Fax: 01–41–15–04–47. E-mail: Company-Formation@wanadoo.fr.

Foreign Affairs Ltd.

One excellent example of a Paris-based business that initially incorporated in the U.K. is the small but dynamic company, Foreign Affairs, Ltd., which specializes in assisting other companies and individuals to work better in France. Foreign Affairs specializes in public relations, marketing, and community business consulting. With considerable savings and a lot less hassle, Foreign Affairs incorporated in England and is registered to do business in France. With more than 18 years of experience in consulting on business projects in Paris, France, and the European scene, the Foreign Affairs, Ltd. team has helped plan projects, presentations, parties, and press packets; draft documents and contracts; and conduct marketing studies and campaigns. The company practices what it preaches.

Foreign Affairs, Ltd.
3 passage de la Vierge
75007 Paris
Tel.: 06–16–40–55–93
Fax: 33–01–44–18–03–20
foreignaffairs@wanadoo.fr

Understanding French Taxes

U.S. citizens can earn up to $75,000 of tax-free, foreign income. Whether you earned money or not in France, you are obliged to file a U.S. tax return. Forms are available at the U.S. Consulate, 2 rue Saint-Florentin, 75001 Paris. U.S. citizens residing in France are automatically granted a filing extension from April 15 to June 15.

Here's a quick overview of French taxes *(impôts)* and fees.

+ IS *(impôt société):* Corporate tax based on profit.

+ *Impôt sur le revenu* (income tax): Tax returns are due each year usually in February or March, on a date announced by the government. Estimated payments may be made on an annual, quarterly, or monthly basis. For an average salary, income tax represents the equivalent of about one month's pay.

+ TVA *(Taxe sur la valeur ajoutée*—Value-added tax): This is a built-in sales tax of 19.6 percent (it was 20.9 percent!) on most goods and services; 33 percent on luxury items; and 5.5 percent on books. (There is talk of creating a Europe-wide 15 percent TVA.) Although referred to as a sales tax, properly speaking it is not, because it is built into the price of products and services. The TVA is France's greatest source of revenue. Nearly everything bought or sold includes TVA, regardless of the type of product or service or the sector of activity. From the beginning to the end of the chain, it is involved in the transaction. For businesses this is considered a painless tax, since it does not affect profit and the consumer (who usually cannot deduct it) ultimately bears its burden.

+ CSG *(Contribution sociale généralisée):* These two taxes (one of 2.4 percent of gross income and not deductible, the other of 5.10 percent and deductible) are used to help the government maintain the burden of its social services.

+ CRDS *(Contribution à la réduction de la dette sociale):* This tax of 0.50 percent of gross income has the same purpose as the CSG.

+ *Taxe foncière* (property tax): This annual tax on the value of land and housing is paid by the owner.

+ *Taxe professionnelle* (professional tax): Based on square-meter surface space being used for professional purposes, this tax is levied on all businesses for the right to conduct business.

+ *Taxe d'habitation* (or *impôts locaux*—a housing tax): This annual local tax on housing is payable by whoever lives in the property in question, the owner or the tenant.

+ *Rédevance* (television tax): This is an annual user's fee for the right to view public television, which attempts to limit the invasiveness of advertising—so the theory goes. The store that you buy the TV from is required by law to report the purchase.

French tax authorities break down government spending of every 1000 euros in this way:

224 euros	education/professional training/culture/research
151 euros	defense
132 euros	social programs/health/employment/housing
116 euros	municipal and regional aid

109 euros	interest on the public debt
109 euros	security and judicial system
105 euros	economic initiatives
54 euros	France's contribution to the EU budget

The Ministries of the Economy and Budget offer a line of Minitel services concerning finance matters:

3615 Finances: taxes, fees, customs, prices, statistics.

3615 Irservice: a program to calculate your taxes.

3614 Consom: consumer protection information.

3517 Sirene: instantaneous identification of all companies in France.

3617 Verif: a quick way of checking up on the profile of companies in France.

3614 Infogreffe: a quick way of consulting the legal registration, capital, and officials of companies in France and ordering copies of their KBIS (papers of incorporation).

Tax Accountants and Consultants in Paris

Recent changes in American and French tax legislation and the signing of a U.S.–French tax treaty and protocol have prompted requests for the names of tax consultants and accountants. A list is available on www.paris-anglo.com. French law restricts lawyers from advertising and self-promoting. Here are a few of the larger firms. There are lots of smaller ones for expatriates, specializing in employment issues.

International Accounting Firms

Arthur Andersen et Associés, 41 rue Ybry, 92576 Neuilly-sur-Seine Cedex; Tel.: 01–55–61–06–06, Fax: 01–55–61–09–09

Deloitte et Touche, 185 avenue Charles de Gaulle, 92200 Neuilly-sur-Seine; Tel.: 01–40–88–28–00, Fax: 01–40–88–28–28

HSD Ernst and Young, 4 rue Auber, 75009 Paris, Tel.: 01–53–05–85–00

KPMG Peat Marwick, 53 avenue Montaigne, Third Floor, 75008 Paris, Tel.: 01–45–63–15–40, Fax: 01–45–61–09–25

Price Waterhouse Cooper, 34 Place des Corolles, 92908 Paris La Défense 2; Tel.: 01–56–57–58–59, Fax: 01–56–57–57–57

Tax Consultants

Van Ham, Richard CPA, 74 avenue Marceau, 75008 Paris; Tel.: 01–47–23–89–12, Fax: 01–47–20–15–07. When it comes to taxes, Van Ham is the star of the Anglo-American community. Don't wait until the last minute to contact him; he's highly solicited.

De Saxce, Frank T. CPA, 103 avenue Emile Zola, 75015 Paris; Tel.: 01–45–77–58–54, Fax: 01–45–79–70–99

Fredenberger, John C., 109 avenue Henri Martin, 75116 Paris; Tel.: 01–45–04–10–10, Fax: 01–45–04–49–67

Okoshken, Samuel H., 51 avenue Montaigne, 75008 Paris; Tel.: 01–44–13–69–50, Fax: 01–45–63–24–96
Porter and Dunham, 5 rue Cambon, 75001 Paris; Tel.: 01–42–61–55–77, Fax: 01–42–86–94–07
Reuter, Norman, 119 rue Lille, 75007 Paris; Tel.: 01–47–05–01–52
Simonard, Stéphanie, and Charpentier, Paula, 16 avenue George V, 75008 Paris; Tel.: 01–53–23–94–20, Fax: 01–40–70–16–08

International Tax and Investment Portfolio Specialist

Geoff Heywood, Senior Partner Cabinet Heywood International Advisers on Tax and Investment, Economist, U.K. Chartered Accountant and also Management Accountant. Specialist in international tax planning and investment. Member of the French CNPP Compagnie Nationale des Professionnels du Patrimonie. Writer of the book *Investment and Tax in France 2002—The Foreigner's Guide to French Investments, Real Estate Tax Incentives, Reduction of French Taxes.*

Tel.: 01–42–25–65–78, Fax: 0–42–25–65–91; Web site: www.cabinethey wood.com; E-mail: gheyw37141@aol.com

If you are incorporated outside of France, the United Kingdom, Ireland, Luxembourg, or the United States, you'll want to have an accountant who knows the ropes on all sides. Paris-based British Chartered accountant Brian Chancellor is also a French *commissaire aux comptes and expert comptable*. 132 rue Longchamps, 75016 Paris. Tel.: 01–47–04–10–73. E-mail: chancell@club-internet.fr.

Applying for Jobs

Your résumé (*curriculum vitae*, CV) should always be neatly typed, but your cover letter must be handwritten. The French place great importance on the handwriting of a candidate, believing that it reflects and reveals all sorts of information about the character of the applicant (stability, reliability, adaptability, etc.). It is preferable to use black ink, leave correct margins, not change styles midletter, and sign in a natural and full manner. French companies regularly hire or consult graphologists to submit reports on applicants, based on the cover letter or writing samples. Graphologists take into account cultural and educational factors in handwriting. Americans, for example, tend to have legible signatures, whereas the French sign in a hurried way that leaves a mark or symbol, but is rarely readable.

At an interview the trick is to tout one's achievements without showing off, to volunteer very little about oneself but to be prepared to answer very nosy questions—including those that would be illegal in the United States (but are completely acceptable in France). Such questions might include: "Do you intend to marry or have a child soon?" "How long have you been living together?" "Where do you stand on such-and-such a moral issue?" "Do you have a problem working in a department where there are only female employees?" Given this and other differences (choice of clothing, general protocol, etc.), Anglo-Saxons often seek training or at least informal advice before setting off on a series of interviews.

A job offer and acceptance of it is official only when noted in an agreement signed by both the employer and the employee. The specifics of such an agreement (hours, salary, etc.) are dictated by law or by the covenant of the professional or trade group in question *(convention collective).* Very little modification of the agreement is possible: There can be no salary increase or decrease, no major change of work location, no major change in the tasks to be performed, etc. The trial period may be for of one or three months, depending on which the employer offers, and it can be extended only once.

Keeping the Workplace Legal and Safe

Employee rights and workplace safety are monitored by a corps of inspectors from *l'Inspection du travail.* These individuals are in many ways the equivalent of police inspectors. They have the authority to check anyone on the work site in order to, for instance, determine whether they have been declared to the social security administration. They also have the power to shut down factories, offices, shops, and warehouses if they find violations of safety regulations. Although they are also empowered to advise employees on the legality of specific workplace situations, they are often quite backed up with cases and thus might be less accessible for minor matters. But they should be warned of any major illegal conduct by an employer. The *inspecteur du travail* may take a passive or at best neutral position regarding employment conflicts, preferring to maintain workplace stability and not get his office caught in battles between management and labor unions.

The Dismissal Process

There are only a limited number of grounds on which an employee can be dismissed, and the dismissal must follow a strict procedure. The first step is a written request by the employer for a meeting about the situation in question. If this occurs, get yourself informed quickly. At the meeting that follows, the employee can be accompanied by a coworker or union representative. The dismissal must be in the form of a written document containing the legal grounds on which the decision was made as well as a description of the act that led to the dismissal.

The dismissed employee is entitled to severance pay, payment of time worked during the notice period, and accrued vacation pay. There are many nuances here; the application of the law depends on the bylaws of the industry, seniority, age, the conditions of the dismissal, and ability of the affected employee to negotiate.

Layoffs related to the financial situation of the company require government approval. If you've never belonged to a union, you just may decide to do so for the first time.

Teaching

The teaching field in France is largely closed to Americans because teachers in French public secondary schools, and the public universities must be French citizens. At the secondary level the only exceptions are for teaching assistants. Public universities can hire foreigners as visiting professors *(professeurs associés)* or as *maîtres de conférences associés, assistants,* and *lecteurs.* The Franco-American Commission for Educational Exchange in Paris (Fulbright Commission) can provide information on openings for visiting lecturers in France and has a general information sheet on teaching positions in France with useful addresses in both France and the United States. Interested persons may write to Franco-American Commission for Education Exchange, 9 rue Chardin, 75016 Paris; Tel.: 01–45–20–46–54.

A Business Service

Maurice Contal's World Executives is a service that provides newcomers with the expertise to manage French employees and do business with French people. This is done through a one-day course given at client locations or at the chamber of commerce for intercompany seminars. The program includes a short introduction to France, the concept of national cultures, and mental programming. The course includes a study of French management expectations, negotiations, and meetings. Write or call for a brochure. Maurice Contal, World Executives, 13 route du Roi, 78290 Croissy sur Seine; Tel.: 01–39–76–94–04, Fax: 01–39–76–75–63; E-mail: maurice.contal@worldexecutives.com.

A Final Way of Obtaining a Work Permit

The AIPT (Association for International Practical Training) is a private, nonprofit, educational exchange organization that assists with on-the-job training opportunities for professionals and students in a wide variety of fields. Upon completion of the training assignment, the trainee is expected to return to the United States to utilize the skills gained abroad.

Candidates must be at least eighteen years of age at the time of application, and not more than thirty-five. They must have graduated with a degree related to the profession in which they are seeking training. Significant experience in the field may be substituted in the absence of a degree.

AIPT administers two programs of student exchanges and career development exchanges. For the latter, twelve months of previous practical or work experience in the field is usually required, depending on the industry, but a degree in the field may be sufficient.

AIPT requires a working knowledge of the host country's language in most cases, as well as a certificate of good health from a doctor. Inquire about AIPT at

OMI (l'Office des Migrations Internationales)
Mme. Helene Harrari
Service de l'Expatriation
Bureau de Coordination des Offres
44 rue Bargue
75732 Paris Cedex 15
Tel.: 01–53–69–53–29

Unconventional Freelance Ideas

There are many ways to manage working in France even if you do not qualify for any of the legal worker statuses discussed above. You'll have to investigate the legal and administrative nuances for yourself, but these suggestions might help you find a productive way to remain in France.

Stringer: Contact your local or hometown newspaper about sending in articles on aspects of Parisian life.

Representative: Find a company or organization in your home country that might be interested in having a Parisian representative or contact person at no risk and little fixed overhead cost. You could be paid on commission or receive a retainer.

Tourism or commercial officer: Offer to represent your home city, county, or state in France. For example, the city of Omaha, Nebraska, or Newcastle, England, could use you and your address as its Paris address. You could distribute information and promote that city among French tourists and businesses.

Be home while you're away: If you're self-employed you might be able to continue your business with faxes, modems, E-mail, FedEx, etc. (although with some modifications) while you live in Paris.

Write a book and negotiate an advance to hold you over while working on the manuscript in Paris. If a publisher won't advance you, gather the funds from family and friends. You can always pay them back from future royalties.

Lotto: Win. Lotteries can change things.

These jobs require little or no administrative entanglements with the French government. You have an activity, but you do not get paid in France. Of course, neither do you benefit from the labor advantages of working in France. But you're here.

Additional and new ideas are introduced regularly on www.paris-anglo.com.

American write Jeff Berner is currently co-writing a book called *Making a Living in Paris: Your Survival Guide to Launching, Maintaining, and Enjoying an Independent Profession or Business in France.* Check details on www.jeffberner.com.

Studying in France

Being a student in Paris is by far one of the most pleasant ways of spending a year or even six months in the French capital. Undoubtedly, you will learn more out of the classroom than you do in it, and that's part of the reason you've chosen to study abroad. Student life is organized in France differently from what you've been used to, and this, as well, is part of the larger context of learning. Although in a formal sense French universities suffer from the lack of any real campus life, the city itself will become your campus as you learn to make use of the museums and sights, track down the bookstores and movie houses, frequent the theaters and concert halls, and spend long hours talking with a unique mix of international students crowded around café tables.

The adventure comes with its collection of challenges, of course, so be prepared to feel lonely at times, alienated from the culture, linguistically inadequate, homesick, and administratively tortured. This is part of what it means to live outside of your culture. But the peaks by far surpass the valleys. Paris will become a second home for you for life. Guaranteed. First, a little brushing up on the legalities of studying in Paris.

Student Visa Procedures

A student falls into a slightly different category than other foreigners coming to work or reside in France. Non-EU (European Union) students can be in France on either a short- or long-term basis. Nationals of one of the EU countries (with the exception of Spain and Portugal) do not require student visas but must still follow French requirements to obtain the temporary resident permit, or *carte de séjour*. The same regulations apply to nationals from Andora and Switzerland. Spanish and Portuguese students must first solicit a student visa in their home countries and then obtain the *carte de séjour*. If you hold a non-EU passport but you have parents or grandparents who were born in an EU country, you might qualify for a passport from that country. If you do, your legal presence in France is virtually assured.

EU students, as well as Andoran, Austrian, Finnish, Icelandic, Norwegian, Swedish, and Swiss nationals, do not need a visa, but all students except French nationals need a *carte de séjour.*

Most students who are planning to pursue university-level studies in France are required to obtain a student visa (not a tourist visa) before leaving their country of residence. It is not possible to obtain a visa after arriving in France. The French police refuse to "normalize" students who enter France without visas. Once you have arrived in Paris, your university may assist you in completing the necessary formalities that allow you to reside legally in France, although with immigration laws tightening up even sympathetic university administrators may not be able to help.

What Type of Visa Is Necessary?

The type of visa you request depends on two factors: your nationality and the amount of time you plan to spend at a university in France. Since the late 1980s non-EU students intending to study in France for only six months have been issued a six-month or 180-day student visa that enables them to stay in France without obtaining a *carte de séjour.* The visa in itself is the temporary residence permit. However, it must contain this statement: *"le titulaire de ce visa est dispensé de solliciter une"* (or *"le présent visa vaut autorisation de séjour"*). If these magical words are not found somewhere on the visa, you have to follow the *carte de séjour* routine like everybody else. This visa is not granted to all nationalities. Consult your local French Consulate for further information.

If you are applying for at least one year, request a *visa de long séjour pour études.*

How Is the Application Made?

The French consulate nearest you will require the following:

+ A certificate of admission. Most consulates will not issue a visa without a cer-tificate of admission or similar proof of official contact. The visa is valid if you matriculate as a full-time student.
+ A financial guarantee as specified by your consulate. In most countries this will be a letter from your parents or your bank, signed in the presence of a public notary. It will certify that you will have an income of at least 275 euros per month for the duration of your stay in France. The figure is subject to change.
+ A statement proving that your health insurance covers you in France. This is also required for a residence permit and for university registration. (See Health and Insurance).
+ Authorization by a parent or guardian if you are under eighteen years of age.
+ Several photographs as specified by the consulate.
+ Your valid passport (should not expire before the visa does).

In order to avoid unnecessary delays, it is recommended that you write or tele-phone the consulate, requesting exact details concerning the documents required. Since different procedures are in effect for students seeking admission to French universities, if you're attending an American program you must clearly request visa information for study in France *outside the French university system.* Since the time required to issue a visa will vary from consulate to consulate and from country to country, you are urged to apply for your student visa as far in advance of your departure date as possible.

Education: Understanding the French System

Formal education in France begins for many at the age of three months in the state-run *crèches* (nurseries). These tend to be remarkably well-organized and pedagogically sound institutions. Aside from the shared colds and minor illnesses, *crèches* seem to offer only positive factors for French society. Mothers return to their secured jobs, and the kids emerge as well-adjusted individuals. The education of the French palate, too, begins in infancy, as the toddlers begin to be fed a complex menu of everything from filet of sole to calves' brains, artichoke purée to Port Salut cheese. And Evian or Volvic for a beverage.

Between the ages of three and six years, the child can attend the neighborhood *école maternelle* (preschool), which is also state-run and municipally administered.

Instruction at the elementary level, for children six to ten, is the same for all children. It is offered in separate primary schools for boys and girls or in the coeducational schools. Elementary education includes three courses—the preparatory (age six), the elementary course (ages seven and eight), and the intermediate course (ages nine and ten).

French students aged eleven to fourteen are in what is called the first cycle of secondary education, in the sixth, fifth, fourth, and third classes, respectively. For the entire duration of this cycle, the teachers meet periodically for the purpose of determining pupil aptitudes or interests in order to guide the pupils in the type of education best suited to them. At the end of the third level, if the parents follow the advice given, the student automatically enters the recommended section of education. If the parents feel that their child should pursue an education that was not recommended, the child must take an entrance examination.

In the second cycle, for students fifteen to seventeen, pupils are guided according to their aptitudes, their propensities, and their previous work into either one of the short programs, lasting not more than two years, or the long program, which combines vocational training and general education.

Higher education, for students eighteen and older, is offered in private as well as public institutions. The public institutions are of three types: the *facultés* grouped in universities, which are authorized to grant state degrees; the university institutes of technology, designed to train future high-ranking administrators and technicians in industry; and the great scientific and literary institutions for advanced research and study.

Education is compulsory from six to sixteen and is free in state schools. Eighty-three percent of children are in state education; the remainder go to private schools, most of which are run by the Catholic Church. Private education does not carry with it much prestige and can even imply the opposite.

The French educational tradition emphasizes encyclopedic knowledge and memorization. The rigidness of former years, however, has loosened somewhat—great battles, student strikes, and debates over pedagogic issues have played a major roll in the French political climate since 1968. In general all children attend the same kind of state day schools, and the tenacious go on to study for the *baccalauréat*, (*bac* or BAC), which is roughly equivalent to a level of studies one year beyond the American high school diploma This *bac* is a highly important indicator of a student's potential choices in life. At age fifteen or sixteen the more academic children go to a *lycée* (high school) to prepare for the bac, usually taken at age eighteen or nineteen. The *bac* is more of a means to get into a university than a job qualification in itself. Passing the *bac*, however, is essential for access to all upper-level jobs. Failure is a negative status symbol and source of shame in some socially well-placed families.

There are almost a million university students in France. Unlike in the United States, admission to a state-run university is not selective but guaranteed to everyone who has passed the *bac*. Student/teacher ratios are high. There is little personal contact between professors and students, and professors see their jobs as confined to the classroom. The system is centralized, tightly controlled, highly politicized, and ridden by life-sapping internal regulations. The Sorbonne's international reputation stems from the quality of the minds who teach there. The archaic organization of the university, however, might dissuade you for life. On the other hand it might fill you with the sensation of participating in a great and celebrated tradition. Think positive. It has been the focus of many political debates and upheavals in the past two decades.

The French university system is organized into three cycles: the first, second, and third. The first cycle is usually two years, and comprises the DEUG (the first diploma received after two years of study) and the *Licence* (the second diploma awarded after the fourth year). The second cycle, or *maîtrise*, is roughly equivalent to the American master's degree. The third cycle, and clearly the most prestigious in the French system, is the doctoral program, which not long ago offered three different doctoral diplomas. More recently the long and painfully serious *doctorat d'etat* was replaced by the *doctorat d'université*, modeled after the American Ph.D. Prescribed programs are subject to modification with governmental and ministerial changes. For all questions of recognized transferable credits, you must submit a written *dérogation* (appeal) to the university's *Service des équivalences*. Remember to bring not only transcripts but all original diplomas. French universities need to see the stamped document itself.

In 1968, in keeping with the international climate, there were a series of nationwide demonstrations, walkouts, and riots staged by French university students demanding an overhaul of the dated and archaic university system. Since then the scene has relaxed somewhat, and universities have now been split up into smaller, more manageable units. Thus the Sorbonne is now simply a building, beautiful at that, which houses a part of the amorphous Université de Paris system.

A number of programs in Paris run by American colleges include the possibility of study at one of the University of Paris campuses. They can also be contacted directly. A complete list of all universities and schools in France, public and private, is called *Le Guide des Etudes Supérieures*, published by *L'Etudiant* magazine. Another source of information are French consulates around the world, which provide information on specific areas of study in France through their cultural services office.

French Schools

Major Paris Universities

Université de Paris Panthéon Sorbonne—Paris 1
12 Place du Panthéon
75231 Paris Cedex 05
Tel.: 01–44–07–80–00

Université de Paris 2 (Law, Economics, and Social Studies)
12 Place du Panthéon
75231 Paris Cedex 05
Tel.: 01–44–41–57–00

Université de la Sorbonne Nouvelle—Paris 3
17 rue de la Sorbonne
75005 Paris
Tel.: 01–40–46–28–97

Université de Paris-Sorbonne—Paris 4
1 rue Victor Cousin
75230 Paris CEDEX 05
Tel.: 01–40–46–22–11

Université René Descartes—Paris 5
12 rue de l'Ecole de Médecine
75270 Paris Cedex 06
Tel.: 01–40–46–16–16

Université Pierre et Marie Curie—Paris 6
4 Place Jussieu
75230 Paris Cedex 05
Tel.: 01–44–27–44–27

Université de Paris 7
2 Place Jussieu
75251 Paris Cedex 05
Tel.: 01–44–27–44–27

Université de Paris Dauphine—Paris 9
Place du Maréchal-de-Lattre-de-Tassigny
75775 Paris Cedex 16
Tel.: 01–44–05–44–05

Institut National des Langues et Civilisations Orientales
2 rue de Lille
75007 Paris
Tel.: 01–49–26–42–00

Art Schools

Ecole du Louvre
Palais Louvre
75041 Paris Cedex 01
Tel.: 01–55–35–18–00

Ecole Nationale Supérieure des Arts Décoratifs (ENSAD)
31 rue d'Ulm
75005 Paris
Tel.: 01–42–34–97–00

Ecole Nationale Supérieure des Beaux-Arts (Beaux-Arts)
17 quai Malaquais
75272 Paris Cedex 06
Tel.: 01–47–03–50–00

Les Ateliers—Ecole Nationale Supérieure de Création Industrielle
48 rue Saint-Sabin
75011 Paris
Tel.: 01–48–06–56–56

Architecture Schools

Ecole d'architecture Paris—Belleville
78–80 rue de Rebeval
75013 Paris
Tel.: 01–53–38–50–00

Ecole d'architecture Paris—Val de Seine
24 rue Bonaparte
75006 Paris
Tel.: 01–44–07–31–11

Ecole d'architecture Paris—La Villette
144 rue de Flandre
75019 Paris
Tel.: 01–40–36–02–62

Ecole d'architecture Paris—Villemin
11 quai Malaquais
75272 Paris Cedex 06
Tel.: 01–47–03–52–02

Ecole spéciale d'architecture
254 boulevard Raspail
75014 Paris
Tel.: 01–40–47–40–47

Grandes Écoles

The difference between a university and one of the *grandes écoles* is vast. There are about 250 small, autonomous, and elite *grandes écoles*. They train high-level specialists in engineering, applied science, administration, and management studies. The entrance exam for French students requires two or three years' rigorous preparatory study in special post-*bac* classes at the *lycées*. Extremely few foreigners are admitted to the *grandes écoles*. Only 10 percent of the students are women. These schools turn out a high proportion of senior civil servants and industrial and business leaders. One of the most prestigious is the *Ecole Polytechnique*, founded by Napoleon to train engineers for the armed forces. It is still run by the Ministry of Defense and is headed by a general. Other *grandes écoles: Ecole Centrale, Ecole des Hautes Etudes Commerciales,* and *Ecole Nationale d'Administration,* which trains future high-level political types.

L'Institut d'Etudes Politiques (Sciences Po)

More than 800 of the 5,000 students at *L'Institut d'Etudes Politiques de Paris,* or *Sciences Po,* are foreign. You must speak and write French to be admitted. There are several possibilities for courses of study.

Those who already have a master's degree in a related field (political science, economics, history, etc.) can enter the third cycle and obtain a doctorate for further research work in the field or a special diploma *(Diplôme d'Etudes Supérieures Spécialisées)* for preparation for more professional work.

Those who already have three years of university work can enter the second cycle by passing an entrance exam. They receive the *Diplôme de l'Institut* after two years of study.

For students who have completed some university work, such as those on a junior year abroad program, the cycle *d'études internationales* is suitable. It does not lead to a diploma or degree.

The *Certificat d'Etudes Politiques* is a one-year program for international students concentrating on studies of modern France; it prepares those who wish to enter the second cycle.

Further information can be obtained by contacting:
Fondation Nationale des Sciences Politiques
27 rue Saint-Guillaume
75341 Paris Cedex 07
Tel.: 01–45–49–50–50
Fax: 01–42–22–31–26
www.sciences-po.fr

American and English Schools in Paris

The American School of Paris, 41 rue Pasteur, 92210 Saint-Cloud; Tel.: 01–41–12–82–82, Fax: 01–46–02–23–90; headmaster: Dr. Billingsly; enrollment: 940; staff: 100

The American School of Paris, or ASP as the school is more familiarly called, is an independent, nonprofit, accredited day school for boys and girls, from prekindergarten through grade twelve, that offers an American educational program to students of all nationalities (40 percent non-American).

The lower school (grades kindergarten through five) offers an educational program typical of reputable American elementary schools, with emphasis on meeting individual needs. The school has a counselor and teaches English as a foreign language (ESOL). A French language and culture program is included in the curriculum for all students. An extracurricular program of Franco-American activities creates opportunities for older students (grades four and five) to mix with French children.

The middle school offers a program of studies based on an American curriculum. Removed from competition with older students, middle school students are allowed to build relationships among themselves as they prepare for high school. Most school activities are self-contained: Students have their own art, drama, and sports programs. In addition there are frequent class trips and, for seventh and eighth graders, the popular Outward Bound program. The student is the center of teaching and curricular planning. The aim is to provide a varied and challenging educational program that emphasizes academic excellence as well as personal, social, and intellectual growth. While encouraging students to excel, the middle school stresses cooperative behavior and respect for the rights and feelings of others.

The upper school (grades nine through twelve, with an optional thirteenth year) provides a rigorous college preparatory program and extracurricular activities typical of better independent schools in the United States. In addition to a standard American curriculum, the school offers a wide range of advanced-placement courses, an intensive program for non-native English speakers, and the international baccalaureate diploma, permitting entrance to universities worldwide. Eighty percent of any graduating class has taken advanced placement or international baccalaureate courses. Knowledge of French language and culture is stressed, with additional programs in Spanish and German and for francophone students. Facilities include four science laboratories, two gymnasiums, sports fields, a self-service cafeteria, and a 400-seat performing arts center, used for numerous music and drama activities.

Marymount International, 72 boulevard de la Saussaye, 92200 Neuilly-Sur-Seine; Tel.: 01–46–24–10–51, Fax: 01–46–37–07–50.

Marymount School, Paris, accredited by Middle States Association of Colleges and Schools, was founded by the Religious of the Sacred Heart of Mary in 1923. Today it aims to fulfill the needs of elementary school students who will be spending only a few years in France and who wish to maintain continuity with an English-speaking program of education. It is a Catholic, independent school open to boys and girls of all nationalities and religions. It has close ties with other Marymount schools throughout the world.

The students of Marymount range from nursery school through eighth grade, from four to fourteen years old. Math and English classes form the core of the curriculum, along with specialized courses in art, music, science, social studies, computer, physical education, and daily French lessons taught by native-born French teachers. The kindergarten level uses a Montessori approach. There is an English as a second language department, as well as a resource center for children having learning difficulties that cannot be met within the regular classroom. Admission to this class is limited and based upon specific criteria.

Marymount offers a strong after-school activities program set up on a trimester system. It provides opportunities for students to follow interests or needs in the areas of sports, music, drama, dance, karate, and art.

International School of Paris, 6 rue Beethoven, 75016 Paris; Tel.: 01–42–24–09–54, Fax: 01–45–27–15–93; Enrollment: primary school: 154, high school: 225

Founded in 1964, the International School of Paris is a private, coeducational day school, accredited by the European Council on International Schools (ECIS), the New England Association of Schools and Colleges (NEASC), and the French Ministry of the Interior. ISP is a truly international school, with students and staff hailing from thirty-eight countries. It offers an individualized Anglo-American/international curriculum, with instruction in mathematics, the experimental sciences, computing, the social sciences, physical education, the fine arts, and language. Classes comprise twenty or fewer students, and, with the exception of language classes, are all conducted in English. Students who are fluent in English are required to study French language and culture. The program in grades eleven and twelve leads to the prestigious International Baccalaureate (IB) diploma or certificates, or the U.S. high school diploma. Extracurricular activities include drama, soccer, swimming, martial arts, computing, and a Saturday sports club. The school accepts students throughout the school year, provided there is an appropriate space available. Detailed information about the school's facilities, academic program, and bus service is available from the director of admissions.

British School of Paris, 38 quai de l'Ecluse, 78290 Croissy-Sur-Seine; Tel.: 01–34–80–45–94.

Classes at this small coeducational school are taught in English from kindergarten through the equivalent of high school and the first year of college. The academic program emphasizes the French language and prepares the students for entry into preparatory schools and colleges in Great Britain and the United States. The school will arrange for both the General Certificate of Education (advanced and ordinary level) for university entrance and the U.S. college board examination. Bus service is available for the Paris area, and hot lunches are served. Brochures and further information are available at the school.

Bilingual and Transition Schools

Lycée International de Saint-Germain-en-Laye, American Section Proviseur: M. Jean-Pierre Maillard; rue du Fer à Cheval, 78100 Saint-Germain-en-Laye; Tel.: 01–39– 10–94–11 (switchboard); for information on the American section, call 01–34–51–74–85, Fax: 01–39–10–94–04

This *lycée* provides an opportunity for Americans and other foreign children to study in a regular French school and at same time take additional courses in their national language. Foreign children are first given a full year of intensive training in special French classes. They are then ready to join other children of their age group, who are taught twenty-four hours a week in French by French teachers in the normal subjects for a lycée and six to eight hours a week in their own language by teachers from their own country according to national programs in language, literature, history, and culture.

Ecole Active Bilingue, Section Jeannine Manuel (3 addresses), 70 rue du Théâtre, 75015 Paris, Tel.: 01–44–37–00–80; 15 rue Edgar Faure, 75015 Paris, Tel.: 01–44–49–09–43; 141 avenue de Suffren, 75007 Paris, Tel.: 01–47–34–27–72

The Ecole Active Bilingue J.M. is a private coeducational college preparatory day school subsidized by the state and recognized by UNESCO as an "associated school." The aim of the school is to develop bilingualism and biculturalism. In the primary classes, besides the French national program, English is obligatory for all students. It is taught as a foreign language and as a mother tongue. In secondary classes French is the working language and English is taught as a foreign language or a mother tongue by level of proficiency. Science, history, and geography are taught in English or French. The curriculum of students wishing to enter American universities is reinforced by preparation for the college board examinations. Adaption classes for non-French students run parallel with regular French classes, with emphasis on the teaching of French.

The Bilingual Montessori School, 65 Quai d'Orsay, 75007 Paris, Tel.: 01–45–55–13–27; Jardin d'Enfants Montessori, 53 rue Erlanger, 75016 Paris, Tel.: 01–46–51–65–87; 23 avenue George V, 75008 Paris, Tel.: 01–47–20–28–10; info@montessori-paris.com.

The Bilingual Montessori School of Paris was founded twenty years ago as an international, nonprofit, accredited school for children between the ages of two and six. The school allows children to work and develop at their own pace in a stimulating atmosphere that includes music, language, mathematics, geography, science, practical life, history, art, and sensorial activities.

Eurecole (trilingual school), 5 rue de Lübeck, 75116 Paris; Tel.: 01–40–70–12–81

Eurecole, a trilingual European school, opened in September 1989 in the sixteenth arrondissement. Claude Duval, the founder and principal, chose a team of teachers from different European countries to formulate a new pedagogical concept, founded on a balance between sport, art, and study. Each day includes two hours of sports in English, two hours of arts in German, and two hours of study in French for all classes from the nursery (starting at three years) to the seventh grade (nine to ten years). The school offers the possibility of a multilingual and cultural exchange in a specially adapted modern building with a library, gymnasium, and video and computer rooms.

Institut de la Tour, 86 rue de la Tour, 75116 Paris; Tel.: 01–45–04–73–35 Catholic high school. Anglophone section with traditional French education.

Kindergarten and Nursery Schools

United Nations Nursery School *(Jardin d'Enfants des Nations Unies)* 40 rue Pierre-Guérin, 75016 Paris; Tel.: 01–45–27–20–24; ages: two-and-one-half to six years.

The private nursery school was founded in 1951 for the international population of Paris. The program is bilingual. There are preschool activities (prereading, writing, math) as well as music, arts and crafts, and games in a private garden. There are fourteen children per class.

Creche de la Fondation Croix Saint-Simon, 3 rue Oudinot, 75007 Paris; Tel.: 01–43–06–11–16, Fax: 01–47–34–43–88; bilingual nursery school for ages two to six.

The American Kindergarten, 3 bis rue Emile Duclaux, 75015 Paris, Tel.: 01–42–19–02–14; mailing address: 35 avenue de Ségur, 75007 Paris (brochure available).

Since September 1993 The American Kindergarten has been welcoming children of all nationalities from three to five years of age. The class is limited to twenty pupils who are taught by two experienced preschool teachers, both of whom are native English speakers and bilingual in French. In an English-speaking environment, the children learn through play, in activities that stimulate them intellectually, physically, and artistically. They gain self-confidence and independence as well as a sense of responsibility and respect for themselves and others.

La Petite Ecole Bilingue (British), 8 Place Porte de Champerret, 75017 Paris; Tel.: 01–43–80–25–34; from two to six years old (all nationalities).

Rencontres et Echanges (kindergarten and bilingual nursery school), 84 rue de la Folie Mericourt, 75011 Paris, Tel.: 01–53–36–81–10; from eighteen to thirty months.

Les Petits Dragons (international kindergarten), 2 rue Jacquemont, 75017 Paris, Tel.: 01–42–28–56–17; Saint-George's Church, 7 rue Auguste-Vacquerie, 75016 Paris; Tel.: 01–49–52–01–03.

The Lennen Bilingual School, 65 Quai d'Orsay, 75007 Paris, Tel.: 01–47–05–66–55; from two to eight years old. Founded in 1960 as a private kindergarten, the school has continued to fill a growing need for bilingual education. Bilingualism is emphasized and many varied activities are offered—art, music, gym. The teachers are fully qualified with experience in bilingual and international education. There is a French- and English-speaking teacher in each preschool class.

A three-year bilingual primary section has been added covering the first three grades in English and French. The children are prepared to enter French or American school. All the children are given an opportunity to build a strong foundation in both languages. The school accepts children whenever there is space available and offers a summer school as well as vacation programs.

Le Petit Cours, 104 rue Ordener, 75018 Paris, Tel.: 01–46–06–80–33; Enixia, 16 avenue de la Baltique, 91953 Courtaboeuf Cedex, Tel.: 01–64–46–16–58. Bilingual school offering individual approach. Art, theater, sport, science, Chinese, multimedia, nature discovery. For children from two years old.

Art and Music Schools

L'Ecole du Louvre, 34 quai du Louvre, 75001 Paris; Tel.: 01–55–35–18–00.

Ecole Nationale Supérieure des Arts Décoratifs, 31 rue d'Ulm, 75005 Paris; Tel.: 01–42–34–97–00.

Conservatoire National Supérieur de Musique et de Danse de Paris, Parc de la Villette, 209 avenue Jean-Jaurès, 75019 Paris; Tel.: 01–40–40–45–45.

Sources and Other Resources for Students

In the Paris telephone directory the section *"Académie de Paris et Universités de Paris"* contains the address and telephone number of each university's administrative office. For complete information, contact any or all of the following organizations:

Centre National des Oeuvres Universitaires et Scolaires, Service d'Accueil aux Etudiants Etrangers, 69 Quai d'Orsay, 75007 Paris; Tel.: 01–44–18–53–00.

Centre d'Information et de Documentation Jeunesse, 101 quai Branly, 75740 Paris Cedex 15; Métro: Bir-Hakeim; Tel.: 01–44–49–12–00. This national association gives miscellaneous information for young people on subjects such as education, teaching, professional training, employment, sports, and entertainment. It also has a list of French language courses.

Office National d'Information sur les Enseignements et les Professions, 168 boulevard de Montparnasse, 75014 Paris; Tel.: 01–43–35–15–98.

Organisation de Tourisme Universitaire, 39 avenue Georges Bernanos, 75005 Paris; Tel.: 01–44–41–38–50. This is a nonprofit organization established to organize French student travel in France and abroad, and to help foreign students and professors during their stay in France. It offers group tours, accommodations in Paris, and information on summer courses, summer camps, and work camps.

Academic Year Abroad, Reid Hall, 4 rue de Chevreuse, 75006 Paris; Tel.: 01–43–20–91–92. Founded and incorporated in New York in 1961, this organization specializes in planning an academic year abroad for students who are in college or about to enter college. For a fee covering costs, the organization makes all arrangements for tuition, board, and lodging.

Council on International Educational Exchange (CIEE) European Headquarters, 154 boulevard Haussmann, 75008 Paris; Tel.: 01–53–76–04–00.

The principal U.S. organization in study abroad, student work exchanges, voluntary service, and student travel, CIEE is a nonprofit association with more than 220 universities, colleges, and other institutions as members. It promotes international understanding through support services to the academic community. The Paris office oversees activities throughout Europe. Programs in France include University Consortium Study Centers in Paris and Rennes. Specialized study programs for groups of French and European professionals (bankers, teachers, educational officials, social workers, etc.) arranged worldwide, in collaboration with companies, universities, associations, and local and national governments. International faculty seminars for professors and administrators of higher education are also given.

There are summer sessions in most academic disciplines and English language programs (all year) at leading universities, as well as government-authorized work exchanges for bona fide students, and internship opportunities year-round for Americans in France and French in the United States School Partners Abroad provides group exchanges between U.S. and French secondary schools.

Commission Franco Américaine d'Echanges Universitaires, 9 rue Chardin, 75016 Paris; Tel.: 01–44–14–53–60.

This organization administers educational exchanges between the United States and France under the Franco-American Cultural Agreement of 1965 and the Fulbright Program and provides counseling and documentation concerning

French and American universities. The counseling center is open to the public Monday through Friday (except Tuesday) from 9:30 A.M. to 5:00 P.M.

Reid Hall, 4 rue de Chevreuse, 75006 Paris; Tel.: 01–43–20–33–07.

A division of Columbia University and located in a lovely eighteenth-century house, Reid Hall's mission is to foster Franco-American exchanges on the university level. Professors, students, and educational groups become members of Reid Hall, which offers them classroom space, office space, and access to the common rooms and gardens. Many overseas undergraduates and graduate programs are based at Reid Hall, including Columbia University Programs in Paris.

Salon de l'Etudiant

Every year the magazine group *l'Etudiant* organizes a massive trade fair focused on the needs of students. Hundreds of schools and programs set up booths and promote their programs. Wholly worthwhile if you're in the market for a specialized program or if you're looking for a possible teaching job. Contact *l'Etudiant* for details:

L'Etudiant
54 rue Saint André des Arts
75006 Paris
Tel.: 01–43–26–68–16

French Language Schools

Being able to effectively use the French language is probably the single most important tool needed for successfully living in Paris. True, there is so much English heard and used in Paris these days that it's not hard to get by, but you'll miss so much and you'll never feel as if you really belong if you don't at least begin to master conversational French, especially the little words, expressions, and verbal gestures that make drinking in cafés, shopping in the markets, and bantering with new found friends so enriching.

If you come to Paris with only a bit of French and you start taking lessons, be prepared for an ebb and tide of exhilarating sensations followed by utter despair. You'll feel as if you're doing really well, and then around three months into the experience, you'll suddenly feel as if you don't know a thing. This is a sign of real progress. Keep going. Listen. Ask. Repeat. Make mistakes. Jump in head first. As Samuel Beckett always used to say, "Fail better!"

Learning French is the key to truly appreciating Paris. And despite all the headaches, embarrassments, excruciating silences, garbled tenses, and gender mutilations, figuring out how to communicate in French is immensely rewarding—and necessary. Shopkeepers and bureaucrats are friendlier, the complications of life are less overwhelming, and the language offers endless insights into French culture and thinking. Most important, if you speak even a little French, you can start to make French friends, a crucial step toward understanding and enjoying Parisian life.

But how to go about learning French? The most obvious answer is by enrolling in a language school, but it's also possible to meet with a tutor, teach yourself with selfstudy books, or plunge right in by living or working with French people. Of the 13 million foreign visitors each year, more than 100,000 people come to Paris from all over the world each year just to study French, and there are about fifty French language schools, scores of private tutors, and numerous get-togethers that exist solely to help foreigners in Paris become conversant in the local language. The trick is finding out what's best for you. This is especially important for people who need a student visa because they have to register and make a down payment before they even set foot in France.

Because there's so much choice—and because the choice you make will probably influence your whole experience here—it's important to consider all your options carefully. To do this, you have to be realistic. How much French do you have already? How much time and money are you willing to commit to learning French? Are you more interested in spoken, written, or professional French? Do you learn better in groups or on your own? Do you want to achieve perfect French or will French that will just get you around suffice? Would you rather learn by classic schoolroom techniques or through interaction with other people?

This chapter has general information about three of the largest and most well-known language schools: the Alliance Française, the Cours de Civilisation Française located at the Sorbonne, and the French language program at the Institut Catholique de Paris, as well as one smaller school, Accord. The larger schools were chosen because of their size and reputation, while the smaller one was chosen as a sample at random. There's also a section on how to study with a tutor or on your own, and a lengthy but far-from-definitive list of schools that teach French to foreigners.

It's recommended that you check out a number of the schools listed. Although the larger schools often come with a reputation, they also tend to offer big classes, and with careful research, you can probably spend the same amount of money, attend a lesser-known school, and receive a lot more personal attention—or learn with new or unusual teaching tools such as interactive CD ROMs. But be careful: Schools that teach French to foreigners are usually private and completely unregulated by the government, so it's important to check what type of teaching credentials the instructors have and how long the school has existed. (All prices listed are subject to change.)

Alliance Française

For a sound grounding in the basics and a lively, friendly welcome to Paris, the Alliance Française is the institution of choice. Founded in 1883, this private, non-profit teaching organization sprawls between two buildings in the St. Germain neighborhood and is probably the largest French-teaching school in the world. More than 20,000 students attend classes each year in Paris and when you add up their students worldwide, the figure is a whopping 300,000. Many lifelong friendships have been made here and the number of couples that found each other at the Alliance is pleasingly considerable.

Because of its size and solid reputation, many people automatically choose Alliance Française, with good reason. Many of the 135 teachers are excellent, there's a language lab, a 15,000-book library, a housing service, notice boards with job and housing information, organized sight-seeing tours, free conferences on French history and literature, a film society, a restaurant, a welcoming service that matches students with French families for a meal or regular chats, and the cacophonous, exciting atmosphere created by students from 140 countries. As Markovic Aleksandar, a 22-year-old from the former Yugoslavia, says, "The best thing is learning with people from all over the world. I've been studying here for a year and a half, and now I have friends from all the continents."

However, the Alliance's explosive success has its drawbacks. Classes can have as many as twenty-two students and the relatively large class size means there's room for a frustratingly wide range of abilities in a single class. Shy students can be drowned out amid the hubbub. Still, many say the Alliance suits them just fine. Tammy Deacon, a British twenty-one-year-old, is in a class of just fifteen students and has a superb teacher. "We're learning about grammar by talking about it—it's a very good way to learn the grammar and improve your speaking ability at the same time," she says.

Marc Bailly, an Alliance Française administrator, explains that the school's teaching leans toward practical, everyday, spoken French, although advanced classes spend more time on grammar and writing skills. Students say teachers use a variety of teaching methods spanning role-playing and sit-down learning, and homework usually doesn't take more than an hour. In most classes students sit in a circle, and although the teachers keep attendance records, it's no disaster if you miss a few classes. The ambience is relaxed and bantering. Most students are between the ages of eighteen and thirty, and Americans, Japanese, and Germans are the largest nationality groups.

Graduates of Alliance Française repeat one nugget of advice: Not all the teachers are stellar, so keep searching until you find someone that makes you keen to study. The school may balk if you make more than a few changes, but once you've paid it's your right to find a teacher you like. Another important point is that enrollment occurs monthly, which means you'll have new classmates and sometimes a new teacher every four weeks. This is an excellent system for people who are in France for a short period of time or for those who travel frequently, but if you want to study continuously for six months or more, the disruptions can become a nuisance.

Alliance Française
101 boulevard Raspail
75270 Paris Cedex 06
Tel.: 01–42–84–90–00
Fax: 01–42–84–91–00
E-mail: afparis_ecole@compuserve.com
Web site: www.alliancefr.org

The Alliance Française offers a great variety of courses for beginners, intermediates, professionals, French teachers, and others. Placement tests are free and prices for classes vary according to the times and type of course chosen. Contact them for fees.

Cours de Civilisation Française de la Sorbonne

The Sorbonne name and the marbled corridors of the institution itself evoke intensely academic images of devotion to the pursuit of higher knowledge. So it's entirely appropriate that the Cours de Civilisation Française, which is located at the University of Paris-Sorbonne—but not formally connected to the university—has acquired a reputation for rigorous study that includes French culture, literature, and civilization, as well as grammar, phonetics, and writing. "Our specialty is written texts and the history of literature more than conversation," explains Jean-Louis de Boissieu, the assistant director. However, he adds, "We are adding some conversational courses because the students ask for this."

The academic style here is reflected in the enrollment requirements: Students must be at least eighteen, they must have the equivalent of a French *baccalauréat* (a high school diploma), and they usually have to sign up for four-month semesters. The teaching methods are resolutely traditional. Students sit in rows in front of a teacher who writes on the blackboard, there's lots of homework, and grammar and vocabulary tests take place frequently.

Many people, especially those with a university education, thrive in this environment. "The program is very good. It's very thorough, very comprehensive," says Lisa Waldo, a twenty-three-year-old American who studied French in college and is spending a year in Paris perfecting her language skills and working as an *au pair*. But for those who prefer conversational French, this is not the place to be. As Petra Wunderle, a twenty-year-old German student, adds, "The teachers give us excellent explanations, but we don't speak much in class—I don't like that."

Although it's not huge like the Alliance Française, the Cours de Civilisation Française is still large. There are about 120 teachers, about 8,500 students annually, and class sizes vary between fifteen and twenty-five. The average student is university age, twenty-two, and the greatest number of students come from the United States, Japan, and Sweden. As noted earlier, the Cours de Civilisation Française de la Sorbonne is a private, nonprofit program that is located within the famous university but operates independently. However, its sister program, the Centre Experimental d'Etude de la Civilisation Française, which is for graduate-level students, does have a formal connection with the Sorbonne and uses some of their professors.

Besides the regular courses during the university year at the Cours de Civilisation Française, there are also a variety of special summer and winter French courses. Of special interest is the three-month, five-hours-a-day crash course that takes place through July, August, and September. Many foreigners who live here and now work in French swear by this as a swift, sure ticket to fluency.

One final note: The course calendars for the Cours de Civilisation Française are incomprehensible if you don't have any French skills—and confusing even if you do. What's more, some of the secretaries who answer information inquiries over the phone have that haughty, harried Parisian attitude that can make someone with beginner's French feel like hiding under a stone. But if you want first-rate French, don't let these barriers hold you back.

Cours de Civilisation Française de la Sorbonne
47 rue des Ecoles
75005 Paris

Tel.: 01–40–46–22–11, extensions 2664 and 2675
Fax: 01–40–46–32–29
The program here includes a variety of courses, conferences, and seminars. A basic language course runs between ten and fifteen hours a week for four months. Contact them for fees.

L'Institut Catholique

Just up the street but worlds away from the bustle of the Alliance Française is the Institut Catholique de Paris, a private Catholic university with a reputable language program. Within the university lies the Institut de Langue et de Culture Françaises, formed in 1948 with just fifteen students and now educating about 3,000 students a year. The Institut Catholique offers a quiet, serious, but convivial learning atmosphere—a middle ground between the challenges of the Sorbonne and the rough-and-tumble of Alliance Française.

The language program has forty-five teachers and class sizes ranging from eighteen to twenty-five students. The largest group of students here comes from Japan, with Germany and Poland close behind. Director Jean-René Rouquette says that when the program started, most students took classes only six hours a week, but since then the school has changed its approach, following some of the Sorbonne's methods. Now students usually come for a year or a summer and their learning commitment is much deeper.

I sat in on an afternoon class of thirteen very attentive students, mostly Asians, ranging from teenagers to an older woman graciously pushing seventy. The chairs in the small, cozy classroom were arranged in a circle, and the teacher was careful to give everyone a chance to talk. After nearly two hours of solid grammar instruction, with students copying and reciting verb tenses, the rest of the class was devoted to active role-playing and language games.

It was hard to find someone with less-than-glowing reviews of the school. Dalia Yarhi, an Israeli 39-year-old, says, "When I first came to Paris, I went to Alliance Française for three months, but I didn't learn anything. I was in a very big class, and I just couldn't keep up. It was a very bad experience. Then I waited a year, and a French friend who lives here told me this is the best school. I came in July, and I was very happy, and I'm still here." Reem Alhaddad, 25, heard the same superlative assessment of the Institut Catholique from her husband, a cultural attaché at the Kuwaiti embassy. "He told me it was the best school in Paris," she says—and so far, she's had no reason to doubt his judgment.

Institut de Langue et de Culture Françaises
Institut Catholique de Paris
21 rue d'Assas
75270 Paris Cedex 06
Tel.: 01–44–39–52–00
Fax: 01–45–44–27–14
The Institut Catholique has a variety of courses on French language, culture, and civilization, and an intensive summer program. Standard intensive language courses run fifteen hours a week for four months. Contact them for fees.

Accord

Just a hop and skip from the Centre Georges Pompidou are the classrooms of the Accord language school, where you can hear strange and wonderful sounds: singing, giggling, acting, and debating, all in beginner's French that seems remarkably unstilted.

This may well be due to the philosophy of the school's founders, Christine Mestra and Marie-Claude Vacherie, who opened Accord's doors in 1988. "We believe that everyone has the capacity to learn languages, but many people are inhibited. Our role is to use our tools as teacher to encourage them," she says. "We want to create a special environment for teaching, to focus on the individual, to create a place where people can feel good and learn well."

In line with this theory, few grammar books are used at Accord. Instead there's a plethora of talking, reading, and listening, using excerpts from film, television, radio, and newspapers. Student speeches are videotaped with camcorders, and some courses include a weekly theater class. But most important, the classes are small, between seven and fourteen students, so everyone can speak at length. "First we work on oral development, with a lot of work on pronunciation," adds Mestra. "We try and build a good dynamic within the class."

With less than a dozen full-time teachers and about only 1,000 adult students a year, Accord offers the benefits and drawbacks of a small school. I observed two classes where students sat in semicircles in white, airy classrooms, and each class had a lovely ambience: Clearly the students were comfortable with each other and their teacher. However, there aren't extensive library facilities, and if you don't like your teacher, you don't have many options for changing. Many of the students come from Spain and South America, and the age range is broad. French beginners take note: The English-language pamphlet for Accord is refreshingly easy to follow. Again, students here seem content with their choice. "I researched a lot of different schools, and I chose this one because they use an audiovisual method, because it's in the center of Paris, and because we talk in the class about real, everyday topics, and we do lots of games. I really like it," says Sonia Fuentes, 42, a Venezuelan television director living in Paris.

Ryusaku Kubota, a Japanese florist now working in Paris, is equally positive. "I decided not to go the Alliance Française because there were too many Japanese there. I'm very happy here. You have a lot of opportunity to talk in class, to ask questions."

Accord Ecole de Langues
14 boulevard Poissonnière
75009 Paris
Tel.: 01–55–33–52–33
Fax: 01–55–33–52–34
E-mail: accordel@easynet.fr
Web site: www.accord-langues.com
Classes run for ten or twenty hours a week for one month. Contact them for fees.

The Roads Less Traveled

Before you plunk down a hefty enrollment fee and get ready to return to the class-room, stretch your imagination for a moment. With a bit of gumption, creativity, and self-discipline, you can probably design your own personalized language pro-gram—and get a crash course in contemporary French society at the same time.

It goes without saying that the very best way to learn a language is total immer-sion. So try to dream up ways to install yourself in the middle of a French family. Do you know people who live in the country? Offer to paint their roof in exchange for meals, lodging, and kindly pronunciation corrections. Work as an *au pair* in a French family, or make a list of your useful skills—bookkeeping, computer layout, driving, or woodworking, for example—and set up an unpaid internship in French business or a local nonprofit group. The all-time best method, of course, is falling in love with someone French. It works!

Another effective approach is hiring a tutor, but this calls for astute decision making because prices and quality vary enormously. For around only 10 euros an hour, you might find a tutor who's an undergraduate French literature student at the Sorbonne, an underemployed journalist, or an out-of-work refugee from the publishing business. But for between 15 and 30 euros an hour, you'll have access to dedicated, well-qualified professionals who can develop a teaching program espe-cially for you. To find a tutor, scan the copious listings in the bimonthly *FUSAC*, the monthly *Paris Voice*, the bulletin-board at the American Church, and the clas-sified pages of the other English-language publications in Paris. Make sure to search widely, ask for references, and, to save money, ask for free or half-price intro-ductory lessons. Don't forget to think carefully about how you connect with the person: In a one-on-one teaching situation, personal chemistry plays a big role.

The only real drawback to hiring a tutor is the expense, but an easy way to get around this is to find a few friends at your learning level and develop your own classes in the comfort of your home. Divided among two or three people, the hourly costs for a tutor can become reasonable.

Other Tips for Learning French

Set up a weekly language swap with a Parisian anglophone "wannabe." This type of language exchange involves a bit of chance: You might end up meeting with someone who becomes a friend for life . . . or a total nut. When this works, it's an ideal way to learn French, but there have also been some stories circulating about women who have met men for language swaps and got more than they bargained for. So be warned: Always arrange the initial meeting in a public place, like a café or park, not in your home. Scan the local announcements for the names and tele-phone numbers of Parisians searching for language swaps.

The **Centre Georges Pompidou** (19 rue Beaubourg, 75004 Paris; Tel.: 01–44–78–12–33) has a free language lab that is open to the public six days a week on the ground floor of the *Bibliothèque Publique d'Information*. This resource is a real gem: There's a copious catalogue of teaching cassettes and videos on topics ranging from neighborhood life in Paris to the French revolution and those tough-to-acquire telephone conversation and answering-machine skills. Plus, if you're interested, you can also take a stab at any of about one hundred other languages you might be interested in. Maori? Yiddish? Armenian? Provençal? You can learn them all here—just turn up, decide which cassette or video you want, then sign for it and listen or watch in one of the many snazzy lime green language lab booths. The only limitations: Use of the language lab is restricted to an hour per day for each person, and there are often long lines to get into the library.

Konversando. French-English conversation exchange and get-togethers for a small fee (never more than 10 euros). Free trial session. 8 bis, Cité Trevise, 75009 Paris; Tel.: 01–47–70–21–64.

Assimil (Bookstore)
11 rue des Pyramides
75001 Paris
Tel.: 01–42–60–40–66
The Assimil bookstore has scores of self-study books, cassettes, and CDs.

Berlitz France
Main office
3 Square Opéra Louis Jouvet
75009 Paris
Tel.: 01–53–30–18–18
Fax: 01–53–30–18–19
E-mail: info@berlitz.fr
Web site: www.paris-anglo.com, click on Berlitz.

Begun in France in 1907, the Berlitz method, taught all over the world, teaches languages "instinctively," the way a child learns a language, without focusing on grammar. The majority of the students at Berlitz France learn English, but about 15 percent learn French. The method, which is not inexpensive, is a preferred choice by many business people. About 300 teachers, individual classes, and small group classes. Call for locations, hours, and fees.

Business Talk France
134 boulevard Haussman
75008 Paris
Tel/Fax: 01–49–53–91–83
E-mail: btf@club-internet.fr
Formed in 1990, this school teaches French and other languages, with a focus on business French at all levels. With about 200 students enrolled each year and four teachers, there are individual and group classes of between three and six students.

Chambre de Commerce et d'Industrie de Paris
2 Place Bourse
75002 Paris
Tel.: 01–53–40–46–00
Individualized, made-to-measure French classes, mostly used by business people.

Institut Parisien de Langue et de Civilisation Françaises
87 boulevard de Grenelle
Tel.: 01–40–56–09–53
Fax: 01–43–06–46–30
Web site: www.institut-parisien.com
Formed in 1988, the institute enrolls about 2,000 students each year, employs fourteen teachers, and has fifteen students maximum in a class. Ten, fifteen, or twenty-five hours per week, special *au pair* program. Bonus: a class where you can get ninety minutes of civilization per week. Start on any Monday at any level.

For additional language schools and updates, consult www.paris-anglo.com.

MBA and Business School Programs in Paris

The two most prestigious institutions in the Paris area for international commerce and management are INSEAD and HEC.

INSEAD (Institution Européenne d'Administration des Affaires)
boulevard Constance
77300 Fontainebleu
Tel.: 01–60–72–40–00
Fax: 01–60–74–55–00
Web site: www.insead.fr

HEC (Haute Etudes Commerciales)
1 rue Libération
78350 Jouy en Josas
Tel.: 01–39–67–70–00
Fax: 01–39–67–74–40
Web site: www.hec.fr

ESGCI (Ecole Supérieure de Gestion et Commerce International)
25 rue Saint-Ambroise
75011 Paris
Tel.: 01–53–36–44–00
Fax: 01–43–55–73–74
E-mail: rdarmon@esg.fr
Web site: www.esg.fr

IFAM (Institute Franco-Américain de Management)
19 rue Cépré
75015 Paris
Tel.: 01–47–34–38–23
Fax: 01–47–83–31–72
E-mail: IfamMba@cybercable.fr
Web site: www.ifam.edu

ESLSCA (Ecole Supérieure Libre des Sciences Commerciales Appliquées)
1 rue Bougainville
75007 Paris
Tel.: 01–45–51–32–59
Fax: 01–45–55–24–94

Pôle Universitaire Léonardo de Vinci
Etablissement d'Ensiegnement Supérieur Technique Privé
(specializes in management, commerce, technology, and science)
92916 Paris La Défense Cedex
Tel.: 01–41–16–70–00
Fax: 01–41–16–70–99
Minitel: 36–15 DEVINCI
Web site: www.devinci.fr

Other Classes in Paris

Kaplan (test preparation)
3 rue Alexis Carel
75015 Paris
Tel.: 01–45–66–55–33
Web site: www.kaplan.com

Le Cordon Bleu (cooking and wine tasting)
8 rue Léon Delhomme
75015 Paris
Tel.: 01–53–68–22–50
Fax: 01–48–56–03–96

Other Sources

Bibliothèque Publique d'Information (BPI)
Centre Georges Pompidou
19 rue Beaubourg
75197 Paris Cedex 04
Tel.: 01–44–78–12–33
Open Monday, Wednesday, Thursday, and Friday from noon to 10:00 P.M. and Saturday, Sunday, and public holidays from 10:00 A.M. to 10:00 P.M. No registration required. Expect long lines to get in.

L'ExpoLangues
Every winter at La Villette a large fair brings together all the major language schools, foreign language programs and bookstores, publishers, and other related organizations. This is an excellent place to market yourself as a teacher, find a language course, buy language method books and tapes, and meet like-minded people.

ExpoLangues
OIP/Reed
11 rue Colonel Pierre Avia
75015 Paris
Tel.: 01–41–90–47–60

Official Translators and Interpreters

Lori Thicke, long-term resident of Paris and director of Eurotexte Translation Agency, added her comments on issues you might face when dealing with—or becoming—a translator.

So You Wanna Be A Translator?

Sadly, I am not a translator. I run a translation company in Paris, but for me it's the freelance translators who have the great jobs. How many other professions can be exercised via the Internet as easily on a boat in the Mediterranean as in a fifth-floor Clichy walk-up? How many jobs can you do without getting dressed up—or dressed at all, like one translator I know?

Nice work if you can get it. But what does it take to join the ranks of those professional translators, battening down the hatches in Clichy or bobbing off the Côte d'azur?

The fact of speaking two—or more—languages won't make you a translator any more than being able to do a square root will make you an accountant (not, I hasten to add, that I have any firsthand knowledge of square roots). Translation is both an art and a profession, though not one you necessarily have to go to school to learn.

Since 1986 my company, Eurotexte, has worked with literally hundreds of technical translators—and has declined to work with many times more that number. Along the way we've noticed that a) bad translators outweigh good translators by about 30 to one, and b) good translators tend to share the following traits:

Perfect understanding, idioms and all, of a second language (the source language)

Excellent writing skills in the mother-tongue (target) language

A nose for sniffing out what would be a word-for-word (*mot-a-mot*) translation and an ear for the way words should sound to a native speaker

Ethics or, if you will, a belief in a job well done (why else would you spend ten minutes on the Internet just to find one term?)

In-depth technical knowledge in at least one area (such as information technology, beauty products, or electrical engineering; "generalist" translators may be better off trying to break into literary translation, which is another kettle of words altogether).

Assuming you possess the requisite skills and talent to become a translator, who is going to pay you to do it? Basically, your choices are to find an in-house position or to offer your services as a freelancer.

A salaried position can be ideal for a wet-behind-the-ears translator as there is no capital equipment to invest in, and, if constructive feedback is available, it can be an excellent opportunity to hone your skills.

Getting a salaried position will be a little trickier, of course, if you don't have the legal right to work in France. If that's the case, you will have to find an employer interested enough in your skills to go through the expensive and lengthy process of applying for your working papers. To be successful, your prospective employer will have to convince the French authorities that no French or EU citizen could possibly do that job. (Which might be the case if, for example, the position required familiarity with American legal language.)

If you see yourself working from home—or boat—one day, perhaps the life of a freelance translator appeals to you more. To set yourself up as a professional, you'll need:

A reasonably fast computer (preferably a PC)

A modem with a reliable Internet connection

The major software packages (at least Microsoft Word, but having others such as PowerPoint and Excel may lead to more assignments)

A fax machine or fax software

A printer (optional nowadays, unless you are using your computer as a fax machine)

Good general and specialized dictionaries, both monolingual and bilingual (many are now available as CD-ROMS, or on-line)

Translation memory such as *Déjà Vu* or *Trados* (optional, but I predict these will become standard in the future, and again, may mean access to more translation work)

An accounting program or an accounts-friendly assistant (also optional, but since you must keep precise records of your income and expenses and remit sales tax, etc., this could be a lifesaver)

A phone number where you can be reached reliably during office hours (an absolute must)

A legal means of billing your clients.

This last is the most problematic. Even having the legal right to work in France won't dispense with the need to sign up with the French social security authority, URSSAF, which, in exchange for health and retirement benefits, will deduct the same chunk out of your freelance earnings as it would out of your salaried earnings. (The advantage is that you can write off your expenses; the disadvantage is that you get to hold on to the money just long enough to believe it's all yours before the state comes to collect its due.)

URSSAF normally requires a valid *carte de séjour* and the names of three prospective clients before letting you sign on.

Recently so-called *sociétés de portage* have come on the scene as an alternative to signing up with URSSAF. These companies invoice your clients for you (though you still have to find the work yourself), then pay you as an employee. For this privilege of not having to sign up with URSSAF, you'll pay the *société de portage* a fee of around 10% on top of the approximately 40% the government takes. This could be advantageous if you are just starting out or are hopeless about putting money aside to pay URSSAF and TVA, if you're not sure how long you'll stick with translating, or if you plan to work only part-time as URSSAF does have a minimum yearly charge. Should you decide to go this route, look for a *société de portage* that will reimburse you for your out-of-pocket expenses such as computer repairs.

Another method of billing customers is to create an SARL (French limited-liability company)—perfectly legal if somewhat heavy in paperwork. (I know of one entrepreneur who created an SARL and then had the company apply for her working papers, but this is an expensive proposition with no guarantee of success.)

For those translators without valid working papers or a *carte de commerçant* (which is what you'd need to reside in France and run an SARL), the above solutions do not apply.

However, if you are not residing in France and want to work on a freelance basis for French companies, you are under no requirement to sign up with URSSAF and will simply have to make your social security contributions in your own home country. (But make sure your real, non-French, address appears on your bills!) It is, of course, illegal for a French resident to invoice a client using an out-of-France address.

But which companies should you translate for? Assuming you've got the billing issue worked out, then your choice is between working for translation agencies or direct customers. There are pros and cons on both sides.

Direct customers (such as IBM or Air France) generally pay higher rates (most often paying on the word), but they may be harder to obtain as clients. Also they can be tougher to hold on to: If you are their only translator, they may find someone else the first time you are forced to turn their work down.

Translation companies, on the other hand, take it very well if you're too busy to take on their job and will surely call on you another day. They're easy to find—just look in the Yellow Pages or on the Internet. But on the downside, in most cases they will pay you a lower word rate than a direct client.

The best solution might just be a mix of these two, translation companies as your bread and butter and direct clients when you can get them.

Setting up as a translator, whether as a freelancer or an employee, may not be the easiest thing in the world, but if I had the gift for translating I know where I'd be right now.

So You Wanna Find a Translator?

Bad translations are arguably one of France's leading exports. (Not that France has cornered the market.) To add to those ubiquitous menus ("Toes with butter and jam") are the documents and Web sites of major French companies rendered in perfect pidgin English (or German or Spanish or….).

It's hard to go wrong if all you need is a birth or marriage certificate translated. In that case you will most likely be calling on the services of a sworn translator *(traducteur assermenté)* who has been certified by the courts for translating official documents. Contact your embassy or the *préfecture* for a list of translators who could do the job.

However, finding a competent translator for your company is not quite so easy. Whether it's a two-page newsletter or a whole Web site, careless work will make your company look second-rate—and the written word is particularly unforgiving.

First you have to decide whether to look for an independent translator, or a company. I can't claim to be utterly objective, but in my experience with Eurotexte (the first agency in France to receive ISO 9001: 2000 certification, I might add), I would say that a translation company can add considerable value. If it's a good one, an agency will not only find the best translators but will edit them for a letter-perfect product—as even the very best translators make mistakes. They'll handle any Web site engineering or DTP work and won't balk at multilanguage jobs. On the other hand, the majority of translation agencies aren't that quality conscious about their work, so for something small I'd say a good independent translator is better than a bad agency.

But how to find a good translation company? Here are a few pointers:

Ask around for a recommendation—but make sure both the company's quality and timeliness are to be trusted: A great translation won't help you much if it arrives after the deadline.

Ask to see a company's client list and samples of their work.

Ask if the company has any accreditations, such as ISO 9001 quality certification.

If you have a reasonable amount of work to offer, request a short test.

Check out their Web site. I've seen the most egregious on-line errors committed by translation agencies on the very pages that extol their so-called quality.

Make sure their translators work only into their native language and that each translation is edited by a second professional.

But getting a good translation is just a little over half the battle. To help you deal with typesetters who don't understand the language they're working in or non-native speakers who know just enough of a language to be dangerous (e.g., changing "equipment" to "equipments" because there's more than one), you can check out Eurotexte's *Translations: A User's Guide,* which is available free under the heading "Tips & Giveaways" on the Web site www.eurotexte.net.

Translators in Paris

Official translators and interpreters *(traducteur–interprète assermenté)* are licensed to translate and interpret for the various French courts. Translations of documents intended for legal use in the United States must have the translator's seal and signature authenticated by *"Apostille"* at the French *Palais de Justice* (see the Government chapter). The individuals listed on www.paris-anglo.com have informed the U.S. Embassy in Paris that they are qualified to translate or interpret in the languages specified, and that they are sufficiently competent in the English language to provide services to English-speaking clients.

Foreign and Exchange Programs in Paris

There are more than thirty university exchange and foreign study programs in Paris in English and a handful in the rest of France. Some have left; others have newly arrived. Much of the drop in enrollment experienced in the early and mid-1990s has been reversed. The trend in American education and culture in general is away from interest in European study, with students opting for more exotic destinations, such as Africa and Asia. This may be related to the increased focus in North American life on multiculturalism and crosscultural experiences.

University Programs

A short list of institutions has been included below. For a full listing of elementary and secondary schools, as well as French schools offering English-language instruction and American university programs, consult the Paris-Anglophone Directory at www.paris-anglo.com.

Academic Year Abroad
Reid Hall
4 rue de Chevreuse
75006 Paris
Tel.: 01–43–20–91–92

American University of Paris
31 avenue Bosquet
75007 Paris
Tel.: 01–40–62–06–00
Fax: 01–47–53–88–03
(American university education; B.A./B.S. degree; all classes in English)
Admissions/Development Office
6 rue Colonel Combes
75007 Paris
Tel.: 01–40–62–07–20
Web site: www.aup.edu

American University of Paris
Division of Continuing Education
102 rue St-Dominique
75007 Paris
Tel.: 01–40–62–06–14
Fax: 01–40–62–07–17
E-mail: ce@aup–fr
Web site: www.aup.edu

Alumni Associations

The best way to keep in touch with fellow alumni living in Paris is to join the Paris Alumnae/i Network (PAN), which organizes regular events for its members and coordinates with individual university alumni organizations. It also publishes a very informative newsletter called *Panache*. To find out more contact Margaret Brautigam at 01–45–23–00–75 or e-mail her at mbrautigam@compuserve.com.

Arts and Culture
in Paris

Museums in Paris

This section was composed by Sandra Kwock-Silve, Paris art critic, historian, hula dancer, and president of the Paris-based France-Hawai'i Association. Her articles appear regularly in the Paris Voice *and various art publications.*

Since the late eighteenth century when the Louvre was first opened to the public, this world-famous museum has ranked high on most visitors' lists of "things to see in Paris." Recent renovation efforts, coupled with I. M. Pei's glass pyramid, have given the Louvre a more contemporary look. Modern installations now showcase art treasures from the past. Once again Parisians are flocking in record numbers to discover a newly opened wing that highlights sculpture and masks from Africa and the Pacific. However, for adventurous spirits, classics like the *Musée du Louvre* and the *Musée d'Orsay* should suggest only the beginning of a serious museum sampling. There are nearly one hundred museums to discover in and around Paris. Prestigious private and public collections highlight just about every subject imaginable. There are serious museums devoted to the history of wine, fashion, new technology, and the arts from every era, country, and culture. Something is sure to capture your interest in Paris's rich museum world, whether it's a glimpse of the future at *La Villette* or an afternoon stroll through the sculpture garden at *La Musée Rodin.* Visits to the artists' studios will take you to some interesting neighborhoods off the beaten tourist track. And the city's eccentric collection of counterfeits, locks, and spectacles (to name but a few) will keep you exploring.

Major museum exhibitions are an important part of the Paris art scene year-round. The weekly publications *Pariscope, Zurban,* and *Official des Spectacles* have extensive museum and gallery listings of current exhibits. For historical information, the Michelin guide to Paris and the Hachette *"Guide Bleu"* are considered the best sources available.

Consider going on a museum spree with *La Carte musées et monuments*. This special pass allows unlimited access to more than 60 museums and monuments without having to wait in line for tickets. Card prices range from 13 euros for one day to 39 euros for a five-day period. Cards can be bought at the tourist office (121 avenue des Champs Elysées), métro stations, or museums. Some museums are free, or half price on Sundays. Check for interesting student/teacher rates. Teachers are usually admitted free. As a general rule, national museums are open from 9h45h to 17h00 every day except Tuesday. Municipal museums keep the same hours but are closed on Monday. Many museums are closed on public holidays, and smaller collections may close during the month of August.

A list of major museums is followed by a selection of diverse thematic collections such as "artists' studios" or "suggested museum outings for children."

Major Museums

+ *Centre Georges Pompidou (Beaubourg):* 19 rue Rambuteau, 75001 Paris (Métro: Châtelet /Les Halles). Tel.: 01–44–78–12–33 Open: weekdays 12h00–22h00, weekends and holidays 10h00–20h00; closed Tuesday. Museum entrance fee: 5,50/3,50 euros for those under age 25 (proof of age is required); free on Sunday from 10h00–14h00. Contemporary galleries, 5,50 euros.

+ *Musée de l'Armée:* Hotel des Invalides, 75007 Paris (Métro: Latour-Maubourg). Tel.: 01–44–42–37–72. Open daily from 10h00 to 17h00. Closed on holidays. Entrance fee: 6/4,50 euros

+ *Musée de l'Art Moderne de la ville de Paris:* 11 avenue Pres. Wilson, 75116 Paris (Métro: Ièna). Tel.: 01–53–67–40–00. Open daily except Monday from 10h00 to 17h30 and until 20h30 on Wednesday. Entrance fee: 5,50/3,90 euros.

+ *Musée des Arts Africains et Océaniens:* 293 avenue Daumesnil, 75012 Paris (Métro: Porte Dorée). Tel.: 01–44–74–85–01. Open weekdays from 10h00 to 12h00 and 13h30 to 17h30. Weekends from 12h30 to 18h00. Closed Tuesday. Entrance fee: 4,50; Sunday, 3 euros. Aquarium open daily except Tuesday from 10h00 to 18h00. Under 18 admitted free.

+ *Musée des Arts Décoratifs:* 107–109 rue de Rivoli, 75001 Paris (Métro: Palais Royale). Tel.: 01–44–55–57–50. Open daily from 12h30 to 18h00. Closed Monday and Tuesday. Entrance fee: 5,40/3,90 euros. Admission to Dubuffet, donation 3,90.

+ *Musée National des Arts et Traditions Populaires:* 6 avenue du Mahatma-Gandi, 75116 Paris (Métro: Sablons). Tel.: 01–44–17–60–00. Open daily from 9h45 to 17h15. Closed Tuesday. Entrance fee: 3,81/2,59 euros.

+ *Musée Carnavalet:* 23 rue de Sévigné, 75005 Paris (Métro: Saint Paul). Tel.: 01–44–59–58–58. Open daily from 10h00 to 17h35. Closed Monday and holidays. Entrance fee: 5,40/4 euros.

+ *Musée Guimet* (Asian Art): 6 Place d'Iéna, 75116 Paris (Métro: Iéna). Tel.: 01–56–52–53–00. Open daily from 9h45 to 18h. Closed Tuesdays and holidays. Entrance fee: 5,50/4 euros.

+ *Musée de l'Histoire de France:* Hotel de Soubise, 60 rue des Francs Bourgeois, 75003 Paris (Métro: Saint-Paul). Tel.: 01–40–27–62–18. Open daily from 13h45 to 17h45. Closed Tuesdays and holidays. Entrance fee: 3/2,20 euros.

- *Musée National d'Histoire Naturelle:* Jardin des Plantes, 57 rue de Cuivier, 75005 Paris (Métro: Monge). Open daily from 10h00 to 17h00; weekends from 11h00 to 18h00. Closed Tuesday. Zoo: Tel.: 01–40–79–30–00. Open daily from 9h00 to 18h00. Entrance fee: 4,57/3,05 euros.
- *Musée de l'Homme:* Palais de Chaillot, Place du Trocadero, 75116 Paris (Métro: Trocadero). Tel.: 01–44–05–72–72. Open daily from 9h45 to 17h15. Closed Tuesdays and holidays. Entrance fee: 4,57/3,05 euros.
- *Musée de l'Institut du Monde Arabe:* 23 quai Saint-Bernard, 75005 Paris (Métro: Jussieu). Tel.: 01–40–51–38–38. Open daily from 13h00 to 20h00. Closed on Monday. Entrance fee: 4,57/3,05 euros.
- *Musée de Jeu de Paume:* Gallerie Nationale (Temporary exhibitions—Contemporary art). Place de la Concorde, 75001 Paris (Métro: Concorde). Tel.: 01–47–03–12–50. Open daily from 12h00 to 19h00; Tuesday until 20h30. Closed Monday. Entrance fee: 5,50/4 euros.
- *Musée du Louvre:* rue de Rivoli, 75001 Paris (Métro: Palais-Royal Louvre). Tel.: 01–40–20–51–51. Open every day except Tuesday. Permanent exhibitions: 9h00 to 18h00. Wednesday until 21h45. Temporary exhibitions: 12h00 to 20h00. Entrance fee: 7,50/5 euros.
- *Musée de la Marine:* Palais de Chaillot, Place de Trocadero, 75116 Paris (Métro: Trocadero). Tel.: 01–53–65–69–69. Open daily from 10h00 to 18h00. Open holidays. Closed Tuesday. Entrance fee: 6/4 euros.
- *Musée Marmottan:* 2 rue Louis-Bouilly, 75016 Paris (Métro: La Muette). Tel.: 01–44–96–50–33. Open daily from 10h00 to 17h30. Closed Monday. Entrance fee: 6,50/4 euros.
- *Musée de la Mode et du Costume:* Palais Galliéra, avenue Pierre-1er-de Serbie, 75116 Paris (Métro: Iéna). Tel.: 01–56–52–86–00. Open daily from 10h00 to 17h40. Closed Monday. Entrance fee: 6,50/4 euros.
- *Musée de la Monnaie:* 11 quai de Conti, 75006 Paris (Métro: Pont-Neuf). Tel.: 01–40–46–55–35. Open daily from 13h00 to 18h00; Wednesday until 21h00. Closed Monday. Entrance fee: 3/2,20 euros. Free on Sunday.
- *Musée National des Monuments Français:* Palais de Chaillot, Place de Trocadero, 75116 Paris (Métro: Trocadero). Tel.: 01–42–24–10–73. Open daily from 9h00 to 18h00. Closed Tuesday. (Currently closed for renovation work; scheduled to open at the end of 2002.)
- *Musee National du Moyen Age-Thermes de Cluny (ex-Cluny):* 6 Place paul-Painleve, 75005 Paris (Metro: Saint Michel). Tel.: 01–53–73–78–00. Open daily from 9h30 to 17h15. Closed Tuesday. Entrance fee: 5,50/4 euros under 18 admitted free.
- *Musée de l'Orangerie des Tuileries:* Place de la Concorde, 75001 Paris (Métro: Concorde). Tel.: 01–42–97–48–16. Open daily from 9h45 to 17h15. Closed Tuesday. (Currently closed for extensive renovation work; scheduled to open at the end of 2002).
- *Musée D'Orsay:* 62 rue de Lille, 75007 Paris (Métro: Solferino). Tel.: 01–40–49–48–14. Recorded message: Tel.: 01–45–49–11–11. Program information: 01–40–49–48–48. Open daily except Monday from 10h00 to 18h00, Thursday until 21h45, Sunday 9h00 to 18h00. Entrance fee: 7,50/5 euros; Sunday, 3, under 18 admitted free.

✤ *Musée du Petit Palais:* avenue Winston Churchill, 75008 Paris (Métro: Champs-Elysées-Clemenceau). Tel.: 01–42–65–12–73. Open daily from 10h00 to 17h40. Closed Monday and holidays. Entrance fee: 5,18/3 euros.

✤ *Musée Picasso:* Hotel Sal, 5 rue Thorigny, 75003 Paris (Métro: Saint-Paul). Tel.: 01–42–71–25–21. Open daily from 9h15 to 17h15, Wednesday until 22h00. Closed Tuesday. Entrance fee: 6,71/5,18 euros.

✤ *Musée de la Poste:* 34 boulevard de Vaugirard, 75017 Paris (Métro: Montparnasse). Tel.: 01–42–79–24–24. Open weekdays and Saturday 10h00 to 18h00. Closed Sunday and holidays. Entrance fee: 4,50/3 euros.

✤ *Musée de la Publicité:* 18 rue du Paradis, 75010 Paris (Métro: Château d'eau). Tel.: 01–44–55–57–50. Open daily from 12h00 to 18h00. Closed Tuesday. Entrance fee: 4,50 euros.

✤ *Musée des Sciences et de l'Industrie:* Parc de la Villette, 30 avenue Corentin-Cariou, 75019 Paris (Métro: Porte de la Villette). Tel.: 01–40–05–80–00. Open daily except Monday from 10h00 to 18h00. Entrance pass: 7,50/5,50 euros.

Museums in Artists' Homes

✤ *Musée Henri Bouchard:* 25 rue de l'Yvette, 75016 Paris (Métro: Jasmin). Tel.: 01–46–47–63–46. Open Wednesday and Saturday from 14h00 to 19h00. Entrance fee: 3,81/2,21 euros. A tour of this official sculptor's studio is given the first Saturday of each month at 15h00. Bouchard lived from 1875–1960. Academic and decorative sculptures and medals are on view in changing exhibits.

✤ *Musée Bourdelle:* 16 rue Antoine-Bourdelle, 75015 Paris (Métro: Montparnasse); Tel.: 01–49–54–73–73. Open daily from 10h00 to 17h40. Closed Monday and holidays. Entrance fee: 4,50/3 euros. The artist's studio contains a large collection of sketches and sculptures in many styles. Bourdelle lived from 1861–1929. Family portraits, *maquettes,* and casts are on view.

✤ *Fondation Le Corbusier:* 8–10 Square de Docteur Blanche, 75016 Paris (Métro: Jasmin). Tel.: 01–45–27–50–65. Open during the week from 10h00 to 12h30 and from 13h30 to 18h00. Closed on weekends. Entrance fee: 2 euros, under age 12 free. A fine collection of Le Corbusier's *Esprit Moderne* paintings and sculpture is housed in Villa La Roche, designed by the great architect in 1923. Research library. Theme exhibitions organized each year.

✤ *Musée Delacroix:* 6 Place de Furstenburg, 75006 Paris (Métro: Saint-Germain des-Prés). Tel.: 01–44–41–86–50. Open daily from 9h45 to 12h30; and from 14h00 to 17h15. Closed on Tuesday. Entrance fee: 4/2,60 euros. Delacroix's studio and living quarters can be visited to view a collection of prints, drawings, and documents. Theme exhibits are organized at times. Charming garden.

✤ *Fondation Jean Dubuffet:* 137 rue de Sèvres, 75007 Paris (Métro: Duroc). Tel.: 01–47–34–12–63. Open weekdays from 14h00 to 18h00. Entrance fee: 4 euros. Changing exhibitions contrast different periods of this prolific artist's work. The charming house once contained Dubuffet's famous Art Brut collection. Research library.

✤ *Musée National Hébert:* 85 rue du Cherch-Midi, 75006 Paris (Métro: Vaneau). Tel.: 01–42–22–23–82. Open daily except Tuesday from 12h30 to 18h00; weekends from 14h00 to 18h00. Entrance fee: 3/2,30 euros. Drawings, watercolors, and paintings of Hébert (1870–1908). Fine decor and furniture. Special exhibitions feature late-eighteenth-century art.

✤ *Musée National Jean-Jacques Henner:* 43 avenue de Villiers, 75017 Paris (Métro: Malsherbes). Tel.: 01–47–63–42–73. Open daily except Monday from 10h00 to 12h00 and from 14h00 to 17h00. Entrance fee: 4/3,20 euros. A large collection of paintings and drawings by Henner (1829–1920). The exotic decor is a perfect setting for works by this celebrated second-empire artist.

✤ *Musée Gustave Moreau:* 14 rue de la Rochefoucauld, 75009 Paris (Métro: Trinité). Tel.: 01–48–74–38–50. Open daily except Tuesday from 10h00 to 12h45 and from 14h00 to 17h15, Wednesday from 11h00 to 17h15. Entrance fee: 3,50/2,30 euros. Moreau's house and studio contain an extensive collection of paintings and drawings, including *"Salome"* and *"Les Licornes."* During the 1890s it was here that the noted symbolist painter taught future greats like Matisse and Roualt.

✤ *Musée Rodin:* 77 rue de Varenne, 75007 Paris (Métro: Varenne). Tel.: 01–44–18–61–10. Open daily from 10h00 to 17h00. Closed Monday. Entrance fee: 5/3 euros. An important collection that includes some of Rodin's most famous works, such as *"The Thinker"* and *"The Kiss,"* with works by Camille Claudel. Housed in the stunning eighteenth-century Hotel Byron, this museum is surrounded by a large formal garden.

✤ *Musée de la Vie Romantique:* Maison Renan-Scheffer, 16 rue Chaptal, 75009 Paris (Métro: Saint-Georges). Tel.: 01–48–75–95–38. Open daily except Monday from 10h00 to 17h45. Entrance fee: 5/3 euros. The house of Dutch artist Ary Scheffer (1795-1858) is the setting for temporary exhibitions that feature the nineteenth-century Romantic movement. There is a permanent exhibition on the writer George Sand.

✤ *Musée Zadkine:* 100 bis rue d'Assas, 75006 Paris (Métro: Vavin). Tel.: 01–55–42–77–20. Open daily except Monday from 10h00 to 17h40. Entrance fee: 5/3 euros. Free on Sunday. Works on paper and sculptures by the Russian artist Ossip Zadkine are on permanent exhibition in the house where he lived untill 1967. A lovely sculpture garden.

Museums with Unusual Themes

✤ *Musée de l'Avocat:* 25 rue du Jour, 75001 Paris (Métro: Louvre). Tel.: 01–47–83–50–03. Open during the week. An appointment must be made to visit the collection of authentic doccuments and works of art. The correspondance between Zola and Dreyfus's lawyer Labori can be seen, as well as a bust of Gerbier known as "the eagle of the bar."

✤ *Musée Cernuschi:* 7 avenue Velasquez, 75008 Paris (Métro: Villiers). Tel.: 01–45–63–50–75. Open daily except Monday from 10h00 to 17h45. Entrance fee: 4,60/2,30 euros. Free admission on Sunday, except for temporary exhibit. Henri Cernuschi's private collection was unique at the end of the nineteenth century. The treasures include neolithique terra cottas, ancient bronzes, funerary pieces, and fine examples of calligraphy. An impressive collection on the edge of Parc Monceau.

✤ *Musée de la Chasse et de la Nature:* 60 rue des Archives, 75003 Paris (Métro: Rambuteau). Tel.: 01–53–01–92–40. Open daily from 10h00 to 12h30 and from 13h30 to 17h30. Closed Tuesday and holidays. Entrance fee: 4,60/2,30 euros. Stuffed trophies from around the world, including big game hunts from Africa. Guns and art celebrate the hunt in a beautiful historic house.

✦ *Musée de Cinéma Henri-Langlois:* Palais de Chailot, Place du Trocadero, 75116 Paris (Métro: Trocadéro). Tel.: 01–45–53–74–39. Visits with a guide every hour from 10h00 to 17h30. Open daily except Tuesday and holidays. Closed between 13h00 and 14h00. Entrance fee: 5/3 euros. The history of the cinema (1895 to present) is illustrated with documents, stage sets, posters, and costumes worn by Greta Garbo, John Wayne, and others.

✦ *Musée de la Contrefaçon:* 16 rue de la Faisanderie, 75016 Paris (Métro: Port Dauphine). Tel.: 01–56–26–14–00. Open Monday and Wednesday from 14h30 to 16h00 and Friday from 9h30 to 12h00. Free admission. The art of forgery is celebrated in all its forms going back to the Romans. Creators have always worried about imitation of original products; you can smell the difference between perfumes and compare Chanel in Paris with Sanel in Turkey.

✦ *Musée Dapper:* 35 bis rue Paul Valery 75016 Paris (Métro: Etoile). Tel.: 01–45–00–01–50. Open daily from 11h00 to 19h00. Entrance fee: 4,60/2,30 euros. Wednesday free. This private foundation highlights the traditional precolonial arts of Africa. The changing exhibitions on diverse themes such as Pygmie Tapa cloth or Fang masks and sculpture are always superb. The research library can be used by appointment.

✦ *Musée d'Ennery:* 59 avenue Foch, 75116 Paris (Métro: Porte Dauphine). Tel.: 01–45–53–57–96. Open Thursday and Sunday from 14h00 to 17h00; closed in August. Free entrance. A private collection of Asian Art that highlights Netsuke and Kogos fom Japan. Chinese dragons and furniture encrusted with mother-of-pearl create the perfect atmosphere to enjoy this eclectic collection. (Closed for extensive renovations; scheduled to open at the end of 2002.)

✦ *Musée Kwok-On:* 57 rue de Théâtre, 75015 Paris (Métro: Montparnasse). Tel.: 01–45–75–85–75. Open during the week from 10h00 to 17h30. Closed weekends and holidays. Entrance fee: 5,40/5,25 euros. This collection from Hong Kong focuses on all aspects of the theater in Asia with masks, puppets, instruments, and costumes from many different countries. There are changing exhibitions and a fine permanent collection, as well as a documentation center.

✦ *Musée des Lunettes et Lorgnettes:* Pierre Marly, 2 avenue Mozart, 75016 Paris (Métro: La Muette). Tel.: 01–45–27–21–05. Open daily from 10h00 to 18h00. Closed Sunday, Monday, and holidays. Free entrance. An eccentric private collection (housed in a boutique) of several thousand pairs of reading glasses, monocles, and binoculars. An optician's paradise; with rare thirteenth-century examples and new trends.

✦ *Musée de la Parfum:* 39 boulevard des Capucines, 75009 Paris (Métro: Opéra). Tel.: 01–42–60–37–14. Open daily from 9h00 to 17h30. Closed Sunday. Free entrance. This elegant collection tells the story of perfume through the ages. Beautiful glass flacons, vanity cases, and a display that explains the process of extracting oils from plants to create a fragrance.

✦ *Musée de la Serrure:* 1 rue de la Perle, 75003 Paris (Métro: Chemin-Vert). Tel.: 01–42–77–79–62. Open daily from 14h00 to 17h00. Closed Sunday and Monday. Entrance fee: 2,30 euros. Keys and locks through history are featured in this fine Marais house. Ancient bronze keys, gothic locks, and pieces with Dianne de Poitier's emblem are on view. There is a reconstructed locksmith's workshop in the courtyard.

✤ *Musée du Vin:* 5 Square Charles Dickens, 75016 Paris (Métro: Passy). Tel.: 01–45–25–63–26. Open daily from 12h00 to 18h00 and from 20h00 to 23h00 for dinners. Entrance fee: 5,40 euros. Entrance free for diners in museum restaurant (meals with wine from 20 euros). This museum evokes the process of wine making with wax figures. Documents and objects illustrate the long history of wine in France. A glass of wine is included with the visit. Oenological courses are conducted there.

Museum Visits for Children

Most major museums have workshops, tours, and special art-initiation programs for children. These activities include an introduction to the world of robots at La Villette, calligraphy courses at the Institut du Monde Arabe, painting at the Centre Pompidou, and art-appreciation tours at the Musée d'Art Moderne de la Ville de Paris.

These programs change each season. For complete information contact the individual museums, or the following offices:

✤ *Affaires Culturelles de la Ville de Paris:* Hotel d'Abret, 31 rue des Francs-Bourgeois, 75004 Paris (Métro: Saint-Paul). Tel.: 01–42–76–67–00. Open from 8h45 to 18h00. Closed Saturday.

✤ *La Direction des Musées en France:* 34 quai du Louvre, 75001 Paris (Métro: Louvre). Tel.: 01–42–60–39–26. Open daily from 9h45 to 18h30. Closed Tuesday.

Check through this guide's listings for subjects of special interest to your child. Some of the eccentric collections listed under "Unusual Theme Museums" will certainly appeal . . . the thousands of pairs of eyeglasses and the bronze dragons that guard the museum Cernuschi are a big hit with young children. Classics like the *Musée de l'Homme* or the aquarium at the *Musée des Arts Africains et Océaniens* will enthrall toddlers as well as adolescents! There are some wonderful museums in artists' homes, too; everyone loves the *Musée Rodin!*

The following is a list of major museums conceived for children:

✤ *Halle-Saint-Pierre (Musée Max Fournay):* 2 rue Ronsard, 75018 Paris (Métro: Anvers). Tel.: 01–42–58–72–89. Open daily except Monday from 10h00 to 17h30. Entrance fee: 6/5 euros. School groups: 5 euros; studio workshop: 5 euros. There are two museums; a large collection of naive paintings and sculptures from around the world, and a second space created to initiate younger children to museum viewing. Changing theme exhibits with games and artistic activities.

✤ *Musée Grévin:* 10 boulevard Montmartre, 75009 Paris (Métro: Rue Montmartre). Tel.: 01–47–70–85–05. Open daily, including holidays, from 13h00 to 19h00. Open during school vacations from 10h00 to 18h00. Entrance fee: 15,09/12,04 euros. This famous wax museum, similar to Mme. Tussaud's in London, traces French history and highlights twentieth-century figures. There is also a half-hour magic show (Palais des Mirages or Cabinet Fantastique) that runs each day.

+ *Musée en Herbe:* Jardin d'Acclimation (Métro: Sablons). Tel.: 01–40–67–97–66. Open daily from 10h00 to 18h00. Entrance fee: 2/1,70 euros plus park entrance: 3/2,50 euros. This museum was created as a "hands-on" experience to introduce children of all ages to museums. Special theme exhibits are animated by games and diverse activities. Past exhibits have included *"Uluri; les Aborigènes d'Australie"* and *"Sur les Paves de Paris."*
+ *Palais de la Découverte:* avenue Franklin Roosevelt, 75008 Paris (Métro: Franklin Roosevelt). Tel.: 01–56–43–20–21. Open daily from 10h00 to 18h00. Entrance fee: 5,60/3,65 euros. Planetarium: 3/2,50. This fine science museum has been overshadowed by the Cité des Sciences at La Villette but still has a lot to offer in terms of changing exhibits on everything from solar energy to biology. All children love the planetarium.

Galleries

Paris's gallery scene has truly become a movable feast. Some twenty years ago innovative galleries established mushrooming art districts in both the Marais and the Bastille areas, bringing new life to an art world formerly restricted to distinct neighborhoods on either bank of the Seine. As we enter the twenty-first century, the diversity and dynamism of the city's artistic community is reaching out to conquer new territory, thus maintaining the City of Light's position as one of the world's major art capitals.

To have a sense of what is going on in the Paris art world today, one should visit the four main gallery districts and compare art works, trends, and the unique atmosphere associated with each. In 1977 the area around the newly opened Centre Pompidou quickly became a hot spot for avant-garde galleries promoting the newest trends in the international art world. Then during the 1980s, contemporary art stormed the Bastille and every available space was seemingly transformed into an avant-garde gallery. At one point the rue Keller alone could boast of more than twenty street-front galleries! Although a severe economic crisis demoralized the French art market during the 1990s, many dedicated art dealers hung on and devised new strategies for art promotion outside of France. The city now counts 200 to 300 serious galleries showing early modern and contemporary art.

The following list, though far from complete, will give you a good overview of the four main gallery districts. You will find the Right Bank galleries to be more traditional. This is an area noted for art dealers who specialize in old masters and nineteenth-century paintings. There are several galleries of historic interest, such as *Bernheim-Jeune,* which was founded in 1863.

Major postwar art movements from the fifties and sixties were launched in Left Bank galleries. Several scandalous Dubuffet exhibits and many historic Yves Klein events took place in the rue Visconti during the early 1960s. The neighborhood is still talking about how Klein blocked cars and pedestrian traffic for hours with a wall of stacked oil drums!

Galleries in the Marais (and Les Halles) often highlight major artists and international movements, while many Bastille galleries have continued to feature Paris based trends. Since the spring of 1977, several galleries took over space vacated by a French ministry.

Paris galleries are open Tuesday through Saturday during the afternoon from 14h00 to 19h00. All galleries close on Sunday and Monday. Double-check morning hours by phone, as they vary greatly and change often.

Look for the *"Association des Galeries"* listing of exhibitions, which is distributed for free in most major galleries. You can also check the *Pariscope* and *Officiel des Spectacles* for information on current exhibitions.

Right Bank (Métro: Miromesnil)

Artcurial: 61 Montaigne, 75008 Paris, Tel.: 01–42–99–16–16. A unique commercial center on several levels with a museumlike gallery that features twentieth-century masters (Magritte, Picasso, and Saura to name but a few) as well as contemporary artists such as Robert Combas. There is also a fine book store, decorative arts department, jewelry boutique, and poster shop.

Marcel Berheim: 18 avenue Matignon, 75008 Paris, Tel.: 01–42–65–22–23. Specializing in late nineteenth-century painting and early-twentieth-century works (Monet, Renoir, Utrillo, Van Dongen). This gallery opened in 1912 and is still going strong.

Bernheim-Jeune: 83 Faubourg Saint-Honoré, 27 avenue Matignon, 75008 Paris; Tel.: 01–42–66–60–31. Another historic gallery responsible for launching the careers of some impressionists; later showing works by Chagall and Matisse.

Louis-Carré: 10 avenue de Messine, 75008 Paris; Tel.: 01–45–62–57–07. This important gallery shows museum-quality works by such twentieth-century greats as Calder, Chaissac, Léger, and Geer Van Velde.

Fanny Guillon-Laffaille: 4 avenue Messine, 75008 Paris; Tel.: 01–45–63–52–00. This art dealer specializes in works by the Ecole de Paris artists of the 1950s, such as Dufy, Doucet, Estève, and Poliakoff, as well as contemporary works by Chasse-pot, Charpentier, and Tal-Coat.

Lelong: 12–13 rue de Téhéran, 75008 Paris; Tel.: 01–45–63–13–19. This gallery was originally part of an international art network founded by Aimé Maeght (of the Maeght Foundation in the South of France). Internationally known contemporary artists such as Alechinsky, Bacon, Judd, Penck, Serra, Saura, Tapiès, and Voss show in this superb space.

Left Bank (Métro: Odeon)

Claude Bernard: 7-9 rue des Beaux Arts, 75006 Paris; Tel.: 01–43–26–97–07. An important figurative gallery that opened during the 1960s. Such major international names as Balthus, Botero, Tibor Csernus, David Hockney, Lindner, and Andrew Wyeth.

Boulakia: 20 rue Bonaparte, 75006 Paris; Tel.: 01–43–26–97–07. Specializes in COBRA (a famous modern art movement originating in Copenhagen, Brussels and Amsterdam), but always on the lookout for new talent, this gallery, founded in 1971, has shown Christo, Basquiat, Ouattara, and Louise Nesbitt.

Down-Town: 33 rue de Seine, 75006 Paris; Tel.: 01–46–33–82–41. Decorative arts of the forties and fifties as well as works by Pincemin, Claude Viallat, BP, and Takis in this original gallery.

Arlette Gimaray: 12 rue Mazarine, 75006 Paris; Tel.: 01–46–34–71–80. Abstract paintings by young contemporary artists, such as Martine Dubilé, Odile de Frayssinet, or Picard de Gennes, are on view.

Albert Loeb: 12 rue des Beaux-Arts, 75006 Paris; Tel.: 01–46–33–06–87. This respected gallery shows figurative works in all mediums by Caballero, Guinan, Lam, Jeanclos and other established artists of today.

Adrien Maeght: 42–46 rue du Bac, 75007 Paris; Tel.: 01–45–48–45–15. A gallery that has become an institution; showing twentieth-century masters such as Braque, Giacometti, Kandinsky, and Matisse while launching a new generation of artists. Contemporaries include Delprat, Gasiorowski, Kuroda, and Labuauvie.

Darthea Speyer: 6 rue Jacques Callot, 75006 Paris, Tel.: 01–43–54–78–41. An American gallery with an eclectic selection of high quality works in all media. Some of the artists associated with the gallery are Sam Gilliam, Roseline Granet, Stanly Viswanadhan, and Zuka.

Beaubourg/Le Marais (Métro: Hotel de Ville)

Beaubourg: 23 rue du Renard, 75004 Paris; Tel.: 01–42–71–20–50. 3 rue Pierre au Lard, 75004 Paris, Tel.: 01–48–04–34–40. Important gallery promoting contemporary French art, with strong links to the cultural ministry's programs. Major French artists include Arman, Ben, Buren, Garouste, Hains, Klein, Nikki de Saint-Phalle, and Villeglé.

Farideh Cadot: 77 rue des Archives, 75003 Paris, Tel.: 01–42–78–08–36. Avant-garde gallery with many American artists. Among the first to open in the Marais. Artists associated with the gallery include Connie Beckley, Joel Fisher, Rousse, Tremblay, and David Hodges.

Gilbert Brownstone: 9 and 17 rue Saint-Gilles, 75003 Paris, Tel.: 01–42–78–43–21. An Americain gallery, highly active in the field of conceptual work. Promotes the works of Albers, Fontana, Gottfried Honneger, Jesus-Raphael Soto, and Raynaud.

Galerie de France: 52 rue de la Verrerie, 75004 Paris; Tel.: 01–42–74–38–00. A beautiful space on several levels showing works by well-known artists such as Domela, Degottex, Matta, Soulages, and Keiichi Tahara.

Baudoin Lebon: 38 rue Ste-Croix de la Bretonnerie, 75004 Paris; Tel.: 01–42–72–09–10. A well-established gallery that seriously promotes a wide range of styles in one of the Marais's finest spaces. Artists include Ben, Clareboudt, Frydman, Mapplethorpe, Dubbufet, and Bettencourt.

Christian Mollet-Viéville: 26 rue Beaubourg, 75003 Paris; Tel.: 01–42–78–72–31. Telephone or write for an appointment. This well-known dealer promotes minimal and conceptual works by artists such as Carl André, Buren, Sol LeWitt, and Weiner.

Daniel Templon: 1 impasse Beaubourg, 75003 Paris; Tel.: 01–42–72–14–10. Well-known gallery specialized in minimal and conceptual art (Judd, Flavin, and Morris), as well as more exuberant works by Alberola, Chia, Fetting, Rauchenberg, and Salle.

Pierre–Marie Vitoux: 3 rue d'Ormesson, 75004 Paris; Tel.: 01–48–04–81–00. A small space with big talents. The gallery represents Hadad, Ben-Ami Koller, Linström, Mazliah, and Maurice Rocher.

Zabriskie: 37 rue Quincampoix, 75004 Paris, Tel.: 01–42–72–35–47. This branch of the famous New York gallery opened in 1977 to feature photography. Photos by Klein, Friedlander, and Stieglitz can be seen, as well as works in other mediums by Tony Long, Poivret, and Shirly Farb.

Bastille (Métro: Bastille)

Frank Bordas: 2 rue de la Rocquette, 75011 Paris; Tel.: 01–47–00–31–61. Founded in 1978, this respected print editor combines studio work space and gallery in this charming courtyard. Artists associated with the gallery include James Brown, Alechinsky, Chambas, and Hervé Di Rosa.

Durand-Desert: 28 rue de Lappe, 75011 Paris; Tel.: 48–06–92–23. Recently inaugurated, this fine gallery boasts five levels to showcase monumental sculpture as well as works on paper. Artists include: Beuys, Boltanski, Haacke, Flanagan, and Tosani.

Espace d'Art Yvonamor Palix: 13 rue Keller, 75011 Paris; Tel.: 01–48–06–36–70. This small but dynamic gallery is a constant presence at international art fairs. Photography and multimedia works as well as computer imagery by artists Orlan, BP, or Jorge & Lucy Orta.

Jacqueline Felman: 8 rue Popincourt, 75011 Paris; Tel.: 01–47–00–87–71. This renovated factory space opened in 1985 to promote contemporary figurative work by younger artists. An international group of painters working between figuration and abstraction, such as Pierre Nivollet, Masao Haigima, and James Bloedé.

Lavignes-Bastille: 27 rue de Charonne, 75011 Paris; Tel.: 01–47–00–88–18. Spacious, well-established gallery that often has simultaneous exhibits that contrast a wide range of styles from neo-Expressionism to abstraction. Artists include: Fraser, Grataloup, Rauchbach, Sandorfi, Baykam, and Vostell

Salons

Modern art history begins with the rejection of the impressionists by the official French academic *salon*. The subsequent *Salon des Refusés* rocked the Paris art world, and some years later the famous Fauve scandal heralded a new era of modern painting at the *Salon d'Automne* in 1905.

It is curious to remember that the *Salon d'Automne*, considered the most traditional *salon* today, was originally created as a rather violent reaction against the prevailing academic criteria of the time. In 1903 artists Rodin, Jourdain, Renoir, and Cézanne founded a new *salon* that was to serve as an alternative exhibition space for a new generation of artists whose experimental work was not deemed acceptable by the official *salons*.

At the end of the twentieth century, art history repeats itself with the emergence of offshoots from established salons. Artistic quarrels seem to be a lively part of the salon tradition, and today there are at least 35 salons in and around Paris. A current example of this principle is the highly successful salon MAC 2000, which began as a splinter group from the *Salon de la Jeune Peinture.*

The launching of young artists is an important part of of the *salon* tradition. Painters and sculptors from other countries envy the opportunities French salons offer to Paris-based artists. Today the salon tradition continues to interest a large audience of art lovers. Each *salon* is highly publicized by posters about town. The following list includes the most important of the French *salons* currently held in the temporary Quai Branly (75007) convention and exhibition space while the Grand Palais is undergoing renovation efforts. Application requirements and fees vary. Individual salons should be contacted for further information. For Quai Branly Salon information, call 01–44–18–43–21.

+ *Grand Palais:* 2 avenue Winston Churchill, 75008 Paris (Métro: Champs Elysées-Clémenceau). Tel.: 01–42–89–23–13. Until recently the Grand Palais was home for most Paris *salons*. This immense, domed exhibition hall was built at the same time as the Petit Palais for the Universal exhibition of 1900. There are several large exhibition spaces to receive major retrospectives and temporary theme exhibits. Exhibitions are open daily except Tuesday, from 10h00 to 20h00; Wednesday until 22h00. Entrance fees vary.

+ *Salon d'Automne:* quai Branly. For information: Porte C, Grand Palais, 2 avenue Winston Churchill, 75008 Paris; Tel.: 01–43–59–46–07. (15h00 to 18h00). A historic *salon* that maintains the great *salon* tradition. Annually, each November.

+ *Salon des Artistes Décorateurs:* quai Branly. For information: Porte H, Grand Palais, 2 avenue Winston Churchill, 75008 Paris; Tel.: 01–49–59–11–10. Every aspect of interior design. A professional *salon* that involves manufacturers/ artists/designers and decorators. Once every two years during autumn.

+ *Salon Comparaisons:* quai Branly. For information: President: Bernard Mougins, 5 rue du Général de Maud'huy, 75014 Paris; Tel.: 01–43–39–45–06. International *salon* featuring diverse trends. Once every two years in June.

+ *Salon Figurations Critiques:* quai Branly. For information: President: Mme Dors-Rapin, 1 rue Louis-Gaubert, 78140 Velizy-Bas. A *salon* that promotes figurative work. Held during September.

+ *Salon de la Jeune Peinture:* quai Branly. For information: President: Katerine Louineau, 143 boulevard Jean-Jaurès, 92110 Clichy; Tel.: 01–47–31–66–37. A postwar *salon* founded in 1949 that supports painted works by emerging talents. Annual. February.

+ *Salon des Independants:* quai Branly. For information: Porte H, Grand Palais. Tel.: 42–25–86–39. Historic salon founded in 1884. Exhuberant but often very crowded. Highly eclectic selection. Annual. Held during winter (February or March).

+ *Salon de la Jeune Sculpture:* Porte d'Austerlitz, 75013 Paris; Tel.: 01–43–04–68–86. Association de la Jeune Sculpture, 10 Square de Port-Royale, 75013 Paris. A biannual *salon* that takes place during the spring and fall to promote contemporary sculpture of all *tendances* (trends).

+ *Salon de Mai:* quai Branly. For information: Secretary: Jacqueline Selz, 8 ave Victorien Sardou, 75016 Paris; Tel.: 01–42–88–44–01. A *salon* that highlights artists of repute as well as emerging talents. Annual. Held in May.

+ *Salon Grands et Jeunes d'Aujourd'hui:* quai Branly. For information: President: Marylène Dénoval, 12 bis, rue de l'Etoile, 75017 Paris; Tel.: 01–43–80–38–75. A well-respected *salon* with a rigorous selection policy that provides a fine overview of contemporary trends. Annual. October.

✦ **Salon MAC 2000:** quai Branly. For information: President: Concha Benedito, 28 rue du Sergent Godefroy, 93100 Montreuil; Tel.: 01–48–59–19–30. A unique salon that features a series of one-person shows for confirmed artists. Careful selection and high-quality work. Annual. Held in November/December.

✦ **Salon de Montrouge:** Centre Culturel et Artistique de Montrouge. Tel.: 01–46–56–52–52. President: Nicole Ginoux-Bessec, 32 rue Gabriel Péri, 92120 Montrouge. The most important of the *salons* outside of Paris; well known for launching artists. Fine quality of work. Annual. During autumn.

Off the Beaten Track: Art Factories

The *Bateau Lavoir* in Montmartre and *La Ruche* on the edge of the fifteenth *arrondissement*, in which the Cuban painter Alvarez-Rios currently resides, are two classic artist studio complexes that housed a number of modern masters early in the last century. Since that nostalgic period, Paris's real estate has soared and an artist's studio in Paris has gone from being a high-priced commodity to a nearly extinct species. Increasingly, contemporary artists of today are gathering in reconverted factories and warehouses to produce their art.

Most of these large abandoned spaces are to be found in the grimmer parts of the city, or the nearby suburbs. Social security sources suggest there may be more than 40,000 (declared) professional artists living in the Paris region. This staggering figure would account for the growing edge to an already competitive art scene, and the increasing sense of alarm over the scarcity of studio space. In recent years, artists' squats have called media attention to these pressing problems of space.

The following is a list of art factories that may be visited by the general public. There are exhibition programs and open studio visits. It is best to call for an appointment.

Ap'Arté: 12 rue Larrey, 75005 Paris; Tel.: 01–42–17–06–59. The association Ap'Arté runs an exhibition space that also highlights conferences, debates, and studio visits.

Glaz'Art: 7–15 avenue de la Oirte de la Villette, 75019 Paris; Tel.: 01–40–36–55–65. This association, supported by the mayor's office, offers a multipurpose space to highlight diverse artistic disciplines. Painting, sculpture, and ephemeral installations.

Quai de la Gare: 91 quai de la Gare, 75013 Paris; Tel.: 01–45–85–91–91. A former refrigerator warehouse situated between the train tracks and the Seine. More than 250 artists work in diverse mediums in private studios. Lively open-studio events several times a year.

Palais de Tokyo: 13 avenue du President Wilson, 75016 Paris; Tel.: 01–47–23–38–86. Open daily, except Mondays, from noon to midnight. Entrance fee: 5 euros. The newest space for installations and ephemeral creations by young artists.

La Base: 6 bis rue Vergiaud, Levallois, 92300 (Métro: Louise-Michel); Tel.: 01–47–58–48–58. A reconverted factory with a fine exhibition space and an artists-in-residence program. An art center with an international scope, showcasing works produced on the spot by major talents from around the world.

Cinema/Film

American film critic Lisa Nesselson, who moved to Paris from Chicago in 1978, regularly reviews films and covers cinema topics for Variety. *From 1987 to 2001, she chronicled Paris's movie scene in the* Paris Voice. *She also pens a bimonthly* ŒLetter *from Paris, in "Facets Features" (www.facets.org). Nesselson sees some 400 films a year (she has never owned a television set). Here are her comments on filmgoing in Paris.*

As the devout make pilgrimages to Mecca or Jerusalem, so should the true believer in cinema come to Paris. For although movies may be made in Hollywood, only in France are they worshiped. The French themselves are surprised to hear it, but in terms of sheer variety and accessibility to the movies of many lands, Paris is the viewing capital of the world. As the commemorative plaque at 14 boulevard des Capucines indicates, history's first public projection of motion pictures for paying customers (courtesy of France's own Lumière brothers) took place in the Salon Indien of the Grand Café on December 28, 1895.

With its film archives, ciné clubs, repertory cinemas, and fabulous concentration of commercial movie houses, Paris is the perfect place to catch up on more than ten decades of the seventh art. Say, why do they call it that, anyway? Glad you asked. It was in Paris, in 1911, that the Italian critic Ricciotto Canudo declared the cinema to be the seventh art, next in line after architecture, music, painting, sculpture, poetry, and dance. (Every so often someone has the temerity to suggest that television/video might be the "eighth art," but such people are usually found, bound with celluloid and gagged with cathode ray tubes, at the bottom of the Seine.)

When this book was first published in 1993, Paris boasted 314 commercial screens. The figure is now 36 screens for a population of roughly two million. (Manhattan, by comparison, has less than half as many screens.) Paris sports some of the best-equipped theaters on the planet, many of them created or expanded in just the past two or three years. The Ciné Cité Les Halles, with nineteen well-proportioned screens, raked seating, and excellent sound, is the most successful multiplex in the nation. Maverick producer and theater owner Marin Karmitz gave the city's nineteenth arrondissement a huge boost when he opened his soon-to-be expanded six-screen MK2 Quai de Seine complex on the waterfront near the Stalingrad métro. Filmgoers nostalgic for the hole-in-the-wall art-house experience can still find valiant vestiges of that tradition, but even most of the smaller establishments have upgraded their facilities to the extent their budgets allowed. Paris audiences still respect the notion that a public theater is not a private living room—extraneous comments and play-by-play accounts ("He's got a gun! He's going to shoot her! Look, he shot her!") are practically unheard of. And, although refreshments are served at many theaters, you'll never find gum stuck to the floor. Plus, your chances of coming across a film crew or even bumping into a major director or actor while walking down the street, riding the metro, or standing in line for a movie are excellent. That's the good news.

The bad news is that movies aren't cheap. Standard admission hovers at around 8 euros. But the CNC, the government body that regulates all film production and exhibition in France, wants everybody to be able to afford to go to the movies at least once a week. From 1980 to 1992 ticket prices were 30 percent cheaper for one and all on (traditionally slow) Mondays. In 1992 "cheap day" officially migrated to Wednesday, the day on which new films open. Several independent art houses now discount seats on Mondays and Wednesdays, and a few theaters have reverted to Mondays only. If your schedule permits and you're not too discombobulated by the idea of taking in a film first thing in the morning, the first show at some of the city's finest multiplexes costs between 4,50 euros and 5,50 euros—and you're nearly guaranteed a seat. The first show at the UCG Ciné Cité Les Halles can be as early as 9:10 A.M. The first show at the UGC Orient-Express (in the Forum des Halles), the UGC George V (on the Champs-Elysées), the Max Linder and the 5 Caumartin (in the ninth arrondissement), the UGC Cité Ciné Bercy and the Pathé Wepler (in the eighteenth) starts closer to 11:00 A.M. or noon. With bonafide ID cards, there are discounts (tarif réduit) for the unemployed, military personnel, senior citizens, families with three or more children, or students. A valid student ID card (local or international) is worth its weight in gold, since many theaters offer a 30 percent reduction to students at daytime shows Monday through Friday (and some, including the Action cinemas, which pioneered the practice, extend the privilege to every show, seven days a week). The Action theaters (two in the fifth, one in the sixth arrondissement) offer the cheapest seats in town during Happy Hour (pronounced "ah-pee owe-air") on weekdays between 6:00 and 7:00 P.M. when a ticket is just 4 euros. There are other alternatives to paying full price, which will be discussed further along. Since films change on Wednesdays, that's when the weekly entertainment guides hit the newsstands. (These are a better bet than the daily papers for complete addresses and showtimes.) *L'Officiel des Spectacles* is neatly organized and costs only 35 centimes. Some folks prefer *Pariscope* (38 centimes), which offers listings by category (Westerns, comedies, horror films) as well as by neighborhood, in case you get the genre munchies ("I simply must see a Western—and quick!"). When you're scanning the weekly listings or spontaneously ducking into a theater, pay special attention to whether a given film is being presented in VO or VF. VO (*version originale*) means the film will be shown with its dialogue intact (be it English, Danish, or pig Latin) accompanied by French subtitles. VF (*version française*) indicates that the film has been dubbed into French (although some theatres use VF to inform customers that the film is French to begin with). Most of the theaters in the Latin Quarter, in Les Halles, and along the Champs-Elysées specialize in VO prints, as does the spanking-new Ciné Cité at Bercy. The Montparnasse area deals in both dubbed and subtitled fare. The theaters of the Grands Boulevards and Montmartre are almost all purveyors of VF films. If, as is increasingly the case, a French-speaking director (Jean-Jacques Annaud, Luc Besson, Jean-Pierre Jeunet) has made an English-language film *(Seven Years in Tibet, The Fifth Element, Alien Resurrection)*, you may come across the designation VA (*version anglaise*).

As for titles, it's not difficult to deduce that *9 Semaines et Demie* is *9½ Weeks*, but if you don't know your directors and actors, it might be hard to guess that *Voyage au bout de l'enfer (Journey to the End of Hell)* is actually *The Deer Hunter; Aux portes de l'enfer (At the Gates of Hell)* is *Angel Heart; Personne n'est parfait (Nobody's Perfect)* is *Torch Song Trilogy;* and *Un cadavre sous le chapeau (A Cadaver under the Hat)* is *Miller's Crossing.* Sometimes the French release actually improves the original title, as in *Sex Crimes* as a replacement for *Wild Things* or *Sexe Intentions* for *Cruel Intentions.*

Outside the theater, most cinemas list two show times for each presentation, a two-tiered system that the program guides no longer bother to differentiate as precisely as they once did. The first, known as the séance, consists of anywhere from ten to forty minutes of coming attractions and commercials. Theoretically, the houselights are to be only partially dimmed, leaving patrons the option of reading Proust, conjugating irregular verbs, or otherwise ignoring the ads.

However, if you hail from a country where it would probably not occur to the telephone company to use topless women in its advertising campaigns, you may want to direct your attention to the screen, where you're also likely to see a buck naked hunk romping in the surf on behalf of a popular brand of men's underwear or a trendy fragrance. On weekend nights or during the first few days of a film's run, you should definitely arrive before the séance to be assured of a good seat. Otherwise, if the movie's not a runaway hit, you can generally plan to arrive just before the second time listed, for the film itself. Some theaters will sell you a ticket for a specific show up to a week in advance, at the box office, via a proprietary reservation system, or through the nonpartisan phone reservation system Allo Ciné; Tel.: 01-40-30-20-10.

The ubiquitous usherette or *ouvreuse* (so-named because the base of the seats in legitimate theaters had to be unlocked—*ouvrir* being the French verb "to open"—and the usherette, who had the key, was loath to do so unless assured of a tip, or *pourboire*) has, in recent years given way to salaried personnel. The ushers at the major theater chains (Pathé, Gaumont, UCG) no longer expect a tip, but those at art houses and a few first-run cinemas still rely entirely on your generosity. A minimum *pourboire* of 2 FF was the polite standard for decades; the transition to the euros makes 30 centimes a good place to start. Although some multiplexes have installed vending machines or built concession stands, in many theaters the usherettes walk the aisles before the show carrying straw trays stocked with ice cream bars and candy. Take the precaution of opening any potentially noisy wrappers before the feature starts—patrons have been seen coming to blows over one too many crinklings of cellophane.

Whatever the basic ticket price, student *(réduction étudiant)* and senior-citizen discounts run roughly 2 euros cheaper. Interestingly enough, you can expect to pay the same amount of money for an art-house revival of *Citizen Kane* as you would for the very latest Hollywood fare. (After all, the reasoning goes, art is art, whatever its vintage). Stanley Kubrick's *A Clockwork Orange*—the highest grossing film in France in 1972 with 7.6 million tickets sold—was one of the year's top box-office performers upon its re-release in 1992. Pedro Almodovar's complete oeuvre remained in almost constant release in Paris for nearly a decade—meaning the price of a ticket to his earlier films has actually gone up over time—and a Woody Allen retrospective held on to its screen at first-run prices for over a year.

Although American films are often released at roughly the same time in France as they are in North America, there is sometimes a hearty gap, with Disney-animated features, for example, hitting French screens as much as one full year later. Some English-language films, however, come out in Paris before they are released in American theaters. Examples include Clint Eastwood's *Bird and White Hunter, Black Heart;* Jim Jarmusch's *Night on Earth;* Woody Allen's *Shadows and Fog;* Michael Mann's *The Last of the Mohicans;* Jennifer Lynch's *Boxing Helena;*

Bernardo Bertolucci's *Little Buddha* and *Besieged;* Jonathan Nossiter's *Sunday;* Jane Campion's *The Piano;* John Carpenter's *Vampires;* the Angelina Jolie-Antonio Banderas potboiler *Original Sin;* and David Lynch's *Mulholland Drive.*

Although Parisians can be relied upon to smoke everywhere else, smoking is not permitted in movie theaters. Depending on your tolerance for tobacco fumes, this in itself could be a major incentive to spend time at the movies.

The French filmgoing landscape was thrown into upheaval in 2000 when the UGC theater chain introduced it's *carte illimitee* (unlimited card). For a flat-fee subscription of roughly $15 a month (with a minimum 12-month commitment), card owners may take in as many movies as their schedules permit, all-you-can-eat style, at any UGC cinema. When it became clear that UGC was unabashedly after market share, the other chains were forced to cave in and create their own prepaid brand-loyalty schemes. Independently owned theaters have been hard hit by these tactics and many of the smaller art houses are hanging on for dear life. While the cards represent a major savings for frequent filmgoers, they've also introduced the idea (a given in America but never previously said aloud in France) that movies are a consumer item like any other for which one can comparison shop, tailoring one's filmgoing to *where* the movie is playing rather than the possible merits of the movie itself. That's tantamount to heresy in some quarters, and lawsuits are pending to settle whether such deep discounting is, in fact, unfair and therefore illegal.

If you're planning to do a lot of mainstream filmgoing but aren't staying in France for an entire year, you may want to invest in the magnetic debit cards offered by Gaumont (30 euros for five admissions) and UGC (26.15 euros for five individual weekday admissions or 33 euros for five admissions any time, including weekends). For 35 euros the MK2 cinema circuit offers a six-seat card valid for four months, and for 15 euros a three-seat card good for one month. The cluster of five cinemas near the Tour Montparnasse run by the Rytmann family honor the UGC unlimited card in addition to offering their own pre-paid discount card (49 euros for 10 admissions). Certain independent theaters reward repeat customers with one free ticket for a specific number of paid admissions.

After over a decade of steadily eroding attendance figures for French films in France, the downward trend buoyantly reversed itself in 2001, propelled by local faves such as *Amelie, The Closet,* and *Brotherhood of the Wolf* that also registered well abroad. For each film released since 1945, the French have—quite logically—kept track of the precise number of tickets sold rather than the amount of money earned. This makes it a cinch to compare French filmgoing habits from year to year without having to factor in rising ticket prices or general inflation.

Although the sixth *arrondissement* became the city's most expensive real estate in price per square meter in mid-1999 (an honor previously held by the seventh), the sixth is still the friendliest place in town for budget-minded young filmgoers. The scruffy Cinoches offers a discount to people under eighteen whether they're students or not, as do the Arlequin, the Bretagne, and the Saint Germain des Prés, an offer the Action extends to anyone under age twenty, the Racine and Trois Luxembourg to those under age twenty-one, and the Saint-André-des-Arts to anyone under age twenty-five.

Archives (Noncommercial and Miscellaneous Film)

The legendary Cinémathèque Française, an archive and public screening room, was founded in 1936 by film fanatics George Franju and Henri Langlois when they were barely out of their teens. Langlois (1914–77), who believed that every film was a potential masterpiece and collected accordingly, is largely responsible for the grudging acknowledgment that the movies can be art as well as entertainment. One of Langlois's greatest fears was that the Cinémathèque would fall into the hands of government bureaucrats and that, alas, is precisely where the Cinémathèque is headed. Although it remains a nonprofit organization, the Cinémathèque relies on government subsidies and will be incorporated into a movie-themed public center tenetatively slated to open by the end of 2003.

After more than fourteen years of solemn official announcements, the Ministry of Culture announced in June 1998 that a genuine, permanent, final home had been found for what was then called the Maison du Cinéma: the defunct American Center designed by Frank Gehry in the Bercy quarter, at 51 rue de Bercy. Gehry's striking structure was purchased by the city and, as we go to press, is being gutted and completely refitted in order to be reborn as a cultural center devoted to the history, study, and all-around enjoyment of movies. The new entity will somehow incorporate the holdings of the BiFi (see below) and the Cinémathèque, as well as a film museum that, of necessity, will have a fraction of the floor space once enjoyed by the Musée du Cinéma Henri-Langlois in the site-specific installation Langlois created in the sprawling basement of the Palais de Chaillot. (After functioning in a variety of projection spaces around town, the Cinémathèque settled at Chaillot in mid-1963.)

Langlois spent two years creating his museum, which opened in 1972. Various government agencies had long coveted the space it occupied, and the question of dismantling and moving the museum was conveniently settled by a freak fire on the newly restored roof of the Palais de Chaillot on the night of June 22, 1997. Although most of the costumes, posters, set replicas, cameras, projectors, and other cinemabilia—some of it priceless—were heroically hauled to safety during the blaze and after, massive water damage left the premises soggy beyond repair. Although the French Court of Appeals granted full artistic status to the museum's layout—after the fire had left the locale an empty shell—Langlois's loving arrangement of more than 3,000 artifacts was consigned to history's scrap heap. The collections were dried out and crated up to await their eventual new home. Given the wording of preliminary proposals and the institution's slapdash track record under elitist self-serving management throughout the nineties, it is nearly impossible to give the benefit of the doubt to the people put in charge of designing the new museum. While it's entirely possible that the new entity will be a pleasant enough place to hang out once it's finished, the failure to restore the Langlois Museum to its original form and location means international filmdom has been deprived of one of its most precious landmarks.

The Cinémathèque itself, however, may be on the right track again under new director Peter Scarlet, who came to the job after years of running the San Francisco International Film Festival. For the Cinémathèque's one unmistakable claim to fame remains its film collection, estimated at 23,000 titles. Before the general public took it for granted that movies could be had cheaply and easily on TV or video-cassette, the Cinémathèque educated and entertained several generations of film enthusiasts, many of whom went on to become filmmakers. While the 51 rue de Bercy project is under construction, the Cinémathèque's film showings continue at the Chaillot theater (which was revamped after the fire) and at a temporary 200-seat annex. Programs are listed in the weekly guides or may be picked up at the theaters. La Cinémathèque française: Palais de Chaillot Place de Trocadéro (avenue Albert de Mun and avenue du Président Wilson, in the sixteenth); Métro: Trocadéro. Second screen (Grands Boulevards) at 42 boulevard de Bonne Nouvelle, 75010; Métro: Bonne Nouvelle; tickets, 4.70 euros. For members, 3 euros. Tel.: 01–56–26–01–01 (recorded program).

Forum des Images

One locale that gives Parisians exceptional access to unusual fare is the Forum des Images (formerly *La Videotheque de Paris*), which, on its tenth anniversary in October 1998, adopted its new name and christened a new auditorium. Opened in 1988 as a public-access archive of film and video documents concerning Paris, the *Forum des Images*, located underground, offers individual video consoles for research (a state-of-the-art robot can select any of the more than 6,000 films on tap in a matter of minutes). Which means that you can watch *Breathless* (see Jean Seberg hawk the *Herald Tribune* on the Champs-Elysées!) or *Superman II* (witness the thrilling rescue of Lois Lane on the Eiffel Tower!) or dial up vintage newsreels or documentaries depicting any aspect of life in Paris that interests you.

The forum also projects as many as seven feature films daily (often preceded by an appropriate newsreel or film trailer) in its impeccable (if slightly sterile) screening rooms. And it runs excellent theme programming (on subjects from Film Personalities Who Died Too Soon to Public Tranportation in the Movies, in addition to hosting the films from the Directors Fortnight in late May after Cannes, the Strange Film Festival in August, and Les Rencontres Internationales in October. One of the advantages here is that titles are almost always repeated on different days and at different times in the course of a retrospective, which gives you more than one chance to catch a given film. Pay 5,50 euros and stay all day, or become a member and reserve a video console via Minitel. The Forum also maintains a cybercafé. Forum des Images: 2 Grande Galerie, porte Saint-Eustache—Nouveau Forum des Halles; Métro: Chatelet-Les Halles; Tel.: 01–44–76–62–00 information, 01–40–26–34–30 recorded programs.

The auditorium at the Louvre as well as the auditorium at the Institut du Monde Arabe, the cinema at the Musée d'Orsay, the Salle Garance at the Centre Pompidou, the tiny theater at the Jeu de Paume, and the screening rooms of the Swiss, Hungarian, Belgian, and Finnish Cultural Centers are all exceptional resources for adventurous filmgoing.

Outstanding, Unusual, and Historic Theaters

If a recent film got yanked before you had a chance to see it, keep your eye on the listings for Studio 28, one of the most charming movie houses in Paris, if not in the world. Founded in its namesake year of 1928, the marvelous cinema Jean

Cocteau dubbed a masterpiece among theaters, the theater of masterpieces, was trashed by hooligans when Salvador Dali and Luis Buñuel's *L'age d'Or* premiered there in 1930. The studio programs a different film (in VO) every two days. In honor of Studio 28's sixtieth anniversary, veteran art director Alexandre Trauner (who died at age eighty-seven in December 1993) redecorated the slim lobby of this family-run enterprise, which displays molded footprints of film celebrities. The kitschy duncecap lamps in the auditorium and the homey little bar and courtyard are just a few of the reasons to visit Studio 28. Closed on Mondays and most of August.

Studio 28, 10 rue Tholozé, Métro: Abesses or Blanche; Tel.: 01–46–06–36–07; tickets: 6,80 euros, 24 euros for five entries, valid for two months. In October 1988 more than a dozen people were seriously injured when religious fanatics firebombed the Saint-Michel movie theater because it dared to show Martin Scorsese's *The Last Temptation of Christ.* Declaring that no attack on a filmmaker's freedom of expression would be tolerated, the government vowed to help rebuild the theater. It took a while, but the all-new Espace St-Michel opened in October 1991 sporting two screens and a pleasant restaurant/exhibit space. Their programming, which often offers the sole print of a given film, is consistently excellent.

Espace Saint-Michel: 7 Place St-Michel, 75005 Paris; Tel.: 01–44–07– 20–49. As its name suggests, the Latina (20 rue du Temple in the fourth arrondissement) shows films mostly from Spanish-speaking countries. Images d'Ailleurs (21 rue de La Clef in the fifth) specializes in movies by black and third-world filmmakers. The Quartier Latin (9 rue Champollion in the fifth) often programs outstanding Iranian films. The Cinema du Pantheon (13 rue Victor-Cousin in the fifth) is dedicated to hosting serious art-house fare, with bonus lectures and discussions at certain screenings The newly remodeled Archipel, in the tenth arrondissement, does likewise with a repertory lineup. In 2001, Cinealternative (in the eleventh, not far from Republique) began regular programs of thoughtfully programmed short films (18 rue fbg du Temple). The greatest concentration of movies for kids can be found at the Saint-Lambert (6 rue Péclet in the fifteenth), an adorable neighborhood theater.

Every Christmas season the Grand Rex—the city's biggest theater at 2,800 seats, although it boasted 5,000 when it opened in 1932—presents a kitschy show involving dancing fountains and colored lights. (For reasons unknown, programming jets of water to bob and spurt to music is something of a French art form.) The city's only true atmospheric movie palace left in operation (the star-sprinkled ceiling with projected clouds is meant to approximate an exotic evening under the open sky), the Rex sometimes shows features in *grand large,* meaning that a colossal retractable screen takes up most of the extremely comfortable main floor, forcing patrons to scurry into the balcony for a momentous view. The only drawback to the Grand Rex is that foreign films are almost always dubbed into French.

Rex (only the Grand Rex is of interest—the other six Rex theaters are run-of-the-mill), 1 boulevard Poissonière in the second.) An ingenious backstage tour of the cinema called Les Etoiles du Rex gives you a taste of what it's like to run a movie palace the size of a city block and includes a trip in a freight elevator behind the giant screen while a film's in progress—a nifty sensation. You can take the tour on its own (7 euros) or buy a combined ticket that includes a movie (11,70 euros).

If your lifestyle calls for regular exposure to *The Rocky Horror Picture Show*, the ninety-two-seat Studio Galande (42 rue Galande in the fifth) keeps the tradition alive on Friday and Saturday nights.

The Action cinema chain celebrates its thirty-fifth anniversary in 2002. Founders Jean-Marie Rodon and Jean-Max Causse survive in a tough field by displaying almost flawless programming taste and striking fresh prints of film classics.

La Pagode, the only remaining cinema in the seventh (57 bis rue de Babylone) is, as the name implies, housed in a pagoda *(salle japonaise)*, complete with miniature rock garden.

The oldest cinema in Paris still functioning as a movie theater, the Studio des Ursulines, is a charming one-screen venue that feels like a miniature opera house. The programming is always interesting, with a marked preference for personal and independent filmmaking. 10 rue des Ursulines, fifth, Tel.: 01–43–26–19–09.

Mac-Mahon

The Mac-Mahon, on its eponymous avenue beside the Arc de Triomphe in the seventeenth arrondissement, celebrated its sixtieth anniversary in 1998. It was at the Mac-Mahon—liberated at war's end by American soldiers whose headquarters were nearby—that Paris's film-starved cinephiles caught up on more than four years worth of Hollywood pictures they'd been denied during the German occupation. Along with Henri Langlois's Cinémathèque Française, the Mac-Mahon was arguably the most important informal school for Gallic critics and filmmakers-to-be. Godard pays tribute to the Mac-Mahon via a passage in *Breathless*. Down a steep flight of stairs, well below street level, lies the quaint theater, complete with velvet curtain and two Greek statues. (5 avenue Mac-Mahon.)

The Cinéma des Cinéastes, created in October 1996 by L'ARP (the French Association of Directors and Producers), runs an admirable mix of current releases, retrospectives, documentaries, and sneak previews with Q&A in its three-screen theater a block from Place de Clichy. The 315-seat main auditorium boasts exposed wrought-iron beams. With special programs designed for children and a strong policy in favor of showing short films, this is one of the liveliest film venues in town. (7 avenue de Clichy)

Film Festivals and Special Events

There is a film festival under way in one or more French towns or hamlets nearly every day and certainly every weekend of the year. There are festivals devoted to romance (Cabourg), film noir and thrillers (Cognac), Mediterranean cinema (Montpellier), animals (Beauvais), Nordic films (Rouen), Latin American fare (Toulouse), British cinema (Dinard and Cherbourg), American and European independents (Avignon), animation (Annecy), short films only (Clermont-Ferrand), and American fare (Deauville). Most, with the notable exception of Cannes, are only too happy to welcome the general public.

The celebrated Cannes International Film Festival takes place each May (56th edition in 2003). Unless you have friends to put you up and some legitimate connection to the film industry, a trip to the fest could be both costly and frustrating. That said, a certain number of tickets are sold to the general public (or given away by generous souls) for the so-called parallel sections, and film buffs can purchase accreditation for the forum, a sort of festival alongside the festival proper, whose lineup sometimes includes a sleeper or two more interesting than the films in the official competition. Throughout the festival the cultural center called Studio 13 (roughly a twenty-minute walk uphill from the Palais des Festivals) welcomes the general public to meet fest filmmakers and view their work for a token fee.

The annual *Fête du Cinéma* is a cross between trench warfare and the proverbial free lunch. Every theater in town participates and it works like this: Customer pays full admission price at the first movie attended that day and a token fee for each subsequent film. Wear comfortable shoes, pack sandwiches and mineral water, plan your itinerary with stopwatch in hand, and you may be able to fit in five current releases for the price of two. The annual International Women's Film Festival, held in the nearby suburb of Créteil, is completely geared to the general public and assembles outstanding female film talent from all over the world. The twenty-fourth edition was held during April 2002. Films de Femmes, Maison des Arts, Place Salvador Allende, 94000 Créteil; Tel.: 01–49–80–38–98.

Reading Matter

For those who read French, there are dozens of monthly magazines devoted to the cinema, with *Studio, Première, Positif,* and *Cahiers du Cinéma* being the best known. Ciné Live, with a CD-ROM in every issue, is a popular newcomer. The Web sites maintained by *Liberation, Telerama,* and *Le Monde* provide plenty of film coverage. *New:* For the most comprehensive listings of films showing in English, consult Sondra Russell's www.versionoriginale.com. The American edition of *Première* magazine is readily available at the more cosmopolitan news kiosks. The André Malraux public library maintains a very good cinema reference collection and subscribes to all of the major film periodicals.

Bibliothèque André Malraux, 78 boulevard Raspail, 75006 Paris; Tel.: 01–45–44–53–85; open 2:00 to 7:00 P.M. Tuesday through Friday, 10:00 a.m. to noon and 2:00 to 5:00 P.M. Saturday. For serious film research La Bibliothèque du Film, or BiFi, which opened in late 1996, at 100 rue du Faubourg Saint-Antoine in the twelfth, has extensive holdings, particularly when it comes to posters and stills. There is a nominal entry fee; Tel.: 01–53–02–22–30; Fax: 01–53–02–22–39; Métro: Ledru Rollin.

Paris and the Performing Arts

You don't have to be in Paris very long to notice that the French pay much more attention to the sensual side of life than to the practical side. This is good news not only for the late night *bon vivant* who likes to wander home through the empty streets at dawn after a night of major-league clubbing. The daylight hours, too, are often packed with possibilities for tasting a bit of what the Parisians call *la qualité de la vie.* It would take a very dull mind and a seriously withered heart to be bored in this city.

The great battle in Paris over the last two centuries, in art and in life, has been between the avant-garde and classical: the Impressionists, for example, shocking the academics in the 1800s, the Dada and surrealist movements shocking the bourgeoisie in the 1920s and 1930s, the writers of the nouveau roman shocking the reader in the 1950s and 1960s. The avant-garde and the classical act like tides that ebb and flow, one temporarily conquering the other. The waves caused by their inevitable clashes tend to keep things bubbling and interesting for the casual observer and leisurely partaker of all kinds of entertainment, French or foreign. Though much has changed over the decades, Paris remains a place where the new and strange are not only tolerated but also welcomed and even proudly displayed. When it comes to the performing arts, this is still in evidence, just as it is in fashion—which in Paris has become a performing art of its own.

Music in Paris

Choices run from the upper-crust, tuxedo, escargot atmosphere of the old Opéra Garnier to the merely crusty, like the head-bashing rock club Le Gibus near République. There's a lot in between—like jazz, for instance. Paris is one of the world's most jazz-appreciative cities, and France actually has a state-funded National Jazz Orchestra. Even in the years before World War II, black American musicians found the Parisians more appreciative than audiences in the United States, and the trend continues today. The city sponsors a Festival de Jazz each fall (usually in October), but year-round you can watch and listen to some of the best American and international acts at such intimate cellar clubs as New Morning, the two Petit Journal clubs at St-Michel and Montparnasse, the Petit Opportun at Châtelet, and a number of others scattered across the city. Every spring the suburban *département*, Seine St-Denis (93), sponsors an impressive gathering of international blues and jazz artists in a festival called *Banlieues Bleues*, with popularly priced gigs strewn all around the department from Bobigny to Montreuil. Call 01–48–13–12–10 for information and maps.

Experimental, electronic, and avant-garde composition of music and sound occurs year-round at the underground attachment to the Pompidou Center, IRCAM, which attracts musicians, composers, and researchers from around the world.

Parisians are serious jazz aficionados. Most clubs are small, crowded, smoky, and fairly expensive. There is usually a cover, and the price of drinks can seriously unbalance the average checking account. But people don't come to these places to drink, they come for the music, which begins at about 11:00 at night, lasts long and loud through multiple sets, and ends about 4:00 in the morning on weekends. Lots of people stay for the duration. When the band breaks, it's time for a cigarette and loud conversation, in the honorable Paris tradition. And unlike at most American establishments, no obnoxious waiter will force drinks on you and give you the bum's rush if you don't consume enough.

Paris is particularly open to street and métro musicians, although the RATP asks musicians playing underground to register first. Parisians are usually receptive to those who pass the hat—that is, if the music is good.

Classical Music
The music scene is Paris is so rich that one doesn't really know where to start describing it. A free, monthly newspaper devoted to classical music and concert

recitals, available at all concert halls, offers the best listings and news. To obtain a copy or to subscribe, contact *Cadences*, Editions Firca, 29 avenue Corentin Cariou, 75019 Paris; Tel.: 01–40–05–01–67.

Music and Dance Venues

Music and dance lovers are in for a treat. Plan to attend a performance during your Paris stay. In addition to the major venues for concerts, classical music, opera, ballet, and dance listed below, certain churches around the city make good use of their excellent acoustics and sponsor concerts throughout the year, especially in the summer, during the annual Festival Estival. Churches include La Madeleine, Saint-Sulpice, Saint-Séverin, St-Germain-des-Prés, Eglise Sainte-Geneviève, La Sainte Chapelle, St-Augustin, and, of course, Notre-Dame.

Amphithéâtre Richelieu de la Sorbonne
17 rue de la Sorbonne, 75005 Paris
Tel.: 01–42–62–71–71

Auditorium du Louvre
Louvre Museum, La Pyramide, Cour Napoléon, 75001 Paris
Tel.: 01–40–20–52–29
Métro: Palais-Royal

Auditorium du Musée d'Orsay
1 rue de la Légion d'Honneur, 75007 Paris
Tel.: 01–40–49–48–14
Métro: Solférino

Le Bataclan
50 boulevard Voltaire, 75011 Paris
Tel.: 01–47–00–55–22
Métro: Oberkampf
Small concert hall for both big names and emerging ones in the rock, hip-hop, reggae, and other scenes.

Bibliothèque Nationale François Mitterrand
11 quai François Mauriac, 75013 Paris
Tel.: 01–53–79–59–59
Métro: Bibliothèque Nationale

Centre Pompidou
19 rue de Beaubourg, 75004 Paris
Tel.: 01–44–78–13–15
Métro: Rambuteau
Tickets: 8 to 75 euros

Châtelet-Théâtre Musical de la Ville de Paris
1 Place du Châtelet, 75001 Paris

Tel.: 01–40–28–28–40
Métro: Châtelet-Les Halles
Tickets: concerts 10 to 30 euros; operas 10 to 88 euros

La Cigale
124 rue Rochechouart, 75018 Paris
Tel.: 01–46–06–59–29
Métro: Barbès Rochechouart
Small music hall used for eclectic performances, guitarists, reggae, and others.

Cité de la Musique
221 avenue Jean Jaurès, 75019 Paris
Tel.: 01–44–84–44–84 (reservations)
Métro: Pantin
Major venue for classical, modern, contemporary, baroque, and other serious concerts. A bit far out, but worth the visit. Good and inexpensive restaurant on the premises.

IRCAM
1 Place Igor Stravinski, 75004 Paris
Tel.: 01–44–78–48–34
Métro: Châtelet

Maison de Radio France
116 avenue du Président Kennedy, 75016 Paris
Tel.: 01-56–40–22–22
Métro: Ranelagh or Passy
You can attend classical concerts, operas, and performances of the Orchestre National de France, which are broadcast on France Culture.

L'Olympia
28 boulevard des Capucines, 75009 Paris
Tel.: 01–47–42–25–49
Métro: Madeleine
Tickets: usually 15 to 30 euros
This is one of musical Paris's landmarks. Famous French singers, such as Edith Piaf, Jacques Brel, and Yves Montand, have made themselves internationally famous here. Although the chansons françaises once dominated the Olympia's stage, more contemporary acts from a variety of musical backgrounds are now included.

Opéra Bastille
120 rue de Lyon, 75011 Paris
Tel.: 08–36–69–78–68
Métro: Bastille
Tickets: 9 to 100 euros
This contoversial opera house of modern design was created by Canadian

Carlos Ott. Since its first perfomance was given in 1989, there has been a nearly constant storm of criticism not only of its architecture but also of its acoustics and prices. Part of this reaction can be attributed to the expected slamming by Parisians of anything new. There are actually more operas performed here than at its crosstown cousin, the Opéra Garnier. We can't gauarantee it, but there are often discounted seats available for students and seniors fifteen minutes before curtain.

L'Opéra Comique
5 rue Favart, 75009 Paris
Tel.: 08–25–00–00–58 (reservations)
Métro: Richelieu-Drouot
Tickets: 8 to 75 euros
French operas and small-scale performances.

Opéra Palais Garnier
Place de la Opéra, 75009 Paris
Tel.: 08–36–69–78–68
Métro: Opéra
Tickets: 9 to 100 euros
This is the granddaddy opera house of Paris, built during Napoleon III's empire by the then-unknown Charles Garnier. The interior is impressive, including an eclectic mix of architecture and adornment from Gobelin tapestries to a Chagallian ceiling. A large part of its season is dedicated to ballet. Visits, with access to all the public areas of the opera and its library and museum, are allowed every day to 5:00 P.M (4,50 euros; Tel.: 01–47–42–07–02).

Palais des Congrès
2 Place Porte Maillot, 75017 Paris
Tel.: 01–40–68–00–05
Métro: Porte de Maillot
Large performance hall.

Palais Omnisports de Paris-Bercy
8 boulevard de Bercy, 75012 Paris
Tel.: 01–43–46–12–21
Métro: Bercy
Huge and impressive stadium and hall for big groups and international acts. The sloping outer walls of the stadium are lined with real grass!

Sainte Chapelle
4 boulevard du Palais, 75001 Paris
Tel.: 01–42–50–96–18
Métro: Cité or St-Michel

Salle Gaveau
45 rue de la Boétie, 75008 Paris
Tel.: 01–49–53–05–07

Métro: Miromesnil
Small and intimate music hall for chamber music and recitals.

Salle Pleyel
252 rue du Faubourg St-Honoré, 75008 Paris
Tel.: 01–45–61–53–00
Métro: Ternes

Théâtre de la Ville
2 Place du Châtelet, 75004 Paris
Tel.: 01–42–74–22–77
Métro: Châtelet-Les Halles
Tickets: 14 to 30 euros

Théâtre des Champs-Elysées
15 avenue Montaigne, 75008 Paris
Tel.: 01–42–45–38–30
Métro: Alma-Marceau
Tickets: 6 to 77 euros.

Zénith
211 avenue Jean Jaurès, 75019 Paris
Tel.: 01–42–08–60–00
Métro: Pantin
Concert hall for some of the biggest and loudest domestic and international talent.

Popular Music
According to American writer and musician Mike Zwerin, who writes regularly for the *International Herald Tribune* and compiled much of the information in this section, "going out to hear live popular music in Paris is relatively easy although more often than not either expensive or uncomfortable." But the creative explosion on the music scene over the past several years, especially in the area of French rap, North African *râi*, and hip-hop have helped provide fresh alternatives to the classic problems of crowdedness, cost, and smoke.

One of the most interesting musical phenomena of our time is the popularity of what is categorized as world music. In Paris the music of North Africa, black Africa, Latin America, eastern Europe, and the multicultural suburbs mix and meld. The most realistic, if least efficient, way to approach this wide-ranging music is to look in the rock, jazz, or folk categories in any of the city's entertainment guides. Search for African, Asian, or Latin American names you've never heard of. Names like Senem Diyici, Safy Boutella, Papa Wemba, or Sheikh Hamza Shakour. If they've been able to travel, they are either the best or the brightest or at least the most ambitious at home. From wherever they come, these people generally end up in Paris, which, xenophobic twitches notwithstanding, takes pride in its cultural variety. Journals, including *Télérama* (the best of them), list world music separately *(Musiques du Monde).*

The most consistently creative world music programming can be found at Le Passage du Nord-Ouest at 13 rue Faubourg Montmartre in Pigalle. It is a pleasant room, holding 500 to 600 people, mostly seated at tables on tiers, with a reasonable admission and minimum consumption price structure. It also books fusion jazz, New Age flirts such as John Surman, and such aging hippies as Hot Tuna; Tel.: 01–47–57–24–24.

La Chapelle des Lombards at 19 rue de Lappe presents salsa and Brazilian music. It starts late, around 11:00 P.M.; it's usually packed with smoking Latinos, and it can swing. Tel.: 01–43–57–24–24.

The New Morning at 7 rue des Petits Ecuries in the tenth arrondissement can no longer be called a jazz club. It has one of the most interesting and varied programs in town. You must join a disorderly mob outside about an hour before the band hits (the French are not very good at lining up) if you want a table (it's smarter to wait for the second set, around 10:30 P.M., when sleepy squares are heading toward beddie-bye). Many of the 400 to 500 people the place holds stand in back. The ventilating system is inadequate and in the summer the smell of armpit can be lethal. Tel.: 01–45–23–51–41.

Although presenting more world music recently, the New Morning is still more jazz oriented than Le Passage. Such people as Archie Shepp, Pat Metheny, and Foley favor the friendly ownership and management team headed by Madame Fahri, an Egyptian lady of some class who grew up in Cairo with Benny Goodman and Count Basie records and likes to book musicians she likes. Before his death Chet Baker was a regular here. Even though he sometimes wouldn't show up or fell off his chair stoned, Fahri thought he was a "sweet man and a great artist." Armpit or no armpit, you've got to support a place like this. (His Royal Badness Prince likes it, occasionally sneaking in to listen or for a surprise recital.)

Going down the line in venue importance, we come to the Olympia. Jimi Hendrix opened for Johnny Hallyday here in days of yore. Thelonious Monk and Nina Simone worked here. It's a monument. Artistically, it's been more or less downhill since the death of owner Bruno Cocatrix in the 1980s. Now mostly French variety music stars are featured. Of course some people like that kind of thing, including cultural politicians who are lobbying to increase the quota of French music on the media to 40 percent. Yes, there is a quota, but nobody has been able to define exactly what "French" means. Vanessa Paradis singing in English is French, long-time resident Americans-in-Paris singing in French are apparently not. The fight goes on.

La Cigale, L'Elysée Montmartre, and Le Bataclan are three halls where what Ahmet Ertegon called "ruckoids" can hear rock, funk, and reggae attractions too new or intelligent to draw more than 1,500 customers—performers such as P. J. Harvey, Four Non Blondes, Alpha Blondy, and John Hiatt. La Cigale is somewhat less *sauvage* than the others (you sit down). It helps to be young to survive the out-front sidewalk mob scene, which is often suffocating, and the volume inside, which can blow your ears. Entering all three you are body-searched by in-your-face muscle, and once in you get stoned on weed just breathing.

You can find the best local blues bands, about half of them American, seven nights a week in the cave of The Front Page at 58 rue St-Denis. As Brian Eno said, the blues is "25 million people singing the same song." At least those who play here try to swing, and it is a clean and cheap place to meet young people of the opposite sex. Tel.: 01–40–39–92–77.

Another good address for hearing live music while chugging a beer or meeting friends is **Chesterfield Café** at 124 rue La Boétie in the eighth. The café also has a restaurant and an attractive happy-hour special. It is open seven days a week from 9:00 P.M. to 5:00 A.M., with a gospel brunch on Sundays. Tel.: 01–42–25–18–06

As far as jazz goes, the "Round Midnight" days of the romantic caves of Saint-Germain-des Prés with Jean-Paul Sartre and Juliette Greco listening to Bud Powell and Dexter Gordon are over. But a number of jazz cellars remain. The most prominent, authentic, and expensive jazz cave is the plush, intimate, and usually jammed (reserve in advance) **La Villa,** just down the rue Bonaparte from Place Saint-Germain-des-Prés at 29 rue Jacob, 75006 Paris, not far from where Racine once lived. It books interesting groups led by such people as the jazz queen of song Shirley Horn, Ravi (son of John) Coltrane, and Teddy Edwards (who used to accompany Tom Waits). You can't get out of there for much less than 30 euros per person. Tel.: 01–43–26–60–00.

Les Latitudes, Le Montana, and **Le Bilboquet** are also just off Place Saint-Germain, on Rue Saint Benoit in back of the Café de Flore. Generally (there are exceptions) they feature journeyman French jazz at high prices. They are not recommended.

The Right Bank is a laid-back musicians' hangout, a place to go no matter who plays there; the street-level **Le Duc des Lombards** (42 rue des Lombards, 75001 Paris) will cost you 25 percent of La Villa, and the service is much friendlier. You may not be familiar with the names, but the management knows how to book. The odds are with you. There's a friendly dining room upstairs with inexpensive respectable food. Tel.: 01–42–33–22–88. Métro: Châtelet.

On the same street, which is a short one near Châtelet in the middle of town, lies **Le Sunset** (60 rue des Lombards, 75001 Paris) a bit more formal and expensive than Le Duc and more like a tunnel than a cave. You can hear good music if you choose beforehand. Both book a sprinkling of North Americans. Tel.: 01–40–26–46–60.

If you don't mind a little ride, one of the best jazz clubs in, or rather out of, town is the **Manhattan Jazz Club** in the Hotel New York at Disneyland Paris. You get there more quickly and easily than you might think by going to the end of the Marne-La-Vallée RER line and then walking ten minutes. It's comfortable, the sound system is excellent, you can drink for only 9 euros or eat reasonably priced Cajun dishes while listening to such people as the Arkansas bebopper Bob Dorough, Buddy De Franco, Hermeto Pascoal, and the wonderful Antillais bebop pianist Alain Jean-Marie. Tel.: 01–60–45–73–00.

The **Jazz Club Lionel Hampton** in the Hotel Méridien Etoile, near Porte Maillot (81 boulevard Gouvion St-Cyr, 75017 Paris), is a well laid-out, acoustically agreeable and comfortable if somewhat pricey venue to hear jazz, gospel, and the blues. Reserve in advance, and you'll sit at tables with good sight and sound lines to the likes of legendary New Orleans singer/songwriter/producer Allen Toussaint, the post-bebop funk of T. S. Monk, and Linda Hopkins with her Black and Blue Band. The room is off-lobby, and you can hear for free, sitting in one of the very-easy-indeed leather easy chairs (possibly next to a napping Japanese businessman). Tel.: 01–40–68–30–42.

The most complete and reliable French-language jazz and rock listings are also in the mass-circulation *Télérama*, which comes out every Wednesday; they include short descriptions of the music. For a thorough listing of venue and clubs offering jazz to house to rap to räi, pick up a copy of *Nova Magazine*, a bible of up-to-the-minute cultural listings and trends in the city. The English monthly *Paris Voice* offers an excellent feature on musical happenings in the city by Tim Baker.

For those of you looking to buy good and/or hard-to-find used records, there's Crocodisc at 46 rue des Ecoles and its sister shack Crocojazz on the nearby rue Montaigne St-Généviève, both in the fifth arrondissement. If you're looking to pick up an instrument or have one repaired, try the area around the Pigalle métro stop, the Paris equivalent to New York's Forty-eighth Street, where the shops, especially those with electric intruments, are clustered. (The area around the métro Europe near the Conservatoire Nationale de Musique in the eighth behind the Gare Saint-Lazare is studded with classical musical instrument shops.)

For the visiting musician looking to jam, both the Sunset and Duc de Lombard have weekly sessions. Show up with your horn, and most likely you'll get to blow.

For a description of Paris's leading musical radio stations, see the Radio Stations sections in Telecommunications and Media.

Quick Reference Guide to Clubs with Live Music
✦ Le Passage du Nord-Ouest, 13 rue Faubourg Montmartre, 75009 Paris; Tel.: 01–47–57–24–24.
✦ La Chapelle des Lombards, 19 rue de Lappe, 75011 Paris; Tel.: 01–53–27–24–24.
✦ New Morning, 7 rue des Petits Ecuries, 75010 Paris; Tel.: 01–45–23–51–41.
✦ The Front Page, 58 rue St-Denis, 75003 Paris; Tel.: 01–40–39–92–77.
✦ Chesterfield Café, 124 rue La Boétie, 75008 Paris; Tel.: 01–42–25–18–06.
✦ La Villa, 29 rue Jacob, 75006 Paris; Tel.: 01–43–26–60–00.
✦ Le Duc des Lombards, 42 rue des Lombards, 75001 Paris; Tel.: 01–42–33–22–88.
✦ Le Sunset, 60 rue des Lombards, 75001 Paris; Tel.: 01–40–26–46–60.
✦ Manhattan Jazz Club, Hotel New York at Disneyland Paris; Tel.: 01–60–45–73–00.
✦ The Jazz Club Lionel Hampton, Hotel Méridien Etoile, Porte Maillot, 81 boulevard Gouvion St-Cyr, 75017 Paris; Tel.: 01–40–68–30–42.

The Rock Scene
For Paris rock, the choice is between the *salle* (hall, room) where you pay to sit, and the club, where you pay to dance. There's live rock in either spot, but the livelier nights tend to be in the clubs. The big venues for live bands start at the massive Palais Omnisport de Bercy, one of the city's few buildings that has to have its walls mowed, to the belle-epoquish, more human-scale Le Zénith, La Cigale, L'Olympia, or L'Elysée-Montmartre, and the most fashionable *salles*, Le Passage du Nord-Ouest or l'Araphaho. In general Paris is not one of the essential stops on every band's concert tour, mostly because of the lack of big-profit-generating stadiums and the policy of the Paris municipality, which is not concerned with rock music except in closing clubs and/or in unauthorizing gigs in others, so the selec-

tion for live bands is less than you'd see in some smaller North American cities. But the big acts make it through town at one point or another. The best way to get your ticket entrance is to buy them at the main FNAC stores (Forum, Montparnasse) or at Virgin Megastore (or via their Minitel on-line ticket services).

Araphaho
42 rue Eugène Carrière
75018 Paris
Tel.: 01–42–52–38–48
Métro: Place d'Italie

Le Bataclan
50 boulevard Voltaire, 75011 Paris
Tel.: 01–43–14–35–35
Métro: Oberkampf

Palais Omnisports de Paris Bercy
8 boulevard Bercy, 75012 Paris
Métro: Bercy
Tel.: 01–43–46–12–21 reservations
Minitel: 36–15 BERCY

La Cigale
120 boulevard Rochechouart, 75018 Paris
Tel.: 01–46–06–59–29
Métro: Pigalle

Théâtre Dunois
108 rue Chevaleret, 75013 Paris
Tel.: 01–45–84–72–00
Métro: Chevaleret

L'Olympia
2ter, rue Caumartin, 75009 Paris
Tel.: 01–47–42–25–49
Métro: Madeleine

Le Passage du Nord-Ouest
13 rue du Faubourg Montmartre, 75009 Paris
Tel.: 01–47–57–24–24
Métro: Rue Montmartre

Le Rex
44 rue Poissonière, 75002 Paris
Tel.: 01–40–28–08–55
Métro: Bonne-Nouvelle

Le Zénith
211 avenue Jean Jaurès, 75019 Paris
Tel.: 01–42–08–60–00
Métro: Porte de Pantin

Clubs

The club scene is much livelier and more varied. It's where you'll find fashion zombies, celebs and apprentice celebs, and people who just like to get out and move it around. At the classic joints that have been on the scene for years, like Le Palace (now closed) and **Les Bains,** people-watching is at least as important as dancing. The African clubs, like **Le Tango, Mambo Club,** and **Keur Samba,** are for some serious shaking and a taste of the exotic.

And, of course, there are the high-tech discos like **La Scala,** with lots of glass, aluminum, lasers, and decibels in the auditory-damage range. The bouncers in these places tend to be numerous and overtrained in rapid intervention, which is fine if your primary concern is protecting your designer clothes from some drunken zonard but bad news if you're not on best behavior. As a rule, North American clubs and discos tend to be a lot rowdier than the Paris version. Public drunkeness or other overt signs of altered behavior are in *très mauvais goût* (very bad taste) here.

Not to be missed on the music and dance scene is the tiny rue de Lappe near the Bastille, home of **Le Balajo,** one of this area's several ex-tango ballrooms that date from the nineteenth century. The atmosphere on certain nights is surreal in its mix: fortyish prostitutes dancing with African immigrants, French sailors on leave and on the prowl, the young and hip *branché* (connected or plugged-in—the now-dated French word for "in") crowd moving to live and recorded music, sometimes retro, sometimes rock. It's an experience.

As a general rule, the club scene in Paris gets started late, rarely before 11:00 P.M., and sometimes doesn't get rolling until the tiny hours, around 3:00 or 4:00 in the morning, depending on the club. The hard-core spill out at dawn.

Les Bains Douches
7 rue Bourg l'Abbé, 75003 Paris
Tel.: 01–48–87–01–80

Le Tango
15 rue Jules Lamant et Fils
93330 Neuilly sur Marne
Tel.: 01–43–08–20–49

Keur Samba
79 rue de la Boétie, 75008 Paris
Tel.: 01–43–59–03–10

Music and Multimedia Project

PROJECT 101 is a young enthusiastic group dedicated to music, video, and multimedia activities. Music lovers, video fans, and multimedia followers are invited to the "Basement Lounge" every Friday (21h to 2h) and Sunday (18h to 00h) nights.

The group's objective is to create a platform for interactive music and video mixing. Weekly events are more informal gatherings, meant to provide a forum for professionals, amateurs, and fans to exchange ideas and to enjoy new audiovisual programs.

Members pay 8 euros and nonmembers pay 10 euros with an open bar all night long. E-mail: project101@noos.fr. Tel.: 06–09–48–68–57.

Theater in Paris

Dana Burns Westberg, an American theater director and founder of the Compagnie du Horlà, who has been living and working in Paris since the mid-1980s, contributed this section on the Paris theater scene.

If you like theater, you've come to the right city. There are about 150 in and around Paris within métro distance, and some 200 shows a night at the height of the season. France's rich theatrical tradition, like England's and Italy's, goes back to the late Middle Ages. Today the quantity is not always matched by the quality, but there's a lot to savor no matter what your taste. These days, alongside the conventionality of French theater, there is a tendency to make theater of anything (translation: any text), so be prepared to expand your palate.

The three companies of international renown, although not listed in order of size, are Peter Brook's Centre International de Créations Théâtrales, at the Théâtre des Bouffes du Nord; Ariane Mnouchkine's Théâtre du Soleil, which performs in the Cartoucherie in the Bois de Vincennes; and the Comédie Française. The three companies are heavily subsidized, maintain a standing troupe of actors, and tour extensively; the latter two characteristics distinguish them from the pack. But all similarities between them stop here.

Peter Brook—Les Bouffes du Nord

Peter Brook's recent work is characterized by his forays into deconstructed opera, the nine-hour Indian epic *The Mahabharata*, and the international nature of his acting company—many whom have been with him since he abandoned England, set up shop in Paris more than thirty years ago, and undertook perhaps the most famous theater renovation in modern times. No Parisian theatergoer or self-styled culture vulture hasn't passed through the door of Les Bouffes du Nord and seen a production by the author of the slim volume masterpiece *The Empty Space*. And listened to the melting pot of francophonie that is Brook's company. While certain critics still privately whine about the indignity of their French, few dare to question the genius of their enterprise, or that Brook is probably the most important and influential theater artist in any language of the second half of the twentieth century.

Théâtre du Soleil

Emerging from the student and worker uprisings in May 1968, Ariane Mnouchkine's Théâtre du Soleil is now a French institution, housed in the Cartoucherie, a former ammunitions depot in the Bois de Vincennes on the eastern border of Paris. The company is known for kabuki-influenced Shakespeare productions, Hélène Cixous' contemporary history plays on Cambodia and India, and a cycle of Greek tragedies. Communally organized, and influenced by Eastern music and culture, the Théâtre du Soleil has broken new ground while amassing enormous popular support. Their cavernous playing space in the Cartoucherie is transformed for each production; the actors apply their makeup and dress as the audience enters; and the company doubles as ticket takers, ushers, barmen, and waiters before, during, and after each show. They have also built the sets and costumes, and maintain the space. No stars. Not to be missed.

Comédie Française
The Comédie Française, the famous *maison de Molière*, was founded more than three centuries ago by Louis XIV. Productions and costumes are lavish, and two or three plays rotate in repertory throughout the season in its luxurious Salle Richelieu, named after the cardinal who was Louis's top cop for culture. Molière, Racine, Corneille, Marivaux, and Musset are the bread and butter of the company. But at the end of the 1980s, Antoine Vitez bravely expanded the repertory to include modern playwrights (Sartre's *No Exit* was performed, for example), and openings were made for francophone playwrights and directors from the Caribbean, Africa, and North Africa. Since Vitez's untimely death the direction of the Comédie Française has changed twice amid shifting political winds. In 1993 Le Français (as insiders call it) took over the legendary and recently restored Théâtre du Vieux Colombier, to create a home for modern and contemporary work.

Sites
The spirit of Jacques Copeau still roams the Vieux Colombier. Those interested in visiting the theaters associated with other French directors who championed the modernist cause can see productions in their legendary haunts—the Théâtre de l'Atelier still dominates the picturesque Place Charles Dullin in Montmartre; Louis Jouvet's Théâtre de l'Athénée now houses two *salles* near the Opéra; and Lugné-Poë's Théâtre de l'Oeuvre, where Alfred Jarry's *Ubu roi* harbingered the chaos of the twentieth-century, continues on the rue de Clichy. Jean Vilar's home for the influential Théâtre National Populaire is now the Théâtre National de Chaillot, housed within the massive marble interiors of the Palais de Trocadéro in the shadow of the Eiffel Tower. With a little scratching around and footwork, theater buffs can easily discover the Paris of Antonin Artaud, Etienne Decroux, Jean Cocteau, Sartre, Camus, Ionesco, Roger Blin, and Samuel Beckett. Jean-Louis Barrault fought for thirty years along with his wife and partner Madeleine Renaud against government indifference and cultural fads to maintain a home for their internationally known troupe in places such as what is now the Musée d'Orsay, the impressive Théâtre de l'Odéon—now home to the Théâtre de l'Europe—and the Théâtre du Rond-Point at the bottom of the Champs-Elysées.

Trends
Parisian theater is divided into government-subsidized and private, or commercial, theaters. But the marriage of public support and private sponsorship, and an ever-increasing infatuation with showbiz has blurred the distinction between the two in recent years. Market pressure's impact on a long tradition of cultural responsibility has created an uneasy ideal of *rentabilité culturelle*, and a flurry of heavily subsi-

dized/privately sponsored productions with well-known actors in the leading roles, top-heavy publicity budgets, and questionable creativity. Not all have worked. The private, commercial, theaters are making increasing efforts to support new work but are constrained by their fiscal responsibilities. It is very difficult to produce new work or reinvigorated classics with unknown actors and directors; both private and subsidized theater directors are playing it very safely these days, and seek clear, marketable commodities. Production and promotional costs scare all but the very hearty, and these often fall short of cash before they can muster the public attention necessary to sustain a run. Fewer theaters create new work; increasing numbers buy and sell it, once established.

The Théâtre National de la Colline near Place Gambetta has probably the clearest artistic direction of all the Parisian institutional theaters, concentrating on contemporary European work. There are interesting public theaters in the close suburbs that ring the city, such as Saint-Denis, Aubervilliers, Gennevilliers, and Bobigny.

The Parisian boulevard theaters still exist, and their fare can range from beguiling revivals of Guitry and Feydeau to distracting contemporary comedies and farces of varying interest. Ticket prices are very steep, and production values don't always follow suit. It's fairly standard stuff, not so different from that offered up in the capitals of most other countries.

Theater and the Press
The French press is a willing partner in the heavy, expensive publicity and promotion machinery of Paris theater and is often neither objective nor terribly thorough. The large institutions and big-budget productions compete for decreasing space in newspapers and magazines—and for radio and television time—in the same press and media that they are often also soliciting for sponsorship. Showbiz, *quoi. Le Figaroscope*, the Thursday cultural supplement to *Le Figaro* newspaper, is the best place to find out what's happening on the fringes, and it does a very responsible and fair job of covering the shows that have neither the budget to attract the frontline critics nor the financial ambitions of the mainstream cultural venues.

Pocket Theaters
There are pocket theaters galore, where the hearty vie for attention and public with the comedy-oriented café-théâters (something of a French institution). The quality can vary greatly, but excellent work can be discovered with a little determination and a sense of adventure. Many of these venues present as many as three or four shows a day. The worst of these venue directors are indifferent, absentee landlords, but some work without recognition to promote the companies they take in. The fare can range from the almost forty-year, uninterrupted run of Ionesco's *The Bald Soprano* and *The Lesson at La Huchette* (where some of the five original cast members still perform), to plays in English, German, Spanish, and Italian, and student companies.

Theater in English
Although the range of theatrical choice in English expanded in the late nineties, Paris remains one of the few European capitals without an established English-speaking theater. But there is a long-dating underground community of English-speaking theater artists, some of whom work in French as well, and whose work is often of the

highest quality. The names of the companies change constantly, as recent French business-cum-cultural regulations are making it harder for them to continue. But continue they do. The level of acting is very high indeed, though production values are minimal.

Short-timers in Paris, as well as the here-for-the-duration crowd, should definitely take in the Théâtre du Soleil, Brook at the Bouffes du Nord, and the Comédie Française, and something in their mother tongue. The avid and the lifers will see Beckett plays in Paris (and maybe think of doing the same in Dublin), investigate the fringes of the theater scene, and run into Neil Simon and Woody Allen on the boulevard. Children's theater abounds around holidays and school vacations, and Wednesday and Saturday afternoons. *Pariscope* and *L'Officiel des Spectacles* are the best and cheapest source of listings. *Pariscope* includes a several-page pullout from London's *Time Out* in English. The Comédie Française offers one of the best ticket deals in town; fifteen minutes before curtain, you can get upper-balcony seats for next to nothing. The state-run theaters have subsidized ticket prices, and good seats are available for 15 to 23 euros, sometimes less. Private and boulevard theater seats are more. Smaller pocket theaters don't always have small prices. Student discounts are often available, and group rates and bookings abound, particularly at the beginning of runs. You should have yourselves a pretty good time.

Theaters/Spectacles

Paris has 115 theaters offering French and foreign productions. Whether you speak French or not, you may choose to spend an evening at the theater. The following Paris theaters not only offer top-quality performances but will enchant you with their style, decor, architecture, and history. A complete list is available on www.paris-anglo.com.

Comédie Française
2 rue Richelieu, 75001 Paris
Tel.: 01–40–15–00–00
Métro: Palais Royal

Odéon Théâtre de l'Europe
1 Place de l'Odéon, 75006 Paris
Tel.: 01–44–41–36–36
Métro: Odéon

Théâtre National de la Colline
5 rue Malte-Brun, 75020 Paris
Tel.: 01–44–62–52–52
Métro: Gambetta

Bouffes du Nord
37 bis boulevard de la Chapelle, 75010 Paris
Tel.: 01–46–07–34–50
Métro: La Chapelle

Theater Companies that Produce Plays in English
Paris hosts a half a dozen small theater companies playing regularly in English. Pick up a copy of *Paris Voice* for listings. To get tickets you can call the box office directly or go to the theater. Paris also has two same-day ticket offices offering seats at half price: Le Kiosque Théâtre (Place de la Madeleine; Métro: Madeleine); and Parvis Montparnasse (Métro: Montparnasse). They are open Tuesday through Saturday from 12:30 to 7:45 P.M. and Sunday from 12:30 to 3:45 P.M. (Officially, these kiosques are open till 8:00 P.M. and 4:00 P.M., respectively, but do not believe the signs; they close fifteen minutes earlier!)

They accept euro checks or cash only. No credit cards. You pay half price plus a commission of 2,50 euros per ticket. Still very much worth it. Tickets to many concerts and sporting events are available from the ticket service at the Virgin Megastore on the Champs-Elysées; France Billet in the Carrefour and Auchan supermarkets; Galeries Lafayette; and the FNAC stores. Additionally, you can call for information or to reserve at 01–44–68–44–68. Beware: No one speaks English. This service is available on-line at www.ticketnet.fr.

For on-line ticket reservations, www.theatreonline.com has been recommended by a number of readers.

Dear Conjunction
6 rue Arthur Rozier, 75019 Paris
Tel.: 01–42–41–69–65
E-mail: dearconjunction@wanadoo.fr
Contact: Patricia Kesseler
Founded in 1991 by Barbara Bray. Performs British (Pinter, Friel, and Woodehouse) and French (Molière, Beckett, Yasmina, and Reza) plays at the Sudden Théatre.

ACT (English Theatre Company)
51 rue Hoche
92240 Malakoff
Tel.: 01–46–56–20–50
Tours show in English to primary and secondary schools, with a run in a Parisian theater each season to showcase the current repertory.

Acting International in English
55 rue Allouettes, 75019 Paris
Robert Cordier and Leslie Chatterly
Tel.: 01-42-00-06-79
www.acting-international.com

Compagnie du Horlà
21 rue Henri Regnault
92210 St-Cloud
Director: Dana Burns Westberg
Tel.: 01–47–71–23–46
This company produces eclectic work in both French and in English.

The Gare-St-Lazare Players
No fixed address
Contact: Bob Meyer
Tel.: 01–34–79–38–01
This troupe floats around town playing at diverse venues from the cellars of bars to the Théâtre Marie Stuart. Works by O'Neill, Pinter, Beckett, etc., and by writer/director/artist Bob Meyer.

Voices (Association of English and American Actors)
10 bis avenue Jean Jaurès, 92240 Malakoff
Tel.: 01–47–35–19–19
Collective created by anglophone actors and voice artists is now home to at least ten other languages.

Théâtre de Nesle
8 rue de Nesle, 75006 Paris
Tel.: 01–46–34–61–04

Sudden Théâtre
14 bis rue Ste-Isaure, 75018 Paris
Tel.: 01–42–62–35–00

Additionally, the Royal Shakespeare Company and the British National Theatre perform for several weeks during the summer.

Acting Classes in English and French
Studios for Actors
Tel.: 01–42–00–06–79

The Acting Lab
Acting Workshops by Béla Gurshka
Tel.: 01–46–06–66–10

Sudden Theatre
14 bis rue Sainte-Isaure, 75018 Paris
Tel.: 01–42–62–35–00

Dance

The French dance scene continues to be a very healthy one with lots of activity in Paris and the close suburbs. The Théâtre de la Ville programs the big, internationally known dance companies throughout the year. The Opéra Garnier features the work of the Ballet de l'Opéra de Paris, as well as another in-house group, Groupe de Recherche Chorégraphique, formerly headed by Rudolf Nureyev, that is more experimental in nature. Both do very high-quality work. Elsewhere—on a less-exalted level—there is some very interesting dance work shown at the Théâtre de la Bastille, usually during the beginning of the year, as well as at the Ménagerie de Verre and the Café de la Danse, both in the Bastille neighborhood. The Centre

Georges Pompidou programs some interesting avant-garde companies from France and abroad. The numerous smaller dance companies based in and around Paris perform at various locations, sometimes in theaters, often in dance studios scattered across the city. The Studio Regard du Cygne and the Atelier de la Danse offer some of the most exciting modern and contemporary programs in Paris. For ballet, creative movement, jazz, and modern dance classes contact:

Quick Reference—Dance
Opéra-Palais Garnier, Place de l'Opéra, 75002 Paris; Tel.: 01–47–42–53–71.
Studio Regard du Cygne, 210 rue de Belleville, 75020 Paris; Tel.: 01–43–58–55–93.
Théâtre Contemporain de la Danse, 9 rue Geoffroy-l'Asnier, 75004 Paris; Tel.: 01–42–74–44–22.
Théâtre de la Bastille, 76 rue de la Roquette, 75011 Paris; Tel.: 01–43– 57–42–14.

Also of Dance Interest
Estivales Danses
Tel.: 01–46–07–34–50
Paris's only annual performing-arts festival

Paris Quartier d'Eté
Open-air dance festival
Tel.: 01–44–94–98–00

Montpellier Dance Festival
France's leading international dance venue
Tel.: 04–67–60–83–60

For inquiries concerning dance in Paris, contact dance critic Carol Pratl, c/o the *Paris Voice,* 7 rue Papillon, Paris 75009.

Paris Villages
Of a far more rustic nature is the city's annual summer program called Paris Villages. In some neighborhoods, mostly the ones on the eastern side of the city, a bandstand is set up in one of the squares, party lights are strung up, and a retro band complete with accordion and female vocalist plays the old French favorites while everybody from the baker to your *concierge* comes out for a drink and a dance. It's lots of fun, very *vieux Paris.* Not to be missed under any circumstances are the local Bastille Eve dances held at every fire station the night of July 13. Here you can dance the night away to live music that is usually so bad, it's an experience in itself. Everyone in the neighborhood comes out for these, from infants to the elderly. The wine flows, there are games and prizes, neighbors who steadfastly refuse to speak to each other during the rest of the year are suddenly great friends, and the firemen gallantly dance with every available woman or young girl. You will probably learn more about the French character in one evening like this than in a year's worth of observation and study. And you can work off your *gueule de bois* the next day by watching the Bastille Day parade on the Champs-Elysées.

Literary and Art Journals

In addition to *Frank* (www.readfrank.com), the longest-running literary journal published in English in Paris, four new English–language literary magazines have been launched in the past two years—*Kilometer Zero* (www.kilometerzero.com); *Upstairs at Duroc; Lieu* (www.lieuscape.com); and *Van Gogh's Ear*, as well as the *Paris/Atlantic* (edited by the undergrad program at the American University), and *Pharos*, run by Pulitzer Prize-finalist poet Alice Notley's writing workshop. This doesn't count the bilingual journal of poetry in translation, *La Traductière* (http://perso.wanadoo.fr/festrad/), or magazines that straddle two headquarters—*Doublechange* (www.doublechange.com), edited in Paris and New York, and the literary webzine *3am* (www.3ammagazine.com), which stretches between Paris and Seattle via London.

Frank: An International Journal of Contemporary Writing & Art, edited by David Applefield, 32 rue Edouard Vaillant, 93100 Montreuil; Tel.: 01–48–59–66–58; www.ReadFrank.com.

Kilometer Zero (literary magazine, readings, multi-disciplinary arts), 37 rue de la Bûcherie, 75005 Paris; www.kmzero.org.

Pharos (literary magazine), The British Institute, 11 rue de Constantine, 75007 Paris.

Upstairs at Duroc (literary magazine), WICE, 20 boulevard du Montparnasse, 75015 Paris; Tel.: 01–45–66–75–50; wice@wice-paris.org, www.wice-paris.org

Paris/Atlantic (literary magazine), The American University of Paris, 31 avenue Bosquet, 75007 Paris, auplantic@hotmail.com.

Lieu (magazine), www.lieuscape.com.

Readings

Village Voice (bookstore), 6 rue Princesse, 75006 Paris; Tel.: 01–46–33–36–47; www.villagevoicebookshop.com

The Abbey Bookshop, 29 rue Parcheminerie, 75050 Paris; Tel.: 01 46 33 16 24; www.abbeybookshop.com

The Red Wheelbarrow Bookstore: 13 rue Charles V, 75004 Paris. Metro: Saint-Paul. Tel.: 01–42–77–42–17. E-mail: good.reading@wanadoo.fr

Tea and Tattered Pages Bookstore: 24 rue Mayet, 75006 Paris. Métro: Duroc. Tel.: 01–49–65–94–35. E-mail: tandtp@hotmail.com

Shakespeare and Company Bookstore, 37 rue de la Bûcherie, 75005 Paris; www.shakespeareandco.org

The American University of Paris: 31 avenue Bosquet, 75007 Paris; Tel.: 01–40–62–06–00; www.aup.fr

WICE: 20 boulevard du Montparnasse, 75015 Paris. Metro: Duroc. Tel.: 01–45–66–75–50; E-mail: wice@wice-paris.org. www.wice-paris.org

KMZ Venues—seasonal series of literary cabarets; www.kilometerzero.org/venue/

Café de Flore (Monday evening play readings): 172 boulevard Saint-Germain, 75006 Paris. Mètro: Saint-Germain-des-Prés

Double Change's French-English Reading Series: www.doublechange.com

Live Poets Society (monthly readings featuring three poets): Current home base at The Flann O'Brien Pub, 6 rue Bailleul. Métro: Louvre-Rivoli. Tel.: 01–42.60.13.58. Roughly 4 euros donation for the poets. Organized by John Kliphan (103 avenue Philippe Auguste, 75011 Paris)

The American Library in Paris, 10 rue du Général-Camou, 75007 Paris; Tel.: 01–53–59–12–60; www.americanlibraryinparis.org

W.H. Smith Bookstore: 248 rue de Rivoli, 75001 Paris; Tel.: 01–44–77–88–99

Brentano's, 37 avenue de l'Opéra, 75002 Paris. Métro: Pyramides. Tel.: 01–42–61–52–50

Used Books:

San Francisco Book Company: 17 rue Monsieur-le-Prince, 75006 Paris; Tel.: 01–43–29–15–70. www.abebooks.com/home/SFBOOKS/, E-mail: sfbooks@easynet.fr

Writing Workshops/Festivals

Paris Writers' Workshop (summer conference), c/o WICE, 20 boulevard du Montparnasse, 75015 Paris; Tel.: 01–45-66–75–50, pww@wice-paris.org, www.wice-paris.org

Festival Franco-Anglais de Poésie (bilingual poetry festival), 10 rue Auger, 75020 Paris; Tel.: 01–40–09–94–19; festrad@wanadoo.fr; http://perso. wanadoo.fr/festrad

Books about Paris Literary History

The Continual Pilgrimage: American Writers in Paris, 1944–1960, Christopher Sawyer-Laucanno (City Lights Books, 1998).

The Crazy Years: Paris in the Twenties, William Wiser (Thames and Hudson, 1983) and his follow-up: *The Twilight Years: Paris in the 1930s* (Carroll & Graf, 2000).

American Expatriate Writing and the Paris Moment: Modernism and Place, Donald Pizer (Louisiana State University Press, 1997).

Sylvia Beach and the Lost Generation: A History of Literary Paris in the Twenties and Thirties, Noel Riley Fitch (W.W. Norton, 1985).

Note: An extensive list of books on Paris and its literary traditions can be found on www.paris-anglo.com, with on-line ordering facilities from PayPal.

Bookstores

Paris is a sheer delight in its proliferation of small bookshops. And Paris wouldn't be Paris without its rows of *bouquinistes* (bookstalls, where Thomas Jefferson bought the books that would be the basis for the Library of Congress), most of which line the Left Bank *(rive* or *quai)* of the Seine. These are independently owned, mainly by individuals who have a passion for used or rare books. In recent years the quality of the offerings has dwindled to include tacky postcards and cheap prints, but fortunately the integrity of the traditional buying, selling, and browsing on nice days along the Seine has remained intact.

The book as object plays a sacred role in Parisian life. Even the TVA is lower on books than on other objects. In general the quality of book production is higher in France than in North America, with serious covers reserved for quality literature, although now the marketing advantage of flashy jackets has become apparent to literary publishers, who often opt for commercial jackets wrapped around somber covers. The most prestigious literary publishing houses in France include the classic Gallimard, le Seuil, Grasset, and Calmann-Levy, but there are scores of excellent publishers of literary, political, social, and pure science books. Some of the most significant small-to-medium-size literary publishers include Actes Sud, directed by Hubert Nyssen in Arles, which has introduced hundreds of contemporary world authors into the French language; Editions Minuit, founded by the late Jerôme Lindon, a pillar in French intellectual history of this century; POL, founded by Paul Otchakovsky-Laurens; Editions de l'Olivier, headed by Olivier Cohen, who has brought much of contemporary American writing into French; and Christian Bourgois, a dynamic iconoclast that reflects the Parisian flare and daringness to still take artistic risks.

Despite contemporary economic pressures, much effort is made in France to protect the life of the small bookshop and the small publisher. The retail prices of books are regulated so that large outlets, department stores, and supermarket chains cannot simply slash prices. The most you'll ever find a new book marked down is 5 percent. There are remainder chains where prices on coffee-table books are greatly reduced. But French law prevents publishers from selling books for lower than cost price. The FNAC (see the Department and Chain Stores section in the Consumerism Paris chapter) has one of the most exhaustive collections of French and foreign-language books in Paris and is particularly well-stocked with travel books.

Paris has an illustrious and important tradition of English and American expatriate writers, poets, and artists, as well as editors and publishers who have made significant contributions in Paris with their work. This tradition may or may not be the source of your inspiration for coming to live and/or study in Paris; it certainly does generate much of the aura and myth about Paris that attracts tourists and long-term visitors each year. And if this glorious past is what drew you here, you might be disappointed to find a changed Paris. For in-depth discussion of Paris's expatriate literary and artistic history, see Ernest Hemingway's *A Moveable Feast*, Noel Fitch Riley's *Sylvia Beach and the Lost Generation* and *Literary Cafés*, Brian Morton's *Americans in Paris*, Maurice Girodias' *The Frog Prince*, Hugh Ford's *Published in Paris*, and Dougald McMillan's *transition*.

In most cases new books are a lot more expensive than what you are probably used to. The price in euros is not a simple conversion from dollars or pounds; each bookstore has its own markup rate to compensate for shipping and customs charges. So you might want to carry those special copies of books dear to your heart or have them shipped to you from home. There are, of course, libraries and on-line booksellers.

On-line Books and English-Language Bookstores

Paris expatriates and students are ordering their English-language books more and more from Internet sources. But, despite the large selection and cut-rate prices at amazon.com and barnesandnobles.com, the overseas shipping costs kill the price advantage instantly. Some readers claim that ordering from Amazon's U.K. operations represents great savings in the shipping costs. We find that in many cases the local bookshops can act more quickly and economically in obtaining your books, especially those available from the United Kingdom. In addition, bookshops such as Odile Hellier's Village Voice Bookshop (see below) pride themselves on the service that on-line sources cannot provide. The local bookshops also host readings and often print newsletters to help expatriates stay in touch with upcoming titles from the United States, Canada, and the United Kingdom. They deserve your support.

As English speakers and readers, you'll probably be more directly interested in sources of English-language books in Paris. Fortunately, there are a lot of resources at hand. The English-language bookshops in Paris contribute to the vitality of the literary scene. You'll probably want to renew your contact with your language and culture by frequenting some of the following shops on a regular basis.

✦ **Abbey Bookshop**, 29 rue Parcheminerie, 75005 Paris; Tel.: 01–46–33–16–24; Fax: 01–46–33–03–33. This Canadian-owned, small but well-organized and pleasant shop in the Latin Quarter has carved an important place for itself in the English-language literary scene in Paris in the last few years. One of its real advantages is its ability to procure titles from North America in record time. Owner Brian Spence offers his clients plenty of service, including an up-to-date ROM bibliographic search and efficient mail-order capacity. Strong in fiction, poetry, and the humanities. On occasion the Abbey also has readings, usually concentrating on Canadian writers.

✦ **Attica**, 64 rue de la Folie Méricourt, 75011 Paris; Métro: Oberkampf; Tel.: 01–49–29–27–27. Closed Sunday and Monday morning. Attica is an old standby for English books in Paris. More British-oriented than American, Attica in its new location is a densely packed space for new fiction, poetry, journals, and guides. The store also caters to French students looking for English titles for their university English courses—thus a lot of classics and nineteenth-century fiction. Students get a small discount on request. The second location specializes in practical books and language methods.

✦ **Brentano's**, 37 avenue de l'Opéra, 75002 Paris; Métro: Pyramides; Tel.: 01–42–61–77–01, Fax: 01–42–61–07–61; www.brentanos.fr. Open daily from 10:00 A.M. to 7:00 P.M. Closed Sunday. Anglo-American literature, art books, magazines, and newspapers. Brentano's rides on a long and illustrious reputation. Today it serves the French anglophile market and business and tourist crowds interested in English paperbacks and best-sellers. Although less connected to the indigenous anglophone population than some of the other literary bookshops, Brentano's is the only English bookshop in the neighborhood of the Opéra. The back entrance area hosts a large selection of English-language periodicals. Other areas of specialty include American hobbies, arts and crafts, sports, and an impressively complete selection of children's books. Brentano's also hosts signings for prominent authors in Paris and services important events, including Bloom and diverse charities fairs. Brentano's offers an efficient international magazine subscription and mail-order book service.

✤ **Galignani,** 224 rue de Rivoli, 75001 Paris; Métro: Tuileries; Tel.: 01–42–60–76–07. Closed Sunday. Books, guidebooks, maps, newspapers, and magazines. This elegant bookshop is actually the oldest English bookstore on the continent. Its selection of fiction, travel and art books, and cultural periodicals is extensive. Galignani organizes signings and events as well.

✤ **Gibert Jeune,** 10 Place St-Michel, 75006 Paris; Tel.: 01–56–81–22–22. This Paris institution is an especially useful address for students. Gibert Jeune and Gibert Joseph, a three-store operation, specializes in academic and university texts and school supplies and buys used books on the fourth floor. Bring your student ID. There are some English-language books but not a lot. They are rather selective on the books they buy. See San Francisco Book Co. to sell what Gibert Jeune won't take.

✤ **Nouveau Quartier Latin** (NQL), 78 boulevard St-Michel, 75005 Paris; Métro: Luxembourg; Tel.: 01–43–26–42–70. Closed Sunday. Only new titles. NQL specializes in Anglo-American literature and guidebooks and also distributes to its 3000-strong network of bookshops through France.

✤ **The Red Wheelbarrow Bookstore,** 13 rue Charles V, 75004 Paris. Metro: Saint-Paul; Tel.: 01–42–77–42–17. Open daily until 7:00 P.M. Book-loving owner, Penelope, and her team have built a very dynamic and energic literary bookshop that is serving the community well with its fine selection of literature and journals and a packed schedule of readings. E-mail: good.reading@wanadoo.fr

✤ **San Francisco Book Co.,** 17 rue Monsieur le Prince, 75006 Paris; Tel.: 01–43–29–15–70. E-mail: sfbooks@easynet.fr. Hours: Monday through Saturday from 11:00 A.M to 9:00 P.M., Sunday 2:00 to 9:00 P.M. In 1997 Phil Wood and his San Francisco-based partner Jim Carroll opened a new venue for quality second hand English-language books at affordable prices. The space is a bit tight, but customers appreciate this shop for its alphabetized stock and its well-organized selection of fiction and quality nonfiction. There are about 20,000 books. A great advantage here is that Phil buys your books and pays either in cash or a trade credit.

✤ **Shakespeare & Company,** 37 rue de la Bûcherie, 75005 Paris; Métro: St-Michel. No telephone. Open daily noon until midnight. George Whitman's Shakespeare & Company is by far the single most celebrated bookshop on the continent. George has recently turned 95 and is still spry and active. The shop and its owner have remained loyal to the cause of international literature and the solidarity of those who write. Much of its reputation comes from Sylvia Beach's original Shakespeare & Company, which was located nearby on the rue de l'Odéon in the twenties and thirties. It was there that James Joyce's *Ulysses,* published by Beach in 1922, first saw the light of day. Ernest Hemingway, Gertrude Stein, and a whole stable of luminous literati congregated there. Beach's store was shut by the Germans at the beginning of the Occupation. George Whitman, the self-proclaimed illegitimate grandson of Walt Whitman (his father was also named Walt, but a writer of science books in Salem, Massachusetts), resurrected the name in the spirit of the original enterprise, tagging on "the Rag and Bone Shop of the Heart." Everything you hear about the current Shakespeare & Co. is true. It can be unruly, chaotically organized, overrun at times by weirdos and dubious writers, but the bookshop is a living legend and continues to be a wealthy storehouse of fabulous first editions and signed copies of novels and volumes of poetry whose authors came through Paris and gave a reading or book party under the supervision of poetic and iconoclastic George. He is often offering tumblers of iced tea or chipped plates of Irish stew to visiting writers, wanderers, and the mildly down-and-out. The store has thousands of used books and a spotty selection of new titles. It's impossible to predict what you'll find. The prices are high for the new stuff, but can be excellent for used and obscure hardcovers. George will buy your used books and pay you cash if you bring identification. In the warm months the sidewalk in front of the store— exquisitely set in the Latin Quarter opposite Notre-Dame—becomes a favorite hangout for visitors, backpakers, and local riffraff, a scene that will give you a good whiff of the state of contemporary bohemia. And if you are writing poetry or fiction, ask George to be slotted into the Monday-night reading series—a good way to test your voice. The shop sells its own mag called *Paris Magazine*, plus a recently inaugurated literary journal *Kilometer Zero*. George's daughter, Sylvia Beach Whitman, replaced her father at the helm in 2002.

✦ **Tea and Tattered Pages,** 24 rue Mayet, 75006 Paris; Tel.: 01–40–65–94–35; Fax: 01–44–49–94–12. Open Monday through Saturday from 11:00 A.M. to 7:00 P.M., Sunday noon to 6:00 P.M This cozy and friendly spot near Métro Duroc has recently changed ownership. The new shop has taken over the former shop, and has added its own touch. Specializes in used and inexpensive paperbacks. The selection has grown rapidly over the years to more than 10,000 books. The prices warrant a visit.

✦ **Village Voice,** 6 rue Princesse, 75006 Paris; Métro: Mabillon; Tel.: 01–46–33–36–47; Fax: 01–46–33–27–48; Web site: www.villagevoicebookshop.com. Closed Sunday. Open Monday from 2:00 to 8:00 P.M., Tuesday through Saturday from 11:00. A.M. to 8:00 P.M. Founded in 1982 by French owner Odile Hellier, the Village Voice (no connection to the newspaper) continued to prove itself as one of the most significant literary anglophone bookshops in Europe. Tucked into a small street just off boulevard Saint-Germain, the store hosts a lively reading series that has included some of the most important American, Canadian, British, and French authors of our time, including Don DeLillo, William Kennedy, Raymond Carver, Alison Lurie, Mavis Gallant, Louise Erdrich, Edmund White, and Susan Sontag. These readings are free and often conclude with wine and discussion. Odile diligently attempts to stock a rich collection of the newest literary titles from both the United States and the United Kingdom in her bright and pleasant store. The vast collection includes modern and contemporary fiction, poetry, translations in the social and political sciences, philosophy, and women's studies. The store also has a wide variety of literary journals and intelligent magazines—*Times Literary Supplement, New Yorker, Harper's, Paris Review, Frank, Granta*, etc. Paris-related literary titles are now available via PayPal on-line at www.paris-anglo.com.

✦ **W.H. Smith,** 248 rue de Rivoli, 75001 Paris; Métro: Concorde; Tel.: 01–42–60–37–97. Closed Sunday. Part of the major British bookstore chain. Anglo-American literature, cookbooks, guidebooks, maps, and magazines and newspapers. This large, well-stocked, and busy store offers a broad selection of contemporary titles and gift books as well as a vast display of English-language publications. Well situated at the Place de la Concorde. The staff is very helpful and highly knowledgeable about the selection of books available. Hosts book signings and special events.

French Bookstores

As for French literary bookshops, there are scores of excellent ones, with a high concentration in the Quartier Latin of the fifth and sixth arrondissements. A few well-known ones include La Hune (170 boulevard St-Michel, 75005) and Flammarion at the Pompidou Center. The l'Oeil de la Lettre group of literary bookstores is first class; one of them is Librarie Compagnie on the rue des Ecoles next to the Sorbonne.

The FNAC, the largest retail chain of electronic, stereo, and photographic equipment (with plans for European expansion), also has the most extensive collection of books and records in France. This French institution will be your first reference in tracking down books and tapes in Paris. Originally set up as a customer/shareholder-owned collective, the chain was bought by the Pineau group that owns Le Printemps and La Redoute. Although its profit picture may have changed, the spirit of the store has remained committed to quality contemporary culture and generally attracts a well-educated and informed clientele. Here are the main ones. (The FNAC also has an extensive Web site with on-line ordering facilities at www.fnac.fr.)

FNAC Micro,71 boulevard St-Germain, 75005 Paris.
FNAC Forum Halles, 1 rue Pierre Lescot 75001 Paris.
FNAC Montparnasse, 136 rue de Rennes, 75006 Paris.
FNAC Etoile, 26 avenue des Ternes, 75017 Paris.
A list of specialized bookshops appears in the directory on www.paris-anglo.com, ranging from cinema, photography, and cuisine to eroticism, music, and government publications..

Libraries *(bibliothèques)*

France's new national library, the Bibliothèque de France, is the largest library complex in the country. Situated on the Left Bank in the thirteenth arrondissement and connected by the new Line 14 of the métro, the library is the most extensive research facility in France, replacing many of the functions of the old and elegant Bibliothèque nationale (BN) on the rue Richelieu. In the great tradition of politicians aspiring to leave their mark via great architectural achievements *(Les Grands Travaux)*, the Bibliothèque de France has been added to the cityscape. The library opened in 1997 at a cost of more than 7 billion francs (one billion euros), and houses books, recordings, film, videotape, and some 12 million catalogued files; in addition there is space for 3,500 readers who have access to 11 million books that are served up at 150 delivery stations through an 8-kilometer-long monorail system.

Bibliothèque National de France
11 quai François Mauriac
75013 Paris
Tel.: 01–53–79–59–59
Tel.: 01–53–79–57–02 to reserve books
Tel.: 01–53–79–59–30 Centre ISSN (periodicals)

The library, whose buildings are shaped like open books, is essentially divided into two parts, the Haut Jardin, which is accessible to the public (sixteen years old and up), and the Rez Jardin, which is reserved for research. Access to the Haut Jardin costs 3 euros a day or 30 euros for an annual pass. This part of the library is open from Tuesday to Saturday from 10:00 A.M. to 8:00 P.M. Call for Sunday hours.

Access to the Rez Jardin requires an interview at which you must prove your need to conduct research in this facility. There are three kinds of passes: the day pass at 3 euros, the twelve-day pass for 30 euros, and the annual pass at 45 euros. There are reduced rates, but few expatriates qualify for them. The Rez Jardin is open on Tuesdays through Saturdays from 9:00 A.M. to 8:00 P.M. It is virtually impossible to be authorized to take books out of the library.

The library is accessible by public transportation by the Métro Line 6 at the Quai de Gare stop or Line 14 at the Bibliothèque de France stop. The Nos. 89 and 62 bus lines serve the library as well.

The library offers the public a year-round program of cultural events and exhibitions. Call the main number and follow the voice prompts to hear the schedule of events or to receive the calendar of events by mail. The recording is in French only.

In dealing with other libraries in Paris you may find the same sort of inconvenience as in other areas of daily life, such as shopping. The inconvenience in this case stems from a certain degree of inaccessibility and an inherent lethargy that take a little time to adjust to. If you are coming from a small university where you had your own library desk at which you could camp out until early morning hours, you may find the adjustment difficult. You may have to keep a more civilized schedule when it comes to your treks to the library. The libraries frequently have quite limited hours. One exception is the Bibliothèque Publique d'Information at the Pompidou Center, which is open until 10:00 P.M., but which can be so jammed that you'll give up hope.

Limited hours are not the only handicap in getting research done or a term paper finished, for most libraries do not allow you to borrow books. These libraries only offer consultation *sur place* (books don't leave the library). So be prepared to take good notes. Laptop computers can be helpful here. You may or may not find working photocopy machines.

Some libraries require that you register and obtain a card to enter and consult books. Be prepared to have to wait in a line when you go. You'll need some identification, such as your passport and proof of address and a couple of photographs. Another thing to be aware of is that in many libraries you are not free to browse through the stacks. Instead, you must go to the *salle des catalogues* and fill out a description of what you are looking for *(fichier)*. An employee, in one of those omnipresent blue smocks that sets workers apart from white-collar employees, will look for the book and send it to the *centre de distribution,* where you collect it.

The library at the Sorbonne is a fascinating place to visit but a frustrating place to use. It can take up to twenty minutes to obtain each book. Don't expect to do much research around lunchtime. In addition, special permission must be obtained for access to the reference section.

There are a number of excellent libraries though in Paris with extensive collections and priceless resources and archives. Here are the major ones:

American Library in Paris, 10 rue du Général-Camou, 75007 Paris; Tel.: 01–53–59–12–60; Fax: 01–45–50–25–83; E-mail: alparis@cybercable.fr. Director: Kay Rader. Open Tuesday through Saturday from 10:00 A.M. to 7:00 P.M. The largest collection of English-language books in Paris. Membership allows you to check out books but is required for admittance. Annual: 88 euros individuals, 70 euros students, 120 euros family. Daily consultation fee: 10 euros You need to bring a recent photo, student identification if applicable, proof of residency in Paris (such as telephone bill), and another piece of identification to register. This library owns 80,000-plus volumes and more than 700 periodicals and journals. It was one of the legendary stalking grounds of Hemingway, Fitzgerald, and Henry Miller in their Paris days.

Bibliothèques et Discothèques de la Ville de Paris, 31 rue des Francs Bourgeois, 75004 Paris; Tel.: 01–42–76–40–40. This is the central administration of the city of Paris's fifty-five municipal public libraries. They can give you information on your local libraries. (The *discothèques* in the title implies that it is a recordings library, rather than one to dance in.)

Discothèque des Halles, Forum des Halles, 75001 Paris; Tel.: 01–42–33–20–50. Huge library of music, records, and CDs.

Bibliothèque Nationale de France, 58 rue de Richelieu, 75002 Paris; Tel.: 01–63–79–63–79. Minitel: BIB NAT. Métro: Bourse or Palais Royal. Open Monday through Saturday from 10:00 A.M. to 7:00 P.M. Known as the BN, this library houses one of the world's most important and complete collections of books, periodicals, manuscripts, and archives. Dark, dense, and serious, the BN is only accessible to doctoral students and researchers with letters of accreditation. The BN also has its own bookstore located in the Galerie Colbert.

Gaining access to the BN's reading rooms may be a vital step for those who've come to Paris to do research. A *carte de lecteur* is required for regular entry. A *laissez-passer*, good for two consecutive days, can be obtained for a one-time entry, upon presentation of identification and two photos. The *carte de lecteur* requires a letter from a university or official organization justifying your need to use the BN, along with your ID and student card, if applicable. A card allowing eight entries in a year costs 5,50 euros, twenty-four entries 12,50 euros; it is valid for two years. Half price for students under twenty-seven. The number of people allowed at one time in the sumptuous grand hall is limited and constantly controlled. You may have to wait in a small antechamber at the entrance until someone leaves.

Bibliothèque Publique d'Information, Centre Georges Pompidou, 19 rue Beaubourg, 75004 Paris; Tel.: 01–44–78–12–33. Open Monday, Wednesday, Thursday, and Friday from noon to 10:00 P.M. and Saturday, Sunday, and public holidays from 10:00 A.M. to 10:00 P.M. Closed Tuesday. *Consultation sur place.* Open access to books. No registration required.

Bibliothèque Sainte Geneviève, 10 Place du Panthéon, 75005 Paris; Tel.: 01–44–41–97–98. Open Monday through Saturday from 10:00 A.M. to 1:00 P.M.

Personal library card is required; you can obtain one Monday through Friday before 5:30 P.M. and on Saturday between 2:00 and 5:30 P.M. Bring a photo and identification; no charge. *Consultation sur place.* Distribution center.

British Council Library, 9–11 rue de Constantine, 75007 Paris; Tel.: 01–49–55–73–00. Open daily from 11:00 A.M. to 6:00 P.M. and Saturday from 10:30 A.M. to 4:00 P.M. Despite a loud controversy, this library has announced its closure in 2002.

English Language Library for the Blind, 35 rue Lemercier, 75017 Paris; Tel.: 01–42–93–47–57.

Record/CD Libraries *(discothèques)*

About twenty-six Paris libraries specialize in lending records, cassettes, or CDs. Contact the *Direction des Affaires Culturelles* at the Paris city hall to find out the discothèques in your district (Tel.: 01–42–76–40–40). They publish a booklet entitled *Bibliothèques Discothèques de La Ville de Paris* specifying which libraries have this option. Some discothèques require that you present the needle from your turntable for inspection before they lend you records.

To buy or trade CDs, try O'CD at 26 rue des Ecoles, 75005 Paris; Tel.: 01–43–25–23–27; Métro: Maubert-Mutualité. Open until 9:00 P.M. Prices range from 2,50 to 13 euros. The shop has listening stations.

You can also find many record shops—including tapes and CDs—located on the Boulevard St-Michel between the Boulevard St-Germain and the Seine on the west side of the street.

Sports and Recreation

Although Parisians have become more fitness conscious in the last decade, recreational sports in Parisian life have not yet approached the levels they enjoy in America or even Britain. The closest you'll see in Paris to the jogging phenomenon in New York's Central Park or along Boston's Charles River is in Luxembourg Gardens and along the *Promenade Plantée*, between the Bastille Opéra and the Bois de Vincennes. The air quality in Paris is far from ideal for running, although the Bois de Vincennes and Bois de Boulogne are vast, lush, relatively pollution-free and well-marked for runners.

In France, you're either *sportif* (athletic) or *non-sportif*. So make up your mind. *Non-sportifs* outnumber the *sportifs*, and a great many smoke cigarettes (indeed, many *sportifs* smoke as well). The *sportifs* tend to be very *sportif* and often belong to clubs, where they regularly swim, ride, work out, or play tennis or squash. Other *sportifs* only "spectate" *le foot* (football/soccer) matches and horse racing, read the newspaper *l'Equipe*, and hang around the special cafés with PMU (off-track betting) marked on the awning. Several sports events in France are of great importance: the Tour de France international bicycling race; the Paris–Dakar international car rally; the French Open tennis matches at Roland Garros; the Paris Marathon for runners; Europe Cup soccer; and, more recently, World Cup Rugby! The 1998 World Cup Soccer championship victory for France over Brazil in the then brand-new Stade de France at Saint Denis marked the pinnacle of athletic achievement and pride for France for decades. (The 2002 results in Korea were disappointing!) Millions of Parisians poured into the streets and celebrated for days and nights, making the scene on the Champs-Elysée the largest *fête* since the Liberation of Paris in World War II. (You can visit the Stade de France; consult www.stadedefrance.fr for details.)

Certain sports such as cycling have a historic significance in France and are widely practiced by amateur specialists. Throughout the French countryside you'll see cyclists with their skintight outfits and colorful helmets pedaling up and over the hills. The sport has suffered serious setbacks, though, due to scandals involving dopage, unauthorized drugs showing up in the blood and urine of competitors. The French also care deeply about car racing, with Alain Prost having attained near-hero status. Horse racing, too, is popular, with major tracks located in the Bois de Vincennes and Longchamp in the Bois de Boulogne.

Sports, in general, still maintain the remnants of social and class order. Golf, for example, which is on the rise in France, is still an elitist sport and remains prohibitively expensive. Golfing in France for your average North American hacker can become a highly serious experience. One duffer from New Jersey invited by a French colleague to play at her club was sent away because he didn't have an official handicap and, worse, hadn't purchased golfing insurance, a requirement for all those wishing to tee up in France.

Basketball has gained tremendous status over the last few years, capturing the popular imagination of the country's youth, following the widely televised games of the U.S. "Dream Machine" at the Olympics in Barcelona and in Atlanta, and then in 2000, when the French team won the Silver Medal by valiantly challenging the rather-arrogant U.S. team in the finals in Sydney. The NBA has even opened up corporate offices in Paris to further promote and market professional basketball in Europe. At a time when more and more idle youths find themselves on Paris (and suburban) streets, more and more hoops are going up. The body skills, though, have been replaced by the Jordanesque desire to dunk (*smatch*). France can so far boast of several players in the NBA, with Tariq Wahad being the best known. For pickup basketball games, go to the courts in the Champ de Mars on Sunday mornings or to the Jardins de Luxembourg any afternoon. The celebrated Franco-American sportcaster for CanalPlus, George Eddie, has greatly helped to elevate American professional sports among French spectators.

In the last few years the French have become more interested in playing American baseball and football. The Japanese have organized a complete league of baseball players in Paris and play in the Bois de Vincennes. Canal Plus regularly broadcasts *Monday Night Football* and other sports events.

Since the popular ascent of Yannick Noah, now a fading pop singer, tennis has become more and more available to the masses. To book a court at one of the numerous public tennis complexes around the city, you need a *carte de Paris tennis;* pick up the application at your local city hall. It's not that easy to get a court where and when you want it; the only way to ensure you get the court you want is to phone (or book by Minitel: 3614 Paris) early in the morning exactly one week in advance—the earliest you're allowed to book a court. Each reservation costs around 3 euros, which you pay when you arrive for your game. It's also possible to join a sports club that has tennis facilities, but like in any city, this can prove expensive.

University Sports

French university team sports, which are run by clubs and student organizations, tend to be only moderately organized and modestly equipped. There are no scholarships to entice middle linebackers or power forwards to the Sorbonne. A few years back the starting five for the basketball team there included two short Americans, a scrappy Mexican, a Japanese forward who owned no white socks, and a lanky French student who was more or less flat-footed. University sports can be serious, fun, and recreational, but rarely obsessively played. All participants, however, must have proper enrollment cards, health certificates, and insurance forms. Anyone who shows up at a university sports complex in gym clothes but without an active student card is not likely to be admitted. Always carry identification with you. University exchange programs have a variety of facilities available to them and organize games and matches with French university teams and sports clubs. Your local city hall *(mairie)* has an extremely extensive booklet (in French) detailing practically everything about sports in Paris—everything you need to know and then some.

Exercise and Sports

Paris offers plenty of resources to the athletic crowd. For up-to-date sports information, including upcoming sporting events, call Allô-Sports (Tel.: 01–42–76–54–54)—a recorded phone line in French operating from 10:30 A.M. to 5:00 P.M. Monday through Thursday and from 10:30 A.M. to 4:30 P.M. on Friday.

Two main chains provide everything athletes need in the line of sports equipment: Décathlon, 94 rue de Rivoli, 75004 Paris; Tel.: 01–44–54–81–30; and Go Sport, 1 rue Pierre Lescot, 75001 Paris at Les Halles; Tel.: 01–40– 13–73–50. Call for other locations.

For specialized sporting equipment for cycling, jogging, swimming, climbing, camping, etc., try Le Vieux Campeur, 48 rue des Écoles, 75005 Paris; Métro: Cluny or St-Michel; Tel.: 01–53–10–48–48.

Jogging

The notorious problem with "uncurbed" dogs has been brought under control in many parts of the city with the introduction of motorized municipally-operated vacuums that suck up a lot of the seventy tons of dog excrement that's deposited on Parisian sidewalks each year. In the less wealthy areas of town, these machines don't seem to make the rounds quite so often.

Joggers are best advised to run in Paris streets with great caution (unlike former president Clinton, who insisted on jogging through Place de la Concorde at rush hour on his state visit to France in 1996). For your safety and the future of your lungs, you may prefer to jog in one of Paris's lovely parks or in either of the two large forests at the eastern and western edges of the city, the Bois de Vincennes and the Bois de Boulogne, respectively. Both are easily accessible by métro. If you love to jog, one of your most memorable jogs will be the time you spend lapping around the lake and chateau in the Jardin de Luxembourg in the Latin Quarter.

Bowling

If you're into bowling, you'll find lanes. Call for hours, prices, and exact addresses.
Bowling de Paris: Tel.: 01–53–64–93–00
Bowling International Stadium: Tel.: 01–45–86–55–52
Bowling Etoile Foch: Tel.: 01–45–00–00–13
Bowling Front de Seine: Tel.: 01–45–79–21–71

Bowling de Montparnasse: Tel.: 01–43–21–61–32
Bowling Mouffetard: Tel.: 01–43–31–09–35

Swimming

If you feel like going for a swim, you'll find excellent public facilities in almost every arrondissement. Entry is generally 2,50 euros. The Piscine Suzanne-Berlioux in the Forum des Halles, impressively located underground in the center of Paris, offers rink hockey, handball, basketball, volleyball, badminton, tennis, dance courses, and martial arts, in addition to its pool facilities. It is accessible to the handicapped as well.

Piscine Suzanne-Berlioux
4 Place de la Rotonde, 75001 Paris; Tel.: 01–40–26–10–51. Métro: Les Halles. Entry: 4 euros.
Piscine Saint-Merri, 16 rue du Renard, 75004 Paris; Tel.: 01–42–72–29–45. Métro: Hôtel de Ville or Rambuteau. Entry: 2,50 euros (closed Monday).
Piscine Armand-Massard, 66 boulevard du Montparnasse, 75015 Paris; Tel.: 01–45–38–65–19. Métro: Montparnasse.

Aquaboulevard
During the summer months when the days are hot and heavy, an outing to Aquaboulevard, an elaborate complex of swimming pools and recreational facilities, may be just what's in order.
4–6 rue Louis Armand, 75015 Paris. Métro: Balard, Porte de Versailles. Tel.: 01–40–60–10–00.

Fishing and Boating

There is some fishing in the Seine and Marne Rivers, as well as in the ponds at the Bois de Vincennes and Bois de Boulogne, but considering the need for licenses and the specific equipment required to nab a *poisson*, we advise you to limit your fishing experiences to the restaurants. You can rent canoes in the Bois de Vincennes and Bois de Boulogne.
Barques du Bois de Boulogne: These medium-sized rowing boats on Lac Inférieur fit a maximum of five people. Rental is by the hour (8,50 euros), a deposit of 30 euros (cash or euro check, no credit cards) is required, and all boats must be back by 6:00 P.M.

Hiking

There is more nature in Paris than you'd be able to discover on your own. Short side trips from Paris place you in dense forests laden with royal history. The most natural park inside Paris is the Buttes-Chaumont, which has rugged hills and even a few stalactites in a cave. This is the largest Parisian park, English-styled and as beautiful as it is romantic. Created under Napoleon III by the designer Adolphe Alphand, it is a colorful landscape of about 5,000 acres with more than half a million trees. Check out Sybill's Temple on the top of a 89-meter cliff. Tel.:

01–42–40–88–66. Take Métro Line 7 bis and get off at the Buttes-Chaumont–Botzaris stop.

For serious (and even casual) hikers, there is an entire set of *Grandes Randonnées* (grand hike trails) that radiate from Paris in distances as short as a several-hour hike to those as long as a several-*week* hike. Each route is specifically designated and is marked (markings on trees, etc.) per the standard hiking marks known to practitioners around the world. A good bookstore will have booklets entitled *GR (Grande Randonnée)* followed by the number of the trail. The booklets correspond to each designated GR trail and contain excessively detailed maps and descriptions of each ("Walk 25 meters and come to a tilted rock next to a red mill. Turn right. Walk 3 meters and turn left. . ."). These GRs are known worldwide, and hikers come from all over the globe to hike them.

Health, Sports, and Gym Clubs

Over the last several years, there has been a dramatic upsurge of interest in health clubs and fitness centers. Garden Gym is well adapted for younger people, with seven locations around Paris, while Gymnase Club, with its twenty-five locations, is the largest and thus a bit more impersonal. Currently, Gymnase Club offers a twelve-month membership to students at 215 euros. Most university programs, organizations, and companies have been offered special discounts for their members, employees, or students. Note that the Paris gym club scene can be overcrowded and less than comfortable. The finer touches that often are found at even moderately priced American clubs—abundant, clean towels, hair dryers, private lockers, saunas, steam rooms—are frequently not part of the deal. Check out the club first. One advantage to these chains is that you can frequent any location with your membership card.

Gymnase Club Nation, 16 rue des Colonnes du Trône, 75012 Paris; Tel.: 01–43–45–93–12.

Gymnase Club, 10 Place de la République, 75011 Paris; Tel.: 01–47–00–69–98. Métro: République. Entry: 8 euros per day.

Although it's possible to get a good workout in Paris, fitness *à l'américain* is a fairly new concept in France. There are, however, several prominent gym clubs with locations across the city offering workout rooms, saunas, whirlpools, and all the stuff you're used to back home. A wave of health clubs has opened in the last five years. There is no word in French for fitness, so Parisians say *"le fitness."* Note that these almost never supply towels, and if they do, they're not large, and you have to pay extra, usually 1,50 euros. Facilities tend to be less spacious than you're perhaps used to. You'll find stairmasters, treadmills, stationary bikes, free weights, and aerobics classes.

Many of the municipal pools have workout equipment but access usually requires an additional fee. For example, the Piscine Club Pontoise-Quartier Latin (19 rue de Pontoise; Tel.: 01–55–42–77–88; Métro: Maubert-Mutualité) costs 11 euros per day for their well-equipped gym and 4 euros per day for the pool. The American Church (65 quai d'Orsay; Tel.: 06–08–31–86–65; Métro: Invalides) offers aerobic classes (7 euros per class, Monday through Saturday).

One of the best clubs in France, the centrally located Espace Vit'Halles, has a younger clientele and offers a wide variety of programs with personalized training (weight lifting, aerobics, stretching, yoga, circuit training).

Espace Vit'Halles, Place Beaubourg, 48 rue Rambuteau, 75003 Paris; Tel.: 01–42–77–21–71. Métro: Rambuteau. Entry: 16 euros per day (credit cards accepted).
Open Monday through Friday from 8:00 A.M. to 10:00 P.M., Saturday from 10:00 A.M. to 7:00 P.M., and Sunday from 10:00 A.M. to 4:00 P.M.

You don't have to be a hotel guest to enjoy all the services offered by Le Ritz Health Club—16-meter pool, squash, hammam, Jacuzzi, free weights, circuit training, exercise and yoga classes—but the day pass just might be more than you'd pay for a hotel room!

Le Ritz Health Club, 15 Place Vendôme, 75001Paris; Tel.: 01–43–16–30–60. Métro: Opéra. Entry: 110 euros per day

A Word on Cycling in Paris

Hailing from Oklahoma, Marie Doezema, literary editor and waitress, shares her most exciting two-wheeled experiences in Paris.

Back in my days of high school French, I spent countless hours staring at a poster adorning the wall of the classroom instead of fully concentrating on the subjunctive. It was a black-and-white photograph, a typically romantic depiction of French country life. The main actor in the photo, a bicycle. On the bike, a jolly Frenchman, beret perched jauntily on his head, a baguette (probably still warm) tucked into the front basket. All the best of France rolled into one: beauty, freedom, food. . . . Certainly, it is in image that has remained with me, even subconsciously, for when I found myself living in Paris after college, I began to crave a bicycle like never before. Perhaps part of the desire for wheels was my admiration, even awe, of the ubiquitous motorcyclists in Paris: their freedom, ease, and devil-may-care attitudes as they weave in and out of traffic and navigate through crevices seemingly too small for even the tiniest of poodles still impresses me. Perhaps, too, it was a desire to be free of the métro, always too hot when you're bundled up in winter and even more stifling as you gasp your way through the crowds in summer. And there's just nothing like the feeling of your own set of wheels, with the open road before you. Open road, a relative term. It's true that the streets of Paris are a far cry from the pristine country road in the photograph from high school French. Nevertheless, having a bike in Paris can change your perception of the city quite drastically. At once, the city seems much bigger and much smaller. Bigger because of the infinite number of discoveries at the tips of your pedals: neighborhoods you didn't know existed, small paved alleyways, parks and courtyards that don't (fortunately) make it into all of the maps and guidebooks. But at the same time, the city seems smaller because it begins to make sense in a new way. If the city before was composed of the bright numbered squiggles of the map in the métro, distances you used to traverse in the dark tunnels of the underground become real streets with people, shops, cafés, liveliness. You can decide when and how you want to go somewhere instead of waiting for the métro or bus, transferring lines, searching for taxis late at night. And, of course, it's not just a matter of practicality: In good conditions (taking weather and traffic into consideration), riding a bike in Paris can be a rather sublime activity. For getting started on your life à vélo, here are a few pointers.

First things first, finding a bike. Though you might be tempted by the idea of a shiny new bike, it's recommended not to be too flashy. Though the threat of bike theft shouldn't keep you in a constant state of worry, the sightings you will have of mere parts of bikes tethered to posts around the city will keep you realistic. No need to tempt people to steal the frame and leave the wheels. A good lock is a must. The U-shaped kryptonite locks are your safest bet, because they're much more foolproof than chain locks, which are easier to cut. When you do lock up your bike, lock it to a sturdy enough object. This may seem obvious, but sometimes seemingly sturdy objects are not what they seem. Signposts and light posts are prime parking spots, and, of course, motorcycle/bike hitching posts, though not overly abundant, are designed expressly for your needs. Many people tie up to the iron grating by the métro entrances, and while these are certainly sturdy landings, they're one of the few places specifically *interdit* for bike hitching, so beware. When you do lock up your bike, make sure to go through both the frame and wheel with your lock.

There are many bike shops in Paris, good sources for both buying and repairing, but also for advice. O'Vélo Ville, on boulevard Richard Lenoir near the Bastille, has a good selection of bikes, both new and used. Prices are reasonable and service is excellent. If you buy a bike, it should come with a guarantee of at least three months. Also, the *mairie* in each arrondissement often has information on routes and bike events in Paris. There is also *Le service vélo de la RATP*, which rents bikes, gives guided bike tours, and is a source of information and advice. Every Sunday in Paris, various sections of the quai along the Seine are closed off to cars, reserving temporarily less-polluted air and space for cyclists, pedestrians, and rollerbladers. Similarly, the increasingly trendy Canal St. Martin is closed to cars on Sundays, creating a friendly neighborhood atmosphere for bikes and people, embraced by the canal on one side and artsy shops and café terraces on the other. Much of the route along the canal, from the nineteenth arrondissement all the way to the Bastille, has its own bike lane, a rather rare treat, because bike lanes in Paris are often shared with buses, a seemingly disparate coupling. Paris might not be as bike friendly as such cities as Amsterdam, but it is becoming increasingly accommodating as more people are beginning to use bikes. Keep in mind that bikers, like buses, are expected to follow traffic laws: That means paying heed to traffic lights, one way streets, and maintaining a well equipped "vehicle." A good light is essential and will make you exponentially safer if you ride at night. A bike pump, too, is never a bad idea.

The good news, too, about biking in Paris is that your visions of yourself careening through the French countryside are not so far off. There are special compartments on the RER that accept bikes, which means your explorations on bike need not end at the Périphérique. Versailles by bike, for instance, can be a lovely springtime activity. So, stick your *plan de Paris* in your saddlebags (or not, just let your whimsy take you where it will), and *bon vélo!*

Bike Rentals and Tours

This list includes shops with the best English-speaking staff and guides we are aware of in Paris. Night excursions have light-equipped bikes. The shops also service and repair bikes.

Au Réparteur de Bicyclette, 44 boulevard Sébastapol, 75003 Paris; Tel.: 01–48–04–51–19

Paris Vélo Rent a Bike, 2 rue Fer à Moulin, 75005 Paris. Tel.: 01–43–37–59–22; Fax: 01–47–07–67–45. Three-hour tour about 23 euros; nighttime tour about 30 euros.

Bicloune, Vélos d'occasion (used bikes), 93 boulevard Beaumarchais, 75003 Paris; Tel.: 01–42–77–58–06.

Paris à Velo, 4 rue Fer à Moulin, 75005 Paris; Tel.: 01 –43 –37 –59 –22. Three-hour tour about 23 euros; nighttime tour about 30 euros.

Paris a velo c'est sympa, 37 boulevard Bourdon, 75004 Paris; Tel.: 01–48–87–60–01.

RATP Bikes

The RATP organizes city tours of Paris by bike between March and September. They rent you bikes for only 5 euros, and en masse you tour the capital. For details, call 01–53–46–43–77. Note that in the summer months, the French railroad company, SNCF, rents bicycles at almost every train station in the country with interchangeable pickup and drop-off points. For information, contact SNCF at:

Maison Roue Libre
95 bis rue Rambuteau, 75001 Paris
Tel.: 01–53–46–43–77
Fax: 01–40–28–01–00
Open from 9:00 A.M. to 7:00 P.M. every day, year-round. Rental prices are very reasonable (3 euros per hour, 12 euros per day, including insurance) and guided tours with several different theme options are available for a small additional fee.

Shipping Your Bike

For information on shipping your bike with you, call your airline. Charter flights tend to be stricter with baggage requirements and are not equipped with bike boxes. Once you get to Paris, you shouldn't have much problem. Carrying bikes on the French trains is not only permissible but free (though you may encounter some restrictions on what time of day bikes are allowed on trains; consult www.sncf.fr for details).

For tour operators specializing in cycling trips to France, request a copy of the Maison de la France's *Easy Reference Guide to France* on the Web at www.france tourism.com or by calling (202) 659–7779.

Inline Skating

By far the hottest Paris sport to grasp the imagination of both residents and visitors is inline skating, a fascinating, fast-paced, and original way to see the city by day and night. Twenty years ago there were barely 10,000 inline skaters in all of France. Today you'll have a hard time going a day without seeing one, winter or summer. With the advent of roller mania, many associations and group outings have been organized to bring together practitioners of all levels and interests. If you are a beginner, several rental and instruction options are available. Roller Squad Institute (Tel.: 01–53–61–21–35) offers ninety-minute lessons for 10 euros per hour every day except Monday and Friday and organizes excursions leaving from Invalides on Saturday and from Trocadéro every Sunday, both at 3:00 P.M. Nomades (37 boulevard Bourdon in the fourth arrondissement; Tel.: 01–44–54–07–44, Métro: Bastille) not only rents inline skates but offers lessons for 15 euros per hour on Saturday and Sunday mornings starting at 10:00. For more advanced bladers there is the three-hour outing that leaves from Place d'Italie every Friday night at 10:00. See their Web site www.Pari-roller.com for more information (in French and English). Other skate rentals: Bike 'n Roller (137 rue St-Dominique, 75007 Paris; Tel.: 01–44–18–30–39) and Franscoop (47 rue Servan, 75011 Paris, Tel.: 01–47–00–68–43).

One of the most successful bike-tour operations is Bullfrog Bike Tours, which organizes guided tours of the city of very comfortable bikes. Tell them that the author of *Paris Inside Out* sent you!

24 rue Edgar Faure, 75015 Paris
Tel.: 01-56-58-10-54
E-mail: bullfrogbikes@hotmail.com
www.BullfrogBikes.com

Golf

There are private and public golf courses in the Paris area, but you'll need a car to get to them. Count on courses requiring all players to purchase insurance before stepping up to the first tee. Greens fees were expensive in the past but have lined up these days with good North American courses. If you do play golf, you may be pleased to note that some of the most sumptuous courses on Earth are found within an hour of Paris. Consult www.golfinginfrance.com. Here are a few choices:
+ Golf Chantilly: Tel.: 03–44–58–47–77
+ Golf Club de L'Etoile: Tel.: 01–43–80–42–05
+ Golf Disneyland Paris: Tel.: 01–60–45–68–90

There are miniature golf courses in the Bois de Vincennes and Jardin d'Acclimatation.

Horseback Riding

Centre Equestre de la Cartoucherie in the Bois de Vincennes, 75012 Paris; Tel.: 01–43–74–61–25.

Selected Sports Contacts in the Paris Area

Baseball Fédération Française Baseball Softball et Cricket. Tel.: 01–44–68–89–30

Basketball. Espace Vit'Halles. Tel.: 01–42–77–21–71 (Saturday mornings at 11:00 at nearby gym)

Boxing Fédération Française de Boxe. Tel.: 01–53–24–60–60

Fencing Ligue d'Escrime de l'Académie de Paris. Tel.: 01–49–23–40–50

Football (American) Fédération Française Football Américain. Tel.: 01–43–11–14–70

Ice Skating Patinoire des Buttes Chaumont. Tel.: 01–44–16–60–00
Rugby Fédération Française de Rugby, Tel.: 01–53–21–15–15
Squash Squash Quartier Latin. Tel.: 01–55–42–77–88

Parks

Paris has fabulous parks for strolling, sunning, and passive recreation. The idea of the park in France differs from its North American equivalent in that Parisian green spaces are aesthetically planned, surveyed, and regulated. Lawns are for looking at, not walking on or hosting picnics. A uniformed guard with a whistle will let you know if you step out of line by using the public space for ball playing or frisbee. Parks are for strolls, for reflection, reading, lovers' rendezvous, concerts. . . . Paris parks usually close at dusk and are locked. The following are some of the major parks in Paris.

Bois de Boulogne, sixteenth *arrondissement;* métro: Porte de Neuilly, Porte Dauphine, or Les Sablons. This park has existed as a green wooded space for centuries. It once stood just inside the fortified boundary of Paris. Now it has been transformed into 2,000 acres of varied terrain that includes a rose garden, a museum, two world-famous race courses, a small zoo, a polo ground, a Shakespeare Garden (where all the plants mentioned in the Bard's plays can be found and his plays are staged in the summer), two lakes, broad avenues for bike riding, and paths for jogging or bicycling. You can even stay here in the campground. The Jardin d'Acclimatation has a small zoo, a playground, and a restaurant where you can share your table with the goats and chickens on Wednesdays. Nearby is the Musée des Arts et Traditions Populaires. There are boats for hire in the Lac Inférieur, and the nearby Parc de Bagatelle has a castle, flower garden, and pickup softball games. At night the park changes character, though. Crime and vandalism are not unheard of, and a most interesting variety of outdoor prostitutes and a hybrid of Brazilian transvestites flourish. Due to the increased number of AIDS cases, the police have begun an unprecedented crackdown on the prostitution in this park and have closed it to motor-vehicle access at night.

Bois de Vincennes, twelfth *arrondissement;* métro: Porte de Charenton or Chateau de Vincennes. Noted for its Parc Floral, hippodrome, and stables, this park has two lakes with rowboats for hire, biking and jogging paths, a medieval castle, playing fields, three fine restaurants, and Paris's largest zoo. An annual ecological fair called La Marjolaine also takes place here.

Jardin des Plantes, fifth *arrondissement;* métro: Jussieu or Gare d'Austerlitz. This lovely park houses a formal garden, a botanical greenhouse, a natural history museum, a hidden gazebo, and a zoo.

Jardin du Luxembourg, fifth *arrondissement;* métro: Luxembourg. Located at the edge of the Latin Quarter along the boulevard St-Michel, this garden/park captures the contrasts of modern Paris, with its joggers, wooden toy sailboats, wrought-iron park chairs, *guignol* (puppet shows), pony rides, tennis courts, and *pelouse* (lawn) specially designated for infants (you will even find an area where only parents with small children are allowed to enter). The gardens are formal in the classical French style, with long open vistas and a central fountain. On the north side the Chateau du Luxembourg, built by Marie de Medici in 1615 (and German headquarters during the Occupation), now houses the French Senate and an art museum. In recent years the *jardin* has been enlivened by controversial "column" sculptures and with contemporary sculpture exhibits.

Palais Royal, first *arrondisement;* métro: Palais-Royal. In the classic but now out-of-print and difficult to find Nairn's Paris, Ian Nairn describes the "luminous melancholy" of the elegant home and gardens of the Duc d'Orléans as "surely among the greyest joys in the world."

Parc des Buttes-Chaumont, nineteenth *arrondissement;* métro: Buttes-Chaumont. Lesser known to tourists and visitors, but absolutely charming, with two restaurants, exotic trees, and deep ravines. This is a great park for runners who may relish the challenges of the park's hills.

Parc Monceau, boulevard de Courcelles, eighth *arrondissement;* métro: Monceau. One of the loveliest spots in Paris, set amid exemplary bourgeois apartments. You'll find artificial waterfalls and ponds, glades, and romantic statuary. Nearby (63 rue de Monceau) is the Musée Nissim de Camondo, a completely preserved eighteenth-century mansion.

Parc Montsouris, fourteenth *arrondissement;* métro: Cité Universitaire. Elegant formal park located near the Cité Universitaire, the residential campus for international students in Paris. The unusual templelike structure, pavillon du Bey, for which the park was known, was destroyed by fire. The Cité Universitaire is the closest you'll find in Paris to the American-style university campus, organized according to national houses, such as the Fondation des Etats-Unis, Casa de Cuba, Sweden House, etc.

Jardin des Tuileries, first *arrondissement;* métro: Tuileries. Contains more than twenty original Rodin sculptures. Excellent for midday strolls between Place de la Concorde and the Louvre. At night the terrace area overlooking the Seine is one of Paris's main locations for gay encounters.

Children in Paris

Paris is a wonderful city for children. And the adults trying to stimulate, entertain, and educate them. In fact, children are the best catalyst for getting adults to learn about and participate in a foreign culture. (There are two million-plus inhabitants of greater Paris under the age of eighteen, and about five million more visit each year.) First, while you should remain cautious, you must understand that the city is not dangerous. You don't have to clutch your kids in fear, as you may feel necessary in large American cities. The French don't have to print pictures of missing kids on milk cartons, fortunately. Occasionally, there are cases of violence and perversion that make the national news. But you can feel relatively secure about bringing up children in Paris or visiting the city with your little ones.

Children are more often than not included at dinner parties—even New Year's Eve parties—and are regularly taken to restaurants. Children's menus exist in many, but not most, restaurants and consist of a slice of ham or two Strasbourg sausages, fries *(frites)*, and an orange juice. Let the kid pick à la carte!

Several books exist on experiencing Paris with children, most notably in French, *Le Paris des Tout-Petits* (Editions Diane de Selliers), *Le Guide de l'Enfant à Paris* (MA Editions), and in English, *Kidding Around Paris* (John Muir Publications).

Better than those is a local guide written and published by Message, a group of anglophone parents who formed a support organization for bringing up children in Paris (Tel.: 01–39–73–48–61).

The bird market, stamp market, and flower market, along with the annual La Marjolaine ecology fair, are all wonderful activities. For the more adventurous the *égouts de Paris* (Paris sewers; entrance on the Pont d'Alma) and the *catacombes* make for memorable and interesting visits.

No Paris apartment/house bans kids, and almost none forbids pets.

If you want to take your child fishing, there are possibilities, but the rules, regulations, and licensing fees, which vary by site and the kind of fish you're angling for, tend to kill all the excitement of being out in the open air. But you can dangle your rod in the Seine or Marne without much hassle.

Children's clothes in Paris are beautiful and well made but very expensive. Good finds for clothes can be made at the flea markets. Agence des Enfants puts out a catalogue of goods and services for children called *Si Tu Veux* (Tel.: 01–42–60–45–42).

Some of the best things to do with kids include the Jardin d'Acclimatation in the Bois de Boulogne; the Jardin du Luxembourg, which has old-time *manèges* (merry-go-rounds), pony rides, puppet shows, and jungle gyms; and the Parc Floral in the Bois de Vincennes. The theme parks are always a treat, although expensive and time consuming. Aside from Disneyland Paris there is Mirapolis and the very French Parc Astérix, about an hour north of the city.

The Ménilmontant district is the Paris of *The Red Balloon*, a children's film classic.

The museums make for superb outings. The Egyptian collection at the Louvre, the sculpture garden at the Rodin Museum, the Musée de l'Homme, and the Musée des Arts Africains et Océaniens are all sure bets. One single father discovered after taking his four-year-old to the Louvre that kids can read hieroglyphics! They're pictograms. Only the educated minds of schooled adults find that ancient form of writing culturally alienating. (See the Arts and Culture in Paris chapter.)

Wednesday afternoons (usually at 4:00 P.M.) there are the traditional *guignols* (marionette) shows in many small theaters in the major parks. Bring your kids to these, and you'll really feel like you're participating in the Paris you've come to discover. Don't worry that the program is in French; your kids will understand and love it. Check the weekly *Pariscope* or *l'Officiel des Spectacles*, available at newsstands, for locations and times. And you'll improve your French by learning the esoterica of the infantile world.

The Cité des Sciences at La Villette offers an excellent simulated *chantier* (construction site)—off-limits for adults—for kids to play and "work" in. And kids usually enjoy Aquaboulevard, a water park with a huge aquatic landscape of cascades and wild vegetation.

Disneyland Paris

On April 12, 1992, compulsively on schedule, EuroDisney (later changed to Disneyland Paris for marketing reasons) opened its imported pearly gates in the Marne Valley, 32 kilometers east of Paris, on a site that is said to be a fifth the size of the capital. In what was one of the largest press campaigns in the history of the world, this fantasy theme park was greeted with the buzz of rampant media attention, popular conversation, and occasionally heated debate. One radical French intellectual called Disneyland Paris a "cultural Chernobyl," which the press enjoyed but which the Disneyland Paris chairman dubbed a disillusioned communist response. Attracted by the wave of 12,000 new jobs, a revved-up local economy, and the coming of state-of-the-art technology couched in inoffensive family entertainment, French officials and the public have shown much enthusiasm and optimism for the park, despite the high entry prices—up to 40 euros for adults and 23 euros for children per day. Today, the park is the largest attraction in Europe with 12 million visitors yearly.

In 1993 Disneyland Paris announced dreadful financial news, a runaway deficit that sent the stock tumbling and rumors of collapse echoing throughout the world. No one really knew if the park was in the trouble they claimed or if they were crying wolf as part of some larger marketing/financial strategy that would ultimately translate into even greater profits for the company.

Part of the growing pains comes from Disneyland Paris's lessened lure during the sometimes very cold off-seasons and the French reluctance to spend a day at a theme park that doesn't serve wine or beer in its restaurants. Puritan values have never been greatly appreciated by the French, especially Parisians. In any case the organization seems to have pulled out all the stops and introduced new features to the park, rendering the experience even more complete. The resort so far features a theme park with thirty-five attractions, six hotels, a campground, a twenty-seven-hole golf course, a jazz club, and a nighttime entertainment center with nightclubs, restaurants, and shops.

Since opening a decade ago, the park has added a dozen new attractions. In 1996 the park opened the classic Disney attraction "Space Mountain," locally named "Discovery Mountain," sending visitors through loops, corkscrew turns, and even a shower of meteorites—all in the darkness of deep space.

If the park offers swatches of European, hand-woven Aubusson tapestries, Victorian gas lamps, and better cuisine than its American counterparts, the neighboring hotels and Festival Disney entertainment center are definitely American.

Festival Disney has a country-western saloon, a New York–style deli complete with lox and bagels, a 1950s-type diner with waitresses in poodle skirts (without the poodles) and roller skates, a sports bar with American beer and snacks, and more.

Reaching the resort is not as complicated as it may seem (Paris métro authorities decided not to name the RER station "Disneyland Paris"). You have to follow signs on the RER A Line for "Marne-la-Vallée/Chessy." Once you've landed there (thirty- to forty-five-minute ride from Paris stations), the park is a two-minute walk away. If you're driving, it's best to follow the Georges Pompidou Express road past Bercy and the Gare de Lyon to hook up to the A4 highway. It's about a forty-five-minute drive to exit 14, Parc Disneyland Paris. There are also shuttle buses direct from Charles de Gaulle and Orly Airports. Since Disneyland Paris is still adapting to its new home in Europe, it's best to check ahead for the latest opening hours, admission prices, etc. (Tel.: 01–64–74–30–00, park information; 01–60–30–60–30, hotel information and reservations; 36–15 DISNEY on your Minitel, or www.disneylandparis.com; you can also write to Disneyland Paris Reservations, BP 100, 77777 Marne la Vallee Cedex 4). The best book on the park is Bob Sehlinger's *The Unofficial Guide to Disneyland Paris.*

Culinary Paris

Eating in France is a ritual that can reach religious proportions. No other city in the world has a greater density of eating establishments per square meter than Paris. Nothing of importance happens in France without food, somehow, being included. Remember the important but unwritten rule: Anything you do at the table that enhances your enjoyment of a meal is permissible. If you're motivated by pleasure and aesthetics, you'll never be ill-judged.

For advice and information on everything food related in Paris, Patricia Wells's *The Food Lover's Guide to Paris* is an excellent resource. It has information on food shopping, restaurants, and cafés, as well as comprehensive restaurant recommendations, including hours of operation, restaurants open on weekends, restaurants open after 11:00 P.M., restaurants open in August, and restaurants with sidewalk tables or outdoor terraces, as well as cross-listings by price, regional specialties, and location. Her book is a must for frequent restaurant goers and food lovers. Another fine reference are the Zagat's series, also available at www.zagat.com.

Café Culture

Cafés are places where people go to be among friends and acquaintances. They are meeting places, solariums (the French are notorious sun-worshipers), or shelters from bad weather; places to sit, talk, dream, make friends, make out, or eat. They are also handy for their telephones and toilets. Café- and bar-sitting are an integral part of daily French life. Knowing a little about how cafés function will save you from a lot of surprises. First of all, the large, well-situated cafés on the Champs-Elysées, on the Boulevard Saint-Germain at Saint-Germain-des-Prés, at Montparnasse, along all the major boulevards, and in the Latin Quarter are expensive. But remember, you are not paying for your cup of coffee or glass of beer as much as for your right to sit in a pretty spot for as long as you like and talk, read, watch, or daydream. If you're spending 2,50 euros for an *espress* (espresso) or 3 euros for a *demi* (a quarter pint of draft beer), think of it as rent for the time and space. The prices of drinks in cafés depend on whether you're standing at the bar (*comptoir*), or *zinc* (counter bar), or sitting—and then, of course, on where you're sitting (only *bar américains* have seats or stools at the counter). Drinks are less expensive if you are served at the bar. The outside terrace is always the most expensive. The prices of drinks go up after 8:00 P.M. Also, you can order some drinks at the bar that you cannot order when seated. A glass of draft lemon soda (*limonade*), the cheapest drink available and very refreshing on warm days, can be ordered only when you're standing at the bar. Otherwise, you get the more expensive and overly sweetened bottled lemon soda. No matter where you're sitting or when, the tip is always included. Although not required or even really expected, it is customary to leave the copper-colored coins (*la feraille*) in your change as a little extra tip. At the counter, you'll be presented with a little plastic dish for payment, which is then flipped over to signify that the barman has collected from you. At the tables, the *serveur* leaves a slip of paper from the cash register indicating what you owe. Usually you pay at the end of your stay, but sometimes the *serveur* (not to be called *garçon*, even though old guidebooks will still indicate so) will come around to collect as he goes off duty. When you've paid he'll crumple or slightly rip the paper, indicating that you've paid.

Cafés are open very early for coffee and croissants. Ask for a *tartine*—a buttered stick of *baguette*—to dunk in your coffee. *Très Parisien* and the best deal in France.

The most common beverage in a café is obviously *un café* (coffee), and the nuances need enumeration and explanation: When you just want to sit and talk, read, write, or pass away the time and you don't want to spend much, order *un café*. (Although French coffee in cafés is notably stronger and more flavorful than American or British coffee, it is widely understood that café coffee is not excellent in quality. Go to a *brûlerie* to buy the best quality ground coffees.)

Quick Guide to Café Coffee

café noir, un café (espress)—classic strong coffee served in a tiny cup
café noir double or double espress—twice the dose of an espresso
café au lait—espress with mostly steamed milk
petit crème—espress with steamed milk
grand crème—larger version of the petit crème
café noisette—espress with a dab of milk
café allongé—espress with extra hot water, also called *un café long* or *un café américain*
café serré—espress with half the normal amount of water
Very weak coffee is humorously labeled *jus de chaussettes* (sock juice)

In the daily cycle of most cafés, there are three periods of peak activity: at breakfast time (before 9:30 A.M.); at lunch (between noon and 2:00 P.M.); and before dinner at the *heure de l'apéritif (apéro)* aperitif hour (from about 5:30 to 7:30 P.M.) It is not unusual to see two different sets of regulars at different times of day, one at breakfast and lunch and the other at the aperitif hour. Between peak periods customers come for a rest from their work, to meet other people, or simply to sit alone with their thoughts.

The choice of beverages in a Parisian café is superb. The French make popular drinks by mixing syrups with either Vittel mineral water or milk. Thus, you can order a *Vittel menthe* (or *menthe à l'eau*) or *Vittel grenadine*, or a *lait fraise* or *lait grenadine*. As for beer, you can order un *demi* (eight ounces), un *sérieux* (pint), or une *formidable* (liter). Or a *panaché* (a mixture of draft beer and draft lemon soda), a popular summer drink that foreigners acquire a taste for after four or five tries. A final twist on the *panaché* is called a *pinochet*, which is a *panaché* with grenadine.

Some Popular Drinks

un thé au lait	tea with milk
un thé citron	tea with lemon
un thé nature	plain tea
un chocolat chaud	hot chocolate
un chocolat froid	chocolate milk
un citron pressé	fresh-squeezed lemon juice (comes with water and sugar)
une orange pressée	fresh orange juice (comes with water and sugar)
un jus de fruits	fruit juice
une bière en pression	Many cafés specialize in this certain brand of beer on tap, usually marked clearly on the café's awning.
un demi, un demi pression	a quarter-liter of draft beer
un demi Munich	a quarter-liter of German beer
une bière	a beer in a bottle

Wine

You should not judge French wine by what is served in most cafés (other than the Nouveau Beaujolais when it comes out each fall). Cheap café wine is seldom very good, and the carafed rosé is often very bad. Cafés normally serve wines in two sizes of glass, *un ballon* (large) and *un petit* (small). For a more complete discussion, see the Wine section, later in this chapter.

Some Popular Wine Drinks

un blanc sec	(petit or dry white wineballon)
un kir	white wine and *crème de cassis*
un kir clair	white wine with just a touch of *cassis*
un kir royal	a kir with champagne instead of white wine

Aperitifs

There are a variety of aperitifs served in cafés, usually served over ice with a twist of lemon. These drinks are mixed with water and sometimes *sirop de menthe (un perroquet)*. A martini in France is not the dry thing with the olive; it's a brand of vermouth ordered by itself as an aperitif. Ice is provided only with certain cocktails, whiskey, Pernod, pastis, or Ricard (a glorious Mediterranean anise aperitif that pours out rich and yellow and goes cloudy when mixed with water). Great on a hot afternoon on a café terrace with Lawrence Durrell's *Justine* in hand. If you prefer bottled water, there's Perrier or Badoit on the sparkling side *(eau gazeuse)*, and Vittel and Vichy on the flat side *(plate)*. The only mixed drink served correctly in most cafés seems to be a *gin-tonique*. Other drinks include *un grog* (hot rum with lemon, water, and sugar), *un cognac* (brandy from Cognac), *un armagnac* (brandy from Armagnac), *un calvados (un calva)* (apple brandy from Normandy), and *une poire Williams* (pear brandy).

A word on café-restaurants: If the tables are set with cloths, they are reserved for those wishing to dine and should not be taken if you plan to have only a drink, snack, or small salad.

Café Services

Toilets and telephones are always found in cafés—usually downstairs in the *sous-sol*, S/S, or somewhere at the back. If you want to use the rest room of a café without consuming anything, you have the law on your side. But getting away with it can sometimes be another matter. Be somewhat discreet. In chic cafés there might be a toilet attendant that has a plate out for a tip. Some toilet stalls require a coin, but most don't. Although they are becoming rarer, the old Turkish toilets (hole in the porcelain floor with spots for your feet) are still common. They are a bit hard to get used to but a highly Parisian experience. Just get ready to jump out of the way before you pull the flusher if you want to avoid flooding your feet. Toilet paper is usually available, but not always, and very often a stiff, crinkly kind that is not very comfortable or practical.

Telephones in cafés usually take coins for local calls, but some cafés, mostly the smaller or older ones, still have booths with regular phones and the barman has to activate the line for you. You have to ask for a line out for each call *(Est-ce que je peux avoir la ligne, s'il vous plaît?)*. You pay afterward at the bar, where there is a counter, usually 30 or 40 cents per unit.

Shops, Markets, and Foods

You may be struck by the charming inconveniences of the Parisian shopping system. Although large supermarkets and mall-style complexes have cropped up all over, especially in the suburbs, anyone who has spent time in North America might find French supermarkets both fascinating and annoying, an enigmatic combination of grandeur and chaos with contradictions galore—lots of space with spotty selections, bright aisles and poorly maintained shelves, great slogans and surly or ill-trained service.

First and foremost, remember to bring along your own shopping bags, basket, or backpack. Only thin and tiny baggies are given away, and they are practically useless for any major shopping. Stronger ones are available in supermarkets but will cost you at least 0,30 euros. Also, remember that most businesses (except supermarkets) close between noon and 2:00 P.M. or between 1:00 and 3:00 P.M. Most small shops and grocery stores are closed on Mondays. One of Paris's greatest resources, though, is its proliferation of wonderful little shops and street markets. The lack of many large supermarkets *(grandes surfaces)* in convenient Paris locations often means having to frequent these small neighborhood shops, which necessitates organization and a deeper understanding of Paris fare and habits as well as waiting to be served in line after line. Though these circumstances may be discouraging at first, going to the markets and different shops is a valuable way of taking part in and enjoying a very basic aspect of daily Parisian life. The subtle varieties found in these shops prove to be intriguing as you discover that the merchant *(commerçant)* is an expert who can give you all sorts of interesting tips. Going frequently to the same baker or butcher can also be helpful—merchants are quick to remember a face.

The larger supermarkets tend to feel like open-air markets that have been roofed in and stocked with army-sized quantities. The largest chains are Carrefour, Auchan, Monoprix, Franprix, Prisunic, Inno, Continent, Casino, and Mammouth (the old and famous chain Felix Potin no longer exists). And there's Ed, the cut-rate bargain-brand chain, where they don't provide plastic shopping bags at all. Everybody has a favorite and least favorite, but many shoppers agree that the Monoprix seems to have a more progressive attitude toward service, quality, and variety. This, though, depends on the particular store you frequent. During its annual, two-week American special you can stock up on salsa and chips, Paul Newman salad dressing, and Budweiser in cans and bottles. Often the food section of supermarkets is upstairs or in the basement of a department store. Don't expect much service in French supermarkets. There are no baggers and your tender goods can get smashed as you scramble to bag them yourself while the checkout clerk rushes you to pay up so he can move on. Don't try to make a special request in the meat section; there is no meat manager. And the produce manager will not mark down your bunch of bruised bananas. A typical response to "Where can I find spaghetti sauce?" might be "I don't know" or "We don't carry it." Don't be surprised if a store clerk doesn't try to find what you're looking for or if no one is mopping up the splattered jar of pickles. To get a shopping cart you need a 1 euro to release it from a locking mechanism. You get the coin back when you return it and relock it onto the others.

The internal organization of food and products may be disorienting at first. In the really large stores, the grocery sections often flow directly into housewear, hardware, clothing, and garden centers. If your image of Parisian grocery shopping has been limited to the quaint cheese shop followed by the beautiful bounty of the *pâtisserie*, you should treat yourself to a hectic visit to a massive supermarket in the *banlieue* (suburbs) to fully appreciate the daily or weekly habits of the *Français moyens* (French middle class), where industrial croissants are purchased in cellophane packs of fifteen. Häagen-Dazs and more recently Ben & Jerry's have carved out places for themselves in the ice-cream section of these stores.

There are also chains of frozen-food stores scattered around town. The best known is Picard. The home-delivery service is Eismann.

Les Commerçants (shopkeepers)

There is a wide range of shops in each Parisian neighborhood and the differences are sometimes very subtle, especially when food is concerned. This section explains the chain of names often seen on shop awnings. A *Boulangerie-Pâtisserie-Confiserie*, for example, will have bread, pastries, and fine candies.

Boulangeries

Most *boulangeries* sell prepared sandwiches, mini pizzas, quiches, onion tarts, and *croque-monsieurs* (a sort of grilled ham and cheese—the classic French common food available at all hours in all cafés; the *croque-madame* is the same thing topped with a sunny-side up egg) for about 3 euros. They'll microwave food for you on request.

It'll take some time before you become agile with all the nuances in the French boulangerie. The bread alone will stun you in its variety. The *baguette* is probably the best deal in France. The following are a few main items:

Baguette: (flour, water, yeast, and salt) weight (250 grams) and price (0,65 euros) are government regulated, but you'll get to know the great ones from the good ones.

Demi-baguette: half a baguette, around 0,32 euros

Bâtard: same weight as a baguette, but shorter and less elegant, made from the squatty end of the rolled-out dough

Pain au levain: sourdough bread. Usually found in health food or specialty stores and relatively expensive. Sold by weight. Delicious with fresh butter and wonderful with pâté or rillettes (minced pork)

Boule: round loaf, either small or large

Chapeau: small round loaf topped with a chapeau (hat)

Couronne: ring-shaped baguette

Le fer à cheval: horseshoe-shaped baguette

Ficelle: thin, crusty baguette of about 125 grams

Fougasse: a flat, rectangular-shaped bread made of baguette dough filled with onions, herbs, spices, or anchovies

Miche: large, round country-style loaf

Pain de campagne: a white bread dusted with flour, giving it a rustic look (and a higher price) or a hearty loaf that may be a blend of white, whole wheat, and rye flour with added bran. Also called *baguette à l'ancienne* or *baguette paysanne*. It comes in every shape, from a small, round individual roll to a large family loaf.

Pain complet: bread made partially or entirely from whole wheat flour

Pain fantaisie: "fantasy bread"—any imaginatively shaped bread

Pain de mie: a rectangular, white, eggy and crusty sandwich loaf used for toast

Pain aux noix and pain aux noisettes: unsweetened rye or wheat bread filled with walnuts or hazelnuts

Pain aux raisins: rye or wheat bread filled with raisins, not to be confused with the sweet bun version

Pain de seigle: closest thing to pumpernickel bread in a boulangerie. Two-thirds rye and one-third wheat flour

Pain au son: a dietetic bread that is quality-controlled, containing bran flour

Pain viennois: milk and sugar are added to the baguette dough for a finer texture.

Pain brioché: a rich dough made with milk, eggs, and sugar. Brioche comes in a variety of sizes and shapes. Proportionately expensive, but a real delight for those lazy mornings. Great to dunk in *café au lait.*

Note: you will often hear customers asking for their bread *bien cuit* (well done and crusty), *pas trop cuit* or *bien tendre* (less baked and doughier). You can also ask for *"une baguette coupée en deux"* (a *baguette* cut in half). This facilitates transportation and prevents the bread from breaking en route. All of your requests, whether they be at the bakery, the cheese shop, or the hardware store, should of course be accompanied by a smile and followed by *"s'il vous plaît,"* two things that will go a long way toward making any transaction simpler and easier. Also, get accustomed to carrying your bread in your hand, bag, or under your arm. Bread is seldom wrapped or bagged. Sometimes, in the more bourgeois boulangeries, your *baguette* will come with a square of tissue paper wrapped around the center where you are to grasp the bread. If you ask for a second square of paper, you'll probably get a strange look—if not an outright *non*. Don't worry, though, in four centuries there are no documented cases of anyone getting sick from unprotected bread.

Note: If you ask for your bread sliced on the slicing machine, expect to pay an additional half an euro. It's annoying, but that's the way it is. Don't even bother complaining.

After bread, the most common items in the boulangerie include the following:

Croissant ordinaire: These are the crescent-shaped puff pastry rolls now found all over the world. If the points are curled toward the center, the croissant has been made with margarine and has not been glazed with butter before baking. Price is always about 10 cents less than the *croissant au beurre*. *Croissants* were first made by French chefs for the rulers of the Ottoman Empire; the shape is based on the Turkish crescent in the Ottoman flag.

Croissant au beurre: These croissants have their tips pointing straight out, signifying their pure butter content. Richer and definitely worth the extra ten cents.

Pain au chocolat: a rectangular flaky pastry filled with a strip of chocolate. If you are lucky enough to catch a batch coming out of the oven, the chocolate will still be warm and soft—a favorite afterschool snack for youngsters.

Pain aux raisins: a round, spiral-shaped croissant cooked with raisins and a light egg cream.

Croissant aux amandes: topped with slivered almonds and filled with a rich almond butter paste.

Chausson aux pommes: a turnover with applesauce inside.

As for individual *gâteaux*, most boulangeries that are also *pâtisseries* offer:

Millefeuilles (Napoleon): puffed pastry with pastry cream
Éclairs: chou pastry filled with chocolate or coffee cream
Religieuse: same as éclair but shaped like a nun's hat
Tartelette aux fruits: small fruit tarts

Croissants are usually purchased in the morning, cakes in the afternoon or evenings. Boulangeries also sell *bonbons* (candy) by the piece to kids, as well as soft drinks and bottled water that are cool but never really cold. It's nearly impossible to get a napkin. Not all boulangeries are open on Mondays, so expect lines for bread on that day. Also, if you wait too long on Sundays, by midday it might get a bit tough to find bread. Most boulangeries sell out their bread every day. Some boulangeries freeze unsold *baguettes* and rebake them later at a slight compromise of taste and texture. You can detect this by the pattern of cracks on the sides of the *baguette* crust. Don't make a scene; just change *boulangeries*.

Boucheries

Although Europe has been plagued these past years with health scares related to beef from England and dioxin-tainted chickens and pork from Belgium, the food supply in France is still high quality, and the beef, especially the *charolais* (a high-quality type of French beef), remains quite good. The Parisian butcher shop has its own array of idiosyncrasies. Most butcher shops sell pork, beef, mutton, lamb, veal, and liver, and some sausages, *pâtés*, poultry, rabbit, and game. Specialized poultry such as turkeys, pheasant, pigeons, and Cornish hen should be bought in a *marchand de volaille*, a neighborhood poultry shop. If you see a butcher's shop with photos of thoroughbreds on its walls, you're in a *chevaline*, where horse meat is sold. Horse is reputed to be the finest meat on the market. Try some. You can buy steaks, roasts, hamburger meat, etc. The shops usually have a gold horse's head over the door.

The cuts of meat are particular to France. Steaks are not precut, nor is chopped meat previously packaged. If you're used to thick steaks, you have to ask for one *très épais*. French meat is very tasty but on the whole not as tender as U.S. beef. Fewer hormones, though! The superior cuts of beef—*côte de boeuf, entrecôte, filet mignon*—are expensive. Pork, though, is excellent and relatively cheap, as are certain cuts of lamb and mutton. Don't be alarmed by scrawny slabs of lean red meat hanging above bellowed cutting boards on nasty aluminum hooks. The blood-stained butchers cut steaks out of these hanging slabs as they go. Fresher. Chopped steak for *tartare* should be purchased just before eating. Supermarkets have meat departments, but there is no bell to ring to call for the butcher. You can't make special requests. If you want your steak thicker, go to a butcher shop.

A Word on Chicken

The concept of the species is far more specific in French culture than in the Anglo-Saxon world. One French traveler who recently flew on the New York–Paris TWA flight was amused when the in-flight meal arrived. The stewardess asked, "Meat or fish?" "What kind of fish?" he replied, upon which she looked at him as if he were a Martian. "Fish fish." Didn't they know in America that salmon is not sole! he wondered.

Well, with chicken the distinctions are even finer. A *poulet*, exclusively male, is a grown-up *coquelet* that becomes either a *chapon* or a *coq*, depending on if he is spared his maleness. A *poularde*, on the other hand, the female, is an adult *poulette* that has never met up with a *coq*. Had she, though, she'd not be a *poularde* but a *poule*.

On the whole, French chicken is superior to U.S. and U.K. chicken. You can tell by the color, the smell, the skin *(chair de poule)*, and the taste. In France, there is a significant distinction between *poulet, poulet fermier,* and *poulet industrielle. Poulet fermier,* though, can mean two things: either the bird is a *poulet plein air,* which means he has spent his life in a two-square-meter coop and has been fed grain and milk, or he is a *poulet liberté,* the highest-quality chicken, and was able to freely run, although fed the same grain and milk. Yellower chickens are corn-fed, while whiter chickens are wheat-fed. It's doubtful if you'll ever need to know this, but in France the law stipulates that a chicken must be at least eighty-one days old before being killed. In the United States broiler chickens live no longer than six weeks! The label of poulet fermier will indicate the age.

The label on eggs, too, will have you either perplexed or on the floor in laughter. Tell me the difference between "bio" eggs from hens allowed to move around freely—*"libre parcours,"* and those *"en liberté"* and I'll make you a free omelet!

In the meantime, here's some meaty vocabulary:

bœuf	**beef**
bavette	tender steak
bifteck	ordinary thin steak
bourguignon	cubed beef stew
châteaubriand	porterhouse steak
faux-filet	sirloin
entrecôte	rib steak
steak haché	ground beef
rosbif	roast beef
tartare	ground beef with zero percent fat
tournedos	filet wrapped in fat
mouton/agneau	**mutton/lamb**
brochette	skewered
carré	roast rack
côte	chops
épaule	shoulder
gigot	leg of lamb
noisette	choice loin
selle	saddle
porc	**pork**
andouillette	(pork) belly sausage
boudin noir	blood sausage
jambon	ham
épaule	less expensive ham, from the shoulder
jarret	pork knuckle
pied	foot
rôti	roast
travers	spare ribs
veau	**veal**
blanquette	stewing meat
escalope	cutlet
paupiette	rolled and stuffed
riz de veau	sweetbreads
triperie	**tripe**
cervelle	brain
coeur	heart
foie de génisse	young cow's liver

gésier	gizzard
langue	tongue
rognons	kidneys (*note:* not to be confused with *reins*—human kidneys)
gibier	**wild game**
lapin	rabbit
lièvre	wild hare
marcassin	baby boar
sanglier	adult boar
volailles	**poultry**
poulet	chicken
coq	rooster
coquelet	young rooster
poule	hen
cuisse	thigh
suprême	breast
dinde	turkey
dindonneau	young turkey
caille	quail
canard	duck
magret de canard	breast of duck
oie	goose
pintade	guinea hen
pigeon	pigeon

Charcuteries

These are France's delis. The sliced meats, fish, seafood in aspic, smoked salmon, avocados with crabmeat, pâtés, salads, fancy vegetables, and prepared dishes are always a savory delight. These stores tend to be expensive but highly pleasurable. They offer a whole gamut of dishes guaranteeing instant culinary success when entertaining or when you want to treat yourself to something tasty and beautiful. When buying cold cuts, order by the number of slices, indicating if you want them *fine* (thin). When buying pâtés and terrines, you indicate the quantity by where the clerk places the knife. To avoid buying more than you want, state, *"un peu moins que ça, s'il vous plaît."* Cold cuts are often precut and servers don't like cutting additional slices. Insist.

Epiceries

Literally "spice shops," *épiceries* are simply grocery stores that sell a little bit of everything. In most *quartiers* there are independent grocers as well as one or several chains. The ones owned and operated by North Africans usually stay open late—often until midnight in some of the outlying neighborhoods. This is convenient for finding munchies and beverages late at night.

Poissonneries

The variety of fish available in Paris is remarkable. The French eat a lot more fish per capita than North Americans or the British. After a number of visits to your local *poissonnerie*, you'll learn the names of the fish and decide which ones you like best and which are the best buys. Whole fish are cleaned and scaled by the fishmonger at your request for no extra charge; crab and shrimp often come precooked. Sprigs of fresh parsley are given away, too, if you ask for them, especially with the purchase of mussels, which are particularly French and make for an extremely reasonable meal. Purchase one liter per person. You can scrub the shells quickly and dump the shiny black mussels into a big pot of chopped shallots and garlic with a tad of cayenne pepper; dump in half a bottle of cheap white wine and steam the mussels until they open. Toss in some chopped parsley at the end and serve. Don't eat the ones that don't open. Drink white wine with the dish and mop up the briney wine and shallot broth with hunks of *baguette*. Two people can have a great time for about 4,50 euros. Lobster is prohibitively expensive, especially the langouste sort, which comes in from the Antilles. Small, frozen Canadian lobsters are available in good supermarkets at very reasonable prices. Smoked salmon *(saumon fumé)* is abundant and excellent. To avoid the very high prices, you can opt for the less-expensive sea trout, which resembles salmon in color, texture, and taste. Smoked salmon is very popular, eaten on *blinis* and with *crème fraiche*.

fruits de mer	seafood
coquilles St-Jacques	scallops
crabe	crab
tourteau	rock crab
crustacé	shellfish
crevette	shrimp
langoustine	sea crayfish
homard	lobster
huitres	oysters
langouste	spiny lobster
moules	mussels
praires	venus clams
oursin	sea urchin
bigorneaux	periwinkle
bulots	whelk
coques	cockle
poisson	fish
anchois	anchovy
bar	bass
barbue	brill
cabillaud	cod
morue	dried salt cod
congre	eel
calamar	squid
haddock	smoked haddock

éperlan	smelt
hareng	herring
lotte	monkfish
merlan	whiting
raie	skate
rouget	mullet
sole	sole
saumon	salmon
thon	tuna
truite	trout

A Word on Oysters

At bistros and brasseries you'll often see an impressive wet bar outside of the restaurant on the sidewalk, adorned with huge platters of crushed ice and seaweed, on which raw oysters, clams, *langoustines*, and other unidentifiable shellfish are being opened and placed by hearty men in rubber aprons. A lot of ritual and pageantry surrounds ordering and eating a platter like this. If you are a shellfish fanatic, you should definitely experience this during your Paris stay. Check the restaurant listings for *fruits de mer*.

You'll probably never understand all the sizes, grades, and types of oysters offered on the menu, but here are a few simple pointers. The *creuses* are the fatter ones in the deeper, rougher shells; the *plates* are the leaner ones in the flatter, smoother shells. Restaurants offer both the *creuses* and *plates* in several sizes. (The pens or beds in the oyster parcs in which the shellfish are raised are called *claires*.)

creuses: huîtres de parc (smallest), *fines de claires* (medium), *spéciales* (largest)

plates: Belon (small and elegant), *Marennes* (greenish color)

When in doubt go for six or twelve *fines de claires* for starters.

Crèmeries/Fromageries

Charles de Gaulle reportedly once said: "How can anyone govern a country with more than 400 different cheeses?" The pungent cheese shops *(fromageries)* offer a wonderful sampling that you should take advantage of. Try the *chèvre* (goat cheese), especially the fresh *(frais)* ones that are covered in *cendres* (ash). Fromageries also sell fresh butter, cut off of huge mountains in chunks; *fromage blanc* (white cheese that falls between sour cream and smooth cottage cheese); *crème fraîche* (a wonderfully rich, slightly sour cream that is used generously in sauces and on desserts); and fresh milk. Whole and skim milk also comes in vacuum-packed cartons that need not be refrigerated and can last for many months unopened (this milk is labeled *longue conservation* or *sterilisé*). Eggs, only brown ones, are also bought in the *crèmerie* in packages of six or by the unit. French "Swiss" cheese is *Emmentaler*. Swiss cheese from Switzerland is *Gruyère*.

fromage	cheese
vieux cantal or mimolette	cheddar
fromage frais	cream cheese
chèvre	goat cheese

râpé	grated cheese
Gruyère, Emmentaler,	Swiss cheese
St-Moret, Fribourg	
lait	milk
lait fermenté léger	buttermilk
lait frais	fresh milk
homogenisé	homogenized
demi-écrémé	low-fat milk
lait écrémé	skim milk
lait stérilisé, longue	sterilized milk
conservation	
lait entier	whole milk
yaourt	yogurt
maigre	no fat
nature	plain
nature sucré	plain but sugared
aux fruits	with fruit

A Note on Quality Chocolate

When a friend from California set out to make a simple chocolate sauce for a dessert after returning home from a period spent in France, she discovered that Hershey Bars don't melt—they bubble and crack like melted plastic. The cocoa content is less than 3 percent. The cheapest supermarket-brand chocolate in France has at least 20 percent cocoa, often from 40 to 50 percent. The chocolate bought in specialty shops can contain as much as 80 percent! The more cocoa, the higher quality the chocolate—unlike ice cream, where more fat content equals higher quality. So quality on the whole is higher and, with it, importantly, come a new set of expectations that will change you for life. Your taste buds just might reawaken. After a year or so in Europe, it's doubtful that you'll be able to chomp on North American chocolate (or guzzle the formerly favorite Milwaukee beer, or savor bagged and doughy sandwich bread).

Some particularly good chocolateries:

La Maison du Chocolat
225 rue du Faubourg St-Honoré, 75008 Paris; Tel.: 01–42–27–39–44
56 rue Pierre Charron, 75008 Paris; Tel.: 01–47–23–38–25
8 boulevard Madeleine, 75009 Paris, Tel.: 01–47–42–86–52

Lenôtre (www.lenotre.fr)
28 rue St-Dominique, 75007 Paris; Tel.: 01–47–53–94–12
48 avenue Victor Hugo, 75016 Paris; Tel.: 01–45–02–21–21

Marquise de Sévigné
32 Place de la Madeleine, 75008 Paris; Tel.: 01–42–65–19–47
62 rue Seine, 75006 Paris, Tel.: 01–40–46–02–01
For the crème de la crème of fine sweets and specialty items, a tour of the

famous and pricey Fauchon at Place de la Madeleine is a must, although the effect has been spoiled a bit by the introduction of banal American products that seem exotic in France. The marketing of North American groceries in France—from nacho chips and salsa to Paul Newman salad dressing—has been a trend over the last few years. Even OceanSpray fresh cranberries are now available in Paris in November. More and more shops specializing in the importation of American and Tex-Mex food items have entered the Parisian scene. And the outcrop of corresponding restaurants has continued to flourish since the late 1980s.

Food Markets

Paris offers three kinds of food markets: the permanent street markets, the moving open-air markets, and the indoor markets. In all of these markets, unless you are encouraged to do so, you should not touch the produce, which is carefully displayed for everyone's enjoyment. You should, however, feel free to specify exactly what you want and to banter freely with the often flamboyant merchants. It's not a bad idea to count your change. To check the addresses of all major markets and to situate them on street maps, please consult www.paris-anglo.com.

The street markets are open Tuesday through Saturday from 9:00 A.M. to 12:30 or 1:00 P.M. and normally close for the rest of the day. On Sundays they are open from 9:00 A.M. to 1:00 P.M.

The moving markets appear in various neighborhoods on fixed days. They often include clothing and other articles as well as food. These are open from 7:00 A.M. to 1:30 P.M.

Les Marchés Biologiques (Organic Markets)

Les Marchés Biologiques are the equivalent of old-fashioned country farmers' markets. From thirty to fifty independent organic farmers set up stalls on the weekends in Boulogne and Joinville (Parisian suburbs easily reachable by RER), where they sell organically grown fruits and vegetables; homemade breads; dried fruits and nuts; pork and pork products; farm-raised chicken, ducks, and geese; and natural wine. You'll also find stands selling freshly made pizzas, whole-wheat breads, apple or pear cider, goat cheeses, sausages, beer, and dried flowers. Go early for a good selection.

✢ **Marché Boulogne:** 140 route de la Reine, 92 Boulogne-sur-Seine. Métro: Boulogne-Pont de Saint-Cloud, or via the No. 72 bus. Open from 8:00 A.M. to 4:00 P.M. the first and third Saturdays of each month.

✢ **Marché Joinville-le-Pont:** Place Mozart, 94 Joinville. Métro: RER Line B to Joinville, then via the suburban No. 106 and 108N buses. Open from 8:30 A.M. to 1:00 P.M. the second and fourth Saturday of each month.

✢ **Marché Sceaux-Robinson,** rue des Mouille-Boeuf. Métro: RER Line B to Robinson. Open every Sunday from 8:30 A.M. to 1:00 P.M.

Restaurants

There is no reason for not eating well in Paris (although it has become easy to do so). Learning how to eat very well, with good value, maximum ambience, and exciting variety is an art that requires some basic understanding, critical skills, and a fair amount of experience. It has become increasingly easy to pay a lot for nothing particularly great. And in Paris it's not certain that you'll be impressed by the service offered in inexpensive or moderately priced eateries. The better news is that top Michelin star chefs are opening less-expensive bistros that make high quality food and service available to more people (for example, Jacques Cagna's Rôterisserie d'en face, 2 rue Christine, 75006 Paris; Tel.: 01–43–26–40–98; and Guy Savoy's La Butte Chaillot, 110 avenue Kléber, 75016 Paris; Tel.: 01–47–27–88–88). The trend in three-star restaurants these days is toward homestyle bistro classics (*pot-au-feu*, etc.). And remember that it's gauche to order a double Chivas before a great dinner—it numbs the taste buds. Order a coupe de champagne, currently the fashionable cocktail—probably explained by the fact that in 1993 twenty-one top champagne producers signed an agreement to lower prices to restaurateurs.

Restaurants are run by a *patron* (or *patronne*) who on the whole regards the position more as one of host than businessperson. As in all human interactions in France, a smile and a polite bonsoir monsieur/madame, lots of *s'il vous plaît* and *merci bien* during service, and an *au revoir monsieur/madame, merci* when leaving will serve you well in getting friendly service and recognition when you return. The idea of the quick meal is not really understood, so don't get impatient if service is slow. It's hard to rush service in Parisian restaurants. And waitresses and waiters don't work for tips—15 percent is always included. *Service compris* means that the 15 percent is built into the prices; *service non compris* means that it will be automatically added to the bill. Be careful not to tip on top of the tip, other than a few coins you leave in the dish as a token of your pleasure.

A word about the strictness of eating hours. As of about 11:30 A.M. or noon, most restaurants have their tables set for the rush of lunchers. In Paris, 1:00 P.M. is the heart of the lunch rush hour. Generally, you must be seated for lunch no later than 2:00 P.M. if you want to eat anything more than a sandwich or a *salade composée* (mixed salad), 2:30 P.M. at the extreme if you're lucky. In the provinces lunch is served between 12:30 and 1:00 P.M. At 2:00 you could beg and plead and offer your firstborn child and still be refused a hot meal. Between 3:00 and 6:00 P.M., it's pretty much impossible to have a sit-down meal. An early dinner would be at 7:00 P.M.; a normal time to dine would be between 8:00 and 9:00 P.M. But later than 9:30 (9:00 in the provinces) is getting dangerous again. At 11:00 it's too late, except in pizzerias, *couscousseries,* some brasseries and bistros, and some American-style restaurants in Paris. There are exceptions, of course, as noted in Patricia Wells's book.

As the New Yorkization of Paris deepens at the beginning of the twenty-first century, a global consensus of quality and service is forming. Paris has shown a new openness to theme restaurants, fewer formal rules for dining, and even a taste for off-hour eateries (a number of twenty-four-hour establishments have cropped up).

The typical French meal—from simple to elaborate—is graceful and balanced: an opening course, a main dish, cheese, a dessert, and coffee. And, of course, wine. Most diners ask for a pitcher of tap water (*un carafe d'eau, s'il vous plaît*) with their meal. This is highly expected. No real need to order a bottle of mineral water unless you prefer it; Paris city water is perfectly fine. Don't expect ice cubes though—very little ice is consumed in France. It's hard, if not impossible, to purchase cubes by the bag. The French are not in the habit of drinking their beverages at extreme temperatures; they say that when something is very cold or very hot, the flavor is less pronounced. And flavor is of primary importance, *n'est-ce pas* ? (The French are often disappointed by the fruits and vegetables found in American-style supermarkets. The huge colorful waxed objects are visually pleasing but the flavor is often bland.) So, don't expect ice with your water. Paris's culinary diversity and the keen attention Parisians give to food should contribute to the richness of your experience. There are about thirty guidebooks on Paris in which eating establishments are featured. (The famous Zagat series launched its Paris guide several years ago; it is useful, but the sampling is still a bit too sparse to give you a well-balanced report.) Here are a few operating principles when selecting a restaurant, followed by a few of *Paris Inside Out*'s favorites.

Selecting A Restaurant

+ In general don't plan on eating in a large café on a major boulevard. You'll pay a lot of money for quickly prepared, average food and for rapid, not particularly careful, service. Slapped-together salads at high prices are standard fare. If you're caught between hours and you're famished, use the café for a quick *croque-monsieur* (3 to 4 euros) or an *oeuf dur* (hard-boiled egg with salt) for less than 0,75 euros at the counter.

+ Distinguish yourself from the unknowing tourist. Running shoes, guide books, cameras, and loud voices are giveaways. Asking for adjustments to a fixed dish is taboo. As for ketchup, learn to settle for mustard. Many small restaurants do have it, but they're not obliged to provide it. And the French mustard is so flavorful you should try a dab or two if you're not in the habit. *Note:* The cheaper Dijon mustard (that comes in jars that can be used as glasses when the mustard has been finished) tends to be wickedly strong.

+ Read the menu posted outside before entering. It's uncool in Paris to be seated and then change your mind.

+ Be prepared in advance to be squeezed into tight tables and booths. Paris restaurants can be densely packed, but privacy is respected. Don't get too annoyed if in a half-empty restaurant your expressed preference for a larger table is refused. If you're a party of two, you will not be given a table for four. Nonsmoking sections, despite a law passed in 1993, are often nonexistent, although more and more Parisians are beginning to realize that some people don't like smoke.

+ *Steak tartare* is raw, but delicious. *Carpaccio* (thinly sliced, cured beef) is also raw. It's very uncool to order these unknowingly, be repulsed, and then try to send it back. Sending something back signifies that there is something very wrong with the dish.

+ If the food (or service) is absolutely horrible, don't eat it—and leave. Have an iron stomach and down it, or head for the door. If you eat half, you can't complain. A waiter or *maître d'* may end up arguing with you that your *magret de canard* is fine when you contend that it's inedible. There will be no recourse, no refund, no apologies, no free meal your next time back.

+ Avoid the Champs-Elysées area unless someone else is paying. And even then suggest somewhere else unless dining at a known establishment. The price to quality ratio is often poor.

Le Menu

The lunch or dinner created daily by the owner or chef of a restaurant is called *le menu*. Don't confuse menu and carte; the French carte is the English "menu." The French *menu* is a fixed menu usually consisting of an appetizer, a main dish, and a dessert; it is often the best bargain and the most promptly served. There may be one or more *menus* to choose from, each a bit more complex or complete and expensive. You can still find little restaurants with menus under 8 euros, but these are getting rare. Some couscous restaurants or Chinese or Vietnamese restaurants have menus around this price. These are generally in the less-chichi neighborhoods, but a number still linger in the Latin Quarter.

The hot dish of the day is called *le plat du jour* and may very well consist of roast veal and a heap of braised Brussels sprouts, or a thin steak and some French fries, or salted pork with lentils.

If you try to order something *à la carte* that breaks the rhythm or balance of the meal, you may find that the service becomes less *agréable*. This will be true if you try to order two appetizers (called *entrées*, because they are your entry into the meal)—or want to share a dessert—or request anything original, personal, or outside of the way that things are usually done. So beware.

When ordering red meat be aware that the French *cuisson* (cooking *degrees*)—*saignant* (rare), à point, (medium rare), and *bien cuit* (medium well)—tend to run rarer than you're used to. The French medium is the North American medium-rare on the rare side. So either compensate accordingly or let the chips fly (you may find that you've been eating overcooked meat for years).

French Regional Restaurants

This is just a sampling. The *Time Out Eating & Drinking Guide* on sale at most kiosks offers a thorough and up-to-date listing of restaurants, bistros, and pubs. *The Unofficial Guide to Paris* (by the same author!) offers around fifty selected restaurants with full descriptions,

Alsace
Chez Jenny
39 boulevard du Temple
75003 Paris
Tel.: 01–44–54–39–00
Open daily until 1:00 A.M. Sauerkraut, sausage, and beer.

Auvergne
Ambassade d'Auvergne
22 Grenier St-Lazare
75003 Paris
Tel.: 01–42–72–31–22
Open daily for lunch and dinner. Hearty specialties from central France.

Pays Basque
Auberge Etchegorry
41 rue Croulebarbe
75013 Paris
Tel.: 01–44–08–83–51
Closed Sunday. Dinner only. Basque paella and savory omelettes topped with Bayonne ham.

Normandie
Chez Fernand/Les Fernandises
17–19 rue de la Fontaine-au-Roi
75011 Paris
Tel.: 01–48–06–16–96
Closed Sunday and Monday. Lots of cream and butter; don't miss the home-cured Camemberts.

Provence
Campagne et Provence
25 quai Tournelle
75005 Paris
Tel.: 01–43–54–05–17
Closed Sunday and for lunch on Monday and Saturday. Reasonably priced southern bistro food from Chef Gilles Epié, who runs the fancier Miraville restaurant across the river.

Savoie
Au Savoyard
16 rue des Quatre-Vents
75006 Paris
Tel.: 01–43–26–20–30
Open noon to 2:00 P.M. and 7:00 to 11:00 P.M. Excellent cheese and beef fondue and raclette.

Good Value

Your best bet is to ask friends and colleagues for their favorite places and scout them out. And try new restaurants, too, as part of your process of becoming Parisian. Again, consult the *Time Out Eating & Drinking Guide* and read about new places cited in *Télérama*. You'll start accumulating your own list of places that are perfect for each occasion. Let us know what you like and what you don't, and tell us why. We'll share these insider tips with readers in our next edition. You can also go onto www.paris-anglo.com, read the restaurant reviews, and suggest your own. Here are a few suggestions to get you started.

Chartier
7 rue du Faubourg Montmartre
75009 Paris
Tel.: 01–47–70–86–29

This is a late-nineteenth-century gem that, despite its abundant tourist crowd, has preserved its authenticity. Extremely casual, inexpensive, and lively. You're often seated with strangers with whom you share baskets of bread and conversation. A large selection of typical, everyday French home-style dishes. The small wooden drawers in the walls were for the linen napkins of the regular customers. Waiters, often feisty and entertaining, tally up the bill from memory on the paper table-cloths. Get there before 9:00 P.M. Crowded, but worth it from time to time.

Le Café du Commerce
51 rue du Commerce
75015 Paris
Tel.: 01–45–75–03–27
Another restaurant in the Chartier style. Open every day. Always a good bet when you're in the fifteenth arrondissement.

Le Polidor
41 rue Monsieur Le Prince
75006 Paris
Tel.: 01–43–26–95–34
Very reasonable prices, traditional cuisine, and old-Paris ambience.

Le Petit Saint Benoît
4 rue St-Benoït
75006 Paris
Tel.: 01–42–60–27–92
Also very "old Paris." Traditional cuisine such as *hachis parmentier* (meat-and-potato hash) and cassoulet. Jean-Paul Sartre, Simone de Beauvoir, and, more recently, Marguerite Duras were frequent customers.

Chez Julien
16 rue du Faubourg St-Denis
75010 Paris
Tel.: 01–47–70–12–06
Pleasant, fashionable in-spot in a less-chic part of town. Plan on spending a bit more. Ornate decor. Don't miss the *profiteroles* for dessert.

Roger la Grenouille
26 rue des Grands Augustins
75006 Paris
Tel.: 01–43–26–10–55
Great spot for fun-loving bawdiness with style, excellent French provincial cooking served up with popular casualness. *Coq au vin* and *canard à l'orange* stand out. So do the not-so-timid waitresses. Good house wine. Order the designed-to-be-embarrassing dessert special for those highly puritanical friends.

Le Gamin de Paris
51 rue du Vielle du Temple

75004 Paris
Tel.: 01–42–78–97–24
This Marais restaurant has fine food, soulful atmosphere, and a sinful chocolate mud pie. Ask for Sammie, the manager; he knows how to lay on that special extra touch. Closed Fridays.

Le Procope
13 rue de l'Ancienne Comédie
75006 Paris
Tel.: 01–40–46–79–00
Believed to be the oldest restaurant in Paris. A popular meeting place for both politicians and intellectuals during the French Revolution. Le Procope was redone at the time of the Bicentennial (1989).

Chez Papa
3 rue St-Benoît
75006 Paris
Tel.: 01–42–86–99–63
Traditional French cuisine served in a cozy, chatty atmosphere.

A Note on Weight

You may wonder how it is that in a country with such a passion for food, everyone seems underfed. With so much sugar being consumed, how can the population be so uniformly *mince* (thin)? It is true that much of what one associates with classical French food is the rich sauce, the buttery and sweet bakery delights. But these do not constitute the average diet—they are special treats. As in every aspect of French life, moderation is important.

A second reason for the relatively petit waistlines is that Parisians are obliged to be rather active in their daily routines. There is less reliance on cars, there are more steps to climb, more stops on the shopping circuit, and fewer hours glued to televisions. The emphasis on form also contributes; mealtimes are adhered to rather strictly, unlike many Americans' haphazard snack times, missed meals, and dinners in front of the TV or at the desk. Also in France personal style and the public self are taken seriously. The French don't like going out if they don't look great. Physical appearance is important. Lastly, over the past few years a whole new generation of lower calorie prepared dishes with "lite" *(allégé)* on the packaging has appeared in Parisian supermarkets.

American Food

No one comes to Paris in order to eat burgers, pizza, and Tex-Mex, but Paris is getting more and more of this—some good, some highly derivative and worthless. Still, for those nostalgic moments when you're *croque-monsieured* to death, and tripe doesn't fit the bill, you'll be reassured to know that there are fifty-plus American-style restaurants in Paris. The number keeps growing as North American entre-preneurs and their local clones keep opening up new ones. Pizza Hut is here in a big way, having invested heavily in promoting the name and conditioning the pub-lic. Parisians, you see, eat record amounts of pizza. Häagen-Dazs has revolution-ized the ice-cream scene, becoming ubiquitous by investing huge amounts in reeducating the public that ice cream can be eaten year-round, and that American ice cream is superior to the commercial French brands. The local Bertillon ice cream found on the Ile Saint Louis, though, is by far the best-tasting ice cream in the city, but the portions are microscopic (and there are no calorie-packed top-pings). Throughout the city you can find everything from ribs to root beer, chile to cookies, although a few cultural culinary icons, such as bagels and the bottomless cup of coffee, are still rare. A few old standbys include Joe Allen, Cactus Charly, Café Pacifico, Indiana, Canyon's Café, O'Cantina, Chesterfield Café, Café Oz, Lizard Lounge, Spicy, the Bagel Place, Chicago Pizza Pie Factory, Harry's New York Bar, Marshall's, Rio Grande, Sam Kearny's, Hollywood Canteen, and The Studio. Although the cuisine at these places is fairly authentic, they tend to fill up with a certain type of trend-seeking French clientele that emulates the look of "the American way of life." They also tend to be on the expensive side and haven't quite captured the spirit of the huge American portion, although over the last five years things have improved. Your best bet for locating these places is to comb through the *Paris Voice, FUSAC,* and *The Irish Eyes,* all of which are free, easy to find, and filled with the latest ads for restaurants, pubs, and cafés eager for your company.

For commercial peanut butter, crumpets, cornmeal, or brownie mix, try the General Store at 82 rue de Grenelle, 75007 Paris or the Real McCoy at 194 rue de Grenelle, 75007 Paris. Also, the American specialty shop Thanksgiving sells great pecan pie.

International Cuisine

Paris is an international crossroads for cuisines from all corners of the world, from Kurdish to Korean. You can almost trace the colonial history of France in the restaurants of its capital, from North Africa to Vietnam to the Caribbean to west Africa to the Middle East. For the purchase of exotic and esoteric foods and goods from the Third World and politically correct collectives, try Bertrand Tellier's Arti-sans du Monde, 20 rue du Rochechouart, 75009 Paris; Tel.: 01–48–78–55–54.

Lebanese

Currently, one of the best international cuisines in Paris comes from Lebanon. With the political upheaval and economic instability there, there has been a veri-table exodus of Lebanese wealth from Beirut and subsequent investment in Paris. Lebanese businesspeople have preferred to invest substantially in Paris knowing at least that their capital is protected against runaway inflation and the risk of violence and terror. Lebanese restaurants in Paris tend to be at once elegant and casual, and the quality, quantity, and prices are favorable.

Chinese

Paris has hundreds of Chinese restaurants, a number of which can be a good deal for days when your wallet is thin. Many, especially those in the Latin Quarter, can be extremely reasonable if you order the menu. On the whole the best and most authentic Chinese food in Paris is concentrated in two of Paris's Chinatowns: the thirteenth arrondissement between the Place d'Italie and Porte de Choisy; and Belleville in the northeast part of the city. Many Chinese restaurants are actually run by Vietnamese. The result is a mixed bag of Vietnamese, Chinese, and Thai influences, overpowered by the tastes and demands of the French palate. Go to the thirteenth or Belleville for the real thing. There are too many to list. (See the section on Chinatowns in Paris.)

Japanese

The Japanese have recently been investing heavily in France, from eighteenth-century chateaux to Paris real estate, especially in the area around Opéra (rue Ste-Anne), which has become a kind of Japanese quarter with many Japanese restaurants and luxury boutiques. There are lots of new Japanese restaurants around the Opéra as well as in the St-Germain area.

Greek

The Latin Quarter is noted for its Greek restaurants, complete with extravagant window displays of brochettes of seafood, stuffed eggplant, and suckling pig. Also complete with aggressively affable male hosts beckoning the tourists. Many of these restaurants are actually connected to the same kitchen. A trade secret! These places serve reasonably priced, sometimes good food. Fun to do once in a while.

Russian

Russian cuisine, which is often vodka-assisted, makes for a very satisfying change from the humdrum of daily food. Paris hosts a number of excellent, although a bit pricey, Russian eateries in the great tradition of Russian intellectual presence in Paris. Tolstoi lived on the rue de Rivoli for a while. Parisians have come to love *blinis* with smoked salmon and *crème fraîche*.

Karlov
197 rue de Grenelle
75007 Paris
Tel.: 01–45–51–29–21
Dinner only. *Blinis*, borscht, shish kabob, romantic decor, and live gypsy music.

Central European / Ashkenazi Jewish

Jo Goldenberg
7 rue des Rosiers
75004 Paris
Tel.: 01–48–87–20–16

Open until midnight. Noisy and boisterous; great chopped liver and pastrami. Famous, but overrated.

Chez Marianne
2 rue Hospitalières-St-Gervais
75004 Paris
Tel.: 01–42–72–18–86
Excellent falafel and assortment of meats, smoked fish, salads, and pickles (Marianne's Tunisian mother-in-law's recipe). Marianne and her eclectic literary-business*mensch* husband, André, are the stars of the Jewish quarter. The restaurant has become almost too busy to be fully appreciated, so go early or late, or reserve.

Italian

La Castafiore
51 rue Saint-Louis-en-l'Ile
75004 Paris
Tel.: 01–43–54–78–62
Open daily. Great pasta and veal in candlelit restaurant created by a British/U.S. team of ex-ad agency execs.

Mexican

Ay Caramba
59 rue Mouzaïa
75019 Paris
Tel.: 01–42–41–23–80
Delightfully out of the way in the nineteenth, this cantina-style restaurant is sprawling and lively with regulars and real Mexican music.

Scandinavian

Flor Danica
142 avenue des Champs-Elysées
75008 Paris
Tel.: 01–44–13–86–26
Open daily for lunch and dinner.

Vegetarian

The choice for vegetarians in Paris is limited, but new restaurants seem to appear every week as health consciousness becomes more a la mode.
Banani (Indian Restaurant)
148 rue de la Croix Nivert
75015 Paris
Tel.: 01–48–28–73–92
Closed Sunday. Service until 11:00 P.M. Indian food, wide variety of curries.

Rayons de Santé
8 Place Charles Dublin
75018 Paris
Tel.: 01–42–59–64–81
Closed Friday evening and Saturday.

Resto U

Students can also take advantage of the French university-run student restaurants called Resto U, managed by the CROUS *(Centre Régional Oeuvres Universitaires Scolaires de Paris);* Tel.: 01–40–51–37–13. These are crowded and noisy, but the food is plentiful and really cheap. You'll need to purchase tickets, available in the lobby of each of these establishments.

Fast Food

Fast food, which is anything but truly fast, has unfortunately overrun the Paris cityscape in the last five years, especially McDonald's, which bought out Burger King, with impressive franchises along the high-rent Champs-Elysées. French businesspeople, office workers, students, and kids flock to these meccas of American hamburger prestige. At lunchtime it's often nearly impossible to get into one of these places, especially on Wednesdays, when school is out and youngsters line up for their Happy Meals. The golden-arches decor often suffers a transatlantic sea change. Two great examples of marketing kitsch: McDonald's-Sorbonne (with fake bookshelves filled with fake editions of classic literature) and McDonald's-Versailles (glossy beige marble walls). McDonald's has flourished wildly in Paris and even has cornered a share of real prestige, after a rocky period in the 1970s when the emperor of fast food pulled out of France due to the shoddy standards of local franchises.

Les sandwiches are commonplace in Paris as more and more Parisians give up the Latin tradition for long meals in favor of the pursuit of more healthful and individual pleasures or simply to save time. Sandwiches usually consist of a third of a baguette with either butter and ham, pâté, cheese, or *rillettes,* a flavorful but fatty paste made from duck, pork, or goose—delicious with those crispy and vinegary cornichons (pickles). In a café a sandwich will cost you from 2,50 to 3,50 euros. Again, be careful about asking for variations. A student who asked for lettuce on a ham sandwich was charged double. *"Mais Monsieur, vous avez commandé un sandwich fantaisie,"* he was told. When you see signs for *Poilâne* bread, take advantage of the occasion. This coarse sourdough bread is both a tradition and delicacy in French culinary life.

When the weather is fine, or at least not too gray and sad *(triste)* as Paris can often be, you can always buy some bread, cheese, and *charcuterie* (deli goods) and sit in one of the parks—but not on the grass, which is part of the landscaping and off-limits. Or you may want to sit down by the Seine. In the fifth *arrondissement* it's pleasant to duck into the Arènes de Lutèce, an uncovered Roman amphitheater that is hidden behind a row of apartment houses on the rue Monge just below the Place Monge. In the seventh *arrondissement* the Champ de Mars, the open space below the Eiffel Tower, is lovely. Other options include the Luxembourg Gardens, the Bois de Vincennes, the Bois de Boulogne, the elegant Parc Monceau, or wherever there is a likely looking bench.

You will see customers in restaurants, cafés, and even McDonald's paying with coupons called *chèques déjeuner,* usually worth about 5 to 8 euros. Employers offer these to their personnel at half price as an additional benefit. Establishments that accept them have stickers on their windows.

A Word on Pizza à la française

Parisians eat pizza often for lunch and dinner in Italian-style restaurants. Pizzas in France have been designed for one, meaning you never share a pizza in pizza restaurants. And Parisians don't eat pizza, or much else for that matter, with their hands. Pizzas come with an oily bottle of olive oil with hot peppers swimming at the bottom. You sprinkle this oil on your pizza, usually making the pizza more oily than hot. Your choice of toppings in Paris pizzerias is almost always the same; the combinations have been pre-selected for you and named. The basic pizza, a *Marguerite,* consists of cheese and tomato, and maybe a few black olives. Other standby varieties include *Quatres Saisons,* which has four toppings—ham, mushrooms, cheese, anchovy; and *Reine,* which has ham and mushroom. Other possibilities include capers, four cheeses, sausage, and even an egg. Asking for substitutions will confuse most waiters, but try if you like, and always ask for extra cheese. Pizza, until the arrival of Pizza Hut, has not had the social, junk-eating quality to it that surrounds American campus life. After a pizza in a restaurant, you're pretty much expected to have a dessert and coffee. No one just eats a pizza and splits.

Typical Dishes and Special Foods

The following is a sampling of specialties commonly found in France.

Bouillabaisse: a Mediterranean-style fish stew with tomatoes, saffron, mussels, shellfish, and the catch of the day. Each version is different from the last one, depending on the whim of the creator. Good ones are becoming hard to find. Two other regional variations of seafood soup are *bourride* and *chaudrée.*

Cassoulet: A casserole of white navy beans, shallots, and a variety of meats such as pork, lamb, sausage, and goose or duck, originating in the Languedoc region of France. Perfect for the winter.

Couscous: Specialty of North Africa originally brought to France by colonialists. A hearty blend of mutton, chicken, and a spicy beef sausage *(merguez)* in a light stock with boiled zucchini, carrots, onions, turnips, and chickpeas. It is spooned over a fine semolina-like base, called couscous, from which the dish gets its name. A hot, red paste called harissa can be stirred into the broth.

Fondue: A Swiss Alps specialty popular in France, especially in the ski regions. There are two types: bourguignon beef—small chunks of beef cooked on long forks

in pots of hot oil and accompanied by a variety of sauces; and Savoyard cheese—
cheese melted and flavored with kirsch or white wine, lapped up with chunks of
stale French bread on long forks.

Raclette: A dish consisting of melted cheese scraped onto potatoes, pickles, and
ham. The cheese is melted at the table and served on tiny plates.

Farce: Spiced ground meat, usually pork, used for stuffing cabbage (chou farci),
green pepper *(poivron vert farci)*, or tomatoes *(tomates farcies)*.

Hachis parmentier: Mashed potatoes and ground meat topped with a béchamel
sauce and served in a casserole.

Moussaka: A Greek casserole dish combining slices of eggplant, tomatoes, and
ground lamb, baked with a béchamel topping.

Paella: A Portuguese and Spanish dish with a rice base, saffron, pimiento,
chicken, pork, and shellfish, cooked in a special two-handled metal pan.

Choucroute: Of Alsatian origin, this dish is often served in brasseries because it
is a good accompaniment to a strong draft beer. It consists of sauerkraut topped
with a variety of sausages, cuts of pork, ham, and boiled potatoes.

Pot-au-feu: Boiled meat and marrow bone with vegetables in a broth.

Cooking Schools

Le Cordon Bleu, one of the great clichés of Paris, continues to be a leader in the culinary arts, offering four *diplômes,* the most ambitious being *le grand diplôme Cordon
Bleu.* With La Varenne no longer in business in Paris, *le Cordon Bleu* is at center
stage; 8 rue Léon Delhomme, 75015 Paris; Tel.: 01–53–68–22–50.

The other main cooking school available to anglophones is the celebrated *Ritz
Escoffier Ecole de Gastronomie Française,* 38 rue Cambon, 75001 Paris; Tel.:
01–43–16–30–50.

Wine

*No insider's guide to French life would be complete without some special commentary
on wine and its place in daily life. The following section was prepared by Petie and Don
Kladstrup, longtime residents of France (Normandy) and wine lovers and collectors.*

Nearly the first act of King Louis XI, upon subduing the obstreperous Duchy of
Burgundy and dragging it back into France, was to confiscate the entire 1477
vintage of Volnay wine. It must have been a good year.

Since then wine in France has become even more important, and no one can
hope to understand or participate in the life and culture of France without knowing something about it. Happily, it is not necessary to be an expert to be an amateur (lover) of wine because everybody in France seems to drink wine, from the
toddler at Grandma's for Sunday lunch to the Grandmas and Grandpas themselves. Almost all dinners include a glass or two, and even many lunches are
accompanied by wine. However, as the pace of French life quickens to keep in
step with the rest of the world, fewer and fewer working people have either the
time or the desire for a two-hour lunch with all the trimmings. Those who do

include a glass of wine frequently "baptize the wine" *(baptiser le vin)* by adding some water to it. Heresy, of course, for serious wine lovers and a mortal sin if the wine is anything but a *vin de table* (table wine).

It is probably the prevalence of wine that made the idea of a weekend bash of drinking parties almost nonexistent in France. The difference between young people's attitudes toward drinking in the United States and in France was summed up by one U.S. college student who had been raised in France. "In France," he said, "my friends and I used to go out on Saturday night to have a good time and occasionally somebody got drunk. Here in the United States, everybody seems to go out to get drunk, and occasionally somebody has a good time."

The legal drinking age is sixteen, but enforcement is so rare as to be nonexistent, so it is almost never an issue. Small children run down to the neighborhood grocery store for the dinner wine, and bars have no ID checks. Of course, the driving age in France is eighteen, and since public transport of some sort is available around the clock in the Paris area, many of the concerns about drinking and driving are eliminated.

So, like nearly everything else in France, wine has become an art form and an economic force. France produces nearly half of the wine made in Europe, and because of the high quality—and higher prices—French wine accounts for approximately three-quarters of the money generated by European wine sales.

The French drink French wine almost exclusively, but the wine makers do worry about the impact of lowered trade barriers in the European Union. Those with the most cause for worry are the makers of the medium-range of quality, because in that area, Italy, Spain, and Portugal can compete with lower prices. The makers of the famous wines from Bordeaux, Burgundy, and Champagne need only worry about having bank accounts that accept all currencies!

Figuring out French wines can seem intimidating, but in reality it is easier than trying to decipher the wines of most other countries. That is because the French wines are regionals, that is, named for the region in which they are produced. Almost every other country uses varietal names, so that you have to master the names of grape varieties before you can order. Horrible when you discover that the pinot noir (black pinot grape) can make a white wine, and that there is a *cabernet sauvignon, a sauvignon blanc,* and a *cabernet franc* grape, all of which make different kinds of wine. Isn't it nice to know that champagne is just champagne no matter what grape they make it with? And while burgundy wines can be either red or white, they stay burgundy. The same is true for all the wine regions of France—Bordeaux, Alsace, the Loire, Provence, the Rhone Valley. If you know those names, you are already on your way and can make the big connection of brain to palate with tasting and trying the different regions' selections.

Although wine does not have to be expensive to be good, it is unfortunately true that most good wines are priced more highly than poor ones. Unfortunately true, as well, is the fact that France makes a lot of bad wine, and if a bottle costs under 3 euros, you are almost assured that it won't be very good. That doesn't mean that it may not be enjoyable in certain circumstances, like an impromptu picnic or for washing down a pizza—just don't serve it at a dinner party or bring it as a gift to one.

Wine seems to absorb and enhance its setting, so get some advice from your local wine merchant or a knowledgeable friend before presenting a host or hostess with an accidental bottle of plonk. In fact don't take wine at all if you don't know your host or hostess very well. Instead, send flowers with a nice note of thanks the morning after the party. If you are the host, don't be afraid to consult wine merchants before buying your dinner party wine (wine is the only acceptable dinner party drink aside from water in France).

Decide what food you are serving before you select the wine and be prepared to tell your wine merchant the details. Don't be surprised to be asked how you are preparing the chicken you said you were going to serve. And don't be timid about your budget. If you can spend only 3 or 4 euros, say so, and if you have a merchant who grumbles or complains, take your business elsewhere.

The Nicolas wine stores found all over France have a good, solid selection of wines at all price ranges. In the past the Nicolas chain was almost as famous for its artistic ads as for its wine, which was considered the best buy in France. That was especially true at Christmastime, when it had a huge "Saint" Nicolas promotion, bringing out of its massive *caves* (cellars) special old wines and offering them for sale in limited quantities for reasonable prices. Alas, those days have gone the way of the wooden métro cars, and the mighty chain has been sold and resold, with those famous caves going to one buyer and the stores to another. Still, the individual stores have good wines, decent prices, and extremely knowledgeable owners/salespeople. And some of the ads are still rather nice. To get a feel for the old ones, stop in at the Nicolas store on the Place de la Madeleine, which is decorated with copies of the classic ads. (Lest you think I exaggerate, those ads were so good there was a museum exhibit of them a few years ago.)

A wonderful place to buy wine is the Cave du Château, 17 rue Raymond du Temple, Vincennes (Tel.: 01–43–28–17–50). The owners are an enthusiastic couple who can go into great detail about any wine in their store, and they have lots of good, inexpensive ones. There is nothing fancy about the shop, and they deliver if you are ordering more than a couple of bottles (most wine stores do the same).

At the other end of the scale is Vins Rares, a gorgeous boutique of gorgeous wines. It is run by a charming, English-speaking Swede named Peter Thustrup. His stock of wines includes vintages from the last century as well as more recent classics; it is the place to go if you want a wine from a specific year or vineyard for a special event. The wines are reasonably priced for what they are, but no 1929 wine comes cheap! Vins Rares can be reached by calling 01–45–01–46–01 (11 rue Pergolèse, 75116 Paris).

A word about vintages. Vintage just means the year it was harvested. Some years are better than others, but any wine with a year attached to its label (and most French wines have that) is a vintage wine. It has nothing to do with quality. Most wine stores hand out vintage charts that rate the years and tell which vintages are ready to drink. The exception to the vintage rule is champagne, which is dated only in the years the makers consider to be extremely good. Otherwise champagne can be made from a blend of grapes from more than one year. Vintage champagne is, of course, more expensive and should be better than others, but because of the blending, the big champagne houses (Moët—pronounce the "t," Bollinger, Mumms, Roederer, Taittinger, Mercier, Lanson) never make bad champagne. Of course, you may not like all of it. Each house has its own style, so it's just a matter of finding the style you like. And the finding is fun.

Champagne, like all the wine regions, has strict controls on the wine bearing its *appellation* (area name). The wine is made only from grapes grown in that region. Wines are labeled *Appellation d'Origine Contrôlée* (AOC) or *Appellation Contrôlée* (AC). If a French wine does not have one phrase or the other, it probably does not have much to recommend it. It may be a blend of any old grapes, including very cheap ones imported from North Africa.

Then there is the system of *crus classés* (classed levels of quality). These are a fairly good guideline to quality, but they haven't been redone in years, so many are out of date. But theoretically, at least, at the bottom of the heap are the *vin du pays* (country wines) and the *vin de table* (table wines). At the top are the premier grand *cru classé* (great first growths). There are lots of nice exceptions at the bottom levels as vineyards change hands and ideas, and there are some at the top that need to have their pedigrees examined, a cry you will hear from wine lovers, and even some growers, on a regular basis. Most resistant to change are the big vineyards of Bordeaux. These wines in their square-shouldered bottles are some of the big economic powers in France, with large amounts of hectares per vineyard, and major distribution organizations behind them. While many of those unclassed or labeled "fifth growths" when the classifications were done in the nineteenth-century would like to have the whole system reopened, those at the top are happy. Most of the premier *crus* have stayed that way, or become even better, but some have slipped disastrously and only nostalgia and hope keep them in the running.

Wine is subject to fads, which can work in the favor of the discerning and financially cautious drinker. Currently out of fashion are the wines of the Loire Valley, which is very good news for people who like good wines that are inexpensive, because many of the Loire wines are of outstanding quality. For whites from bone-dry to very rich and sweet, look to the wines from Vouvray. Two very good makers are Gaston Huet and Prince Poniatowski. They both also make good sparkling wines at very low prices, generally about 7,50 euros a bottle. If you can't afford a good champagne, these are marvelous substitutes, a little more full-bodied and richer, but still sufficiently light and bubbly to make any event special. Huet and Poniatowski also make sweet wines that can last until your grandchildren are senior citizens. These cost more, but can be a wonderful souvenir of France, especially when accompanied by some *foie gras*. For a lovely cheap red, try the Touraine, made by the Chateau du Petit-Thouars. This seems to get better with each vintage.

Myths surround wine. Some provide good guidelines, while others can be shunted aside—for instance, red wine with red meat, white wine with white meat. That is a good starting point, but lots of chicken dishes are better with red wine, and even some fish is better that way. Just keep trying combinations to see which you like better. Another myth: Wine doesn't travel. That is definitely true for poorly made wines, but good wine doesn't mind a trip. It just likes to have some time afterward to recover. Of course, no wine likes to sit on a dock in the sun for several hours, so if you want to ship wine, make sure you are dealing with good people who know what they are doing. Don't hesitate to take a bottle or so with you, though, as long as you carry it. But remember that the wine that tasted wonderful on a hot summer day on the Côte d'Azur may give little pleasure on a cold, blustery day in a *chambre de bonne* in Paris. Don't blame the wine for that!

When serving wine, get clear glasses, the bigger the better. Don't fill them up; leave plenty of room for the aromas to swirl around. With champagne, avoid the flat-shaped coupe (modeled after either the breast of Helen of Troy or of Madame de Pompadour, depending upon the myth you're listening to), and look for the long graceful flute that shows off the bubbles and avoids creating the big head of foam that attacks your nose in the flat glass. You can keep the foam down even more by pouring against the side of the glass instead of directly into the bottom of it. Don't worry too much; sparkling wine makes everything sparkle.

If you want to pursue wine further, look into the courses taught in English at the Cordon Bleu school by James Lawther.

Most of all, taste and enjoy. That is the only true way to learn about wine.

Wine Tasting

The Centre d'Information de Documentation et de Dégustation, Découverte du Vin, (30 rue de la Sablière, 75014 Paris; Tel.: 01–45–45–32–20) offers wine tastings and information about other tastings.

A Selection of Cafés, Bars, Bistros, and Brasseries

The following establishments have been listed here for their original style and glorious tradition. Be prepared to pay a premium, though, for the reputation. These places should become part of your working knowledge of Paris, but they probably won't become daily hangouts. If they do, you'll find yourself watching tourists watch other tourists. But it is undeniably pleasant just to sit on the terrace and enjoy the moment. Bring out-of-town visitors for a look at the grand style they associate with Paris. For a more complete list of cafés with illustrious literary lore, see Noel Riley Fitch's little book *Literary Cafés of Paris*.

La Coupole, 102 boulevard Montparnasse, 75014 Paris; Tel.: 01–43–20–14–20.

Le Sélect Montparnasse, 99 boulevard Montparnasse, 75006 Paris; Tel.: 01–45–48–38–24.

La Closerie des Lilas, 168 boulevard Montparnasse, 75006 Paris; Tel.: 01–40–51–05–81.

Café Les Deux Magots, 6 Place St-Germain-des-Prés, 75006 Paris; Tel.: 01–45–48–55–25.

Café de Flore, 172 boulevard St-Germain, 75006 Paris; Tel.: 01–45–48–55–26.

Le Balzar, 49 rue des Ecoles, 75005 Paris; Tel.: 01–43–54–13–67.

Irish Pubs in Paris

The presence of the Irish in Paris, although not new (Samuel Beckett, James Joyce), has increased over the last several years, primarily due to the ease of movement between the two EU countries. As a result an outcrop of Irish pubs has joined the cityscape. A complete list can be found on www.paris-anglo.com. Otherwise, pick up a copy of *The Eyes*, Irish-Paris's free weekly.

Wine Bars, Landmarks, Late-Night Places, and a Few Favorite Places to Drink

Undoubtedly, you will establish your own favorite places to drink, hang out, meet people, and commune with the city. Here is a short, diverse list of favorites that can make daily life in Paris truly delightful. Finding your own favorites among them will be a matter of personal taste.

La Tartine, 24 rue de Rivoli, 75004 Paris
One of the oldest, most reasonably priced, and best wine bars in Paris. Also serves great *pain Poilâne* sandwiches. Art-deco interior, which seventy years of cigarette smoke has mellowed.

Café de l'Industrie, 16 rue Saint Sabin, 75011 Paris
Good; "in," in an "in" *quartier.* Eccentric decor, good food.

Le Cochon à l'Oreille, 15 rue Montmartre, 75001 Paris
The walls of this café are covered with painted tiles showing the old Les Halles market. Early in the morning you can share breakfast (or a last drink if you've been out all night) with the butchers from rue Montmartre.

Le Clown Bar, 114 rue Amelot, 75011 Paris
Next to the Cirque d'Hiver, this tiny café has its original painted ceiling depicting clowns and circus entertainers.

Brasserie de l'Ile St-Louis, 55 quai Bourbon, 75004 Paris
Stand at the bar and try one of the white Alsatian wines while listening to the street musicians on the Pont St-Louis. There is a beautiful old coffee machine at the bar.

Le Petit Gavroche, rue Sainte-Croix-de-la-Bretonnerie, 75004 Paris
On the corner of the bar of this café/restaurant is one of the few remaining examples of the water holders used in the ritual of absinthe drinking (its sale was prohibited in 1915). Water was dripped onto a sugar cube and into the absinthe.

Le Train Bleu, Gare de Lyon, 20 boulevard Diderot, 75012 Paris
Sweep up the curved staircase from the inside of the station and through the revolving door into one of the most astonishing *fin de siècle* interiors in Paris. To the left is the bar with its soft leather sofas and atmosphere of luxury and calm. While most of the travelers below sit in orange plastic chairs drinking overpriced demis, you can be sipping a Pimms, wearing a linen suit and sporting a panama hat, dreaming of taking the Blue Train to the Mediterranean. The restaurant, a national historic site, has maintained its elegance amid sprawling frescoes, but the prices are high and the cuisine has slipped.

Au Général Lafayette, 52 rue de La Fayette, 75009 Paris.
Popular French beer bar trying to look like an English pub. Great selection

of beers and even greater selection of beer mats, mugs, memorabilia, and old Guinness posters.

The Frog & Rosbif, 116 rue St-Denis, 75002 Paris

Happy Hour Monday through Friday 5:00–8:00 P.M., Saturday 6:00–9:00 P.M.; all pints 3,80 euros. This is Paris's only English pub. Celebrated for its own micro brewery with such beers on tap as Inseine (best bitter), Frog Natural Blond (lager), Dark de Triomphe (stout), Parislithic (ruby ale), and Trente huit (wheat beer). This large corner bar near the red-light district is lively and fun. Also has a new location in the Village Bercy and another on the rue de Princesse, but the bawdy rue Saint-Denis wins out in atmosphere.

Le Fumoir, 6 rue l'Amiral Coligny, 75001 Paris

Hours: daily 11:00 A.M.–2:00 P.M. If you're hunting for the hot spots . . . this hybrid just opposite the Louvre delivers excellent cocktails in a deluxe atmosphere. Elegant wood bar captures the style of this networking nest for an in crowd of creative and ambitious regulars.

Harlem Hôtel (Café Oz), 8 rue St-Denis, 75001 Paris.

Since DJ Ivan Smagghe from Radio Nova and Dr. Eguobhum got hold of the turntables at the Australian Café Oz and created the Harlem Hotel nights on Thursdays, the bar is now a club to be. "The early music & drinking experience."

La Palette, 43 rue de Seine, 75006 Paris.

Hours: Monday through Saturday 8:00–2:00 A.M. Closed in August and one week in winter. This is a favorite meeting spot for painters, sculptors, photographers, gallery people, art lovers, and neighbors. Always lively and rarely pretentious, La Palette represents the best of the area. The paintings on the wall in the back depict the ageless waiters. The wines are excellent and reasonably priced. This is one of the best spots to be at midnight in November when the Beaujolais Nouveau is legally released.

China Club, 50 rue de Charenton, 75012 Paris.

Hours: Sunday through Thursday, 7:00 P.M.–2:00 A.M., Friday and Saturday 10:30 P.M.–3:00 A.M. (concerts); Happy Hour 7:00–9:00 P.M. Classy French colonial–style Chinese restaurant with a high-class cocktail bar upstairs and, on most evenings, a DJ in the cellar. If you go upstairs to the *fumoir chinois,* you'll be seduced by the laquered walls and the discreet and dark seating. You could be in Hong Kong or New York.

Harry's New York Bar, 5 rue Daunou, 75002 Paris

Open 10:30–4:00 A.M. You probably aren't interested in hanging out at an American bar in Paris, but this one is such a fixture on the Paris bar scene that you might want to make an exception and ultimately call it your own. Established in 1911, Harry's Bar, then called New York Bar, the oldest cocktail bar in Europe, still retains much the same feel and decor—college banners on the wall, lots of dark varnished wood, and photographs of regular Ernest Hemingway fishing and hunting. Allegedly the birthplace of the Bloody Mary, and regulars swear by them, but the experienced bar staff do an impressive job with all the cocktails (mixing exactly the right measure effortlessly). A bit pricey, but good value nevertheless. Food. Piano bar downstairs (where George Gershwin played "An American in Paris" while F. Scott Fitzgerald drank till he'd collapse). Harry's enjoys a regular clientele of expats, foreign journalists, and the American-loving French who have great stories and share a common feeling of belonging here. The bar is famous for the phonetic spelling of its address: *Sank Roo Doe Noo*, which was created to help English-speaking customers direct taxi drivers to the bar. Duncan McElhone, the grandson of the founder, Harry, recently died after managing the bar in the great tradition for many years. The place is legend.

Consumerism in Paris

Although you didn't come to Paris to shop—as many short-term visitors do —living in the French capital obliges you to become an instant and constant consumer. Knowing how and where to make your purchases in a foreign city, especially this one, takes a lot of time and experience. As we've said repeatedly, France is not a service society, and although some progress has been made in the area of customer relations, you'll be continually surprised at how often you'll feel mistreated, ignored, or abused as a customer.

Remember that in France it is nearly impossible to get customer satisfaction over the telephone. You either have to write or make a trip to make your case in person. If you are properly prepared for this large cultural difference, the displeasure can be somewhat tamed.

Beyond that, it must be said that Paris is a haven for shoppers of all sorts. The steady flow of quality produce, wine, cheese, handcrafted goods, and luxury goods (silk scarves and ties, jewelry, leather work, designer clothes) makes it a delight to stroll through Paris's numerous boutique districts.

Open-Air Markets

Almost as gratifying and interesting as museums, Paris's open-air markets require some of your valuable time. You'll be impressed with the selection of fresh fruits and vegetables, meats, cheeses, and fish as well as the colorful vendors that scream out their specials to attract shoppers. Although supermarkets have gained a significant amount of market share, most Parisians still rely on their local market several times a week for their fresh produce. One of the most fun aspects of these markets is the identification of produce that you don't find at home. Some visitors have a hard time with the hanging ducks and unplucked hens, the slippery eel, and little containers of veal brains! Others are in their element. Note the variety of greens that Parisians consume, dandelion leaves and lamb's lettuce; the size of the arti-chokes, fennel, and endives; and the long thick stalks of leeks. Every season has its share of produce, and in Paris much joy comes from seeing the first strawberries or cherries or melons. The autumn brings with it an awesome range of wild mush-rooms—*cêpes, chanterelles, pleurotes,* and *bolets.* In the summer you should really try some *mirabelles* and *questches,* two wonderful fruits. As a tourist, you probably won't be buying fish in the market, but you'll certainly be wowed by the urchins and *tourteaux,* the mountains of mussels and the slabs of salmon and monkfish. Parisians not only eat a lot of fish, they eat a large variety of fish. Each *quartier* (neighborhood) has its own market. Most are open either in the morning (till 1:00 P.M.) or in the afternoon (1:00–7:00 P.M.). For a complete listing of food markets, see the Culinary Paris chapter.

Flea Markets

Paris's flea markets *(marchés aux puces)* are a major source of pleasure and explo-ration for both the neophyte and the initiated. Every couple of months, make a point of getting up early on a Saturday or Sunday, and slum through the crowded alleyways filled with old clothes, odds and ends, furniture, records, and tools.

✤ **Porte de Montreuil:** avenue de la Porte de Montreuil, twelfth arrondissement; Métro: Porte de Montreuil. Saturday, Sunday, and Monday. This is probably the least touristy of the flea markets. Located on the eastern edge of Paris at the newly revamped Porte de Montreuil, this market is noted for its huge, cluttered tables of used clothes. If you're not overly bothered by the idea of rummaging through old clothes and are filled with patience, you may find high-quality sweaters, skirts, dress shirts, ties, etc., wrinkled, but of fine materials and for tiny prices. One and a half euros, for a shirt, for instance. Of course there's also inferior-quality clothing, as well as loads of old junk, some fine antiques, and piles of useless bric-a-brac. You may not be able to bargain quite as much as you imagined, but you usually can get things for 20 to 30 percent less than the ask-ing price. It's not improper to try in any case. (There is talk of closing down the Marché de Montreuil in the near future.)

✤ **Porte de Vanves:** avenue Georges-Lafenestre, 75014 Paris; Métro: Porte de Vanves. Open Saturdays and Sundays from 8.30 A.M. to 1:00 P.M. The quality of the objects—real bric-a-brac, Art-Deco mirrors, brassware, earrings and pen-dants, and drawings—is superior to what's found at the other flea markets, but the prices reflect this.

✤ **Saint-Ouen:** rue des Entrepots, 75018 Paris; Métro: Porte de Clignancourt. From Porte de Saint-Ouen to Porte de Clignancourt in the eighteenth arrondissement. Open Saturday, Sunday, and Monday from 9:00 A.M. to 6:00 P.M. The oldest and most popular flea market of Paris divided in several mar-kets, second-hand or brand-new cloth, military surplus in Marché Malik (now a national monument), antiques in Marché Serpette, and others. A full range of new and old items ranging from trinkets to luxurious antiques. You have to wade through a lot of junk to find the good stuff, and you have to arrive early if you hope to find something great at a small price.

Other Remarkable Markets

✤ *Marché de la Porte des Lilas:* 75019 Paris; Métro: Porte des Lilas. Sunday and holidays. Produce.

✤ *Marché de la Place d'Aligre:* Place d'Aligre, twelfth arrondissement; Métro: Ledru-Rollin. Daily from 9:00 A.M. to noon. One of Paris's best and least-expensive open-air markets. Produce.

✤ *Marché aux Fleurs:* Ile de la Cité, 75001 Paris; Métro: Cité. Daily assortment of fresh flowers and exotic plants.

✤ *Marché aux Oiseaux:* Same location as the *Marché aux Fleurs.* Sunday mornings. Bird *amateurs* (lovers) from all over bring their birds to sell, trade, and exhibit.

✤ *Marché aux Timbres:* 75008 Paris; Métro: Rond Point des Champs-Elysées/Georges Clemenceau. Sunday mornings. Stamp collectors, phone card, postcard, and *pins* collectors all unite to trade and sell.

Marjolaine

Each year in late October, an organization called *Nature et Progrès* sponsors the Marjolaine, an ecological fair held in the Parc Floral de Paris in the Bois de Vincennes. The Marjolaine, which was the first European ecological fair, promotes agriculture, eating, and lifestyle that respect the environment and health. These are the most green-conscious folks you'll ever meet in the Paris area (Greenpeace included, which never regained its earlier popularity after the sinking of the Rainbow Warrior in New Zealand by French intelligence agents). At the fair you'll find everything from banks that fund ecological projects to organic vegetable collectives that will deliver weekly baskets of the real stuff to a drop-off point in your neighborhood. The Marjolaine is a lot of alternative fun, and a healthy escape from the hedonism of café smoke, heavy meals, and the I-me foolishness of Parisian daily life.

Fashions and Shopping

Since polls declare shopping as the second or third most popular activity of foreign visitors, a word on the sport is needed. There are plenty of books and mags offering their favorite tips on the most "in" of the latest boutiques. Consult them if that's your passion. Hermès and a few other of the most exclusive couturiers open their doors each spring for a few hours for bargain-basement sales. Here the most dignified and cultivated ladies from Paris, New York, and Tokyo are transformed into ape women, scraping, pushing, and biting their way to the tables of marked-down silk scarves.

Shopping Zones and Favorite Streets

The following zones and highlighted streets in Paris offer prime shopping opportunities.

Place des Victoires/rue Etienne Marcel
A preferred hub for fashion-design houses and trendsetters. Here you'll find Jean-Paul Gaultier, Adolfo Dominguez, Montana, Miki House, Kenzo, Esprit, Thierry Mugler, Comme des Garçons, and more. Don't miss the historic Galerie Vivienne covered passageway, the rue Etienne Marcel, the rue du Louvre, and the rue Jean-Jacques Rousseau. The streets around the central post office and the rue de Montmartre are chockablock with wonderful, original finds.

Les Halles
Les Halles, in the heart of the city, the central produce market for the city before it was transformed into a commercial mall complex, is so trendy that no guidebook can keep up with the openings and closings. Lots of great little finds mixed in with a large helping of tackiness. I prefer the little streets in the area to the multilevel indoor mall, except that inside the mall you'll find the FNAC for books and CDs and concert tickets. Check out the rue Montmartre, the rue du Jour, rue de Turbigo, the rue Pierre Lescot, and the rue St-Denis.

Le Marais
More old-world than Les Halles, the Marais is studded with great boutiques offering clothes, objects, art, and accessories. Stroll along the rue Vieille du Temple, the rue Sainte-Croix de La Bretonnerie, rue du Roi de Sicile, rue des Ecouffes, rue des Rosiers, rue Pavée, rue de Sévigné, the Place de Vosges, and without fail the rue des Francs-Bourgeois, one of Paris's best shopping streets.

Saint-Germain-des-Prés
Elegant, up-market shops for the very chic. Visit the rue du Bac, the rue de Sèvres, the boulevard Raspail, the rue Jacob, the rue des Saints-Pères, Passage de rue Saint-André des Arts, rue de Grenelle, rue du Cherche-Midi, rue Madame, rue du Vieux-Colombier, rue du Four, rue de Rennes, rue Saint-Sulpice, rue de Seine, and, of course, the boulevard Saint-Germain, where you'll find Hugo Boss, Sonia Rykiel, Kashiyama, Miyake, and the cosmetics wizard, Shu Uemura. The rue Bonaparte and the area surrounding the Place Saint-Sulpice offer a wealth of great fashion and household delights.

Boulevard Haussmann, rue Saint-Honoré, La Madeleine
Welcome to the top-top, the chic of the chic. In this area, also referred to as the Golden Triangle, you'll find all the world's leading haute couture fashion brands as well as Paris's top department stores.

Along the boulevard Haussman you can't help but find the Galeries Lafayette and Le Printemps. Stroll the rue de la Paix, and enter the Place Vendôme. Here, aside from the Ritz, you'll find Guerlain, Armani, and Chanel (rue Cambon). Around the Madeleine you'll encounter Ralph Lauren, Cerutti 1881, and the catering meccas Fauchon and Hédiard. I like the Maille mustard shop on the Place for very original and affordable savory gifts. Lagerfeld and Lanvin as well as Joan & David are on the rue du Fauboug Saint-Honoré, along with Hermès, the makers of mythic silk scarves, and Yves Saint Laurent and Christian Lacroix. Follow along the rue Saint-Honoré. We won't say these shops are expensive, but one visitor from

Boston hot for a new leather jacket found that the sales tax alone (19.6 percent) on the one she had picked out was beyond her budget.

The Champs-Elysées
The avenue is still impressive despite the repeated invasions of Häagen-Dazs, McDonald's, the Disney Store, Virgin Megastore, and Planet Hollywood. The spokes off the avenue host some of the most elegant old money in the fashion industry. Wander down the avenue George V and the rue François 1er. Then strut along the avenue Montaigne, where Valentino and Guy Laroche, Christian Dior and Nina Ricci, Chanel and the world's most copied brand, Louis Vuitton, have set up shop and studios.

The Bastille
New and innovative designers and fashion folk have progressively moved east. The Bastille is still the hub of this side of Paris, but the more interesting trendsetters have ventured farther east by now: Oberkampf, Bercy 2, rue du Faubourg St. Antoine, Cour St-Emilion, Nation, Ménilmontant, Montreuil. . . . Start at the Bastille and follow the rue de la Roquette and the rue de Lappe, head up the rue de Charonne, and wander down alleys and lanes like the Passage Thiéré.

Passy/Avenue Victor Hugo
Upscale shopping haven in the lively part of the sixteenth arrondissement. Kenzo, Chipie, and others are here, including the famous cake maker Lenôtre. Don't miss Passy's brand-new shopping center.

Department Stores
Paris department stores (Grands Magasins) are famous and historic. Only in Paris could a department store also be a registered national monument. Such is the case with Le Printemps on the boulevard Haussman, which dates from 1865 and hosts an exquisite stained-glass dome. Even nonshoppers don't mind wandering through this Paris landmark. All the stores offer special services for international shoppers: English-speaking staff, gifts, maps, fashion shows, and, of course, shipping services and détax procedures. Both Le Printemps and Galeries Lafayette are accessible directly from the métro, without even going into the street. The same is true for the BHV next to the Hôtel de Ville.

If you get to your last day in Paris and haven't yet bought your gifts, give yourself a few hours in one or several of these stores. If you group your purchases from the same store and on the same day, you will be able to benefit from a VAT tax refund, provided your purchases total a minimum of around 200 euros.

Le Printemps
64 boulevard Haussman, 75009 Paris; Tel.: 01–42–82–57–87; Métro: Havre-Caumartin. Open till 10:00 P.M. on Thursday. Fashion shows every Tuesday (year-round) and Friday (April to October) at 10:00 A.M.

To obtain a 10 percent discount card, an invitation to the fashion shows, and a free map of the city, request a shopping kit in advance by sending a fax to Marketing Challenges Inc. at (212) 529–8484.

Galeries Lafayette

40 boulevard Haussman, 75009 Paris; Tel.: 01–42–82–34–56; Métro: Chaussée d'Antin. Open till 9:00 P.M. on Thursday. You can also get a haircut, a facial, or a manicure. The Galeries Lafayette gourmet supermarket is not only a great place to stalk the finest produce in the city, it's a great place to buy unique culinary gifts, or to step up to one of ten counters for a specialty lunch. Like Le Printemps, it offers discount cards, free fashion-shows, and maps. Call International Marketing at 01–42–82–37–66 for details.

BHV (Bazar de l'Hôtel de Ville)

52–64 rue de Rivoli, 75004 Paris; Tel.: 01–42–74–90–00; Métro: Hôtel de Ville. Open Monday, Tuesday, Thursday, and Friday from 9:30 A.M. to 6:30 P.M., Wednesday till 9:00 p.m. and Saturday till 6:00 p.m. This department store is convenient if you're in the Marais or the Latin Quarter. What's really special about the BHV is the basement, Paris's largest and most complete hardware and houseware store. Visitors have less reason to go here, but if you're imaginative you'll find all sorts of great ideas for your house and for gifts, like new handles or knobs or brass fittings and trim for the kitchen. Café Bricolo in the basement is a real find.

Samaritaine

75 rue de Rivoli, 75001 Paris; Tel.: 01–40–41–20–20; Métro: Pont Neuf. Open till 10:00 P.M. on Thursdays. This Paris landmark located between Châtelet and the Louvre is spread over four buildings. The kitchen department is particularly good. After you've finished shopping, head to the rooftop terrace of Building No. 2. You can enjoy a beer or a coffee here while you take in one of the best views of the city. The great advantage of this vantage point is that you're standing on something you'd prefer not to see! The fifth-floor restaurant, Toupary, a play on words, offers one of the most romantic tableside views in Paris.

Le Bon Marché

22 rue de Sèvres, 75007 Paris; Tel.: 01–44–39–80–00; Métro: Sèvres-Babylone. This is Paris's oldest department store, and it prides itself on being the only one on the Left Bank. A recently opened emporium of cosmetics called the *Théâtre de la beauté* is said to be among the best in the city.

Department and Chain Stores

FNAC. A leading upbeat chain (formerly a politically correct cooperative) for books, records, photo, video, audio, and electronics equipment, with after-sales and photo service all over the city. An institution in France. Vast variety, with prices 5 percent lower than suggested retail. Also a major outlet for concert tickets. Major locations at Montparnasse, Les Halles, Champs-Elysée, Wagram, the Bastille (music), and boulevard St-Germain (computers and electronics). Check Minitel 3615 FNAC or www.fnac.fr.

Darty. A large appliance chain with a wide variety of brands at reasonably good prices. Noted for service, home delivery, guarantee, and repair services—the first post-sales service in Paris. Salespeople wear blinding red jackets.

Tati. A working-class department store for inexpensive clothes. Montparnasse and Barbès locations. Opened cut-rate quality jewelry outlets, Tati d'Or and a New York store.

GAP. Since the mid-1990s the crackerjack U.S. clothing retailer GAP has opened a succession of highly successful stores in Paris. As a North American in Paris, you might be attracted to the unique feature that items bought in the United States can be returned or exchanged for full value at any Paris shop.

Rentals of All Sorts

Power Tool Rentals

RS, 95 rue de Charonne, 75001 Paris; Tel.: 01–43–71–45–35. Plus five other locations. Rent everything from power screwdrivers to wallpaper removers and jigsaws.

Kiloutou. With sixty agencies in Paris, this is the city's best source of rentals of building tools, pumps, paint sprayers, soldering and plumbing equipment, power tools, cleaning equipment, etc. The name sounds like Qui loue tout, "who rent everything." Call Tel.: 01–44–69–95–00 or consult the Minitel (36–15 KILO-UTOU) for a list of locations, equipment, prices, and conditions.

Computer Rental (PCs and Macs)

Amac, 4 rue de la Sorbonne, 75005 Paris; Tel.: 01–44–07–11–75.

TVA (value added tax)

Sales tax on goods and services, better known as TVA in France, is steep—19.6 percent for most consumer goods and services and 33 percent for luxury items, including certain food specialties. (The exorbitant price of gasoline is a result of hidden taxes totaling 74 percent!) Books and plumbing, on the other hand, as well as a few other amenities, are taxed at only 5.5 percent.

Although tourists and short-term visitors are entitled to refunds of the sales tax paid on purchases of goods being taken out of France, if you live in France you cannot technically de-tax your purchases. Many residents, though, play as if they are tourists leaving with their gifts and successfully de-tax their goods at the airport.

The TVA authorities are serious and severe. If you are working in France and sell any goods or services, you must invoice the TVA and pay it to the TVA administration. Although illegal, sometimes goods or services will be offered to you for espèces (cash), which means that the sale will not be declared, an invoice not given, and TVA not collected. In any case TVA occupies a prominent role in the consciousness of the French.

For purchases that are being taken out of the country, a part of the TVA can be recovered (récupéré). Anyone over fifteen years old who is a foreign resident when spending less than six months in France can benefit from this tax rebate. To be eligible, purchases from any single store must amount to at least 300 euros including tax for foreign nationals or 425 euros for EU citizens. The purchases can be cumulative. Be careful in that stores apply the law differently. The Musée de Paris gift shop at Les Halles, for example, requires that cumulative purchases be made on the same day. Items that cannot be de-taxed include tobacco, medicines, firearms, unset gems, works of art, collectors items and antiques, private means of transport (cars, boats, planes and their equipment), and large commercial purchases.

To benefit from the duty-free allowance, ask the vendor at the point of purchase to give you a three-slip form called a *bordereau* (export sales invoice) and an addressed, stamped envelope. Non-EU nationals must present the de-taxed purchases, the three slips (two pink, one green), and the stamped envelope provided by the shop to the French customs agents at the airport, border crossings, or train crossings. At the airport there is a window marked DETAXE, where you may be asked to show your purchases. Do not pack duty-free items in your checked baggage; if they are not available to be shown to customs, you risk being denied the tax refund. If you leave the country by train, have your three slips validated by the customs agent on board. French customs will keep the pink copies and send them in the envelope directly to the point of purchase, which will then reimburse you the amount indicated. (It is best to make purchases with your credit card to avoid astronomical fees for changing refunds into local currency.) Keep the green copy for your files. Sometimes you will be reimbursed at the time of purchase, but you still must go through the above process. It's best to ask. EU residents get a yellow invoice consisting of three copies, two yellow and one green. All three must be validated by the customs agent at your home destination. Send the two yellow slips to the Bureau des Douanes de Paris-La-Chapelle, 61 rue de la Chapelle, 75018 Paris. Keep the green slip for your files.

The *Tabac*

Le tabac (tobacco shop) plays a curious but dynamic role in daily French life. The *tabac*, clearly marked with an elongated red diamond-shaped street sign, has a monopoly from the state to sell cigarettes, cigars, and tobacco. You cannot buy cigarettes anywhere else in France. In exchange for this privilege, the tabac, which is usually also a *café*, performs certain services at face value, such as selling postage stamps, lottery tickets, parking meter cards *(carte de stationnement)*, telephone cards, and tax stamps. If you need some stamps for letters or cards, you can easily buy them from the cashier in a *tabac*. Don't expect total cooperation, however, if you want postal rates for Senegal, for example. That's not their job. A *carnet* of stamps is a unit of ten basic letter stamps for France (often sold in little booklets or on convenient, self sticking *(auto-collant)* pages. One basic letter stamp (for France or any of the EU countries) currently costs 0,46 euros.

Outside every *tabac* you will find a nearby mail box (always yellow and usually divided into two parts—Paris and its suburban codes and the rest of the world).

Single envelopes and writing paper can also be purchased in a *tabac*. This is handy when you have to mail something off in a hurry. You have envelope, stamp, and mailbox at hand—but you have to know the postal rates yourself.

The *tabac* also handles, in many cases, off-track betting (PMU) and sells lottery tickets *(Loto)*. Lottery sales have increased rampantly in the last few years.

Mail-order Catalogues

There are essentially two national mail-order catalogues from which the French order everything from bedroom furniture to bathing suits: La Redoute (Tel.: 08–92–35–03–50, 0,46 euros per minute; lots of pickup points around the city) and 3 Suisses (Tel.: 08–36–67–15–00, toll free; to order directly from the catalogue, 08–36–67–36–36; Web site: www.3suisses.fr).

To Order Tickets for Concerts, Theater, and Sporting Events

FNAC Musique
4 Place de la Bastille
75012 Paris
Tel.: 01–43–42–04–04

FNAC Forum des Halles
1 rue Pierre Lescot
75001 Paris
Tel.: 01–40–41–40–00
www.fnac.fr

Virgin Megastore
52 avenue des Champs-Elysées
75008 Paris
Tel.: 01–49–53–50–00, Tel.: 01 44 68 44 08 telephone reservations
Minitel: 36–15 VIRGIN
Web site: www.virgin.fr

Returns and Refunds

Paris businesses rarely if ever give cash refunds *(remboursements)*. In fact, it's rather recent that you could even get store credit. For a number of historical reasons, the "customer is always right" adage never really caught on in France, and although refund policies are becoming a bit more flexible, it's best to avoid exchanges or returns *(retours)*. Ask the store's policy on returns and exchanges before you buy. The arrival of the American clothing chain the GAP somewhat revolutionized the concept of retail public relations in France. You can buy a sweater at the GAP on rue de Rivoli and return it for a full cash refund in Houston, Texas. *Très rare* in Paris.

Usually if something doesn't fit or doesn't work, you can exchange it for another size (or color or such) provided you have the sales receipt and the original packaging, and even then it's not a guarantee.

Returning food items to supermarkets is unheard of in Paris.

Deposits or down payments *(les arrhes or an acompte)* are sometimes refundable but usually not. Always ask for the conditions of a sale before putting money down.

Anglo-American Clubs and Organizations in Paris

There is probably no city on Earth other than London that has as many English-language community activities and organizations as Paris. The support structure in the areas of business, culture, social issues, health, politics, and education is vast. Here is a list of clubs and organizations compiled from numerous sources, including the U.S. Embassy and American Chamber of Commerce listings, as well as the Paris-Anglophone directory.

Alcoholics Anonymous (English-speaking group), American Church of Paris, 65 Quai d'Orsay, 75007 Paris; Tel.: 01–46–34–59–65. This internationally known organization holds regular meetings at the American Church, American Cathedral, and several other locations in Paris. Call for schedule of meetings.

American Aid Society, c/o United States Embassy, 2 rue Saint-Florentin, 75001 Paris; Tel.: 01–43–12–47–90. The American Aid Society of Paris is a private, nonprofit, volunteer organization founded in 1922. Although the American Embassy provides office space for the society, donations are its sole source of financial assistance for Americans in temporary difficulty in France. A limited number of grants for elderly, disabled, or sick Americans residing in France are also funded through gifts.

American Cathedral, 23 avenue George V, 75008 Paris; Tel.: 01–53–23–84–00. General information: secy@american-cath.asso.fr. The American Cathedral hosts numerous service organizations and groups, such as The American Cathedral Club, which is a social club for members of the cathedral. Activities include dinner meetings with public speakers including theologians, the American ambassador, and other persons having an interest in the American Cathedral community.

American Chamber of Commerce in France, 156 boulevard Haussmann, 75008 Paris; Tel.: 01–56–43–45–67; Fax: 01–56–43–45–60; Web site: www.amchamfrance.org; E-mail: office@amchamfrance.org. Founded in 1894 (the oldest American Chamber of Commerce outside the United States), this private not-for-profit organization promotes Franco-American economic relations. Through the board of directors and various committees, it serves as both a forum for the professional community and a representative body for U.S. business in France. Activities include conferences, seminars, professional forums, luncheons, and new-member cocktail receptions. Special-interest committees include information technologies, communication services, trade and industry, laws and public affairs, small business, professional women, and young executives program, plus others. The chamber publishes a newsletter and a membership directory that includes a list of American companies in France. It has local affiliates in the larger French cities.

American Club of Paris, 34 avenue de New York, 75016 Paris; Tel.: 01–47–23–64–36; Fax: 01–47–23–66–01. Founded at the time of Benjamin Franklin, it was first called The American Club in 1904, as the successor to several American men's clubs (today membership is open to women). Principal activity consists of lunches with prominent French and international guest speakers in the fields of science, the arts, politics, diplomacy, and literature. Also holds a monthly breakfast meeting on the theme "Meet the Ambassador of . . ." Lunches and breakfasts take place at a private club, the Cercle de l'Union Interalliée. Theater, concert, opera, ballet evenings, and various tours are also organized. There is a formal dinner at the residence of the U.S. ambassador every two years. Membership applications require the sponsorship of two members of the club and the presence of the prospective member at a membership cocktail. There is no clubhouse or other physical facility.

American Friends of Blérancourt, 34 avenue de New York, 75016 Paris; Tel.: 01–47–20–22–28. This is a historical and cultural organization that arranges events at the Château de Blerancourt.

American Hospital of Paris, 63 boulevard Victor Hugo, 92202 Neuilly-sur-Seine Cedex; Tel.: 01–46–41–25–25; Fax: 01–46–24–49–38. Since it opened its doors in 1910, the American Hospital of Paris has grown into a modern, 187-bed healthcare facility, offering a full range of diagnostic and treatment services. A private, not-for-profit institution, it has been recognized as conforming to the exacting standards of the American Joint Commission on Accreditation of Healthcare Organizations. The majority of treatment and administrative staff are bilingual (English/French). More than thirty specialties are represented by 150 specialists in the outpatient department. The emergency room is open twenty-four hours a day, 365 days a year for medical, surgical, and dental emergencies.

American Legion, Paris Post 1, 22–24 boulevard Diderot, 75012 Paris; Tel.: 01–44–74–73–42. This veterans' organization was founded in Paris in 1919 and now has worldwide membership of more than three million members. Meetings are on the third Saturday of each month at 10:30 A.M.

American Library in Paris, 10 rue du General Camou, 75007 Paris; Tel.: 01–53– 59–12–60; Fax: 01–45–50–25–83; alparis@noos.fr; www.americanlibrary inparis.org. Open Tuesday through Saturday from 10:00 A.M. to 7:00 P.M. Metro: Alma Marceau or Ecole-Militaire. Founded in 1920 (and frequented by the likes of Hemingway and Henry Miller), the American Library in Paris, a nonprofit membership institution, is open to the English-reading public of all nationalities. Various types of memberships are available; consultation by nonmembers is possible for a daily user's fee. The library houses a 90,000-volume collection including fiction, nonfiction, and reference works, and more than 7,000 books for children and young adults. A modern research center provides CD-ROM indexes and a periodicals collection of 450 titles, some of which date from the nineteenth-century. The children's services department features a weekly story hour on Wednesday for pre-schoolers, as well as programs for toddlers and young adults. In addition, the library offers a monthly Evening with An Author lecture series (free and open to the public), which in recent seasons has presented Betty Friedman, Diane Johnson, Edmund White, Mavis Gallant, Jerome Charyn, David Guterson, and William Wharton. Stop by for a tour or orientation. Branches are located in Angers, Toulouse, Montpellier, and Nancy.

American University of Paris, 31 avenue Bosquet, 75007 Paris; Admissions Tel.: 01–40– 62–06–00; Fax: 01–47–05–34–32. www.aup.edu.. Founded in 1962, the American University of Paris is a fully accredited liberal arts university offering degree programs in eleven fields of study. See Studying in Paris.

American Women's Group in Paris (AWG), 32 rue Général Bertrand, 75007 Paris; Tel.: 01–42–73–28–72, Fax: 01-42-73-36-74. This club offers social and cultural activities promoting Franco-American friendship. The organization was founded in 1953 and has about 400 members. Activities include monthly luncheon meetings with prominent speakers, educational courses, guided tours, and new-member coffee receptions. The club sponsors various fund-raising activities in order to finance scholarships awarded annually to French students for study in the United States at the university of their choice.

Amherst College Alumni Association. E-mail: david@paris-anglo.com.

Association of American Wives of Europeans (AAWE), 34 avenue de New York, 75016 Paris; Tel.: 01-40-70-11-80; Fax: 01–47–23-32-97; E-mail: AAWEParis@ wanadoo.fr., www.aawe.org. Founded in 1961, AAWE is a nonprofit organization based in the Paris area. The majority of its 600 members are Americans married to Europeans. The association seeks to encourage understanding among people of the United States, France, and Europe; to protect the U.S. citizenship of its members and their children; and to promote American traditions, culture, and language. AAWE publishes a newsletter and an annual membership and professional directory for members only. Its *Guide to Education* lists the bilingual/English language schools throughout France and contains information on bilingual education as well as the French school system. *Guide to Living in France* assists English-speaking people in France by providing information on marriage, divorce, retirement, wills and inheritance, real estate, care for seniors, job hunting, etc. AAWE also publishes a bilingual cookbook that features American desserts, from chocolate chip cookies to Key lime pie. All are available from the office. An annual Christmas bazaar is its main fund-raising activity, with proceeds donated to pre-selected charities and scholarships.

Association of Americans Resident Overseas (AARO), 34 avenue de New York, 75116 Paris; Tel.: 01-47-20-24-15; aaroparis@ aol.com; members.aol.com/ aaroparis/aarohome.htm. Since its establishment in 1973, this issues-oriented organization has been protecting the basic rights of overseas Americans. With members living in twenty-plus countries, AARO concentrates on such issues as voting rights, citizenship, taxation, health care, and business competitiveness. Members are eligible to apply for AARO's group medical health care plans.

British Institute, 11 rue de Constantine, 75007 Paris; Tel.: 01–44–11–73–73; Fax: 01–44–11–73–82. www.bip.lon.ac.uk.

Canadian Women's Group in Paris, Canadian Cultural Center, 5 rue de Constantin, 75007 Paris; Tel.: 01–45–51–35–73. Also, Ile de la Jatte, 3 allée Claude Monet, apt. L2–24; 92300 Levallois-Perret; Tel.: 01–47–48–91–25. Vice president: Lynn Trapnell.

Canadian Cultural Center, 5 rue de Constantine, 75007 Paris; Tel.: 01–44–43–21–90; Fax: 01–47–05–43–55.

The Counseling Center at The American Cathedral, 23 avenue George V, 75008 Paris; Tel.: 01–47–23–61–13; Fax: 01–47–23–95–30. The center is staffed by experienced and qualified psychotherapists working with adults, adolescents, and children with a wide range of problems and concerns. Individual, family, and couple therapy is offered by appointment Monday through Friday. Messages received are answered promptly.

Comité La Fayette, 177 rue de Lourmel, 75015 Paris; Tel.: 01–44–23–93–71. Comité La Fayette was founded on May 20, 1924, the anniversary of the death of the American Revolutionary hero. The comité develops Franco-American exchanges. Every year it organizes a ceremony in front of the statue of La Fayette.

Council on International Educational Exchange (CIEE), 112ter rue Cardinet, 75017 Paris; Tel.: 01–58–57–20–50. www.councilexchanges-fr.org. The main U.S. organization in study abroad, student work exchanges, voluntary service, and student travel, CIEE is a nonprofit association with more than 300 universities, colleges, and other member institutions. It promotes international understanding through support services to the academic community. The Paris office oversees activities throughout Europe. Programs in France include international study programs for students age eighteen and older; work-exchange programs, and many others. See the Travel and Tourism chapter.

Daughters of the American Revolution, Rochambeau Chapter, 22 rue de Quatre Fils, 75003 Paris; Tel.: 01–48–04–32–16. Laurence Chatel de Brancion l.chateldebrancion@free.fr. Members are descendants of participants in the American Revolution; their aim is to maintain Franco-American friendship. The group participates in various American ceremonies on July 4, Memorial Day, and Thanksgiving.

Democrats Abroad France, 57 rue Vasco de Gama, 75015 Paris; Tel.: 01–45–54–99–91. www.democratsabroad.org. Represents the Democratic Party in France, and enables American voters residing in France to directly exercise their rights in the U.S. political process and, if they choose, to participate in the activities of the Democratic party.

English Language Library for the Blind, 35 rue Lemercier, 75017 Paris; Tel./Fax: 01–42–93–47–57; ellb@worldnet.fr; home.worldnet.fr/ellb. The library provides audio books to English-speaking blind and visually-handicapped subscribers living in France and other countries outside the English-speaking world. This service is entirely supported by private and institutional donations. Volunteers are always needed, in particular volunteer readers to add new books to the 1,400 titles in the catalogue.

FACTS, 190 boulevard de Charonne, 75020 Paris; Tel.: 01–44–93–16–32; Facts Line: 01–44–93–16–69 (Monday, Wednesday, and Friday 6:00–10:00 P.M.) FACTS provides AIDS counseling, treatment information, support, and education to Americans and English-speaking people of all nationalities in Paris. The FACTS-Line is a help line for English speakers concerned about HIV and AIDS. **Foch Foundation (Fondation Maréchal Foch)**, Pavillon Balsan, 40 rue Worth, 92151 Suresnes; Tel.: 01–45–06–29–24; Fax: 01–46–97–04–39. Founded in 1929 by prominent French and American citizens, the Foch Foundation is a private, nonprofit Franco-American organization that offers financial and logistic support to the needy requiring hospitalization.

Fondation des Etats-Unis, 15 boulevard Jourdan, 75690 Paris Cedex 14; Tel.: 01–53–80–68–82; Fax: 01–53–80–68–99 (administration); fondusa@iway.fr. Founded in 1927 with private donations, this French equivalent of the international houses on American campuses provides lodging and cultural facilities to American graduate students, professors, and researchers. The foundation also accepts French and other nationalities. Located in the Cité Internationale Universitaire de Paris (CIUP), it has 270 single rooms.

France-Amériques, 9–11 avenue Franklin D. Roosevelt, 75008 Paris; Tel.: 01–43–59–51–00. www. france-ameriques.org. france-ameriques@wanadoo.fr. This private, nonprofit organization was founded in 1909 to foster better relations between France and the nations of the Americas. It offers many facilities to its members: restaurant, lounge, bar, garden-terrace, library, and four large drawing rooms suitable for banquets, cocktails, business lunches, or dance evenings. Numerous economic, cultural and social events take place in the club, which is located in a nineteenth-century mansion of authentic Second Empire decoration. France-Amériques is also a debating club on economic and geopolitical matters. Several other Franco-American organizations and university clubs, such as the **Harvard Club of France**, are housed in its building.

France–Etats–Unis, 39 boulevard Suchet, 75016 Paris, Tel: 01–45–27–80–86. france.usa@wanadoo.fr. This French-American friendship organization with chapters throughout France was founded in 1945 to better inform the French about Americans, and Americans about the French, through discussions and conferences. Publishes a quarterly newspaper.

France-Canada, 5 rue de Constantine, 75007 Paris; Tel.: 01–44– 43–21–90.

Franco-American Commission for Educational Exchange (Fulbright program), 9 rue Chardin, 75016 Paris; Tel.: 01–44–14–53–60 (Administration); 08–36–68–07–47 (Educational Advisory Center, 0,34 euros per minute); Minitel: 36–17 USAETUDES (0,53 euros per minute). cfa@fulbright-france.org, www.fulbright-france.org. The commission administers educational exchanges between the United States and France under the Franco-American Cultural Agreement of 1965 and the Fulbright program. Counseling and documentation concerning French and American universities.

Franco-American Institute (Institut Franco-Américain), 7 quai Chateaubriand, BP 2599, 35059 Rennes; Tel.: 02–99–79–20–57; Fax: 02–99–79–30–09; www.rennet.org/ifa.htm. Founded in 1961, this USIA-sponsored binational center advises Americans on administrative procedures, education, real estate purchases, crosscultural business transactions, travel, exchange programs, and the politico-economic climate in the region.

Inter-Allied Club (Cercle de L'Union Interalliée), 33 rue du Faubourg Saint-Honoré, 75008 Paris; Tel.: 01–42–65–96–00; Fax: 01–42–65–70–34. The club provides luncheon and indoor sports facilities and, as the name implies, includes members from various nations. The American Club and certain other groups hold their meetings or luncheons at the club.

International Association of American Minorities (IAM), 3 route de Chaufour, 78270 Cravent; Tel.: 01–34–76–18–75. The association is a nonprofit, nonpartisan, educational and cultural organization whose principal objectives are to study the concerns of minorities living in the United States, to highlight minority achievements, and to promote communications and relationships across racial and ethnic lines. Activities include panel discussions and public forums, as well as gala events in honor of special guests.

International Counseling Service (ICS), 65 Quai d'Orsay, 75007 Paris; Tel.: 01–45–50–26–49. Founded in 1977 in the belief that counseling is more beneficial when provider and recipient share the same language and cultural roots, the service is staffed by qualified, bilingual mental health professionals and offers individual, family, couple, and group therapy for adults, adolescents, and children, by appointment. The office, located at the American Church, is open weekdays all day and Saturday mornings. A twenty-four-hour answering service records messages, answered promptly. The first interview is free of charge.

Junior Guild of the American Cathedral, 23 avenue George V, 75008 Paris; Tel.: 01–53–23–84–00. This is a multicultural charity organization for women that gives financial assistance to many families. Funds are raised by rummage sales held in May and November at the cathedral and by a gala at the residence of the U.S. ambassador. Luncheons with a variety of programs are held each month.

Junior Service League of Paris, Mona Bismarck Foundation, 34 avenue de New York, 75016 Paris; Tel.: 01–53–23–84–00; Fax: 01–45–27–32–64. This nonprofit organization of international women serves the Paris community in the areas of child welfare, health, and the arts. The league publishes a book that helps newcomers adjust to daily life in Paris.

La Leche League France (LLL), BP 18, 78620 L'Etang La Ville; Tel.: 01–39–58–45–84 (answering service). LLL is an international organization with several French groups and one English group in the Paris area. Meetings are held monthly for all mothers interested in learning about breast-feeding. The LLL manual "The Womanly Art of Breast-feeding" can be ordered at the above address in French or English. Members also receive a bimonthly journal containing advice, the latest research findings, and testimonials on all aspects of breast-feeding. There are also regular toddler meetings for the older nursing child, and couples meetings.

The Liberal Democrats Association (UK), 31 rue Brunel, 75017 Paris; Tel.: 01–48–76–90–29 or 01–44–09–71–20. Contact John Gallop. Founded in 1988 to provide a focus for all those interested in truly democratic politics in Britain and in participating in the democratic development of Europe as part of a European network of liberal democrat groups.

Lions Club International, 295 rue St-Jacques, 75005 Paris; Tel.: 01–46–34–14–10. maisonlions@compuserve.com. Secretary: François Leduc.

Message Mother Support Group, Contact: Sallie Chaballier (Tel.: 01–48–04–74–61) or Oona Cadorin (Tel.: 01–39–65–79–29) 9:00 A.M.–4:00 P.M./ Monday–Friday. Message is an international English-speaking group for pregnant women, new mothers, and families with young children. Founded in 1984, it currently has about 900 members throughout Paris and its suburbs. Annual membership fee includes a quarterly bulletin, regular area meetings, baby and toddler groups, and breast-feeding counselors. Evening events and social activities without children, and some including husbands, are also organized. A working mothers' group meets on a monthly basis in the evenings, often with guest speakers. A special problems register provides information based on members' experiences, and information on hospitals, clinics, and medical practitioners. Preparation for parenthood classes is available in English to Message members. *The ABCs of Motherhood in Paris,* now in its third edition, is a 210-page guide to living in Paris with a baby or young children.

The Mona Bismarck Foundation, 34 avenue de New York, 75016 Paris; Tel.: 01–47–23–38–88; Fax: 01–40–70–92–10. The aim of this nonprofit American organization is to encourage and promote international artistic, scientific, and educational activities, particularly those that further Franco-American friendship. The foundation is housed in the magnificent Paris town house of the late Countess Bismarck, with four imposing salons for exhibitions, concerts, and receptions.

Organization for Economic Cooperation and Development (OECD), 2 rue André-Pascal, 75775 Cedex 16; Tel.: 01–45–24–85–00; webmaster@oecd.org, www.oecd.org.

OECD British Delegation, 19 rue Franqueville, 75016 Paris; Tel.: 01–45–24–98–28.

OECD Canadian Delegation, 15 bis rue Franqueville, 75016 Paris; Tel.: 01–45–27–62–12.

OECD US Mission, 19 rue Franqueville, 75016 Paris; Tel.: 01–45–24–74–77. Head: Ambassador Denis Lamb.

Office of American Services, 2 rue Saint Florentin, 75001 Paris. Tel.: 01–43–12–45–01 or 01–43–12–23–47 .

Reid Hall, 4 rue de Chevreuse, 75006 Paris; Tel.: 01–43–20–33–07. Reid Hall, a division of Columbia University, is a lovely eighteenth-century house whose mission is to foster Franco-American exchanges on the university level. Professors, students, and educational groups become members of Reid Hall, which offers them classroom space, office space, and access to the common rooms and gardens. Many overseas undergraduate and graduate programs are based at Reid Hall.

Republicans Abroad, 01–43–06–10–27.

Rotary Club of Paris, 8 passage Cardinet, 75017 Paris; Tel.: 01–47– 66–06–03.

Saint Ann's Guild, Tel.: 01–53–23–84–00. This women's organization of the American Cathedral supports children's, women's, and family activities through a Sunday school, nursery, and youth groups, and provides a monthly forum for discussing issues of interest to its members.

Sisters, 271 rue St-Denis, 75002 Paris; Tel.: 01–42–21–00–73; Fax: 01–42–21–00–26. This nonprofit association of black women in France, founded in January 1993, provides a forum for social and professional networking, information exchange, shared experiences, and a support group. It promotes black culture and gives members the opportunity to discover France from a black perspective by learning about other black cultures and lifestyles.

Sons of the American Revolution (SAR), 20 rue Bosquet, 75007 Paris; Tel.: 01–40–62–97–19; sarfrance@free.fr. The French branch of the SAR was created in

1926 by an ancestor of Comte de Chambrun. Members are descendants of participants in the American Revolution; their aim is to maintain Franco-American friendship. The group participates in various American ceremonies on July 4 and Memorial Day.

S.O.S. HELP, BP 239–16, 75765 Paris Cedex 16; Tel.: 01–47–23–80–80. SOS HELP, founded in Paris in 1974, offers the English-speaking community in France a telephone support service every day of the week, including holidays, from 3:00 to 11:00 P.M. Its objective is to provide an anonymous, confidential , nondirective, nonjudgmental telephone crisis line/suicide prevention listening service. The service is staffed by English-speaking volunteers and the psychotherapists who train them.

UNESCO, United Nations Educational, Scientific, and Cultural Organization, 7 Place de Fontenoy, 75352 Paris 07 SP; Tel.: 01–45–68–10–00, Fax: 01–45–67–16–90; www.unesco.org.

United Service Organizations (USO), 20 rue de la Trémoille, 75008 Paris; Tel.: 01–40–70–99–68; Fax: 01–40–70–99–53; usoparis@compuserve.com, www.uso.org. Open seven days a week. USO serves visiting American military personnel and their families. Hotel reservations, discount tours, nightclub and theater tickets, transportation information, and APO mail drop are among the services offered. The Paris USO operates temporary fleet centers in northern French ports during U.S. Navy ship calls.

Volunteers of the American Hospital of Paris, 63 boulevard Victor Hugo, 92202 Neuilly-sur-Seine, Tel.: 01–46–41–25–48.

Women of the American Church in Paris (WOAC), 65 Quai d'Orsay, 75007 Paris; Tel.: 01–40–62–05–00. This organization provides opportunities for women to meet together in friendship and to assist newcomers to make a successful transition to life in Paris. Six neighborhood coffee groups meet monthly, and various other social, cultural, and religious programs are offered throughout the year. An orientation program for English-speaking newcomers to Paris is held the first three Tuesdays in October. The Information Center, an information and referral center, is organized and administered by the group, with the on-site support of the International Counseling Service. The Information Center is located in the Franco-American Community Center of the American Church in Paris. It serves as a clearinghouse for the collection and dissemination of information pertinent to English-speaking people in Paris, maintains a comprehensive database of resources available for people in need, and provides volunteer opportunities for interested individuals.

WICE, 20 boulevard du Montparnasse, 75015 Paris; Tel.: 01–45–66–75–50; Fax: 01–40–65–96–53; Métro: Duroc or Falguiére; Monday–Friday, 9:00 A.M.–5:00 P.M.; wice@wice-paris.org; www.wice-paris.org. WICE (formerly Women's Institute for Continuing Education) is a nonprofit multinational association offering educational programs in English in art, studio arts, history, politics, personal and professional development, literature and writing, living in France, and English as a foreign language. In conjunction with Rutgers University, it offers a university certificate in teaching English as a foreign language. Each summer it sponsors the weeklong Paris Writers' Workshop, taught by prize-winning authors form the English-speaking world. In addition to paying reduced prices on courses,

WICE members have access to French-English conversation groups, a bilingual book group, a resource library and lending library, and discounts at a number of museums, stores, and activities in Paris. The association is run by volunteers.
YMCA, 14 rue de Trevise, 75009 Paris; Tel.: 01–47–70–90–94.
YWCA (main office), 22 rue de Naples, 75008 Paris; Tel.: 01–53–04–37–47; Fax: 01–42–94–81–24. This organization, while similar to the YWCA in the United States, is affiliated with world Alliance YWCA in Geneva. The youth hostels are for young women between eighteen and twenty-six years of age. They offer permanent or temporary lodging. Breakfast and dinner are included. During the summer there is no age limit and a short stay is possible.

Religious Organizations

Although France is a traditionally Catholic country, religion does not play a highly visible role in Parisian life or values. Church and state formally separated in 1905, and the debate over public (or secular, *laïque*) vs. parochial education in France flares up periodically. A recent government decision to permit municipal mayors to decide whether they will allocate public funds to private schools polarized the nation. The Paris area, of course, has some of Europe's most astonishing cathedrals and churches, although these treasures are more architectural and art monuments than religious sites. They are also important for their series of classical and sacred music concerts. Attending mass at Notre-Dame or l'Eglise de St.-Germain-des-Prés, for example, however, can be memorable and highly spiritual. Just being in the presence of the stained-glass windows of the cathedral at Chartres is a religious experience. As in all big cities, the opportunities for worship are numerous. Here's a list of what Paris offers in English.

American Church in Paris
(services for all Protestant denominational)
65 Quai d'Orsay, 75007 Paris, Tel.: 01–40–62–05–00

American Cathedral of the Holy Trinity
(Episcopalian/Anglican services)
23 avenue George V, 75008 Paris, Tel.: 01–53–23–84–00

Baptist Church
48 rue de Lille, 75007 Paris, Tel.: 01–42–61–13–95

Saint Joseph's Church (Roman Catholic)
50 avenue Hoche, 75008 Paris, Tel.: 01–42–27–28–56

Christian Science Church
36 boulevard St-Jacques, 75014 Paris, Tel.: 01–47–07–26–60

Church of Jesus Christ of Latter-day Saints
23 rue du Onze Novembre, 78110 Le Vesinet, Tel.: 01–39–76–55–88

Church of Christ
4 rue Déodat-de-Sévrac, 75017 Paris, Tel.: 01–42–27–50–86

Church of Scotland
17 rue Bayard, 75008 Paris,Tel.: 01–48–78–47–94

Consistoire Israëlite de Paris (synagogue)
17 rue St-Georges, 75009 Paris, Tel.: 01–40–82–26–26

Emmanuel Baptist Church
56 rue des Bons-Raisins, 92500 Ruiel Malmaison, Tel.: 01–47–51–29–63 or
01–47–49–15–29

Second Church of Christ
58 boulevard Flandrin, 75116 Paris, Tel.: 01–45–04–37–74

Third Church of Christ
45 rue la Boétie, 75008 Paris, Tel.: 01–45–62–19–85

Church of Jesus Christ of Latter-day Saints (Mormon)
64–66 rue de Romainville, 75019 Paris, Tel.: 01–42–45–28–57

Great Synagogue
44 rue de la Victoire, 75009 Paris, Tel.: 01–45–26–95–36

International Baptist Fellowship
123 avenue du Maine, 75014 Paris, Tel.: 01–47–49–15–29 or 01–47–51–29–63

La Mosquée (Moslem)
Place du Puits de l'Ermite, 75005 Paris, Tel.: 01–45–35–97–33

Mosque Abu Bakr As Siddio
39 boulevard de Belleville, 75011 Paris, Tel.: 01–48–06–08–46

Liberal Synagogue
24 rue Copernic, 75016 Paris, Tel.: 01–47–04–37–27

Living Word Christian Fellowship
21 rue Gallieni, 78230 Le Pecq, Tel.: 01–39–76–75–88

Quaker Society of Friends
114 rue de Vaugirard, 75006 Paris, Tel.: 01–45–48–74–23 (Sunday silent meditation service)

St. George's Anglican Church
7 rue August-Vacquerie, 75016 Paris, Tel.: 01–47–20–22–51

St. John's Lutheran Church
147 rue de Grenelle, 75007 Paris, Tel.: 01–47–05–85–66

St. Joseph's Roman Catholic Church
50 avenue Hoche, 75008 Paris, Tel.: 01–42–27–28–56

St. Mark's Anglican Church
31 rue du Pont Colbert, 78000 Versailles, Tel.: 01–39–02–79–45

St. Michael's Church (Anglican)
5 rue d'Aguesseau, 75008 Paris, Tel.: 01–47–42–70–88

Unitarian Universalist Fellowship of Paris
7 bis rue du Pasteur Wagner, 75011 Paris, Tel.: 01–30–82–75–3

A Note on Anti-Semitism

Violence in the Middle East has contributed to worries about escalated tension between France's prominent Muslim and Jewish communities. Although there were some incidents of racially or religious-oriented violence in France in 2002 it is overwhelmingly believed that there is no substantial increase in anti-Semitism in France, nor any justifiable reason to boycott the country on fear of religious discrimination. Much of the problem originates in an information-disinformation battle that appears to be politically motivated.

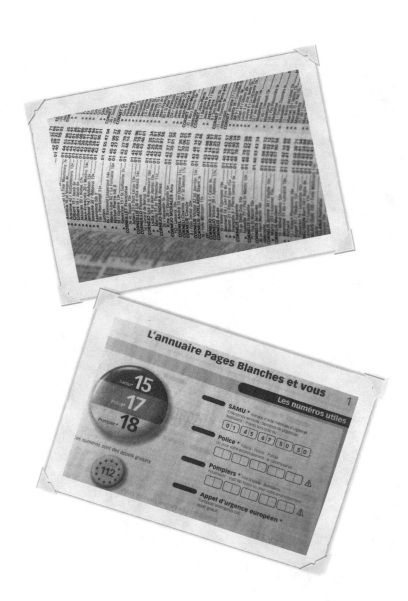

Resources

Useful Telephone Numbers

Ambulance: 01–42–63–70–70
Bus Information (in English): 08–36–68–41–14
Central post office (twenty-four hours): 01–40–28–76–00
Charles de Gaulle Airport: 01–48–62–22–80
Chronopost (La Poste's international next-day courier service):
    01–49–27–90–74
Customs information center: 01–42–60–35–90
Directory information
    Ile de France (Paris region): 12
    International: 00–33
Drug crisis center: 01–42–25–40–00
Emergency Numbers
    Fire Department: 18
    Medical Emergencies: 15
    Police Secours: 17
    Poison center (twenty-four hours): 01–40–05–48–48
    Rape Crisis Hotline 01–53–79–04–41 (toll free)
    SAMU Ambulances (Paramedic ambulance service): 01–45–67–90–00 or
        medical emergency number
    SOS Attack (assistance to victims of assault): 01–47–07–97–97
    SOS Cardiologues (emergency service for heart patients): 01–47–07–50–50
    SOS Dentists: 01–43–37–51–00
    SOS Locksmith (twenty-four hours): 01–47–07–99–99
    SOS Médecins (twenty-four-hour emergency medical house calls):
        01–47–07–77–77; 01–43–37–77–77
    SOS Oeil (eye emergencies): 01–40–92–93–94

SOS Pregnancy: 01–45–82–13–14
Enfance et Partage (Hotline for Kids in Trouble): 08–00–05–12–34 (toll free)
Le Bourget Airport: 01–48–62–12–12
Lost/Stolen Credit Cards:
American Express Card: 01–47–77–72–00
Carte Bleue or VISA: 02–54–54–67–63
Diner's Club Card: 01–40–23–58–00
MasterCard/Eurocard: 01–45–67–84–84
Lost and Found: 01–55–76–20–20
Lost animals: 01–43–55–76–57
Lost property *(objets trouvés):* 01–55–76–20–20
Minitel directory: 36–11
SNCF: 08–92–35–35–35
Orly Airport: 01–49–75–52–52
RATP (public transport): 08–10–03–04–05 (for information)
Restaurant information: 01–43–59–12–12
Search for hospitalized persons: 01–40–27–30–81
Taxis Bleus: 01–49–36–10–10
Taxis Radio Etoile: 01–47–39–47–39
Telephone companies (long-distance carriers):
AT&T: 08–00–99–00–11
Canada Direct: 08–00–99–00–16 or 08–00–99–02–16
MCI/Worldcom: 08–00–99–00–19
Sprint/Global One: 08–00–99–00–87
Telephone Complaints France Telecom, Repairs: 13
Telephone—To find out who called your number while you were out: 31–31
Telephone—To block your outgoing phone number from the recipient: 36–51
Telephone/Online Services from France Telecom: 0 800 36 47 75.
Theater information: 01–49–52–53–54
Time: 36–99
Tourist office: 01–49–52–53–54
Wake-up calls (electronically programmed): * 55 * plus the time in four digits
(i.e., 7:30 A.M.=0730), then your number.
Weather information (Meteo): 08–99–70–11–00 (Paris); 08–92–68–02–75.

Paris Web Information

Finding information about Paris on the Web has never been easier! For those of
you living, studying, or working in Paris, or traveling to Paris, check out www.paris-
anglo.com. *Paris Inside Out* updates will be posted here.

For Museums in Paris

Beaubourg: www.centrepompidou.fr
Le Louvre: mistral.culture.fr/louvre/
Musée d'Orsay: www.musee-orsay.fr

Paris Modern Art Museum: www.cofrase.com/artforum/mamparis/
Comprehensive list of museums and art galleries: www.paris-anglo.com/
guide/entertainment
Personalized museum tours: www.parismuse.com
Walking tours: lisa.pasold@wanadoo.fr

For Sight-seeing and Monuments

Les Champs-Elysées: www.champselysees.org
La Place Vendôme: www.place-vendome.net
Montmartre: www.montmartrenet.com
Interactive photographic journey in Paris: www.paris-anglo.com/zoom
La Tour Eiffel: www.tour-eiffel.fr

For Embassies, Consulates, and Administrations

General Consulate of France in the United States: www.france-consulat.org
U.S. Embassy in Paris: www.amb-usa.fr
Embassy of France in Washington: info-france-usa.org
Tips and advice on French administrative procedures: www.paris-anglo.com/
guide/dailylife/legal

For Practical Information

Getting around in Paris: www.paris-anglo.com
Postal Services (in French): www.laposte.fr
RATP (Métro, buses, RER): www.ratp.fr
SNCF (Trains): www.sncf.fr
Eurostar: www.eurostar.com (08–92–35–35–39)
Telecommunications: www.francetelecom.fr

For Doing Business in or with France

American Chamber of Commerce in France: www.amchamfr.com
Chamber of Commerce and Industry in Paris: www.ccip.fr
France Business Practices: www. worldbiz.com/bizfrance.html
Invest in France: www.investinfrance.net
U.S.-based French activities: www.afusa.org (Alliance Françaises USA)

Information Available to the English-Speaking Community

The Office of American Services at the U.S. Consulate (2 rue St-Florentin, 75001 Paris, Tel.: 01–43–12–22–22; Fax: 01–42–61–61–40) provides free of charge the following pamphlets:

The British Community Committee (c/o Mme. Beryl Jones, 17 villa Chaptal, 92300 Levallois-Perret; Tel.: 01–47–58–81–42) provides the following publications upon request: *Digest of British and Franco-British Clubs, Societies and Institutions* (free), and a *Quarterly of British Community Social Events* (15 euros).

For a Selected Bibliography of the Best Books on Paris and Related Paris-oriented Literary Titles (provided by the Village Voice Bookshop), go to www.paris-anglo.com.

A Few Key Source Materials Available from the Paris Tourist Office (125 avenue des Champs-Elysées)

Hotels
Paris & Ile de France, Published by the Office de Tourisme et des Congrès de Paris. A complete list of Paris hotels with addresses, emails, web pages, star rankings, handicapped access, etc.

Venues
l'Officiel des Reunions d'Affaires, Chambre de Commerce et d'Industrie de Paris. A comprehensive list of venues, conference rooms, ballrooms, business meeting places, châteaux for hire, reception halls, etc.

Fairs/Exhibitions in France
Trade Exhibitions, Congress and Exhibition Centers in France. Published by Le Moci. Annual listing. Tel.: 01–53–90–20–00; info@foiresaloncongress.com.

The Center for Awareness and Action
78 boulevard Magenta
75010 PARIS
Tel.: 01–40–05–94–94
TheCenter@soulworks.com
Contact: Libby Robinson
Business networking breakfasts, training programs, community projects, personal development, etc.

Other Key Sources of Paris Info

Newsletters/Publications/Sites
✢ *Bonjour Paris,* edited by Karen Fawcett, www.bonjourparis.com or www.bparis.com
✢ *Parlerparis,* edited by Adrian Leeds, www.parlerparis.com. Published by Bill Bonner's International Living (Agora).
✢ *Paris Notes,* edited by Mark Eversman, www.parisnotes.com or marke@paris notes. com.
✢ *Paris Pocket Guide,* iculture@noos.fr
✢ *This City,* edited by Claire Downey, thiscity@compuserve.com.
✢ www.paris.org, edited by Norman Barth.
✢ Polly Platt's seminars, www.pollyplatt.com
✢ Netcapricorn.com, French-based advertising, directed by Cyril Toullier (toullier@netcapricorn.com)

Expressions/Slang

Here is a selected list of French colloquial expressions and some *argot* (slang), selected on the the basis of what you might hear in daily conversation or in the street. Although these and others are useful to know, be absolutely sure you understand the context and appropriate usage before using them yourself.

à table	the meal is served (be seated)
aie!	ouch!
argot	slang
berk	yucky
bêtise	stupidity, foolishness, nonsense
bof!	(a noise used to say "I don't know")
bon courage	chin up!
bonne chance	good luck
bonne continuation	keep up the good work
branché	hip/in
c'est absurde	that's absurd
c'est chouette	It's really great, fab
c'est comme ça	that's just the way it is
c'est dingue	that's crazy
c'est drôle	that's funny, strange
c'est foutu	it's over, it doesn't work, it's broken (for events/people/objects)
c'est génial	that's great, brilliant
c'est impec	that's impeccable, that's perfect
c'est intéressant (in business)	that's a good deal, opportunity, investment
c'est marrant	that's funny
c'est pas la peine	it's not worth it
c'est pas mal	it's not bad, rather good (used as a compliment)
c'est pourri	that's rotten
c'est ridicule	it's/that's ridiculous
c'est super	that's super
ça boum	it's hopping (as in a party)
ça cocotte	it smells strongly (perfume)
ça gaze, ça baigne	everything's going great
ça m'énerve	that unnerves me, annoys me
ça m'est égal	It's all the same to me
ça marche	it works, it's ok
ça me gêne	that bothers me
ça me gonfle	that bothers me (literally, that makes my head swell)
ça ne me dit rien	I'm not in the mood, that doesn't ring any bells
ça peut aller	I'm ok (a positive but unenthusiastic response to ça va?)

ça chlingue	that stinks
ça suffit	enough!
chacun son tour	each his turn
con, connard	idiot, clod
connasse	tart, stupid bitch
connerie	rank stupidity
coucou	hi
coup de foudre	to have a crush on
couper la poire en deux	cut the pear in half (split something in half, compromise)
d'acc (d'accord)	all right, ok
dégage	get the hell out of here!
dégoûtant	disgusting (polite form)
dégueulasse	disgusting (slang version)
elle me fait craquer	she drives me crazy (as in love)
engagé	committed
ferme ta gueule	shut your face/trap
flipper	to flip out, to freak out
fous le camp, barre-toi, casse-toi!	piss off, beat it, get lost (very vulgar)!
fous moi la paix	leave me alone, leave me in peace
franchement	frankly
grosses bises	hugs and kisses
il a perdu les pédales	he's lost control, he's nuts
il a un grain	he has a screw loose
il est culotté	he's nervy, cheeky
il est gonflé, il exagère	he's got a hell of a nerve
il faut profiter	to take advantage of something
j'ai d'autres chats à fouetter	I have better things to do
j'en ai assez	I've had enough!
j'en ai marre	I'm fed up with (this, it, him/her, everything)
j'en peux plus	I can't go on like this
je craque	I'm giving in to temptation, I can't resist any longer
je m'en fiche, je m'en fous	I don't care a hoot
je n'ai pas envie	I don't want to, I don't feel like it
je suis crevé, KO	I'm dead tired, beat
je suis raide	I'm stoned, high
je suis saoûl(e), je suis bourré(e)	I'm drunk
je t'embrasse	I kiss/hug you (for ending friendly phone conversations or letters)
la bagnole, la caisse	the car
la nana, la gonzesse, la meuf	chick, girl, babe
le boulot	job, work
le fric, le pognon	bread, money
le gars, le mec, le type	guy
les fringues, les sapes, nippes	duds, clothing

ma frangine, mon frangin	my sis, sister; my bro, brother
merde	shit
mince (replacement for merde)	darn
mon cul	my ass
mon pote	my buddy, pal
ne quittez pas	hang on, don't hang up
ne t'inquiète pas	don't worry
on laisse tomber	let's forget it
on s'apelle/on se téléphone	we'll call each other (call me/ I'll call you)
p cul (PQ)	toilet paper (TP)
plouc	country hick
putain	whore (holy shit)
punaise (replacement for putain)	thumb tack (oh, damn)
quel bordel	what a mess!
salaud, salope	dirty bastard; son of a bitch; slut, bitch
saloperie	filthiness
si tu veux	it's okay with me
sois pas vache	don't be nasty
ta gueule	shut up (literally: your snout/face; vulgar)
tais-toi, taisez-vous	shut up
tant mieux	so much the better
tant pis	too bad, that's the way it is
truc/machin	thingamajig, whatchamacallit
tu parles!	no kidding (sarcastic)
un clope	a butt, cigarette
un flic, les flics , les poulets	a cop, the cops, the fuzz, the pigs
une toile	a film
va te faire cuire un oeuf	go jump in a lake! (literally: go fry an egg)
vachement	tremendously, very, extremely

Index

E

tickets, 373
Time Out, 211, 348
time, 387
Tissot, 118
title search, 117
tobacco shops, 372
toilettes, 129
Toullier, Cyril, 390
Toupary, 370
towing, 170
TPS, 202
traducteur assermenté, 263
Traductière, 306
traffic patterns, 171
Train Bleu, 361
train discounts, 54
train reservations, 51
train stations, 50
train travel, 53
Transeuro Desbordes, 138
Transferring Funds, 182
transition schools, 247
translators, 261
transportation, 153
Travel and Tourism, 41
traveler's checks (lost), 103
tripe, 339
Trocadéro, 110
TV tax, 141
TVA, 45, 223, 232, 371
twelfth arrondissement, 110
twentieth arrondissement, 111
typical dishes, 355

U

U.K., 231
U.S. Embassy, 221
UBC, 197
UCG, 281
UNESCO, 37, 382

unfurnished apartments, 127
United Nations Nursury School, 248
United States Embassy, 71
Université de Paris, 243
universities, 243, 265
university sports, 318
Unofficial Guide to Disneyland Paris, 329
Unofficial Guide to Paris, 347
Upstairs at Duroc, 306
urban landscape, 98
Urban Transportation, 153
URSSAF, 262
US Embassy, 61
USA Today, 210
useful telephone numbers, 384
using the métro, 155
USIT, 55
USO, 382

V

vacation time, 7, 224
value added tax, 371
Van Gogh's Ear, 306
Van Ham, Richard, 233
Vanden Bos, John, 211
VAP, 59
VCR, 202
veal, 339
vegetarian food, 353
VF, 281
Video, 202
Videothèque de ParisCannes, 285
Vietnamese, 113
Vieux Campeur, 319
Vigipirate plan, 105
vignettes, 167
Villa, la, 295
Village Voice, 306, 311
Villette, La, 111, 267
vin de table, 357

About the Author

DAVID APPLEFIELD, an American writer originally from Boston, has been living and working in Paris for nearly twenty years. Author of two novels, two Paris guidebooks, and the Paris newsletter *My Mercredi*, he also writes for the *Paris Voice*, teaches at Sciences Po in Paris, works for *The Financial Times* in French-speaking Africa, and hosts a weekly radio program on Paris's "RadioinEnglish." David also finds the time to edit the international literary journal FRANK, publish the Paris Web site www.paris-anglo.com, and lecture and consult on issues relating to living and working in France. He and his family live in Montreuil-sous-Bois, on the eastern edge of Paris.